The
Mystery
Lover's
Companion

The Mystery Lover's Companion

ART BOURGEAU

CROWN PUBLISHERS, INC., NEW YORK

ACKNOWLEDGMENTS

These are the folks who helped me on this book.
Without the aid of their good looks, keen minds, and sophisticated opinions,
the whole thing would have been a damn sight more difficult. Many thanks to
Rebecca Stefoff, Robert Carson, Patricia J. MacDonald, Frank Webb, and
A. C. Hohnke.

Published by Crown Publishers, Inc., 225 Park Avenue South, New York, New York
10003 and represented in Canada by the Canadian MANDA Group

CROWN is a trademark of Crown Publishers, Inc.

Manufactured in the United States of America

Library of Congress Cataloging-in-Publication Data
Bourgeau, Art.
    The mystery lover's companion.
    1. Detective and mystery stories, English—History and criticism—Handbooks,
manuals, etc. 2. Detective and mystery stories, American—History and criticism—
Handbooks, manuals, etc. I. Title.
PR830.D4B68   1986   823'.0872'09   86-4511
ISBN 0-517-55602-2

10 9 8 7 6 5 4 3 2 1

First Edition

To Mom, with love

Contents

Introduction

E_DGAR ALLAN POE HAD NO IDEA of the literary force he was unleashing when he invented the detective story. Since the initial appearance of "The Murders in the Rue Morgue" in the early 1840s, the mystery story has never diminished in popularity. Since then, over a quarter of a million mysteries have been written, with more and more coming each day.

Many bookshops devoted solely to the mystery have sprung up across the United States and in Canada. Each of these shops bears the very distinct imprint of its owner and, depending on the depth of its selection of used books, carries anywhere from 5,000 to 25,000 titles. When confronted with such a massive selection, many new customers will develop a glazed expression and concentrate on only a small part of the stock, such as Agatha Christie or Mickey Spillane books, missing the opportunity to expand their horizons by trying new authors.

I know that glazed expression well, for as proprietor of Whodunit?, Philadelphia's mystery bookstore, I see it every day. Unlike at other bookstores, where people are happy to browse in morguelike silence, at a mystery bookstore many more customers will actively seek help in picking a book to buy.

When they do solicit my opinion, a few questions help to significantly narrow the field of possible suggestions. The first question is, "What kind of mysteries do you like?" People generally have a strong preference for one of four categories: the American mystery, the English mystery, the Thriller, or the Police Procedural. Some would argue for more categories, such as suspense, romantic suspense, and European mysteries, but I think four categories does the job nicely.

Now that we have figured out what the customer wants to read, how do we determine what to recommend? A good mystery contains four vital elements: the main character, the plot, the action, and the atmosphere.

The most important element in a mystery is the main character. If the reader doesn't get behind the main character almost from page one, then the greatest plot in the world will not satisfy. Successful main characters are created by an author's unashamedly mixing fantasy, fact, hero worship, and quirks until the mixture comes out right. Most readers think the character is modeled on the author. This is seldom so. While Mickey Spillane does look like Mike Hammer, Agatha Christie certainly does not look like Hercule Poirot, and Dorothy Sayers bears only a passing resemblance to Lord Peter Wimsey.

No, characters are their own little people. Often they will start out as an emotional extension of the author, such as John D. MacDonald's Travis McGee or Robert Parker's Spenser, and they will remain good and faithful friends to their creator. Other times, for seemingly no reason, a character will turn on its creator, making his life miserable for many of the same reasons that used to make it happy. When that happens, he has no choice but to destroy the character, as in the case of Conan Doyle's Sherlock Holmes, Freeling's van der Valk, and in a gentler sense, Christie's own magnificent Hercule Poirot. But however troublesome the character may be, an author's success is more directly reflected in the success of this main character than of any other element in the mystery.

The next most important element is the plot or the story. Forget about originality when judging a story. There are no new stories; they have all been written countless times. But there are fresh approaches, new gimmicks, quirkier motives, better clues, and more imagination. The worst offender of all in the mystery field is the Ross Macdonald little-girl-lost story. An embarrassingly high percentage of current, hard-boiled detective stories use this device. When Ross Macdonald did it, it was fresh and beautiful. Now, through repetition, it is a bit stale, and freshness is the key to a good story.

To judge how well an author writes action, it is first necessary to determine whether the book was meant primarily for a male or female audience, for the two sexes have different views as to what constitutes action. For men, action consists of movement, which may take one of three forms: movement from place to place, violence, or sex. While women basically agree, they add a fourth form of action—social interaction.

To illustrate social interaction, let me use Helen MacInnes as an example. Her characters are always well drawn, her story lines gripping, and her atmosphere impeccably staged. The plot moves along—building, building, building—as the hero and heroine move across Europe amid clouds of intrigue, but instead of spine-tingling chases, or dark-alley attacks, nothing ever happens but endless lunches at little roadside restaurants. Yet, by most female readers, Helen MacInnes is considered an action writer.

The way to judge the other three forms of action—movement, violence, and sex—is to ask yourself the question, "Does the action move the story, or is the action the whole story?" If it is the latter, then the writer did not do as good a job as he could have.

Last, but most influential is the atmosphere, which covers everything else—such as location, supporting characters, subplots, time period, weather, humor, and food and drink. While the atmosphere is never as critical to the lack of success of a particular book as a bad story or a poor main character, the skillful use of atmospheric details can take an average book and turn it into a most pleasant evening.

No writer is a master of all these elements, from the main character all the way through the plot, the action, and the atmosphere, but there are certainly ways to determine who does it better. For this reason I have established a rating guide to help you decide whether you want to read a book reviewed herein. An explanation of the guide follows this section. It is simple and, like the reviews throughout the book, reflects only my taste. Please feel free to disagree; disagreement is good for the soul.

I sincerely hope that this book will help and amuse novice and veteran mystery fans alike. The time spent reading the books reviewed here was time lovingly given, and the friends made, both real and fictional, a wealth unto themselves.

Rating Guide

†††††
A True Classic

††††
Excellent

†††
A Good Job

††
Could Be Better

†
Only Read This One When You're Drunk

THE
AMERICAN
MYSTERY

THE 1920S AND 1930S WERE A TUR-
bulent time in America. A time famous for flappers, gangsters, Pro-
hibition, bathtub gin, and the Great Depression. A time when brash
young writers like Hemingway, Fitzgerald, and Wolfe cut their literary
teeth in the gin mills of two continents. And it was the time of the
true birth of the American mystery.

From the first, the American mystery could be divided into two
groups: the "Western" and the "Eastern" detective novels.

The western, or hard-boiled detective novel, created in California,
is a uniquely American art form, and its hero may be thought of as
an extension of the American cowboy. Typically, the main character
is a private eye in his mid-to-late forties, who is divorced, asexual,
friendless, unable to hold down a real job, and on the verge of bank-
ruptcy. Yet he clings steadfastly to the belief that it is the world, rather
than he, who is out of step.

As he sits in his run-down office on the shabby side of town, his
self-examination is interrupted by a potential client. We know that the
client is a loathsome creature by the fact that he is wearing cologne.
(If it is a female client, *beware*, for the designing woman always means
double trouble for the western private eye.)

The client wants our hero to find a missing person, usually a
daughter, who has fallen in with bad company. (In the 1940s, it was
gamblers; in the 1950s, beatniks and jazz freaks; in the 1960s, it was
hippies; in the 1970s, it was political activists; in the 1980s, religious

9

cults.) The private eye looks down his nose at his client, registers his distaste, but accepts the job because of his financial straits.

Finding the missing person is easy and is usually accomplished by about page 70, but somewhere along the way an innocent bystander—like a crippled newsboy—is killed. The detective is fired between pages 70 and 100, but he refuses to quit until *he* knows all the answers. For the next hundred pages, he goes from place to place, leaving a trail of bodies in his wake. Clues are less important than movement.

In the end he discovers the mystery involves a deep, dark family secret, usually sexual in nature. (Incest is rather popular at the moment. An overview of the hard-boiled novel tends to show us what sexual taboo was in vogue at the time of writing.) Whether justice was actually served remains somewhat murky, but the private eye is usually satisfied in his own way.

Although the stories are often clichéd, there is comfort in knowing what you are getting. Dashiell Hammett, Raymond Chandler, Ross Macdonald, and Mickey Spillane are the four greatest, western mystery writers of all time.

Meanwhile, on the opposite coast, the eastern detective novel was developing simultaneously. Bearing no resemblance whatsoever to the western, the eastern detective novel owes its inspiration to Britain and British writers like Conan Doyle, Chesterton, Christie, and Sayers.

The detectives were usually amateur, but like Ellery Queen, often enjoyed an unusually close relationship with the police. Some, like S.S. Van Dine's Philo Vance, were dapper, handsome men, while others, like Rex Stout's Nero Wolfe, were less sexually appealing but still exuded winning charm. Some operated alone, while others, like A. A. Fair's Bertha Cool and Donald Lam, operated in partnerships, or like Lockridge's Mr. and Mrs. North were married. Their occupations covered a wide range, but were generally white collar in nature.

The locked-room mystery, or a variation of it, is the standard plot, with the ingenuity of the story deriving largely from the murder method and the alibis of the suspects. If it seems a bit like a cheerful parlor game, that is what it is meant to be—a couple of hours of amusing misdirection, similar to a magic trick. But whether the plot is cunningly constructed or more simple, and whether the setting is New England, New York, or the South, one thing usually holds true—it is murder among the "nice" people.

During the late 1950s the eastern mystery novel went into a decline which lasted until the late 1970s, when publishers and writers alike found there was indeed a substantial market for the more genteel mystery. And with a trace of updating, a number of top quality women writers, such as Jane Langton, Charlotte MacLeod, Lucille Kallen, Jane Dentinger, and Amanda Cross, rushed in to fill the void.

Now that balance is restored, it doesn't matter if we are dealing with a western gumshoe or an eastern little old lady in Maine, the American mystery is alive and well.

A

ADAMS, HAROLD. The author of a series of mysteries about Carl Wilcox, an ex-con, all set in South Dakota. Wilcox is not so much a detective as a hero in the *film-noir* tradition. Although his work slightly resembles that of James M. Cain and Cornell Woolrich, Adams departs from their style by having a continuing character and avoiding their sense of bleakness.

Murder. 1981. Carl Wilcox comes home from prison to find himself the central figure in a pitchfork slaying which smacks of a lovers' triangle. †

Paint the Town Red. 1982. A more ambitious plot than *Murder*, in which Eleonore, the bad woman, and her gunsel show up looking for mob money stashed in Corden, S.D. Naturally, Eleonore is a past mistake of Carl Wilcox's, and the memory has helped pass the long South Dakota nights. †††

The Missing Moon. 1983. The local moonshiner is found unconscious next to a woman's body, and Carl Wilcox sets out to clear his name. ††

ALDYNE, NATHAN. *Vermillion.* 1980. Amateur detectives Valentine, a gay bartender, and his lady friend, Clarisse, solve a gay murder in Boston's famed "Combat Zone." †††

ALDYNE, NATHAN. *Cobalt.* 1982. Quite simply the best gay mystery ever written. Once again, after their initial appearance in *Vermillion*, Valentine, the gay bartender, and Clarisse, his lady friend, are confronted with murder. This time it is summer in Provincetown, and the murder is that of a young hustler. ††††

ALDYNE, NATHAN. *Slate.* 1984. Clarisse and Valentine decide to open a gay bar named "Slate" in Boston. Before they can complete renovations, they find the body of a murdered, gay gossip columnist in the bar. Not as good as either of the other two Aldyne novels. ††

ALEXANDER, KARL. *Time After Time.* 1979. Jack the Ripper escapes Victorian London in H. G. Well's time machine and winds up in modern-day San Francisco, a perfect place to continue his rampage. H. G. Wells, a peace-loving man, chases him. Wells falls in love with a young woman, and the object of his desire also becomes the object of Jack's desire. †††

ALLEN, STEVE. *The Talk Show Murders.* 1982. Television personality Steve Allen has written a cute mystery filled with a lot of name-dropping of famous people, in which guests on talk shows are being murdered right on the air. ††

ALVERSON, CHARLES. *Goodey's Last Stand.* 1975. A well-written, but conventionally plotted, California hard-boiled detective story in which police-outcast turned detective Joe Goodey tracks down the killer of Tina D'Oro, a San Francisco nightclub dancer. Along the way he stops off in Chinatown, hobnobs with criminals, and even runs into an evil doctor. †††

ANGUS, SYLVIA. She has produced only a few mysteries, but they are highly enjoyable for their good writing and excellent use of background and setting.

Death of a Hittite. 1969. The hero's adventures begin in Constantinople and continue when he joins an archaeological dig in a remote part of Turkey. A new skeleton is unearthed in a very old grave, obviously as a result of a murder. Angus deftly blends the prehistoric past, a WWII adventure, and a modern-day mystery in this suspenseful tale. ††††

Dead to Rites. 1978. Angus's main character in this book is an imperious widow, Mrs. Wagstaff, who is a bit like Miss Marple, but with muscles and a libido. Her fondness for mystery novels and her incurable curiosity about her fellow travelers help her solve two grisly ritual murders at a Mayan temple in Mexico. ††††

ANTHONY, DAVID. *The Midnight Lady and the Mourning Man.* 1969. Private eye Morgan Butler, filling in for an old friend, investigates a campus burglary at an Ohio college. The case quickly becomes more complex with the death of a beautiful coed, who is the daughter of an important senator. ††††

ANTHONY, DAVID. *Blood on a Harvest Moon.* 1972. A classic in which retired detective, now turned farmer, Morgan Butler is lured back into harness by his ex-wife who wants him to locate her missing second husband. †††††

ARMSTRONG, CHARLOTTE.   Her forte might be called the domestic-fantastic. Her suspense novels feature resolutely cheerful everyday characters—housewives, hatcheck girls, high school science teachers—who stumble into surrealistic or frightening cases of madness, conspiracy, or espionage. Fearful anticipation of mayhem may keep you on the edge of your seat, or the pervasive tone of manic coziness may set your teeth on edge.

The Dream Walker.   1955. Psychic prophecies intertwine with political blackmail in this look at the dark side of occultism. Armstrong's gift for the telling detail that illuminates a scene is stronger than her ability to concoct convincing motives.   ††

A Dram of Poison.   1956. This one has all the ingredients of a good household thriller: a mature husband, a young wife, a sly, bitchy sister-in-law, a handsome neighbor, and a science lab complete with poison. Simple characterization keeps it from being as good as it could have been.   †††

The Witch's House.   1963. A distraught wife must find her mysteriously missing husband despite inefficiency on the part of the local police. Two plots—one a somewhat improbable mystery, and the other involving an implausible madwoman—don't quite mesh.   †

Mischief.   1963. One of her best, this tale shows the potential for terror in an event as commonplace as leaving a child with a new babysitter for an evening. Tension is built up by the claustrophobic setting, a New York hotel room. †††

ARNOLD, MARGOT.   The drawback to this series, featuring amateur detectives Toby Glendower and Penny Spring, is that each book involves such radical shifts in locale that I feel the need to pack my suitcase before starting to read.

Exit Actors, Dying.   1979. Toby Glendower and Penny Spring find the body of a beautiful movie star in an ancient Greek amphitheater, but the body vanishes before the police arrive.   ††

Zadok's Treasure.   1980. During an Israeli excavation, Toby Glendower's old friend, William Pearson, is tortured and murdered. Toby and Penny make it their business to find the killer.   ††

The Cape Cod Caper.   1980. Penny is in Massachusetts and Toby is in Italy investigating the same murder.   †

ASIMOV, ISAAC.   A man of humor and style, and a damn fine writer.

Murder at the ABA.   1976. The author has a great time poking fun at the publishing world in this delightful tale of the murder of an author at the annual, gala book show of the American Booksellers Association. The amateur detective and hero is Darius Just, a not too highly regarded writer who, in his pursuit of truth and justice, treads on the toes of just about everyone, including Isaac Asimov himself. ††††

Tales of the Black Widowers, ††††, *More Tales of the Black Widowers*, †††, and *The Casebook of the Black Widowers*, †††, are all short-story collections featuring six men and their waiter who gather at a particular restaurant each month to solve mysteries and enjoy each other's companionship. The stories are great fun and show Asimov's skill in a fine light.

†††

B

BANDY, FRANKLIN. *Deceit and Deadly Lies*. 1978. The story of a man and his lie detector. ††

BANKS, OLIVER. *The Rembrandt Panel*. 1980. Despite killing off one of the book's more appealing characters, the author, a noted art critic, in his first mystery provides a feeling of authenticity as Amos Hatcher, art association investigator, follows the death-strewn trail of a priceless Rembrandt. †††

BANKS, OLIVER. *The Caravaggio Obsession*. 1984. Amos Hatcher is back in an art theft and murder concoction involving international terrorism. After a friend's murder in New York, Hatcher follows the trail to Italy and to a show featuring the brooding work of the 16th-century artist. †††

BARDIN, JOHN FRANKLIN. The author of three early psychological suspense novels. In the introduction to the *Omnibus* (the only way these stories may be obtained), Julian Symons classes Bardin as an important forerunner of Highsmith and on a par with Poe himself.

The Deadly Percheron. 1946. A troubled young man, wearing a red hibiscus in his hair, comes to a psychiatrist seeking help from the little people who plague him into doing embarrassing things. The psychiatrist thinks they are a figment of his imagination until he meets one of them. ††††

The Last of Philip Banter. 1947. Philip, an adman with contemporary problems, discovers a manuscript which mixes the past with the future. Much to his horror, the future part begins to come true. †††

Devil Take the Blue Tail Fly. 1948. Bardin's masterpiece about the breakdown of a young woman. A classic. †††††

BARING-GOULD, W. S. *Nero Wolfe of West Thirty-fifth Street.* 1969. A fictional biography of Nero Wolfe. Not as good as the author's *Sherlock Holmes of Baker Street*, but still excellent. ††††

BARNES, LINDA. *Bitter Finish.* 1983. Michael Spraggue, a wealthy private eye, movie actor, and partner in a vineyard, comes to the aid of Kate Halloway, his partner, who is accused of murdering a man whose body can't be identified. Lenny Brent, their winemaker, is missing, and soon a second body turns up. †††

BARNES, LINDA. *Dead Heat.* 1984. While acting in Shakespeare at the Harvard Rep, Michael Spraggue tries to keep a high-profile senator from being murdered during the Boston Marathon. ††

BARTH, RICHARD. *The Condo Kill.* 1985. Barth writes about old people in New York, a topic I find thoroughly depressing. This is the story of a landlord trying to evict two old people from a condemned building. ††

BAXT, GEORGE. In the late 1960s Baxt created Pharaoh Love, a campy, ultra-gay detective, who talked like a 1950s beatnik and got involved with a series of troublesome young men. Daring for their time, the Pharaoh Love novels now strike some readers as dated and affected, but they are still worth reading.

A Queer Kind of Death. 1966. Pharaoh Love prances on stage in this giddy tale of murder in a gay world that hadn't yet been mass-marketed into middle-American stylishness. The plot doesn't hold water, but the author's strength is in creating wildly eccentric characters and presenting them in rapid-fire, surreal succession. ††††

Swing Low, Sweet Harriet. 1967. Pharaoh Love is back, coping with his own wayward lover and also with a gaggle of aging film queens, who are ripe for a comeback, but so is a long-forgotten murderer. A wry story with overtones of tragedy despite its facetious tone. †††

A Parade of Cockeyed Creatures, or Did Someone Murder Our Wandering Boy? 1967. Like the previous two, this is essentially a book of the 1960s, reminding us that drugs and pop psychology were still new and exciting then. The detective, Max Van Larsen, is an angst-filled, Jules Feiffer type of character, who is the perfect investigator for this tale of destructive family relationships. †††

The Affair at Royalties. 1971. The author switches to a British locale for this story of an American woman mystery writer who wakes up in a London hospital with a severe case of amnesia. She learns that she was found in the kitchen of her English country home, drenched with blood and clutching a knife, but no corpse was found. With the help of a Scotland Yard detective, she tries to regain her memory and find out whether she has committed murder. ††††

The Dorothy Parker Murder Case. 1984. Baxt tries his hand at a Stuart Kaminsky style story filled with notables from New York in the 1920s. Dorothy Parker tries to clear George S. Kaufman's name when a murdered show girl is found in his apartment. †††

BECK, K. K. *Death in a Deck Chair.* 1984. A light, frothy, period piece with a locked-room setting and a good heroine. The climax has an interesting touch, as it involves a rather obscure point of the story. †††

BERGER, PHIL. *Deadly Kisses.* 1984. A 1930s period piece in which reporter Harry Krim investigates the death of a beautiful female star found dead in a pond. ††

BERGER, THOMAS. *Who Is Teddy Villanova?* 1977. An almost surreal presentation of the hard-boiled-detective-and-the-missing-person story. Very offbeat. I liked it, but it's not for everyone. ††††

BERGMAN, ANDREW. The author of two very good 1940s mysteries featuring Jack LeVine, private eye. They are well plotted and breezy.

The Big Kiss-off of 1944. 1974. It is New York late in WWII, and Jack LeVine investigates the murder of a chorus girl who is a former porno star. ††††

Hollywood and LeVine. 1975. Jack LeVine seeks the warmer climate of California, where he stumbles into a plot right out of Stuart Kaminsky, featuring Nixon, Bogart and Bacall, Ava Gardner, and others. †††

BERNE, KARIN. *Bare Acquaintances.* 1985. A nicely done first novel in which Ellie Gordon goes through a divorce, loses weight, finds herself, and gets a job in a law firm. A feminist attorney is murdered, and Ellie, in her new-found freedom, decides to play amateur detective. †††

BERNE, KARIN. *Shock Value.* 1985. Ellie Gordon comes to the aid of a friend in public relations at a nuclear power plant, who is accused of murdering her womanizing boss by electrocuting him. †††

BIGGERS, EARL DERR. Author of the Charlie Chan series (or Charles Chan to those of us who feel he is due a bit more respect). In the novels, Mr. Chan is far from the buffoon pictured in the famous movies. The series is very well written and should be read by fans of Christie, Carr, and Ellery Queen.

The House Without a Key. 1925. Dan Winterslip, the black-sheep son of a Boston family, now in Hawaii, is murdered, and all the suspects are at sea when the crime occurs. ††††

The Chinese Parrot.   1926. A string of pearls holds the key to the death of a mysterious millionaire, who collects strange pets. Mr. Chan goes undercover in the desert to find the answer to a clue spoken in Chinese—by the parrot.

†††††

Behind That Curtain.   1928. Now in San Francisco, Mr. Chan comes to the aid of the police when they are baffled by the murder of a visiting Scotland Yard detective.   †††

The Black Camel.   1929. Mr. Chan solves the murder of Sheila Fane, a rich Hollywood star.   †††

Keeper of the Keys.   1932. Charles Chan is invited as the extra guest at a Lake Tahoe dinner where the other four male diners have all been married to the same woman. During dinner someone kills that woman.   †††††

BLOCH, ROBERT.   *Psycho.* 1959. The classic story of Norman Bates and his motel.   †††††

BLOCK, LAWRENCE.   A very versatile author who has written several series, including the hard-boiled Matt Scudder and the lovable burglar Bernie Rhodenbarr. All his work is first rate and deserves a read.

Matt Scudder series:

In the Midst of Death.   1976. Scudder helps out a dirty cop, formerly on the take, in a hooker murder.   †††

The Sins of the Father.   1976. A hooker is found murdered. A homosexual is arrested, and later found hanged in his cell. Not my favorite Scudder story.

†††

A Stab in the Dark.   1981. A very nicely plotted story of a serial killer who stabs his victims through the eyes. Scudder figures out the clues, but I didn't. I guessed wrong.   ††††

Bernie Rhodenbarr series:

Burglars Can't Be Choosers.   1977. The first of the Bernie Rhodenbarr novels. Bernie is caught burgling an apartment. He pays the cops to look the other way, but then they find a body, and Bernie has to run for his life.   †††

The Burglar Who Studied Spinoza.   1980. Bernie Rhodenbarr decides to steal a valuable coin collection that turns out to have only one coin in it. After going to the trouble to steal it, he then has to face the problem of what to do with it.   †††

The Burglar Who Painted Like Mondrian. 1983. This is the most complex of the Bernie Rhodenbarr series, because of the story's parade of eccentric characters rather than the art caper itself.   ††††

Other novels:

The Girl with the Long Green Heart. 1965. A well-written story about two lovable con men and a beautiful woman who set out to swindle a pompous upstate New York businessman in a Canadian land scheme. Unlike many of Block's books, there is little humor here.   †††

Tanner's Twelve Swingers. 1967. On a trip to the Balkans, Evan Tanner agrees to slip into Russia and smuggle out a friend's girlfriend. However, the number to be smuggled out soon grows to fifteen, and includes a female Olympic team.   ††

BORTHWICK, J. S.   *The Down East Murders.* 1985. The author moves into Lucille Kallen–Phoebe Atwood Taylor territory, as Sarah Deane, English teacher and amateur detective, goes to meet Dr. Alex McKenzie for a summer fling on the coast of Maine, but instead of lobsters, they begin to find bodies.   †††

BOUCHER, ANTHONY.   The famed mystery critic also wrote mysteries. While none of his mysteries are classics, they *are* certainly excellent, following strongly in the grand tradition of Carr and Queen. Finding them today can be a bit difficult, so if you happen across one, don't pass it up.

The Case of the Seven of Cavalry. 1937. When a Swiss humanitarian is killed on an American campus, Dr. Ashwin, a professor of Sanskrit, and Martin Lamb, a graduate student, join forces to find the killer. The only clue is a scrap of paper on which has been drawn an obscure symbol known as the Seven of Cavalry.   ††††

The Case of the Crumpled Knave. 1939. Detective Fergus O'Breen investigates a murder with two completely different sets of clues. Which one is the right set?   ††††

Rocket to the Morgue. 1942. His most famous work. Someone is trying to murder Hilary Foulkes. Detective Terry Marshall and his assistant, Sister Ursula, a nun, race to keep the killer from succeeding.   ††††

BOURGEAU, ART.   It is an immodest thing to review yourself, but modesty has never been my strong suit. My series, featuring amateur detectives Snake Kirlin and F. T. Zevich, is meant to poke a bit of fun at the hard-boiled detective story, and will in no way make you a better person for having read them. If you revere the traditional detective novel, don't read them.

A Lonely Way to Die. 1980. On a fishing trip to Snake's hometown of Cannibal Springs, Tennessee, Snake and F. T. come to the aid of a woman who is running for mayor when someone tries to mix politics and murder.   †††

The Most Likely Suspects. 1981. Snake and F. T. are invited back to Snake's college alma mater for Homecoming Weekend. Sharing the festivities with them is a murderer who is killing off the members of the honor council one by one.   †††

The Elvis Murders. 1985. My favorite of the series. Snake and F. T., now working as free-lancers for a men's magazine, are assigned to cover a contest to find the world's greatest Elvis imitator. The winner of the contest, Radio Johnson, is a charismatic but evil man, and someone in his entourage is trying to kill him. It is up to Snake and F. T. to stop it. There is a locked-room scene in this one.   ††††

Murder at the Cheatin' Heart Motel. 1985. The most popular of the series. Snake inherits a run-down motel on the edge of a swamp when someone murders his elderly aunt. As he seeks revenge for her death, he comes in contact with a variety of offbeat characters, including a husky woman named Dixie, who starts to look better and better to him as the pages turn.   †††

BOX, EDGAR. Gore Vidal wrote three mysteries under this name. All three are fun. The tone is charming, a bit like Rex Stout and a bit like Patrick Quentin.

Death in the Fifth Position. 1952. An excellent ballet murder in which public relations man, Peter Cutler Sargeant, investigates the death of a ballerina, who is killed on stage.   ††††

Death Before Bedtime. 1953. Peter Cutler Sargeant, now doing public relations work for a senator, finds himself out of work when someone blows up the senator.   †††

Death Likes It Hot. 1955. This time it is murder during a weekend at the Hamptons, as Peter Cutler Sargeant continues to hobnob charmingly with the rich, powerful, and effete.   †††

BRADBURY, RAY. *A Memory of Murder.* 1984. An excellent collection of fifteen terror-filled short stories written by Bradbury in the 1940s for pulp magazines like *Dime Detective.*   ††††

BRADBURY, RAY. *Death Is a Lonely Business.* 1985. A well-told tale from a master, in which four bodies are found under unusual circumstances in Venice, California, in 1949. In an atmosphere symbolized by the death and destruction of an amusement park, a private eye and a young writer set out to prove these deaths are murders.   ††††

BRAUDY, SUSAN. *Who Killed Sal Mineo?* 1982. A fictionalized version of the actor's death, in which a New York woman reporter who had known him slightly in childhood sets out to find the killer.   †††

BREAN, HERBERT. *Wilder's Walk Away.* (n.d.) A classic suspense novel in which each member of the Wilder family seems marked for death until Reynold Frame, a young writer, happens on the scene.   †††††

BREAN, HERBERT. *The Traces of Brillhart.* 1960. Magazine writer William Deacon is unwillingly plunged into a maelstrom of curious events when a friend drops by and tells him of a dead man who is dating show girls. Is he really dead, or is the friend crazy?   ††††

BREEN, JON L. *The Gathering Place.* (n.d.) Young, bright Rachel Hennings inherits a used bookstore in Los Angeles and leaves Arizona to claim her inheritance. She moves into the apartment above the store, and the store is immediately burglarized. From there the plot moves into blackmail and murder in an amusing, breezy mystery written by the respected *Ellery Queen Mystery Magazine* columnist.   †††

BRETT, MICHAEL. A good example of the Mickey Spillane school of hard-boiled writing.

Kill Him Quickly, It's Raining. 1966. Rape and murder annoy Pete McGrath, New York private eye, and his beautiful client, the widow of an ex-convict. Then a spy named Smeck gets mixed up in the case. McGrath not only has to find a murderer, he has to persuade his girlfriend to come on a Caribbean vacation for two.   ††

Another Day, Another Stiff. 1967. McGrath goes to Letcher County, Kentucky, to help a tough guy accused of murdering his girlfriend. The private eye from the big city tangles with some good old boys.   ††

We, the Killers. 1967. It is time for crime on campus as McGrath tracks a missing coed and comes up with scandal, blackmail, and murder. He gets an "A" for perseverance.   ††

BRISTOW, GWEN, AND MANNING, BRUCE. *The Ninth Guest.* 1930. A good, early example of the "Ten Little Indians" type of story. Eight guests are assembled by a mysterious host who begins to kill them off one by one.   ††††

BROWN, CARTER. People have been poking fun at Carter Brown for years, but it is hard to argue with success—over 25,000,000 copies sold. In that light, it looks as though there are a lot more people laughing with him than at him. I'm one of those laughing with him. His books are short, breezy, hard-boiled, and fun. There is quite a bit of sex in them, too. He has four main series: Al Wheeler, Danny Boyd, Rick Holman, and Mavis Seidlitz. Mavis Seidlitz is my favorite.

The Dame. 1959. Someone is trying to kill the beautiful movie star Judy Manne. Lieutenant Al Wheeler convinces her to invite the suspects to her house for the weekend. †

Terror Comes Creeping. 1959. Private eye Danny Boyd is hired by a beautiful girl to protect her and her sister from their murderous, rich father; only the other sister doesn't see it that way. †

Murder Is a Package Deal. 1964. A movie actress hires Rick Holman to solve a blackmail problem. The most interesting character in this one is Gilda, a six-foot stuffed doll. †

Tomorrow Is Murder. 1960. While Mavis is appearing on a television show, another guest predicts a man's death, and Mavis finds herself head-over-heels in a case involving people with names like Bubbles Romayne. †

BROWN, FREDERIC. A powerful American writer from the 1940s and 1950s. Today he is most remembered and collected because of his science fiction, but he also wrote a number of mysteries somewhat in the tradition of James M. Cain and Cornell Woolrich.

The Fabulous Clipjoint. 1947. Ed Hunter seeks revenge for his father's death as he hunts a killer through Chicago's South Side. ††††

Madball. 1953. Here Brown uses one of his favorite themes—the Carnival. In a surreal setting, Doc, a phony fortune-teller, nightly peers into his crystal ball, until one special night when the ball held the key to fabulous wealth and a new life away from the sordid, neon-lit world of the Carnie. †††††

The Lenient Beast. 1956. The story of a psychotic mercy killer who has released six people from their pain. Interesting and chilling. ††††

Honeymoon in Hell. 1958. A collection of short stories covering science fiction, mystery, ghosts, demons, and gods. ††††

BUCHANAN, PATRICK. *A Requiem of Sharks.* 1973. This has an interesting beginning when a shark turns up in a swimming pool, but it rapidly degenerates into an average, hard-boiled novel. †††

BURKE, J. F.   *Location Shots.* 1974. Black hotel detective Sam Kelly investigates a murder at the Castlereagh which involves a film crew on location.   †††

BURKE, J. F.   *Death Trick.* 1975. It is the middle of a heat wave in New York, which the author describes with a tropical lushness normally reserved for New Orleans. Hotel detective Sam Kelly and his ex-hooker girlfriend, Madam Bobbie, investigate a murder by garrote in Madam Bobbie's whorehouse. An enjoyable hard-boiled story.   †††

BURNS, REX.   *The Avenging Angel: A Gabe Wager Mystery.* 1983. Detective Gabe Wager investigates a series of murders, each with a clue—the Avenging Angel from Mormon history.   †††

BYRD, MAX.   *Finders Weepers.* 1983. Private eye Mike Haller is looking for a stripper about to receive a large inheritance.   ††

C

CAIN, JAMES M.   If you are not already a fatalist, you will be after a short course of Cain. His characters are so deeply trapped in their grim fates that they don't even know how to struggle. Reading these books gives you the uneasy pleasure of omniscience: you know the character is about to take a fall, but you keep reading because you want to see him hit the ground.

The Postman Always Rings Twice.   1934. Cain's first novel has a reputation for sexiness, but it's really about boredom. The kind of boredom that eats away at you until you are so starved for excitement that you will do anything to break up the monotony. In this case, anything translates into adultery, murder, and divine justice.   †††††

Mildred Pierce.   1941. Cain explores the sexual rivalry between a mother and a daughter, with its ramifications of lust, betrayal, and ultimately murder. The California setting—sunny but seedy—is the perfect metaphor for the way all Cain character's dreams go sour.   †††††

The Butterfly.   1947. This short novel is about a grim, rawboned Kentucky farmer and his illicit (and implicit) love for his daughter. The Kentucky of the time was rough country, and telltale birthmarks, murder, and revenge enter the picture.   †††

Mignon.   1962. Cain's foray into the historical novel is good, but nowhere near as good as his other work. Set in New Orleans in the Civil War, the hero needs money and has to choose between pulling off a colossal crime or serving as the main squeeze in a fancy whorehouse.   ††

The Baby in the Icebox and Other Short Fiction. 1981. A good collection of some of his short stories. †††

CANNELL, DOROTHY. *The Thin Woman.* 1984. A wonderful story in which Ellie Simmons, an interior designer, who is a bit overweight, rents an escort— Bentley Haskell, a writer of trashy novels—to pose as her beau at a family reunion. The pose backfires when her wealthy uncle dies, leaving her his estate if she loses sixty pounds, her beau writes a novel with no smut, and they find a missing treasure. ††††

CAPUTI, ANTHONY. *Storms and Son.* 1985. The story of a father's revenge for the drug-related death of his son. The story was a bit too much from the stream-of-consciousness school of writing for my taste. ††

CARKEET, DAVID. *Double Negative.* 1980. Words can kill, and this book shows how. The story is set in an institute for language research in Wabash, Indiana, and hinges on a most unusual clue—but a fair one. With its engagingly oafish narrator, its bizarre office politics, and its wild humor, it is somewhat similar to Kingsley Amis. The motive is a bit farfetched, but it is so much fun that it doesn't matter. ††††

CASPARY, VERA. *Laura.* 1942. One of the great classics. What more need be said, except that it is the story of a tough cop who falls in love with a dead girl he has never met. †††††

CASPARY, VERA. *Bedelia.* 1945. A beautiful loving wife is gradually revealed as a female Bluebeard in this suspenseful domestic drama. †††

CASPARY, VERA. *A Chosen Sparrow.* 1964. A young Jewish girl marries a wealthy man who turns out to be an ex-Nazi and a homosexual. The promised terror and suspense never really develop, but the novel does offer a well-crafted study of the psychology of a concentration camp survivor. †††

CHANDLER, RAYMOND. One of the most famous and highly regarded of all American mystery writers. Next to Dashiell Hammett, he made the most important contribution in forging the truly American style of the California hard-boiled detective. Chandler's strength lay in his writing style rather than his plots. In fact, his plots are long, rambling affairs, which often do not work and are next to impossible to describe in brief form. But his tone, his ability to set a scene, and his description of people, places, and scenes is unsurpassed in all of detective fiction.

The Big Sleep. 1939. The idle rich are not so idle after all. Gambling, drugs, pornography, and blackmail are just for openers in one of Chandler's most complex novels. ††††

Farewell, My Lovely. 1940. My favorite description in all of Chandler occurs on the first page as Marlowe is "hired" by a huge ex-con, named Moose Malloy, to find his missing hooker-girlfriend, Velma. ††††

The High Window. 1942. The search for a rare coin brings Marlowe face to face with a cast of particularly unsavory characters: thieves, blackmailers, and others who crawl out from under rocks. ††††

The Lady in the Lake. 1943. Philip Marlowe's search for a missing woman turns up murder, blackmail, and official corruption. †††††

The Little Sister. 1949. Mousy, little Orfamay Quest comes to Marlowe for help in finding her long-lost brother. He wades through murder and drugs in his quest for the missing Orrin. †††††

The Long Goodbye. 1953. This story deals with alcoholism and contains some of Chandler's best writing. Hired to baby-sit a drunken novelist, our hero wades through the low habits of the upper crust. †††††

CHESBORO, GEORGE C. Author of one of the most interesting detective series of the past twenty years. His detective, Dr. Robert Frederickson, formerly Mongo the Magnificent, is a dwarf with a circus background. The plots are so far-out that they could be updates of the old pulps, but they are beautifully written and great fun.

Shadow of a Broken Man. 1977. The first Mongo novel. A man who is married to the widow of a famous architect hires Mongo to make sure the architect is really dead. There is a scene in the book which requires a suspension of belief, but you won't mind. ††††

City of Whispering Stone. 1978. The weakest of the Mongo stories. Mongo tangles with circus people and the Shah of Iran's secret police. †††

An Affair of Sorcerers. 1979. Mongo battles evil so incarnate that it reeks of *The Exorcist* as he comes in contact with people obviously under evil spells. ††††

The Beasts of Valhalla. 1985. Chesboro's most ambitious plot to date. Mongo investigates the death of his nephew who had invented a game based on *Lord of the Rings.* The search brings him up against monsters, evil geniuses, and a fortress in the Arctic. My hat is off to him for his cleverness. ††††

CLARK, MARY HIGGINS. One of the best suspense writers working today.

A *Stranger Is Watching.* 1977. Ronald Thompson is convicted of a series of brutal murders. Steve, the husband of one of the victims, falls in love with Sharon, a journalist who strongly opposes capital punishment, an issue which threatens their relationship as they wait for Thompson's execution. But they are not alone. Outside, in the dark, a stranger is also waiting. ††††

A *Cry in the Night.* 1982. Her most gothic tale. Jenny, a divorced mother of two, works in a Manhattan art gallery, where she meets the brooding artist of her dreams. He sweeps her off her feet and takes her to the wilds of Minnesota where, beneath the snow, everything is not coming up roses. †††

CLARK, PHILIP. Clark's novels of murder in the South read a bit like Tennessee Williams. They are mainly dialogue, virtually fleshed out plays, and are almost devoid of atmosphere.

Flight Into Darkness. 1948. After the death of his wild son, Henry Sturdevant gives up his bid for the presidency, leaving his younger son Hallon to unravel the blackmail scheme and find the murderer. ††

The Dark River. 1949. Janet and Murray Rossler have a huge fight. Later Murray is found dead in the study. The police say suicide, but Janet knows better. ††

CLOTHIER, PETER. *Chiaroscuro.* 1985. Artist Jacob Molnar drops out and goes into seclusion to pursue his painting until a young painter of little talent brings him evidence of murder and an art scam involving a giant of 20th-century art, a friend of Molnar's. Molnar tries to ignore it, but when the young painter is also killed, he has no choice but to leave his painting and find the killer. †††

COLLINS, MAX ALAN. *True Crime.* 1984. The title is somewhat misleading. It gives you the idea, when coupled with the photos in the text, that this is a true story. It isn't. It is a hard-boiled novel set in the 1930s in Chicago, somewhat along the lines of Stuart Kaminsky. †††

COLLINS, MAX ALAN. A *Shroud for Aquarius.* 1985. Mystery writer Mallory gets a late-night call from the sheriff of an Iowa town asking him to come to the site of a murder. The victim is an old friend of Mallory's, a woman he grew up with. The sheriff wants an update on how the old hippies are faring today— a bit of the usual left wing versus right wing so often found in the hard-boiled novel—but it's not a bad read. †††

CONSTINER, MERLE. *Hearse of a Different Color.* (n.d.) An intricate tale of multiple murder set in a small Tennessee town. Things are not what they seem. The solution is tricky and the killer well hidden. ††††

COONEY, CAROLINE B.   *Rear-View Mirror.* 1980. A good tense story in which Susan Setson, out for a stroll, comes across an escaped convict who is dumping infant twins into a river. She rushes to the rescue and becomes trapped in a nightmarish kidnapping.   †††

COXE, GEORGE HARMON.   Author of the Flashgun Casey and Kent Murdock series as well as many stories which appeared in the pulps.

The Glass Triangle.   1940. The Hollywood crowd comes to Boston and Kent Murdock's date with a starlet gets him involved in a scandalous murder case.   †††

The Jade Venus.   1945. Murdock comes home from war duty in Italy and steps into a deadly mystery. The key seems to be an ugly painting of a green Venus, a piece of war loot.   ††††

The Fifth Key.   1947. In the best of the Kent Murdock books, our hero finds himself on the wrong side of the camera when he turns up in a photo, next to the corpse of a naked woman. The setting is the New York radio-broadcasting world in its heyday.   ††††

Murder on Their Minds.   1957. Investigating the murder of an ex-cop and friend, Murdock unravels a case of lace-curtain corruption involving one of Boston's most upper-crust families.   †††

Inland Passage.   1949. This non-series novel is set on a cruise up the inland waterway from Miami to New York. When the captain is killed, the acting captain has his hands full with the cruise and the seven mysterious passengers on board.   †††

CRABB, NED.   *Ralph or, What's Eating the Folks of Fatchakulla County?* 1979. A wildly funny tale of murder in the Florida swamps, loosely based on "The Hound of the Baskervilles."   †††

CRANE, CAROLINE.   *Woman Vanishes.* 1984. After her husband takes a powder in the middle of the night, Pauline learns that he is $40,000 in debt to loan sharks and the interest is $2,000 per week. She decides to take her child and do the same.   ††

CROSS, AMANDA.   A series of genteel mystery novels set in academia and featuring Kate Fansler. They are low in violence and high in scholarly humor. She is well worth reading.

In the Last Analysis.   1964. The first Kate Fansler novel. A student asks Kate for help and winds up being murdered.   ††††

The James Joyce Murders. 1967. I was expecting something on the lines of Jane Langton's *Minuteman Murders,* Innes's *Hamlet Revenge,* or Tey's *Daughter of Time,* but that wasn't what I got. What I got was a light mystery in keeping with the rest of the series. The disappointment was of my own making. ††††

Poetic Justice. 1970. A wonderfully witty story of murder by aspirin set against the university unrest of the late 1960s. Good fun all the way through. ††††

Death in a Tenured Position. 1981. The first woman professor of the Harvard English department is found dead in the men's room. This is Kate Fansler's big chance to find out what the guys do behind closed doors, and she does it beautifully. ††††

CRUMLEY, JAMES. Everyone I know thinks Crumley is one of the powers of the future in the mystery field. I agree with them. My lone complaint is that he has only produced three books since 1976.

The Wrong Case. 1976. The story of Milo Milodragovitch, a hard-boiled detective with a liver like an L. L. Bean boot. I had a hangover for four days after I finished reading it. ††††

The Last Good Kiss. 1978. I hate the ending in this book. If you read it, you should skip the last chapter. I have my suspicions as to why he chose such an ending, but it doesn't excuse it. However, it is still one of the finest detective stories to appear in the last twenty-five years, and the opening page is as fine as there is in the field. The story is simple: Detective C. W. Sughrue is hired to locate Abraham Trahearne, a writer who is off on a drunk. He does, and that's when the fun begins. †††††

Dancing Bear. 1983. That old self-destructive sonofabitch Milo Milodragovitch is at it again. This time he has tapered off in his drinking, but he has discovered something worse—cocaine. He is hired by an old lady—a friend of his late father—to satisfy her curiosity about two lovers she has been observing through binoculars. Milo accepts the assignment, squares his shoulders, snorts up, and takes us into a world filled with machine guns, grenades, and bad people. †††

CURTISS, URSULA. A solid suspense writer of long standing.

The Noonday Devil. 1951. The long arm of coincidence is stretched to the breaking point when a chance meeting with a stranger in a bar puts Andrew Sentry on the trail of the man who can clear up the mystery of his brother's death. The brother was shot while attempting to escape from a WWII prison camp. Was it war or murder? †††

The Deadly Climate.   1954. A good example of the "night of terror" novel in which everything happens in a few, short, terrifying hours. Plucky Caroline Emmett is marked for death after accidentally witnessing a murder, and the house in which she takes refuge also harbors the murderer.   †††

Hours to Kill.   1961. A woman staying alone in the house of her sister and brother-in-law (her former lover) has to protect a frightened child and deal with a series of mysterious, menacing visitors, each of whom is a killer or a victim.   †††

Out of the Dark.   1964. Six children, left alone when the baby-sitter can't make it, invent a new game: they call people on the phone, at random, and say, "I know who you really are and what you did." Naturally one of the victims of their prank is an undiscovered murderer. The kids should have stuck to "Do you have Prince Albert in a can?"   ††††

D

DALY, CARROLL JOHN.   *The Snarl of the Beast.* 1927. Race Williams, New York private eye, goes up against the "Beast," a huge, snarling super-villain who could have made a good defensive lineman for the New York Giants. This novel is more important for the fact that Daly was the inventor of the hard-boiled detective than for its content.   †††

DALY, ELIZABETH.   Light, breezy husband-and-wife mysteries in the tradition of Lockridge's Mr. & Mrs. North series. Set largely in the 1940s, the Henry and Clara Gamadge stories are full of the style and grace of the period.

Unexpected Night.   1940. A few days of golf was all Henry Gamadge had in mind, but his holiday is interrupted when a young man's body is found at the bottom of a cliff. After that, the golf unfortunately has to take a backseat to the detection.   †††

All the Evidence Seen.   1943. While Henry is away, Clara Gamadge rents a summer cabin in the Berkshires. She begins to see visions of the cabin's former owner, a woman who has been dead for a year. When the dead woman's sister is murdered, Clara is accused, and Henry comes hurrying to her side.   †††

Nothing Can Rescue Me.   1943. Evil is everywhere and directed toward novelist Florence Hutter Mason as Henry Gamadge attempts to get to the bottom of things in a country weekend of murder and ouija boards.   †††

Nightwalk.   1967. A night prowler who turns to murder in the quiet village of Frazer's Mill proves to be a handful for Henry Gamadge.   †††

DAVIS, DOROTHY SALISBURY. *A Death in the Life.* 1976. Julie Hayes opens a storefront fortune-telling emporium near Times Square and falls squarely into a murder involving the hookers who parade nearby. A good read. †††

DAVIS, DOROTHY SALISBURY. *Scarlet Night.* 1980. Julie Hayes buys a painting to go over her mantel and becomes involved in an art-smuggling ring. †††

DAVIS, FREDERICK G. *Another Morgue Heard From.* 1954. Schuyler Cole and Lucas Speare leave their New York-based detective agency to help an old school chum of Speare's. They end up in the middle of a hot statewide political fight and murder. Two former accidental deaths come under scrutiny, and Speare cuts his way through the obfuscation to a rather improbable solution. ††

DAVIS, KENN. *The Forza Trap.* 1979. San Francisco private eye Carver Bascombe is hired as a bodyguard for a sexy opera star when rehearsals at the Golden Gate Opera House turn deadly. †††

DAVIS, KENN, AND STANLEY, JOHN. *Bogart '48.* 1979. A period piece in which Bogie and friends race around to stop a plot to blow up the Academy Awards. ††

DAVIS, KENN. *Words Can Kill.* 1984. A Carver Bascombe story in which the black, hard-boiled, California private eye sets out to discover which of several writers is responsible for the death of another writer. ††

DAVIS, MILDRED. A suspense writer of quality. Her work spans a quarter of a century but still retains freshness.

They Buried a Man. 1953. A newcomer to a small town, a newspaper reporter, gradually uncovers a shocking fact about a former mayor who died a year earlier. Although the mayor was the most popular man in town, everyone believes he was also a murderer. The reporter digs deeper to solve an old poisoning and learns the truth about the dead man. ††††

The Voice on the Telephone. 1964. This crowded plot has everything: an airplane blown up by a hidden bomb, blackmail, kidnapping, adultery, murder. The suspense mounts as the police try to nail an elusive killer, who seems to know too much about his victims' pasts. One problem with this book is that it is pieced together from accounts by various characters, which gives it a choppy quality. †††

The Sound of Insects. 1966. A pretty, young, high school biology teacher finds out that life in the suburbs can be as brutal as life among the predatory insects she studies when a suicide and murder disturb her quiet existence. This book is a little heavy-handed with the bug symbolism. †††

Tell Them What's Her Name Called. 1975. Three seemingly accidental deaths are preceded by identical, mysterious phone messages. The young daughter of one of the victims is the only person to suspect that they have been murdered— and that the murderer may strike again. Although the characters and the plot are only average here, a tense, anxiety-producing situation always develops when one helpless person knows the truth but can't get anyone to believe her. †††

• *Some books to read when you wake up convinced that you were meant to own a quaint little bookshop:*

THE BAY PSALM BOOK OF MURDER by Will Harriss
THE BURGLAR WHO LIKED TO QUOTE KIPLING by Lawrence Block
DEWEY DECIMATED by Charity Blackstock
HARDCOVER by Wayne Warga
THE HAUNTED BOOKSHOP by Christopher Morley

DEAN, S. F. X. *Death and the Mad Heroine.* 1985. Stylistically similar to Crispin and Davey, Dean sets an erudite, witty tone as amateur detective Professor Neil Kelly helps a lively young woman clear her father's name in an old shooting. †††

DEANDREA, WILLIAM. Even though he is a scattershot in his choice of subject and character, DeAndrea is one of my favorite, rising young authors. Firmly entrenched in the eastern school of the American mystery, his best work features quirky plots, rather than long-winded moralistic diatribes. Humor and a light, but deft, touch abounds throughout.

Killed in the Ratings. 1978. The first of DeAndrea's novels, about murder in the television world, made me an immediate fan. †††

The Lunatic Fringe. 1980. A warm, humorous story in which Teddy Roosevelt, as police commissioner of New York City, and a cop named Muldoon set out to thwart a group of anarchists. DeAndrea put a lot of effort and affection into this story, and it shows. Everyone I know that has read this book has loved it. ††††

Killed in the Act. 1981. It is the network's fiftieth anniversary and Matt Cobb (from *Killed in the Ratings*), along with a host of Hollywood types, plans to attend. Before they can leave the party, a body is found in the swimming pool. Then a bowling ball is stolen, followed by more murder. †††

Killed on the Ice. 1984. The weakest of the Matt Cobb stories. The television network is taping a special, starring a young skating star, when a psychiatrist is found dead on the ice.   †††

Cronus. 1984. A departure in style for the author, as he moves to the spy field with this Ross Macdonald type of tale involving family and political corruption.   †††

DELMAN, DAVID. *Death of a Nymph.* 1985. Lieutenant Jacob Horowitz journeys to upstate New York to speak at a college. While there he is shot, and the woman next in line for the presidency of the college is brutally murdered. Her body is found with the initials "EX" written in blood on her forehead. While Horowitz recovers, his wife does the detecting honors.   †††

DE LA TORRE, LILLIAN. She wrote, among other things, a play about America's favorite ax-murderess (*Goodbye, Miss Lizzie Borden,* 1948). She also wrote several true-crime books and a number of short stories featuring Samuel Johnson as an early detective.

Dr. Sam Johnson, Detector. 1946. Nine stories rich in superbly researched historical detail and period slang, including extracts from Boswell. Bonny Prince Charlie's ruby, the waxwork of Mrs. Salmon, and the true case of the missing great seal of England are among the doctor's cases.   ††††

The Detections of Dr. Sam Johnson. 1960. Eight more stories told by "Bozzy" and based on real people and events, including Horace Walpole and his famous Gothic estate, a spy from the American colonies, and a missing Shakespeare manuscript. As in the earlier volume, the author has included notes, so that the curious reader can determine just how much of her mysteries really happened.   †††

DENTINGER, JANE. Keep your eye on her. She takes up where Susan Isaacs left off when she so abruptly deserted the mystery field. Dentinger has a great, bitchy sense of humor and a fine eye for New York and the theater scene. Don't miss her.

Murder on Cue. 1983. Jocelyn O'Roarke, an out-of-work actress, lands a role as the understudy to a famous Broadway actress. When the famous actress is murdered, Jocelyn is suspected, and she has to play amateur detective to clear her name.   †††

First Hit of the Season. 1984. New York actress and amateur detective Jocelyn O'Roarke sets out to solve the murder of a vicious critic with a big cocaine habit.   †††

DEVON, D. G.   *Shattered Mask*. 1983. The story of this second novel—murder motivated by a real estate controversy—is better than the first (*Temple Kent*), but I still have not warmed to Temple, the fashion model turned detective. It's probably my prejudice, because the customers like her just fine.   ††

DISNEY, DORIS MILES.   Disney uses everyday Connecticut settings and solid, thoughtful investigators: a detective, an insurance adjuster, a postal inspector. The last, David Madden, is her best. He takes us behind the scenes at the post office and makes sure that—like rain, snow, etc.—even murder can't stop the mailman.

The Last Straw.   1954. A family-man detective probes a case of fraud, disappearance, and murder. It's a sober, methodical procedural investigation, with a tangle of motives—love and the love of money among them.   †††

Unappointed Rounds.   1956. Postal inspector David Madden, whose hobby is collecting stamps, gets involved with the police in a case of blackmail. The setting and characters are genteel, and the postal props of letters and stamps are used effectively.   ††††

My Neighbor's Wife.   1957. This one is a romantic suspense story in which girl meets man, sparks fly, he proposes, and doubts begin. Has he really divorced his first wife? Or has he done something worse? And who will win our heroine's heart—flashy, mysterious Roger or dull, dependable Neal?   ††

The Magic Grandfather.   1966. Seen largely through the eyes of a five-year-old girl, this is the story of two old enemies who live side by side, playing a long-drawn-out game of wits, patience, and revenge. Highly unusual.   ††††

Do Not Fold, Spindle, Or Mutilate.   1970. In what starts as a lighthearted spoof on dating services, a coven of bored bridge-club ladies invents a young blonde and submits her vital statistics to a computer dating service. Unfortunately, the ladies are a little *too* inventive, and the would-be swain a little *too* ardent.
†††

The Chandler Policy.   1973. A murder witness fleeing for his life involves an innocent bystander. Insurance investigator Jefferson DiMarco helps the police unravel a complicated plot. You never dreamed the insurance business could be so dramatic.   ††††

Winifred.   1976. A change of pace for Disney, this book is about the roots of psychic disintegration—madness leading to murder. It traces the emergence of a young woman's psychosis, and while there's not much mystery, there's a lot of suspense.   †††

DOBYNS, STEPHEN. A name to watch among young mystery writers. He gets better with each book, skillfully combining humor, action, and plot. His most popular books are set at Saratoga, around the racetrack, but any resemblance to Dick Francis ends there. His detective, Charlie Bradshaw, is a far cry from the wiry, diminutive heroes who people Francis's work.

Saratoga Swimmer. 1981. A gritty, atmospheric story in which Charlie Bradshaw, a security guard at Saratoga, sets out to solve the murder of his boss, a prominent stable owner. This is the second Charlie Bradshaw story; unfortunately, I could not find a copy of *Saratoga Longshot*, the first, to review here.
†††

Dancer with One Leg. 1983. A well-plotted, grim, police procedural about arson in Boston. This is not a Charlie Bradshaw story, but it is still a very good read. †††

Saratoga Headhunter. 1985. Saratoga detective Charlie Bradshaw reluctantly allows a crooked jockey to stay with him while he is awaiting his turn to testify in court. Before the trial begins, the jockey is murdered and beheaded. Fingers begin to point to Charlie, who in his ever-friendly way, has taken on a sleazy partner, and is helping out an ex-con with his morning milk route while the con goes to visit his ailing mother. The best yet from Dobyns. ††††

DOLSON, HILDEGARD. The inventor of Lucy Ramsdale, a tart-tongued but kind Connecticut widow who takes up criminal investigation and cultivates an intermittent friendship with the local police inspector.

To Spite Her Face. 1971. This is the first Lucy Ramsdale book. Like a pushier Jane Marple, Lucy insinuates herself into the murder investigation at a sedate cocktail party. A nose job has turned an ugly duckling into a swan—and may also have unleashed adultery, jealousy, and other disruptive elements. †††

A Dying Fall. 1973. Lucy's matchmaking plans for the local inspector go awry when the intended bride—the neighborhood millionairess—fixes herself up with someone else, someone who later turns up dead. Mystery clues here are concealed in a barrage of chatty byplay between the characters, but they are there. †††

Please Omit Funeral. 1975. A book-burning zealot rubs a notorious local author the wrong way, then gets rubbed out. Lucy and the inspector investigate. As in all of Dolson's books, Lucy comes off as someone you enjoy reading about, but would probably not want to live next door to. ††††

DOWNING, TODD. *Vultures in the Sky.* 1935. A train speeding through the Mexican desert pulls out of a tunnel, and the passengers discover that murder was committed in the tunnel. It's a classic situation: a closed carload of people, one of whom must be the killer, but all have something to hide. †††

DOWNING, WARWICK. *The Mountains West of Town.* 1975. Nathan Tree, a lawyer and reformed alcoholic, goes to a party for another lawyer—a crusader. At the party, the crusader's missing girlfriend turns up dead, and it is up to Nathan Tree to clear his name. †††

DRUMMOND, JOHN KEITH. *Thy Sting, Oh Death.* 1985. Little old lady and former court reporter Matilda Worthing investigates the death of an operatic tenor from an allergic reaction to a bee sting. This is a very clever idea for a murder. However, for the heroine to even consider a random bee sting as an act of murder is to suggest that she's a tremendously paranoid old lady with too much time on her hands. †††

DUNLAP, SUSAN. *The Bohemian Connection.* 1985. A nice wrinkle on the "missing woman" story as electric-meter reader Vera Haskell turns amateur detective and tries to find a missing friend of a friend. †††

DUNNE, JOHN GREGORY. *True Confessions.* 1977. A disappointing story of two brothers—a cop and a priest in post-WWII Los Angeles—who become involved in the hunt for a solution to a Black Dahlia type of killing. The quality of the writing could have made this a classic if the author had not become bored with his story. ††

E

EARLY, JACK. *A Creative Kind of Killer.* 1984. In New York's trendy SoHo district, private eye Fortune Fanelli tries to find the killer of Jenny Baker, a young woman whose body is left dressed as a mannequin in a boutique store window. †††

EBERHART, MIGNON. Her specialty is young women in mysterious circumstances, usually incriminating ones. Fortunately, the young women are always beautiful, so there are always stalwart males somewhere in the offing, ready to bail them out. Unlike most suspense novels of this kind, Eberhart's are shot through with flashes of humor.

Five Passengers from Lisbon. 1946. Five people board ship at Lisbon, fleeing war-ravaged Europe. The book starts with a shipwreck and goes on from there. One of the passengers isn't what he or she pretends to be. †††

Postmark Murder. 1955. An enigmatic war orphan and a lost relative miraculously returned from the dead are key players in a drama of impersonation and murder. The pathos with which the child is portrayed and the kindness of the main character become a little wearing. ††

Deadly Is the Diamond. 1955. A good Eberhart sampler: four novelettes of murder and mystery, ranging in tone from the droll to the gruesome. All are well done, with good, terse description and tight plots. ††††

Run Scared. 1963. A farfetched tale of blackmail and murder involving a potential president and his future first lady. †

EGAN, LESLIE. *A Case for Appeal.* 1961. Seven witnesses testify against a young woman in a murder trial. She is convicted but Jesse Falkenstein, her attorney, doesn't give up hope as he works to save her from execution. ††††

EGAN, LESLIE. *Against the Evidence.* 1962. Jesse Falkenstein, now married, takes on a case in which a retarded man is accused of murder. ††††

EGAN, LESLIE. *My Name Is Death.* 1964. The wife in a divorce proceeding is murdered and the finger points to her banker husband. It is up to Jesse Falkenstein to clear him. ††††

EHRLICH, COLLIS. *Attack.* 1980. The story of a woman's rape; its strength lies in its minimal violence and sensitive treatment. Much feeling and research are in evidence. †††

ELKINS, AARON J. *The Dark Place.* 1983. Professor Gideon Oliver investigates the death of a hiker, whose body is found in the Washington State Olympic National Park some eight years after his death. From all appearances his death was caused by a spear which is ten thousand years old. A well-written novel deserving attention. ††††

ELLIN, STANLEY. The author of a number of award-winning short stories and a handful of novels. He rarely works in the field of straight mystery and detection; instead, his tales are suspenseful, macabre, and ironic. One of his stories, "The Specialty of the House" (1948), has been widely anthologized and may put you off restaurants for life.

Dreadful Summit. 1948. The title is from *Hamlet*, and, like the play, this is the story of a mentally unstable boy bent on avenging an insult to his father. It is a squalid, gritty, well-contrived book, and the pathetic but dangerous narrator is especially compelling. †††

The Key to Nicholas Street. 1952. A beautiful and free-loving woman in a small-minded town turns up dead. The solution to her murder is pieced together in a collage of revelations and accusations by her neighbors. †††

The Eighth Circle. 1958. This book manages to take the stuffing out of all the

1950s-style, hard-boiled detective novels, while imitating them perfectly. It's the story of Murray Kirk, head of a detective agency in the Naked City, who has the toughness and the patter to be an investigator, but not the moral myopia. His investigation of police corruption and murder is well plotted and well written, if a bit dated. †††††

Very Old Money. 1985. Although its subject matter is an almost gothic story of derangement and revenge, this book is really about relations between the Nouveau Poor (a couple of out-of-work, young teachers who hire themselves out as servants) and the Old Rich (the blind, old patrician woman who hires them). As always with Ellin, it's smoothly written and convincing. †††

ELLINGTON, RICHARD. *Shoot the Works.* 1948. Ellington deserves to be better known. This is a neatly plotted private-eye novel. On the surface it appears to be an average blackmail-and-murder plot, but he has a few tricks up his sleeve, including the ability to hide the identity of the killer amid a small cast. ††††

EMERSON, EARL. *The Rainy City.* 1985. My customers loved this one, so I took it home and settled back only to find it was another private-eye-and-missing-female story. After twenty-five or thirty pages I gave up. ††

EMERSON, EARL. *Poverty Bay.* 1985. In a very Chandleresque plot, Seattle private eye Thomas Black takes on a missing-person case from a bride left at the altar. She wants him to find her missing husband-to-be, who has just inherited $15 million and is caught between bad friends and a bad family. †††

ENGLEMAN, PAUL. *Dead in Center Field.* 1983. Mark Renzler, former baseball player turned private eye, investigates two cases: in one a baseball bat was used as the weapon; in the other a hot hitter on a baseball team is being threatened. ††

ESTLEMAN, LOREN. An author who puzzles me. I've given quite a bit of reading time to him. Some of his work I like a lot, and some of it I have to turn thumbs down on.

Motor City Blue. 1980. Estleman introduces Amos Walker, Detroit private eye. The plot is a reworked series of Chandler/Macdonald clichés, which left me wondering if the whole thing wasn't meant to be tongue-in-cheek. I asked several customers. They weren't sure if it was a parody either. If it was, it is great. If not, it is nowhere near as interesting. ††

Angel Eyes. 1981. I'm still unsure about the seriousness of the series, but suffice it to say that this time Amos Walker gets tangled up with a dancer, a diamond ring, and a crooked union boss. ††

Kill Zone. 1984. The first appearance of Peter Macklin, hit man for hire. A group of terrorists kidnaps a pleasure boat on Lake Erie, and it is up to Peter Macklin to free them. ††

Roses Are Dead. 1985. The second Peter Macklin story. This time a mysterious enemy keeps hiring hit men to kill Macklin. A simple story, but beautifully told. I enjoyed every page of it. ††††

EVANS, JOHN. *Halo for Satan.* 1948. One of the best of the 1940s private eyes, Chicago sleuth Paul Pine becomes involved in a race for a rare religious artifact. A strong ending. ††††

EVANS, JOHN. *Halo in Brass.* 1949. Paul Pine is hired to find a missing girl. One of the most interesting tidbits of the story is his fee—five bucks per day. It shows what has happened to the dollar through the years. ††††

F

FAIRLEIGH, RUNA. *An Old-Fashioned Mystery.* 1983. Readers will either love or hate this puzzler, built around the "Ten Little Indians" idea. A group of guests are invited to spend the weekend on an island off the coast of Canada; one by one they are murdered. Be sure to read the introduction. I loved it. A great job of plotting and a lot of fun. ††††

FEARING, KENNETH. *The Big Clock.* 1946. A minor executive in a large publishing company is assigned to solve a woman's murder, apparently an unpremeditated crime of passion. However, when he begins to achieve results, he finds himself blocked by people in his own organization and is forced to go underground in a desperate attempt to publish the truth and save his own life. †††††

FEARING, KENNETH. *Dagger of the Mind.* 1947. A group of people in an artists' colony are thrown into confusion by the murders of two of their members. Lieutenant Wessex tries valiantly to unravel the intertwined threads of their lives to lay bare the motive for murder. A bold and dramatic effort to present a murder mystery from the various points of view of multiple narrators. ††††

FEEGEL, JOHN R. *Autopsy.* 1975. Myrl Caton is worth a lot more dead than alive, because of his life insurance, but only if his death is not a suicide. It is up to pathologist Jerry Leatherman to sift through the evidence and the suspects to determine whether it is murder or suicide. ††††

FEEGEL, JOHN R. *Death Sails the Bay.* 1978. Medical pathologist Bill Trumbull fakes his own death to be rid of his wife. However, on the sunny Gulf Coast, things go awry. This one reminded me of John D. MacDonald. †††

FENADY, ANDREW. *The Man with Bogart's Face.* 1977. A very funny story in which present-day private eye Sam Marlowe has plastic surgery to make him look like Bogart, and then takes on a case, filled with oddball characters, to find the famed "Eyes of Alexander" sapphires.   †††

FENADY, ANDREW J.   *The Secret of Sam Marlowe.* 1980. Bogart look-alike Sam Marlowe is hired to protect a beautiful movie star. Multiple murders follow in the never-never land of Hollywood, with the author—a film producer himself—interspersing the action with insider, film-colony jokes.   ††

FISHER, BRUNO.   *The Evil Days.* 1973. This is how James M. Cain would have told the story of Adam, Eve, and the Apple. Caleb Dawson's wife, a sexual handful, finds a bag of jewels, which she convinces him not to turn in, and just as in Adam's case, that's when his heartaches begin.   ††

FLETCHER, LUCILLE.   *Eighty Dollars to Stamford.* 1975. David Mark, a teacher by day and a cab driver by night, picks up a fare, a young woman who offers him eighty dollars to drive her to Stamford, Connecticut, wait outside a house while she goes in, and then drive her back to New York. This happens three times, but the third time she doesn't come out. David goes in, finds a body, and realizes he has been framed for murder.   ††

FLUKE, JOANNE.   *Cold Judgment.* 1985. A mad psychiatrist decides his patients are too crazy to live, so he sets out to correct the situation.   ††

FOOTNER, HUBERT.   *The Doctor Who Held Hands.* 1929. Almost unknown today, Footner was a Canadian journalist and author of many adventure and mystery novels. This one, set in New York, features one of the characters from his series: the beautiful Madame Rosika Storey, a private detective. Here she tangles with a psychoanalyst-blackmailer and criminal mastermind. The story has a lot of action and a neat twist in the final paragraph.   ††††

FORD, LESLIE.   Author of a series of mysteries featuring Georgetown detectives Grace Latham and Colonel Primrose. These are well-written mysteries from the 1930s and 1940s, written with a light social touch, and should be "must reads" for fans of Elizabeth Daly and Richard and Frances Lockridge.

Ill-Met by Moonlight. 1937. Colonel Primrose, the chubby detective, meets his sidekick-to-be and platonic pal, Grace Latham, in this adventure. Stormy weather on Chesapeake Bay interferes with their holiday, but the murder of the local vamp puts an even bigger damper on the fun.   †††

False to Any Man. 1939. A blonde and a redhead go after the same man, and one of them winds up dead. It looks like suicide, but Grace Latham and Colonel Primrose discover otherwise. The plot of this Georgetown mystery is partly political, with characters referring to the White House and the Senate, but politics are secondary to more personal motives.   †††

Siren in the Night. 1943. Wartime San Francisco is the setting for this novel, which finds Grace Latham investigating the death of a man murdered in his mansion during an air-raid alert. She runs into several related mysteries—a ghost and a bygone marital tragedy—and also finds herself in danger.   †††

By the Watchman's Clock. 1932. This non-series mystery, set in a small Maryland college, has some of the typical gothic ingredients: a pretty young heroine, a big empty house, and an atmosphere of menace. But it's also a murder mystery, with clues neatly arranged and a straightforward police investigation. A well written academic mystery.   †††

Trial by Ambush. 1962. This story of rape, murder, and revenge is a change of pace for Ford. It doesn't have her series characters or her usual chatty, amusing female narrator. Instead, it's a tense look at a psychotic and the police manhunt he sets off.   †††

FORREST, RICHARD. *A Child's Garden of Death.* 1975. Amateur detective Lyon Wentworth and police chief Rocco Herbert set out to find a killer who has left three bodies—a man, a woman, and a child—and a doll in shallow graves.   †††

FORREST, RICHARD. *The Death in the Willows.* 1979. Amateur detective and children's author Lyon Wentworth, after spending a pleasant day in New York, boards a bus bound for Connecticut, only to have it hijacked by a young man who demands to be taken to New Jersey. In the ensuing confusion, someone slips Lyon a gun and he kills the hijacker, but when the police arrive to investigate, the gun is nowhere to be found.   †††

FORWARD, ROBERT. *The Owl.* 1984. A beautifully written paperback original that reads like a James M. Cain and Cornell Woolrich version of "The Shadow." The Owl, a private eye cursed by permanent insomnia, roams the Los Angeles streets day and night, paying penance for his past sins and bringing criminals to justice—his own way. Warning: This story is extremely gritty and unsettling. Be careful when you read it.   ††††

FOY, GEORGE. *Asia Rip.* 1984. Lars Larsen, the skipper of a Cape Cod boat, investigates the murder of another captain, a close friend of his. There is lots of action and local color in this one. It's hard to put down.   ††††

FRIEDMAN, MICKEY. *Hurricane Season.* 1983. Interesting characterization and the Gulf Coast setting make for a pleasant read about murder in the swamps. Lily Trulock makes a good, middle-aged amateur detective.   †††

FRIEDMAN, MICKEY. *The Fault Tree.* 1984. Marina Robinson's sister, a devotee of a half-baked Indian guru, is killed in India. Marina goes to work for a firm in San Francisco which investigates industrial accidents. As she nears the end of a study involving an amusement park, she begins to receive messages from India, containing information only her sister could have known. Marina abandons her project and returns to a terror-filled India.   †††

G

GARBO, NORMAN.   *Gaynor's Passion.* 1985. If you can imagine combining the brooding intensity of *Crime and Punishment* with *Death Wish*, then you have *Gaynor's Passion*. Artist Richard Gaynor sets out to avenge the death of his sons in a plane crash linked to dirty dealings in the intelligence world.   ††††

GARDNER, ERLE STANLEY.   Best known for his 85–90 Perry Mason novels, Gardner also wrote some 25–30 stories under the name A. A. Fair, about the detective team of Donald Lam and Bertha Cool, and approximately 10 books about D.A. Doug Shelby. I'm a big fan of the A. A. Fair stories. The quality of the writing is far superior to the Perry Mason novels. In tone, they are very much like Rex Stout's Nero Wolfe stories, with Donald Lam filling the Archie Goodwin role, and Bertha Cool coming off very much like Nero Wolfe in drag.

Perry Mason novels:

The Case of the Caretaker's Cat.   1935. The caretaker for a dead millionaire wants to hire Mason to defend his cat against the bickering heirs; the plot ultimately leads to the murder of the caretaker.   †††

The Case of the Golddigger's Purse.   1945. Perry and Della are having a quiet drink when a man approaches him about a case involving a goldfish and a gold-digger. There are other wrinkles to the plot, but those are the two that attracted my attention.   ††

The Case of the Sunbather's Diary.   1955. The daughter of a man convicted of theft hires Perry Mason to help clear him—five years after his conviction—and Perry winds up suspected of murder.   ††

The Case of the Gilded Lily.   1956. Businessman Stewart Bedford is blackmailed for his young wife's past indiscretions. When the blackmailer is murdered, he is the logical suspect and calls on Perry Mason.   †

The Case of the Bigamous Spouse.   1961. A young woman suspects her best friend's husband of bigamy. She survives an attempt on her life, only to be charged with murder. Perry Mason rushes to the rescue.   ††

Novels under the name of A. A. Fair:

Double or Quits.   1941. Donald Lam and Bertha Cool go fishing and meet a doctor, who hires them to find some stolen jewelry. But there's more to it: there's a life-insurance policy with the old double-indemnity clause, and some slick talk about the difference between accidental death and accidental means.   †††

Crows Can't Count.   1946. Donald Lam and Bertha Cool are hired to find out why a man's niece is trying to sell a valuable necklace.   †††

Fools Die on Friday.   1947. A niece hires Donald Lam and Bertha Cool to keep her uncle's wife from poisoning him. When he is poisoned, the wife vanishes, and Donald and Bertha are murder suspects.   †††

Stories about D.A. Doug Shelby:

The D.A. Cooks a Goose.   1941. Doug Shelby investigates a hit-and-run which points to the heirs of an old miser with cans and cans of money in his cabin.   ††

The D.A. Breaks an Egg.   1949. A wheeler-dealer buys a local newspaper and wants Doug Shelby to play ball with him.   ††

GARNET, A. H.   *The Santa Claus Killer.* 1980. An entertaining story in which lawyer Charles Thayer decides to run for mayor against the wishes of his firm. In the process he discovers a nest of political corruption. Lots of action, love interest, and a good Detroit setting.   ††

GARRETT, RANDALL.   An author who combines science fiction and mystery in a strange setting where magic is stronger than science. If you can accept the premise, the plots and characters he creates are fun.

Too Many Magicians.   1967. Garrett's detective, Lord Darcy, investigates a classic locked-room murder in an unconventional setting—a sorcerers' convention held in barely recognizable London. Gambling, espionage, and mind reading enter into the solution.   †††

Murder and Magic.   1979. This collection of short stories continues the adventures of Lord Darcy. With his sidekick, Master Sorcerer Sean O'Lochlainn, he solves cases of murder, theft, and treason. The methods may be magical, but the motives are all too down-to-earth.   †††

GARRITY, DAVE J.   *Dragon Hunt.* 1967. Reading this novel about private eye Peter Braid, you'd think Mickey Spillane wrote it. Mike Hammer actually makes a cameo appearance compliments of Garrity's good friend "the Mick."   ††††

GARRITY (NO FIRST NAME). *Cry Me a Killer.* 1961. Why Dave Garrity is simply known as "Garrity" here is a mystery in itself. Police detective Walter Patterson falls in love with a gangster's girlfriend and decides that to have her he must murder her boyfriend. †††

GAT, DIMITRI. What appeared to be a rising career was suddenly thrown into a tailspin when the author was accused of plagiarism by none other than John D. MacDonald, and his second book was pulled from print. If you can find either of his books, *Nevsky's Return,* or *Nevsky's Demon* (modeled on *The Dreadful Lemon Sky*), grab it. They are both good reads and are fast becoming collector's items.

GAULT, WILLIAM CAMPBELL. A former pulp writer of western, hard-boiled-style mysteries. He had two main series: Brock Callahan, private eye, and Joe Puma, private eye.

Don't Cry for Me. 1952. The story of a playboy on the downhill slide was his first novel. ††

Run, Killer, Run. 1955. An ex-bookie, framed for the murder of his wife, breaks out of prison. On his way to Mexico, he discovers that his friend and lawyer had been sleeping with his wife, and that his case was sabotaged. There is only one chance to clear his name. †††

GAYLORD, OTIS. *The Rise and Fall of Legs Diamond.* 1960. A novel based on the life of one of the smoothest and most ruthless gangsters of the 1930s. He walked on everyone around him, and they loved it—or else. ††

GLAZNER, JOSEPH MARK. His Billy Nevers series is a nice updating of the old Mickey Spillane style. Glazner is nowhere near the writer Spillane was, but that doesn't keep the stories from being good, fast, time-passers in the New York private eye, tough-guy mold.

Smart Money Doesn't Sing or Dance. 1979. Billy Nevers finds a beautiful body in the bath, the body of the woman who has brought him into the art world to bid for a valuable Rembrandt. ††

Fast Money Shoots from the Hip. 1980. Billy Nevers gets involved in the world of movie tax shelters, warm women, hot lights, and murder. ††

Dirty Money Can't Wash Both Hands at Once. 1980. This time Billy Nevers is helping to establish a clinic for the terminally ill, but someone decides Billy should join the patients—with a terminal case of lead poisoning. ††

GODEY, JOHN. A prolific writer best known for his famous novel *The Taking of Pelham One Two Three,* Godey shuns series characters. His work ranges from traditional hard-boiled stories with an edge of suspense—like the early John D. MacDonald books—to humorous capers similar to the novels of Donald Westlake.

The Blue Hour. 1948. Things look bad for Henry Calvert, a heavy cocktailer who loses his wife and almost loses his job. They get worse when he is beaten up and his place ransacked, and he finds himself up to his ears in blackmail and murder. ††

The Fifth House. 1960. Reed Wingate, impulsive young reporter, investigates the mysterious hit-and-run death of a beautiful woman with secretive ties to the rich and powerful. ′ ††

A Thrill a Minute with Jack Albany. 1967. Small-time actor Jack Albany, on a night stroll in New York, finds himself the victim of a mugging by two men. The mugging turns weird, as one of the muggers kills the other, who turns out to be a cop. The remaining mugger mistakes Jack for a member of the gang, and that's when the thrill a minute begins. †††

GOINES, DONALD. Today he is a cult figure among blacks and his books are somewhat difficult to find, even though they have enjoyed very good sales. Some of his noteworthy titles are *Whoreson: The Story of the Ghetto Pimp*, *Black Gangster*, *White Man's Justice—Black Man's Grief*, and *Never Die Alone*.

GOLDSTEIN, ARTHUR D. *Nobody's Sorry He Got Killed.* 1976. When the granddaughter of one of the residents at the Golden Valley Senior Citizens Center is accused of murder, some of the senior citizens ask their resident crime expert, Max Guttman, to lend a hand. A fun read for fans of either Sam Spade or Miss Marple. †††

GOODIS, DAVID. A grim, "mean streets" type of writer in the tradition of James M. Cain and Cornell Woolrich. Within the past couple of years collectors have begun to show interest in his work, and his books—mostly paperback originals— once plentiful, are now getting hard to find.

Behold This Woman. 1947. Less a mystery or even a suspense novel than a bizarre, neon-lit portrait of the sleaze that inhabit the Baltimore dock world. ††††

The Moon in the Gutter. 1953. A picture of a loser too stupid to live—a man who forgives the man hired to kill him, and returns to live with the woman who hired him. †††

GOODRUM, CHARLES A. *Carnage of the Realm.* 1979. A very sophisticated, eastern, drawing-room type of mystery set in a club of wealthy coin collectors. †††

GOODRUM, GEORGE, AND KNOWLTON, WINTHROP. *A Killing in the Market.* 1958. The story of the kidnapping of the daughter of a powerful Wall Street executive. It is a fast, smooth read, but the plot is a bit ambitious for the length of the story.   †

GORDONS, THE. A married couple—Mildred Gordon, and Gordon Gordon (that's right, Gordon Gordon). In their younger days, Mildred was a correspondent for United Press, Gordon was an FBI agent. Together they wrote edge-of-the-seat novels in which the innocent bystander was drawn into a web of danger against his will.

Murder Rides the Campaign Train. 1952. Someone tries to kill the front-runner for the presidency on his campaign train, and accusing fingers begin to point to Jackie Moxas because of her troubled background.   ††

Menace 1962. Beginning in Tokyo and continuing through Hong Kong and Bangkok, an unknown man follows and terrorizes Sherri Jones. She has no idea who it is, or why it is happening. Could it have something to do with Chris, her new boyfriend?   ††

Ordeal. 1976. Sandy Wilcox lives through a plane crash in the desert. There is a fortune in Indian jewelry in the wreck. Outlaws hunt her down and have their way with her.   †

GORES, JOE. A former private eye, Gores, in his DKA (Dan Kearney Associates) series, gives a fresh, new look to the western, hard-boiled novel. With unromantic realism, he discloses what a private eye actually does for a living.

Dead Skip. 1972. The first DKA novel. One of the associates winds up in a coma while repossessing a car, and the rest of DKA sift through his cases to find out who and why. An excellent read.   ††††

Final Notice. 1973. This time DKA find themselves between a blackmail scheme and the Mafia. Although a very good read, it is not quite as unusual as *Dead Skip.*   †††

Gone, No Forwarding. 1978. The weakest of the series. DKA spends a lot of time tracking down witnesses, while someone is trying to have their license revoked.   †††

GOULART, RON. *A Graveyard of My Own.* 1985. A very ingeniously plotted novel of murder in Westport, Connecticut. Comic book artist Bert Kurrie finds the body of another artist while jogging.   †††

GRADY, JAMES. *Runner in the Street*. 1984. A good private-eye novel with a strong Washington, D.C., setting, in which John Rankin investigates the murder of a hooker and the connection with powerful figures on Capitol Hill.   †††

GRAFTON, C. W. *The Rat Began to Gnaw the Rope*. 1943. An excellent story featuring Gil Henry, a Kentucky lawyer, who begins investigating a stock fraud and winds up investigating murder.   ††††

GRAFTON, SUE. *"A" Is for Alibi*. 1982. The well-written debut of female private eye Kinsey Millhone, hired by a woman who has been convicted and imprisoned for the murder of her worthless husband. The woman wants her innocence proven, even at this late date and at all costs.   †††

GRAFTON, SUE. *"B" Is for Burglar*. 1985. In spite of the opening reference to the "had I but known" school of detective writing, the story is much more like Chandler than Eberhart with its emphasis on missing sisters and bad rich people.   †††

GRANT, MAXWELL. Author of the "Shadow" stories. What more need be said?

The Living Shadow. 1931. This is the Shadow's debut. He solves a string of murders, enlists the aid of several loyal sidekicks, appears when he's needed, and then vanishes into the night, delivering a powerful punch to evildoers everywhere. His Lamont Cranston identity is not developed in this first appearance (as it was later to be), but the book's exciting originality is still there fifty years later.   †††††

The Shadow Laughs. 1931. In one of the great original Shadow novels, a counterfeiting gang shakes up New York, murdering a police detective along the way. But, as always, the Shadow has the last blood-curdling laugh.   †††††

The Shadow and the Golden Master. 1939. The Shadow tangles with the arch-villain Shiwan Khan, the Golden Master, who proves too wily for the Shadow.   †††

Shiwan Khan, The Master of Oriental Nemesis. 1939. The Shadow and Shiwan Khan tangle again. This time the Shadow is up to the task.   †††

GREEN, ANNA KATHARINE. One of the pioneers of the field. She was one of the first women ever to have a mystery novel published and, as such, we owe her a tremendous debt of gratitude.

The Leavenworth Case. 1878. It is tough going if you don't like period pieces, but her first and best book is worth reading for its complex plot and the melodrama that made it a best seller a century ago. A prominent businessman is shot to death in his library, and his two beautiful nieces are the logical—if shocking—suspects. The investigation and eventual outcome lead Ebenezer Gryce through an almost Dickensian legal labyrinth. †††††

GREENLEAF, STEPHEN. Author of the John Marshall Tanner stories. They are traditional in the Ross Macdonald, hard-boiled style. A bit too traditional sometimes, but my customers like him.

Death Bed. (n.d.) The first John Marshall Tanner story. †††

Grave Error. 1979. Family scandal among the powerful, an old murder, and a daughter's search for identity keep Tanner busy. †††

State's Evidence. 1982. Tanner tangles with the country-club set and a hit-and-run accident. †††

Fatal Obsession. 1983. Tanner's nephew is found hanged in his hometown. Tanner's brother is an embittered Vietnam vet with past secrets. †††

GRUBB, DAVIS. *The Night of the Hunter.* 1953. One of the true classics of suspense. The story of a preacher, so evil as to defy description, and the nine-year-old boy who discovers his secret and is hunted by him because of it. †††††

GRUBER, FRANK. One of my favorite writers from the fifties. He was funny, hard-boiled, and fast moving. He favored two-man teams for his heroes. The teams he used most were Johnny Fletcher and Sam Cragg, and Otis Beagle and Joe Peel.

The Lonesome Badger. 1954. Otis Beagle and Joe Peel are down to their last dime, and Otis gets the idea to reply to an ad in the personals from a rich woman looking for a husband—only he does it in Joe's name. Joe goes to meet her, and she turns out to be beautiful, but married. When the husband winds up dead, things look bad for Joe. †††

The Limping Goose. 1954. A bill collector catches up to smooth-talking Johnny Fletcher and Sam Cragg, his iron-man companion. After a slight altercation, which the bill collector loses, Johnny and Sam bet that they can do a better job of bill collecting than he. But all hell breaks loose when a playboy is found murdered in the apartment of a show girl they have just visited. †††

H

HALLAHAN, WILLIAM. *The Search for Joseph Tully.* 1974. A mystery and search through the past with horror overtones, as London solicitor Matthew Willow comes to New York to trace the whereabouts of the last living relative of Joseph Tully. He methodically goes about his business, always reaching dead ends, until he discovers an old diary—and then the problems begin.   ††††

HALLIDAY, BRETT.   Although Halliday's Mike Shayne novels do not have the depth or quality of writing found in Mickey Spillane's Mike Hammer novels, Halliday was certainly Spillane's greatest competition in the ultra–hard-boiled school of the 1950s and 1960s. With sales of over forty million from one publisher alone, Halliday had one big thing going for him—he could crank them out fast, and they were always a good read.

Armed... Dangerous...   1966. Shayne, posing as a holdup man, infiltrates a gang of drug smugglers.   †††

Murder Spins the Wheel.   1966. Shayne is called in when a group of thugs threatens a big gambler as he moves money from one location to another to cover some unexpected losses.   ††

So Lush, So Deadly.   1968. Mike investigates the goings-on aboard a yacht whose inhabitants' dialogue sounds like Tennessee Williams imitating Hemingway.   †††

At the Point of a .38.   1974. A beautiful, Israeli secret agent throws herself into Mike Shayne's big old protecting arms when she runs afoul of the Jewish godfather.   ††

HAMILL, PETE.   *Dirty Laundry.* 1978. The story of New York reporter Sam Briscoe, and the murder of a girlfriend.   †

HAMILL, PETE.   *The Deadly Piece.* 1979. Sam Briscoe goes to a concert where a murder occurs in front of 20,000 fans.   †

HAMMETT, DASHIELL.   Praising Hammett is like carrying coals to Newcastle, so I won't bother, except to say that his importance in the field of detective fiction and his influence on other writers cannot be overemphasized.

The Dain Curse.   1928. The only thing interesting about this Continental Op story is that Hammett wrote it, and obviously couldn't figure out how to end it, or when.   ††

Red Harvest. 1929. Hammett's most important work, it is the bridge between the western novel and the modern hard-boiled detective story. It may well be the first novel where the outsider-detective battles a corrupt town.　†††††

The Maltese Falcon. 1930. This is the one they made into the movie and it still holds up. As you read it, you are right there with Bogart and Greenstreet.
†††††

The Glass Key. 1931. I have read that this was Hammett's personal favorite. It is another novel of corruption, only this time it is set in a city and the corruption is political. Ned Beaumont, a political sleazebag, attempts to wrestle control from a group of even sleazier people.　††††

The Thin Man. 1934. Hammett's last novel. It marks a switch in direction from the western hard-boiled to the eastern drawing-room category. In fact, it is almost a play as Nick and Nora Charles conduct the investigation of a murder from the comfort of the Normandie in New York at Christmas.

The Big Knockover. 1966. A posthumously published collection of short stories featuring the Continental Op.　††††

The Continiental Op. 1974. Another collection of short stories featuring the Continental Op.　††††

HANNA, DAVID. *The Opera House Murders.* 1985. The worthless husband of a big-time diva is found murdered at the stage door, just like any other Johnnie. Attorney Tammy Drake investigates, trying to solve the murder before the killer can strike again.　††

HANSEN, JOSEPH. The author of an excellent series featuring gay insurance investigator Dave Brandstetter. There is some truly good writing in these novels, and the plotting is very good, too.

The Man Everybody Was Afraid Of. 1978. Dave Brandstetter investigates the death of a small-town police chief.　†††

Nightwork. 1984. Insurance investigator Dave Brandstetter examines the murder of a teacher with a big life-insurance policy. His investigation takes him to some seamy places, and the good writing creates real tension.　††††

HANSL, ARTHUR. *Freeze Frame.* 1985. A super-bitch is found hanging from her gravity boots with her throat slashed. In places it sounds a bit like Jackie Collins, but it is not.　†††

HARRINGTON, JOYCE. *No One Knows My Name*. 1980. A very well written tale of a psycho killer loose in a theater group in the wilds of northern Michigan. †††

HARRIS, CHARLAINE. *Sweet and Deadly*. 1981. A southern mystery in which Catherine Linton discovers the body of her deceased father's nurse and realizes the auto accident which had claimed the lives of both her parents some six months earlier was no accident. ††††

HARRIS, CHARLAINE. *A Secret Rage*. 1984. A New York model returns to college in Tennessee. However, when she becomes the victim of the rapist terrorizing the small town where she lives with a girlfriend, she gets angry— real angry. With a couple of other women, she sets out to see justice done.
†††

HARRISS, WILL. *The Bay Psalm Book of Murder*. 1983. When a librarian is found dead with a rare volume in his hands, English professor Cliff Dunbar and the beautiful Mona Moore track down a ruthless killer. ††††

HAUSER, THOMAS. *The Beethoven Conspiracy*. 1985. This first mystery by an author in the nonfiction field begins with a triple murder of three New York musicians. In investigating the crime, a police detective sifts through the fragile evidence and the great composer's nine symphonies to find a bizarre motive for mass murder in a Bavarian mansion. †††

HEAD, MATTHEW. He created Hooper Taliaferro, a civil servant working for the U.S. foreign service, mostly in Africa. His rambling tales are strong in local color and feature complicated psychological mysteries solved by Head's missionary detective, Dr. Mary Finney. Despite their murky plots and sometimes lurid motives, Head's books are enjoyable reading because Taliaferro is so easy-going.

The Cabinda Affair. 1949. At the request of the War Contracts Settlements Commission, Taliaferro gets mixed up in the shady dealings surrounding a shipment of valuable mahogany. Long on murder, mosquitoes, and missionaries, the case is neatly managed, and the terse descriptions of West Africa are knowledgeable and vivid. ††††

The Congo Venus. 1950. The lady in question is a beautiful blonde Belgian, murdered at the beginning of this book, which is set in Leopoldville in the Belgian Congo. It's a grisly domestic melodrama, but Taliaferro manages to retain his sense of humor. †††

Murder at the Flea Club. 1955. In a change of scene, Taliaferro and Dr. Finney appear in Paris, where they untangle the knot of motives and alibis surrounding a murder in a seedy bistro. †††

HEALY, JEREMIAH. *Blunt Darts*. 1984. Another Boston private eye, another missing kid. Sound a bit like Spenser? †††

HENSLEY, JOE L. *Rivertown Risk*. 1979. The novel is set in a corrupt town where the judge in a murder trial begins to receive death threats. †††

HENSLEY, JOE L. *Outcasts*. 1981. Attorney Dan Robak defends his cousin in the murder of his girlfriend. His investigations take him to the Grand Hotel where there are some X-rated goings-on. †††

HIGGINS, GEORGE V. If you like Elmore Leonard, you will like Higgins. His strong suit is dialogue; next best are his characters; his weakness lies in plotting. Sometimes his plots are a bit obscure and tough to follow. In that respect, he is more novelist than mystery writer.

The Friends of Eddie Coyle. 1971. The story of a worthless Boston thug. It could be a textbook on how to write a novel about big-city flotsam. †††††

The Judgment of Deke Hunter. 1976. A near unreadable story of a Massachusetts cop and a bank robber. ††

Kennedy for the Defense. 1980. A lively, tough-guy story about Jerry Kennedy, a Boston lawyer. ††††

Penance for Jerry Kennedy. 1985. Jerry Kennedy's whole world seems to be crashing around his ears with friends going to jail, the IRS after him, his wife aloof, and his secretary indifferent. This one is a lot of fun. ††††

HILLERMAN, TONY. The author of two series of mystery novels set on Navaho reservations in the Southwest, Hillerman combines a tremendous knowledge of Indian lore with some very well plotted mysteries. The heroes of his two series are Joe Leaphorn and Jim Chee.

The Fly on the Wall. 1971. A good novel of political corruption on a statewide level, and the investigative reporter who uncovers it. This is not an Indian story. †††

The Blessing Way. 1970. Lieutenant Joe Leaphorn finds a body with its mouth filled with sand. It appears to be the work of the Wolf-Witch, a character from Navaho mythology. †††

Dance Hall of the Dead. 1973. An Indian boy disappears in the night while performing a solitary dance ritual. When his best friend finds out, he disappears too. Joe Leaphorn investigates and uncovers a load of interesting characters in the process. †††

Listening Woman. 1978. Joe Leaphorn investigates the murder of an old man. The trail leads to a bank robbery and a kidnapping plot. †††

People of Darkness. 1980. An old Indian is murdered, and his wife offers Jim Chee a reward to find a box filled with rocks. †††

The Dark Wind. 1982. Jim Chee investigates the murder of a man whose palms and soles have been cut off. †††

The Ghostway. 1984. An excellent story in which the Federal Witness Relocation Program puts a thug on the Navaho reservation without telling anyone. This triggers a series of murders all tied to Navaho legends. One of his best. ††††

HIMES, CHESTER. Himes is best remembered for his novel *Cotton Comes to Harlem*††††, one of a series featuring Coffin Ed Johnson and Grave Digger Jones, a couple of great black cops with Harlem as their beat. Himes could write like a dream. His prose was like music, and I always loved it. He had warmth, style, humor, and a tremendous gift for character and setting. Other favorites of mine are *All Shot Up* ††† and *The Big Gold Dream* †††† (my favorite of them all).

HINKEMEYER, MICHAEL. *A Time to Reap.* 1984. The bloody murder of the local prostitute and one of her sons brings retired sheriff Emil Whippletree back into the murder-solving business. In a German-American community in Minnesota, Emil bails out the new sheriff in a mystery which seems to involve local churchmen. †††

HIRSCHBERG, CORNELIUS. *Florentine Finish.* 1963. A story of multiple murder, stolen diamonds, and chicanery in the New York diamond world. Well told with a good heroine. ††††

HITCHENS, DOLORES. *Footsteps in the Night.* 1961. Sheriff Ferguson investigates murder in a new housing development. ††

HITCHENS, DOLORES AND BERT. *F.O.B. Murder.* 1955. Special agents Collins and McKechnie of the railroad police investigate a number of seemingly unrelated small-time cases which ultimately lead them to a murder. ††††

HOCH, EDWARD D. *The Shattered Raven.* 1969. A story of great fun set at the Mystery Writers of America annual Edgar Awards dinner. Each year an award is given to the mystery writer of the year. This year the recipient is murdered just as he begins his speech (probably by a concerned citizen who has seen too many awards shows on TV). ††††

HOLTON, LEONARD. Author of the Father Breeder series.

A *Pact with Satan*.   1960. Father Breeder thought the woman was crazy when she told him that her dead husband was trying to burn her alive. After all, he had died in a flaming car crash. But then there were the incidents such as the mattress soaked in gasoline and the gas jets left on.   †††

Secret of the Doubting Saint.   1961. Father Breeder gets involved with a big-time TV producer and finds himself suspected of murder over a missing diamond. Like the man says—If you don't know diamonds, know your jeweler.   †††

HOMES, GEOFFREY.   *The Man Who Murdered Goliath*. 1943. Robin Bishop, newspaperman and amateur detective, investigates the murder of businessman Walter Miller, and figures out whether Dick Kilgallen, a man who has confessed to dozens of crimes over an eight-year period, has finally committed one. †††

HORNIG, DOUG.   *Foul Shot*. 1984. This first novel is a bit overplotted. It is a private-eye story which combines adultery, incest, sibling rivalry, and murder with a parade of unlikable characters caught in bizarre situations.   ††

HORNIG, DOUG.   *Hardball*. 1985. Private eye Loren Swift is hired to find out who is making hell for a local sheriff in rural Virginia.   ††

HOYT, RICHARD.   A strong newcomer to the field. Hoyt has written several thrillers, but his best works are his John Denson mysteries. Denson, a private eye from the Washington/Oregon area, is a fine mix of the 1930s values and 1980s human frailties. Good reads for men and women hard-boiled fans alike.

Decoys.   1980. Denson is hired by a beautiful, tough-talking, female private eye to help track down a murdering pimp who is hiding out in Denson's small, snow-bound hometown of Cayuse, Oregon. Denson and the woman work well together. | | |

30 for a Harry.   1981. Denson is hired by a newspaper to discover a blackmailer on the staff.   ††††

Siskiyou.   1983. Denson goes trout fishing in Oregon and hooks into the murder of a beautiful girl.   †††

HUGGINS, ROY.   He did not produce many novels, but he will be long re-membered as the creator of two extremely popular television shows: "77 Sunset Strip" and "The Rockford Files." If you are lucky enough to find anything by him, don't pass it up.

The Double Take.   1946. The initial outing of Stu Bailey, later to become "77 Sunset Strip," is one of the finest of the Chandleresque, hard-boiled private-eye stories ever written.   †††††

Lovely Lady, Pity Me. 1949. Someone was out to get John Swanney. Was it the sleazy private eye, the sexy secretary, or the ruthless millionaire?   †††

HUGHES, DOROTHY B.   A topflight suspense writer.

The So Blue Marble. 1940. Fashion designer Griselda finds herself being used by a set of twins intent on securing a valuable treasure. When she opposes them, the danger spills over to her estranged husband and her sisters.   ††††

Ride the Pink Horse. 1946. A classic novel of revenge in which a Chicago thug pursues a slightly smarter and dirtier Chicago thug to Santa Fe during a fiesta.   †††††

In a Lonely Place. 1950. A masterpiece. A man's mental breakdown is caused by his own jealousy and insecurity, just as luck and a good woman's love brings him success again after a long downhill slide.   †††††

HUGO, RICHARD.   *Death and the Good Life.* (n.d.) An excellent first novel of the James Crumley type. The hero roars around the Northwest from Montana to Oregon as he tries to solve the ax murder of an accountant for a timber mill. In the process, he meets a wonderful world of quirky characters.   ††††

I

IAMS, JACK.   *The Body Missed the Boat.* 1947. A very entertaining novel about the murder of an American consul in French Equatorial Africa. The author's first mystery.   †††

IAMS, JACK.   *A Shot of Murder.* 1950. On their honeymoon in Paris, Rocky and Jane Rockwell encounter murder and a cast of characters which includes an evil doctor, with an even more evil hypodermic.   †††

ISAACS, SUSAN.   *Compromising Positions.* 1978. A whale of a first novel from a woman who has gone on to become a major novelist of general fiction. This lighthearted, but not comic, mystery about the murder of a Long Island periodontist is near perfect in tone with its great bitchy sense of humor.   ††††

J

JACKSON, JON.   *The Diehard.* 1977. An offbeat mystery featuring Detroit cop "Fang" Mulheisen and a corpse, who rings the doorbell wearing nothing but bubblebath foam and a knife in the back.   ††

JAGODA, ROBERT. *A Friend in Deed.* 1977. An absolutely hilarious novel about a New York adman who decides to kill his overbearing, nymphomanical wife by using their pet poodle. When the scheme backfires, and the wrong person is killed, he turns detective. So funny, it could have been written by Tom Robbins. ††††

JAKES, JOHN. *The Seventh Man.* 1958. Chicago reporter Harry Diamond gets a bullet through his windshield as a message to "lay off" his investigation of Chicago crime and its new boss. Think he pays any attention to it? †

JEFFERS, H. PAUL. *Rubout at the Onyx.* 1981. A readable hard-boiled novel set in the 1930s in which private eye Harry MacNeil moves through an average plot, all the while rubbing shoulders with some of New York's greats and near-greats of the period. †††

JOHNS, VERONICA PARKER. *Servant's Problem.* 1963. This time the butler did not do it. No, this time the butler is the detective. Webster Flagg, an elderly black actor doubling as a houseman extraordinary, solves a Manhattan drawing-room mystery. †††

JOHNSON, DIANE. *The Shadow Knows.* 1974. Someone is trying to rid the world of a rather disagreeable woman. Is it her nightly obscene phone caller, her married lover, her ex-husband, or someone even more loathsome? ††

JOHNSON, DIANE. *Dashiell Hammett—A Life.* (n.d.) Possibly the best biography of Hammett, and the only one written with the consent of Lillian Hellman. ††††

K

KALLEN, LUCILLE. One of the up-and-comers in the eastern school of detective novels. C. B. Greenfield is the publisher of a small-town, New England newspaper, and Maggie Rome, the narrator, is his star reporter. A fresh new look, coupled with humor and good writing, makes this series one to be reckoned with.

Introducing C. B. Greenfield. 1979. An excellent debut in which Maggie and C. B. investigate a hit-and-run accident involving a child. ††††

The Tanglewood Murder. 1980. Death mars the Boston Symphony's Tanglewood series, and it is up to C. B. and Maggie to get things back on track. ††††

No Lady in the House. 1982. The third adventure in the series. Good New England atmosphere. Low violence, energetic wit. †††

The Piano Bird. 1984. Maggie Rome discovers murder on a beautiful barrier reef inhabited by some Hollywood types, a charter boat captain, and a female botanist. †††

KAMINSKY, STUART. One of my favorites for a light, fun, energetic read. His stories about Toby Peters, a down-on-his-luck, but not morbid, Hollywood private eye during Hollywood's Golden Years, combine Kaminsky's tremendous knowledge of film and film stars with humor-filled plots and unlikely combinations. Chandler he ain't, and thank God for that. Do yourself a favor and read him.

Bullet for a Star. 1977. In his debut, Toby Peters, former Warner Brothers studio guard turned detective, is hired to clear Errol Flynn of a rather nasty sex scandal. †††

Murder on the Yellow Brick Road. 1977. In the second Toby Peters story, he is hired by Louis B. Mayer to keep Judy Garland's name clean after someone murders a Munchkin on the sound stage of *The Wizard of Oz.* †††

You Bet Your Life. 1978. Hollywood private eye Toby Peters is hired to keep the Chicago mob from killing Chico Marx over a gambling debt. There is a hilarious scene in which Groucho Marx, posing as Dr. Hackenbush, addresses a psychiatrists' convention. †††

High Midnight. 1980. Gary Cooper begins receiving death threats and Toby Peters comes to his aid. In one amusing scene, Toby gets involved in a boxing match with Ernest Hemingway. †††

Catch a Falling Clown. 1981. Toby Peters is called in when an elephant is electrocuted, and Emmett Kelly begins to fear for his life. †††

He Done Her Wrong. 1983. Peters is recommended by his brother to discover who would want to kill Mae West. †††

KANE, FRANK. Author of the Johnny Liddell private-eye series. The stories are quippy, action-filled quickies in the mold of Mike Shayne.

Final Curtain. 1964. A would-be actress is accused of murdering the producer, who lured her to the casting couch and then failed to produce. It is up to Johnny Liddell to set the record straight and collect his pound of flesh. ††

The Guilt-Edged Frame. 1964. Johnny, following his baser instincts with a beautiful woman, finds himself looking down the wrong end of a gun. ††

KANE, HENRY. Among older readers, Kane is known as one of the first to switch from a straight detective format to one including a bit of sex. Today his sex is quite tame, but his stories still hold up. He had a style similar to Frank Gruber. They were well plotted, breezy, humorous reads. His main guy is Peter Chambers.

Don't Just Die There. 1963. Peter Chambers falls for a beautiful actress, but he has rivals in the form of two other boyfriends. After a date they return to her apartment and find a body in the kitchen. They leave for a few minutes to discuss things. When they return, the body is gone.   † †

Nobody Loves a Loser. 1963. Mitch Crane, one of Pete's best friends, comes to him with a tale about a struggle with a jealous husband and an accidental shooting. However, when they get there, the body is that of the wife, not the husband.   † †

The Schack Job. 1969. Peter Chambers renews an old affair with Ursula Schack, an opera singer and the wife of a Greek shipping magnate, then finds himself framed for murder. A sexy one.   † †

Death of a Hooker. 1969. Pete is hired by two separate women to get each of them an extension from the same loan sharks. The plotting is good, but the most interesting part of the story is whether Pete gets the girl.   † †

KAPLAN, ARTHUR. *A Killing for Charity.* 1976. Charity Bay, New York City private eye, is hired by diamond merchants to recover three quarters of a million dollars in missing stones, and gets a bit romantically involved with a cop.   † †

KATZENBACH, JOHN. *The Heat of the Summer.* 1982. A stunning debut. The author writes with total confidence and command of his subject—the story of a nut on the loose in Miami, who calls up a newspaper reporter to brag. While not strictly a police procedural, it is a strong work of investigation by a newspaper and a big-city police department.   † † † †

KAYE, MARVIN. *Bullets for Macbeth.* 1976. In the style of Josephine Tey in *Daughter of Time*, but not quite as good, the author takes on a theater mystery. Amateur detective Hilary Quayle tries to figure out who did it in the present tense, as well as to provide illumination on the identity of Banquo's third murder in Shakespeare's play.   † † †

KAYE, MARVIN. *My Brother, The Druggist.* 1979. Marty Gold, a New York City pharmacist, allows himself to be conned into taking a thirteen-year-old kid to Washington for a convention. The thirteen-year-old is kidnapped, and Marty, in an adventure similar to a Westlake novel, has to get the kid back.   † †

KELLY, PATRICK A. *Sleightly Murder.* 1985. A promising debut in which professional magician Harry Colderwood is hired to explain away some spiritualist mumbo jumbo, but his client is killed, and things start to look bad for Harry.
†††

KELLY, SUSAN. *The Gemini Man.* 1985. A promising debut in which freelance writer Liz Connors, full of warmth and happiness in her new Cambridge, Massachusetts, apartment, find the young woman next door murdered. Liz calls her boyfriend who happens to be a police lieutenant. Solid police work by a new writer, who also happens to work for the Cambridge Police Department.
†††

KEMELMAN, HARRY. He started by writing short stories about Nicky Welt, a chess-playing professor and armchair sleuth, and went on to chronicle the doings of David Small, the rabbi detective. Both the Nicky Welt stories and the Rabbi Small novels rely on logic and deductive reasoning, though the novels have been increasingly concerned with character studies, social commentary, and religion.

Friday the Rabbi Slept Late. 1964. This much-praised first novel introduces young Rabbi Small, who's having trouble with his slick, new suburban congregation. His troubles multiply when a girl is found pregnant and dead in the synagogue parking lot—and the rabbi is the chief murder suspect. The book is as much about Small's struggle to win the confidence of his congregation as it is about the murder investigation, but the parallel plots are smoothly woven together.
††††

Saturday the Rabbi Went Hungry. 1966. Murder on Yom Kippur gives the rabbi a chance to demonstrate not only his detective skills but also his endless store of Talmudic lore.
†††

The Nine Mile Walk. 1967. This book contains eight Nicky Welt stories, in which the professor demonstrates his ability to solve crimes by the use of rigorous, unaided logic. In the title story, Welt uses a chain of logical inferences to solve a crime, before he even knows it has been committed.
†††

Sunday the Rabbi Stayed Home. 1969. Rabbi Small is trying to cope with a bad case of synagogue politics when he is embroiled in another murder, this one involving hippies, drugs, and a black radical. With his buddy, Police Chief Lanigan, Small manages to solve the case, but the real suspense is in the question: Will the temple elders fire him for being insufficiently hip?
†††

Monday the Rabbi Took Off. 1972. Kemelman varies the formula of the Rabbi Small books with this one, substituting Israel for the New England town of Barnard's Crossing, and political intrigue for the usual humdrum, small-town murder.
†††

Tuesday the Rabbi Saw Red. 1973. As the week wears on, Kemelman's plots become more offbeat; Rabbi Small investigates a bombing and a murder in a Christian college. †††

Wednesday the Rabbi Got Wet. 1976. One of Rabbi Small's most endearing qualities is his tolerant empathy. In this book he exercises it on behalf of a young man who, on top of family troubles and a religious crisis, is the chief suspect in a death by poison. †††

Thursday the Rabbi Walked Out. 1978. Rabbi Small comes to the end of the week, still plagued by tiresome temple politics. A notorious anti-Semite is murdered, and the rabbi's congregation seethes with suspicion. Small leads the police to the key that is the key to the crime. ††††

KENDRICK, BAYARD. One of the founders of the Mystery Writers of America, Kendrick was prolific and popular during the 1940s. His best-known books feature blind detective Duncan Maclain who was the basis for TV's "Longstreet."

The Iron Spiders. 1936. Deputy sheriff Miles Standish Rice copes with a deranged mass murderer, a tropical storm, and voodoo in this nicely plotted thriller set in the Florida Keys. The brooding atmosphere of a millionaire recluse's resort on a jungle island is the Florida equivalent of an English country-house setting in an Allingham or Heyer novel. †††

The Last Express. 1937. Captain Duncan Maclain makes his debut in this murder mystery centered on an old, unused subway tunnel. †††

Flight from a Firing Wall. 1966. A Cuban doctor, who has fled to Florida to escape Castro's regime, returns to Cuba to rescue his wife and is promptly thrown into the worst prison on the island. †††

KENNEDY, GEORGE. *Murder on Location.* 1983. A cheery story of a murder on a movie set chock-full of familiar names with George Kennedy in the role of the detective. †

KEZER, GLENN. *The Queen Is Dead.* 1979. A bit like Nicholas Blake's *Corpse in the Snowman,* this book has bodies turning up everywhere in a small Hudson River village at Christmas. It is up to local detective Max Ambrose to sort things out. †††

KIENZLE, WILLIAM. A writer of considerable skill. Kienzle's Father Koesler series of mysteries has proven once again that clergymen always make good detectives.

The Rosary Murders. 1979. The first and best of the Father Koesler stories. Here he tries to stop a psycho on a killing spree in Detroit. The killer always leaves a rosary with his victims. ††††

Kill and Tell. 1984. A weirdo in the confession booth alerts Father Koesler to the possible murder of a big-time parishioner. †††

KING, RUFUS. Although he created several series characters in his years of writing books and stories for the pulp magazines, King's most famous character was Lieutenant Valcour, a French Canadian in the New York Police Department who solves his cases with a blend of Gallic intuition and Anglo-Saxon logic.

Murder by Latitude. 1930. When the wireless operator on a luxury cruiser bound from Bermuda to Halifax is murdered, it's bad luck for the killer that Valcour happens to be on the passenger list. He probes into the pasts of his cruise mates—especially, a lovely and lethal man-eater—but the killer strikes again before Valcour arrives at a solution. King makes nice use of the shipboard setting and the book offers suspense and a lot of dry humor. ††††

Valcour Meets Murder. 1932. In this moody, melodramatic thriller, Valcour returns to his native Canada just in time to witness the murder of an old man—but not the murderer. He spends the night in a very strange household, where everyone seems to have something to hide, and winds up investigating not only the murder, but also the case of a stolen fortune in jewels. †††

The Lesser Antilles Case. 1934. Valcour is called in to investigate the curious and fatal occurrences on a tiny uninhabited Caribbean island while some ship-wrecked tourists were stranded there. Two men were killed by sharks—was it murder, or simply a tragic accident? Only by restaging the calamity and pursuing his clues all the way to the ocean floor can Valcour discover the killer's motive for revenge and the evidence of his guilt. ††††

• *Some books* not *to read in the bathtub when you are alone in the house:*

NIGHT OF THE HUNTER by David Grubb
PSYCHO by Robert Bloch
RED DRAGON by Thomas Harris
THE RED RIGHT HAND by Joel Townsley Rogers
THE SERPENT by David Wiltse

KINGSLEY-SMITH, TERENCE.   *The Murder of an Old-Time Movie Star.* 1983. A fun read about the murder of an old movie star. A little like Stuart Kaminsky.   ††

KLEIN, DAVE.   *Blind Side.* 1980. A good, sports mystery about a psycho in the National Football League who can't get enough violence on Sundays to suit him. Written by a professional sportswriter, it is filled with action and lots of atmosphere.   †††

KLEIN, DAVE.   *Hit and Run.* 1982. Blackmail and murder in the baseball business.   †††

KNICKMEYER, STEVE.   *Straight.* 1976. An excellent story about an ex-cop who turns hit man, and along with his thug-partner, takes on a contract in Oklahoma. Things become sticky when a couple of determined private eyes get on their trail.   ††††

L

LANE, JIM R.   *Static.* 1984. A good read with a different type of detective— Nick West, a Nevada country-and-western disc jockey. Nick tries to speed up the slow country ways of his listeners by changing his show to an all-talk format, and with the ensuing controversy comes murder.   †††

LANGTON, JANE.   One of the best working today. Her New England setting is flawless, her stories beautifully told, and her characters engaging as hell. If the gentle, sophisticated mystery is your cup of tea, then she is the one for you.

The Minuteman Murder.   1964. From a research standpoint, I think this is every bit the equal of Tey's *Daughter of Time.* The setting is Concord, Massachusetts, where the famous shot was heard round the world, and which was also the home of Thoreau, Emerson, and the Alcotts. During a reenactment of the famous shot, there is a murder tied into the past and the famous citizens of Concord.   †††††

Dark Nantucket Noon.   1975. A beautiful woman is murdered during an eclipse of the sun, and a young hysterical woman is accused of the murder. Homer Kelly believes in her innocence, but he still has to prove it.   ††††

The Memorial Hall Murder.   1978. Homer Kelly, visiting lecturer at Harvard, investigates the bombing of Harvard's Memorial Hall and the disappearance of the university's chorus leader.   ††††

Emily Dickinson Is Dead.   1984. The background is the centennial celebration of Emily Dickinson's death in Amherst. Homer Kelly wanders around in a maze of academic bitchiness and clever plotting.   ††††

LATHEN, EMMA. The author of the John Putnam Thatcher series. Thatcher is an investment banker with Sloan Guaranty Trust, and in his role as an amateur detective, he always finds murder in the business world. Each novel deals with a separate industry, and in itself is a nice little lesson in how the other half lives, without being boring.

A *Stitch in Time*. 1968. After a life-insurance company refuses to pay because a surgeon testifies that one of Sloan Guaranty's clients killed himself, the bank orders a second autopsy and they find the body had been sewn up with a handful of hemostatic clamps left inside. ††††

Ashes to Ashes. 1971. A Queens Catholic church agrees to sell a parcel of land to developers for a high-rise apartment building which Sloan Guaranty is backing, but a neighborhood protest group begins to make trouble, and then the head of the group is found dead. ††††

Sweet and Low. 1974. John Putnam Thatcher becomes involved when the commodity specialist for a chocolate company is murdered on the floor of the New York Cocoa Exchange. †††

Double, Double, Oil, and Trouble. 1978. The chief negotiator for a Houston drilling company is kidnapped, and John Putnam Thatcher goes to Zurich to handle the ransom demanded by the terrorists. ††††

Green Grow the Dollars. 1982. The Vandam Nursery and Seed Company is set to rock the world with a winter tomato that doesn't taste like cardboard, until first a lawsuit and then a murder require the help of John Putnam Thatcher. ††††

LAUBEN, PHILIP. A *Nice Sound Alibi*. 1981. This Kentucky murder mystery would have been pretty good with a little more work. ††

LAWRENCE, HILDA. One of the best suspense writers from the 1940s. She deserves much more recognition and praise than she has received lately.

Blood upon the Snow. 1944. This was Lawrence's rather weak debut, but a feeling of terror is created that makes the reader continue. A series of murders on an isolated estate has to be solved by detective Mark East. Although the characters are well defined, the goings-on are so murky it is hard at times to tell who is doing what to whom. There are traces of the mindless terror that will become her trademark. ††

A Time to Die.   1945. The second Mark East novel and much better than the first. This time Mark East has a case of motiveless murder in a small-town setting. There are well-defined characters that you can believe in, and a cleverly hidden killer.   ††††

The Pavilion.   1946. The modern gothic tale at its best. A young woman comes to visit her uncle only to find that he is dead. His death reveals well-concealed murders in the past. The sense of terror and impending doom never lets up. The setting is a small town with a strange, closed feeling that adds to the creepiness.   †††††

Death of a Doll.   1947. Mark East appears again with a motiveless murder in a hotel for women. The setting is claustrophobic, which increases the feeling of dread generated by the author. The characters are diverse, but not sinister, and the simple solution is well-concealed.   ††††

LEE, GYPSY ROSE.   *The G-String Murders.* 1941. Yes, this is *the* Gypsy Rose Lee, the stripper of song and fable. She is both the author and heroine in an amusing tale in which a fellow stripper is found strangled with her own G-string.   †††

LEONARD, ELMORE.   Everyone is touting Leonard as if he's the second coming. He ain't. He's a good writer—always has been, even before he was "discovered"—but reading him is not going to cure baldness, restore sexual potency, or make you a welcome guest at a cocktail party. His plots are all over the place: some cynical, some funny, some hard, even some excellent westerns. But no matter which you choose, you can expect a satisfying read from him.

Valdez Is Coming.   1970. A western. You may remember the movie. The bad guys anger the wrong man, and Valdez gets even.   ††††

The Switch.   1978. A caper novel which is a cross between Donald Westlake and "The Ransom of Red Chief." Lovable thugs kidnap the beautiful wife of a rich man only to find that he doesn't want her back. A fun read.   ††††

La Brava.   1983. A cross between an early John D. MacDonald and an old film on the Late Show. An ex–secret-service agent becomes a photographer and meets one of those beautiful women who make strong men write hot checks.
                                       †††

LEVIN, IRA.   *A Kiss Before Dying.* 1953. Only a master writer like Levin could take this farfetched story, of a family of sisters and their involvement with the same cad, and turn it into the classic it is.   †††††

LEWIN, MICHAEL Z.   A hard-boiled writer who is developing a nice following. He has two series: Albert Samson, an Indianapolis private eye, and Lieutenant Leroy Powder, the biggest prig to ever wear a badge. I like the Albert Samson stories.

The Enemies Within.   1974. Albert Samson is asked to look into the matter of a manuscript which has been held too long by a publisher. This leads to a missing daughter, a murder, and other complications, all resolved in a competent manner by the author.   †††

Hard Line.   1983. Lieutenant Powder has been transferred to the backwaters of Missing Persons, where he demonstrates he can still make waves. He is given, as an assistant, a policewoman who has been shot and paralyzed in the line of duty, and spends the rest of the book making life hell for her as the butt of many a joke and jibe. I found this book too offensive to even rate, and would put it in my top ten all-time, worst mysteries ever written.

Out of Season.   1984. A prominent woman applies for a passport and is denied it because she has no birth certificate. Samson is hired to trace her parents' past, and is drawn into a nightmarish maze of double identities, insanity, and dead people who may still be alive, all woven into a massive cover-up which costs two people their lives.   †††

LEWIS, LANGE.   *The Birthday Murder.* 1945. A bit dated today, but still a highly readable story about murder by poisoning in the Hollywood film community of the 1940s.   †††

LINDSEY, DAVID.   *Heat from Another Sun.* 1984. A Raymond Chandler type of story in which detective Stuart Haydon tangles with the rich, beautiful, and perverse.   †††

LIVINGSTON, JACK.   *Die Again, Macready.* 1984. Deaf private eye Joe Binney is hired to find the missing manager of an actor who has absconded with a quarter of a million dollars.   †††

LOCKRIDGE, RICHARD AND FRANCIS.   Their creations—Mr. and Mrs. North—are two of perhaps the most charming detectives to ever cross a page. For my money they have Nick and Nora Charles beaten hands down for charm, plot, and character.

The Norths Meet Murder.   1940. The debut of Pam and Jerry North. The apartment above them is vacant so they decide to use it for a party, but when they go up to look things over, they find the body of a nude woman in the bathtub.   ††††

Murder Out of Turn. 1940. Pam and Jerry invite Lieutenant Wiegand of homicide to the country for a tennis tournament and a quiet weekend out of the city. He meets a young woman he takes a fancy to, and after walking her to her cabin stumbles across another woman—only this one has had her throat cut. †††

A Pinch of Poison. 1941. My favorite of the series, it is one of the best poisoning novels I have ever read by an American. Lieutenant Wiegand and his girlfriend are having dinner with Pam and Jerry when a call comes through that a woman has been poisoned at a nightclub. Very smooth and tricky. †††††

Murder Within Murder. 1946. A complex case of murder for Pam and Jerry who wade through a group of greedy heirs. †††

LOGUE, JOHN. *Follow the Leader.* 1979. Someone is killing the great golf pros of America, and it isn't funny, especially for a man who enjoys the game. ††

LOGUE, JOHN. *Replay Murder.* 1983. Someone is killing off the college football team. ††

LORE, PHILIPS. Author of a neglected but highly readable series featuring millionaire-turned-detective Leo Roi.

Who Killed the Pie Man? 1975. Mix a touch of the Mafia, some embezzlement, a little incest, and you wind up with the slain bodies of a coed and her professor. †††

The Looking Glass Murders. 1980. Again it is the young coed and the old professor and murder. ††

Murder Behind Closed Doors. 1980. The best of the series. In this locked-room mystery, set in the gay world, a wealthy advertising executive is murdered. ††††

LYONS, ARTHUR. Author of the Jacob Asch series. One of the best of the California private-eye series.

The Dead Are Discreet. 1974. Asch investigates love-triangle murders. The finger points to the husband, but there's more to it than that—there is also witchcraft and pornography. I guess the devil made them do it. ††††

All God's Children. 1975. Jacob Asch is hired to find a missing girl in the world of motorcycle gangs and other weirdos. †††

Killing Floor. 1976. Asch investigates the death of a slaughterhouse owner found dead on his own killing floor. ††††

Dead Ringer. 1977. Asch is hired to find out who is making threats against a down-and-out boxer, then the boxer is killed in a whorehouse. †††

Castles Burning. 1979. My favorite of the series. Asch tracks down the wife and child deserted by a famous artist, finding murder at every turn. ††††

Hard Trade. 1981. A woman hires Asch to follow the man she is going to marry. It turns out the man is gay, and the woman is killed. ††††

Three with a Bullet. 1985. Asch treads gingerly through the world of rock and roll and its inevitable drug scene. Hired to find out who is sabotaging his client's concerts, he spends much of the book discovering corpses. The uncovering of the murderer is a little weak. †††

LYONS, NAN AND IVAN. *Someone Is Killing the Great Chefs of Europe.* 1976. A classic in comedy as world-renowned chef Natasha O'Brien and her husband try to stop a madman from killing the best chefs of Europe, each of whom is noted for a special dish. This is murder among the nice people at its best. I read it the first time and loved it. I waited a couple of years, and then, on a whim, reread it, and came to the conclusion that it couldn't be improved upon. †††††

LYSAGHT, BRIAN. *Special Circumstances.* 1983. A young Los Angeles lawyer takes a case with fifty million dollars at stake. Still wet behind the ears, he gets caught in the middle and is set up for the fall—an idea he doesn't like. ††

M

McCLOY, HELEN. She was married to Brett Halliday, but her mysteries are completely unlike his own hard-boiled "Mike Shayne" tales, being refined stories of detection and suspense among the upper classes. She created a series character for some of her novels: Dr. Basil Willing, a psychologist who assists the New York City District Attorney's office and who uses Freud and Jung, as well as fingerprints and blood types, to solve cases.

Cue for Murder. 1942. This tale of murder onstage is the best of the Basil Willing books. Unlike most theatrical mysteries, which usually involve productions of either *Hamlet* or *Macbeth*, this one is set during a wartime production of Victorien Sardou's melodrama *Fedora*, which offers a unique opportunity for a stage killing. Willing unmasks the murderer through a physical clue—a housefly—and a psychological one—a canary. The plot is watertight, the characters suitably dramatic, and the pace brisk. †††††

A Question of Time. 1971. An ingenious murderer uses a surprising and original mechanism to dispose of a young heiress. Although it seems at first a gothic suspense novel and turns out to be a straightforward murder mystery, this book is well worth reading for its clever and scrupulously fair plot. Basil Willing does not appear.   †††

The Changeling Conspiracy. 1976. This is a non-series novel about a Patty Hearst like political kidnapping and a nasty, very personal murder, neatly intertwined into a fast-moving story. McCloy peoples her books with characters who can and do expound quite knowledgeably on all sorts of recondite topics, from literary hoaxes to brainwashing. While this may not be completely realistic, it adds interest and paves the way for some exotic clues.   †††

The Imposter. 1977. The helplessness of a sane woman falsely imprisoned in a mental hospital is always a good tension builder. This book starts there and goes on to a missing husband, an impostor who replaces him and then disappears, a coded message deciphered by the plucky heroine, and a conspiracy to gain control of a deadly new laser weapon—all this in a Boston suburb.   †††

McCRUMB, SHARYN. *Sick of Shadows*. 1984. Elizabeth MacPherson agrees to attend the wedding of Eileen Chandler, her cousin, who has been recently released from a sanitarium. But as Elizabeth soon discovers, Eileen is not the only one in the family that is crazy. This one is for fans of Charlotte Macleod.   †††

McCRUMB, SHARYN. *Lovely in Her Bones*. 1985. Elizabeth MacPherson goes on an archaeological excavation in Tennessee, where the director of the dig is murdered with a tomahawk.   †††

McDONALD, GREGORY. With the appearance of *Fletch* in 1974, McDonald introduced a new prose style on the mystery scene—the machine-gun delivery. Recognizing that Americans no longer read as an evening's entertainment, but rather as a fill-in sandwiched between other activities (on a bus, in a restaurant, just before going to bed) he began to write in a crisp, clean style which is totally devoid of description and relies heavily on snappy dialogue and biting wit.

Fletch. 1974. Fletch, as an undercover reporter on the California beach, receives an offer from a millionaire to murder him—the millionaire, that is.
        ††††

Confess, Fletch. 1976. This doesn't exactly follow *Fletch*, but it is the second of the series. Fletch, now rich and back from Europe, finds a murdered girl in his Boston apartment. What follows is a great verbal duel between Fletch and Flynn of the Boston Police Department.   ††††

Flynn. 1977. A spin-off of *Confess, Fletch* featuring Boston cop Flynn. It doesn't really get moving like the Fletch series.   †††

Fletch's Fortune. 1978. The series started to weaken slightly with this one. Fletch is intimidated into digging up scandal on a wealthy millionaire. The scene in the church is the best in the book.   †††

Who Took Toby Renaldi? 1980. The story of the kidnapping of the young son of U.N. Ambassador Teddy Renaldi. McDonald's machine-gun style does not lend itself to novels dealing with sensitive subjects.   ††

Fletch and the Widow Bradley. 1981. Fletch finds himself behind the eight ball when he does a news story in which he quotes a man who has been dead for two years.   †††

Flynn's In. 1984. Flynn is called outside his jurisdiction to investigate a murder at a wealthy rod and gun club. By far my favorite of the Flynn series. The author slows his prose style to match the slower pace of the story, and it works well.

                ††††

MACDONALD, JOHN D.   His career began with the pulps in the late 1940s. When they began to die out, he switched over to paperback original novels, and over the years, largely through his highly successful Travis McGee series, he has come to be regarded as a major American novelist. Travis McGee is a Florida boat bum who lives aboard the *Busted Flush* in a Fort Lauderdale marina. Using that as a base, he and his trusted sidekick, economist (no first name) Meyer, launch themselves on adventures, often involving beautiful women, during the course of which they are able to make lengthy and interesting statements about the quality (or lack) of American life, business, and Plymouth gin. Much of his success is due to the fact that Travis McGee is a big brother to all men, no matter how old. When times get tough, all you have to do is to pick one up, and you are instantly transported to the most interesting Florida vacation you will ever have.

Travis McGee novels:

The Deep Blue Good-By. 1964. The first Travis McGee novel. A sleaze named Junior Allen is making life hard for Cathy Kerr. She has no one to turn to except Travis.   ††††

A Purple Place for Dying. 1964. Travis McGee goes to Arizona to help a not so nice woman recover money owed her by her husband. The woman is killed.   †††

The Long Lavender Look.   1970. One of the best of the series. Travis and Meyer, returning from a wedding, are involved in an auto accident when a nude young woman runs out in front of their truck. They wind up in jail as guests of a corrupt Florida town.   ††††

The Turquoise Lament.   1973. Travis goes to Hawaii to help an old friend named Pidge when her ex-football-playing husband tries to kill her.   ††††

The Dreadful Lemon Sky.   1974. My favorite of the series. Travis's ex-girlfriend arrives unannounced and asks him to hide a hundred thousand dollars for her, with no questions asked.   †††††

The Empty Copper Sea.   1978. Travis investigates the drowning of Hub Lawless, an old friend who is heavily insured. Then it turns out that Hub is alive and living in Mexico.   ††††

The Green Ripper.   1979. One of the weaker novels in the series. When Travis's girlfriend is murdered, he goes seeking a religious cult, where he engages in a bloodbath.   †††

Other novels:

The Executioners.   1959. When a convicted rapist is finally set free, he wants revenge on the man who put him behind bars—through the man's daughter.
††

The Girl, The Gold Watch and Everything.   1962. A humorous story involving a magic watch.   ††††

One More Sunday.   1984. A novel about corporate-type corruption in the big business of religion.   †††

MacDONALD, PATRICIA J.   This gives me the greatest pleasure of all the reviews in this book, since this particular author also happens to be my wife. Although the packaging of her books often suggests that they may be horror novels, they are suspense novels in the truest sense. Her heroes are always heroines, but unlike most suspense writers, her work has an extra dimension in that the jeopardy in the story does not necessarily threaten the heroine. More often, it is the family unit which becomes jeopardized in the story.

The Unforgiven.   1981. Freshly released from the nightmare of the cellblock, Maggie Fraser goes to Heron's Neck, a New England island, to begin a new life. There she unfortunately steps on the wrong toes and becomes the target of someone with emotions strong enough to kill.   ††††

Stranger in the House.   1983. A terrific story of a family and the return of a teenage son who had been kidnapped ten years earlier. The family is strained by its readjustment to the boy, and by the fact that the kidnapper is still on the loose.   †††

Little Sister.   1986. A young career woman returns to her hometown to attend the funeral of her father. Once there, she has to make some very hard decisions about the future of her troubled teenage sister. But the heroine is not the only one making decisions about the little sister, as a series of harrowing experiences moves toward a shattering climax.   ††††

MACDONALD, ROSS.   The third most important writer (after Hammett and Chandler) in the development of the hard-boiled detective. His "Lew Archer" stories exhibit a marvelous sense of atmosphere and writing style. The plotting is deep, but predictable, centering around an old murder, a little girl lost, and just a hint of incest. If his work can be negatively criticized, it would be for this unchanging theme which runs through much of his work, a theme which virtually every California, hard-boiled writer has borrowed but not improved on.

The Dark Tunnel.   1944. Not a Lew Archer story. In fact, not even a detective story, but the tale of Nazi espionage on a college campus during WWII.   †††

The Ivory Grin.   1952. Archer takes on a corrupt town in one of the best of the series. His style here is cleaner and more straightforward than in his later work.   ††††

Find a Victim.   1954. Lew Archer stops for a wounded hitchhiker and becomes involved in a Chandler-type story filled with beautiful bad girls.   ††††

The Name Is Archer.   1955. A collection of seven Lew Archer stories published between 1946 and 1955.   †††

The Doomsters.   1958. Archer goes out to pick up the morning paper and finds an escapee from a mental hospital on his doorstep. The troubled young man wants Archer to find out who murdered his father six months earlier.   ††††

The Ferguson Affair.   1960. A muddled story with characters more caricatured than usual for Macdonald's work.   †††

The Wycherly Woman.   1961. Archer searches for the killer who dumped a young woman's body in the San Francisco Bay.   †††

The Zebra-Striped Hearse.   1962. Although a bit dated today, this is one of the classics of the series. Archer is visited first by the stepmother of a young woman who is about to inherit a lot of money, and then by her father, a retired army colonel. The daughter has fallen in love with a young man. The stepmother is for their marriage; the father is opposed. Archer finds himself in the role of family arbitrator as he moves in the California youth culture of beach party movies and blond surfers. †††††

The Far Side of the Dollar. 1965. Archer is hired to find a troubled boy who has escaped from a boarding school that is more prison than school. †††

The Underground Man. 1971. Against the backdrop of a raging California forest fire, Archer finds himself in the middle of a family warring over the young son, in a story which could have been written by Tennessee Williams. Many feel this is Macdonald's masterpiece. †††††

McDowell, Michael. *Jack and Susan in 1953.* 1985. The author has done a nice job in giving us a lighthearted 1950s Nick and Nora Charles, or Pam and Jerry North, type of story that takes Jack and Susan from Manhattan to Havana as they try to solve a murder. †††

McInerny, Ralph. Author of the Father Dowling series.

Second Vespers. 1980. People begin to show interest in Francis O'Rourke, Fox River's famous, dead author. This interest leads to murder and to Father Dowling's playing amateur sleuth. ††

The Grass Widow. 1983. A young woman comes to Father Dowling for help because her estranged husband, a radio personality, has announced on the air his intentions to see her dead. Then she turns up dead. ††

MacLeod, Charlotte. One of the gentler writers. She has two series: one features Peter Shandy, a professor at Balaclava College in New England, and the other features Sarah Kelling, from a Boston family now down on its luck. Her tone is light, breezy, and humorous. Her plots are adequate, as are her settings. She appeals especially to women, and is just the thing to help forget one's troubles.

Rest Ye Merry. 1978. A Christmas mystery and the first Peter Shandy mystery. Peter finds the body of a faculty wife in his living room. The end is a bit obvious, but it is a lot of fun. †††

The Luck Runs Out. 1979. My favorite of the series. There's murder, but there's more as Peter investigates the kidnapping of Belinda, the Balaclava Agricultural College prize pig, and the clues point to a protest group called the Vigilante Vegetarians. ††††

Wrack and Rune. 1982. A good one. Peter Shandy investigates a death by quicklime at a farm. For color there's a Norse curse and a hundred-year-old man. †††

Something the Cat Dragged In. 1983. A toupee is what the cat dragged in, and its owner is dead. Peter Shandy investigates. †††

The Family Vault. 1979. The first Sarah Kelling story. She finds the body of a burlesque queen who has been missing for thirty years. As if that's not enough, the body is in the Kelling family crypt. †††

The Withdrawing Room. 1980. The second Sarah Kelling novel is a little weaker than the first. Sarah is renting out rooms in her Beacon Hill house to make ends meet, and one of the roomers is murdered. †††

The Palace Guard. 1981. Sarah makes the mistake of hobnobbing with the guard at a concert, only to wind up in the midst of art forgery and murder. †††

MADSEN, DAVID. *Black Plume.* (n.d.) Subtitled "The Suppressed Memoirs of Edgar Allan Poe," this novel deals with Poe as the detective who, in the manner of Sherlock Holmes, thwarts a fiendish plot set among the Corsicans of New York. †††

MAILER, NORMAN. *Tough Guys Don't Dance.* 1984. Either you like Mailer or you don't. I like him, so I enjoyed this offbeat story of Tim Madden who wakes up from an all-night binge, only to find he has been tattooed, and there is a severed head on the seat next to him. I've had similar mornings. ††††

MALING, ARTHUR. The author of a series featuring Brock Potter, a stock analyst. Maling is perfect when you have finished all the Emma Lathens and can't figure out who to go to next.

Ripoff. 1976. Brock Potter answers a late-night phone call and not only loses his sleeping partner for the night, but becomes embroiled in a complicated case of counterfeiting, insurance swindles, and murder. He runs afoul of the SEC and the police of two countries, but he does eventually get his love life straightened out. ††††

Shroeder's Game. 1977. The story of a colossal swindle and a white-collar crook who kills to protect his scam. Potter is a carefully constructed "New Man," sensitive as well as tough, a bit like Robert Parker's Spenser. ††††

MALONE, MICHAEL. *Uncivil Seasons.* 1983. The story of murder in North Carolina. It has the usual overtones of Tennessee Williams southern gothic, reek of madness, and a touch of sexual dysfunction in the family, but it is done, oh, so well. Hillston, N.C., and its people fairly jump off the page at you. ††††

MASTERSON, WHIT. *Why She Cries, I Do Not Know.* 1972. A drifter infiltrates a revolutionary group in California to avenge his brother. He is caught in the crosscurrents generated by the radical chic of the affluent, discontented, young who seek to change society to conform to their own fashion. It all leads to an explosive finale. ††

MASTERSON, WHIT. *The Undertaker Wind*. 1973. Templeton, a down-and-out, once famous journalist, licks his drug problem and seeks to come back. A friend gives him the job of investigating the murder of a sheriff in New Mexico. Templeton finds conflicting views about the dead man and becomes involved in a dispute between the authorities and Chicanos over land. A tightly told story with a romance in it. †††

MASUR, HAROLD Q. (aka Hal). Author of the 1940s and 1950s series featuring attorney Scott Jordan. Although cast somewhat in the Perry Mason mold, I feel Scott Jordan is a far superior character to Mason. The books are much better balanced, showing more detective work in progress, and less trial action. The stories hold up beautifully today.

Bury Me Deep. 1947. A beautiful woman is murdered in Scott Jordan's living room, and he is the chief suspect. His only clue is that the dead girl was involved in an inheritance case involving a hundred thousand dollars. †††

So Rich, So Lovely, And So Dead. 1952. Scott Jordan meets a beautiful woman at an art opening. She immediately asks him to marry her, but before they can even test each other physically, she is murdered. †††

Tall, Dark, And Deadly. 1956. Scott defends a man charged with bigamy and the murder of his ex-wife and her chauffeur. †††

Murder on Broadway. 1958. A Broadway producer's main squeeze is killed and Scott Jordan investigates. †††

MATHEWSON, JOSEPH. *Alicia's Trump*. 1980. Alicia Von Helsing discovers her artist-godson's body in his SoHo loft. Around him, all his tarot paintings have been destroyed. The New York police seem uninterested so Alicia turns sleuth in this bright, witty mystery. †††

MATHEWSON, JOSEPH. *Death Turns Right*. 1982. First the publisher of a right-wing magazine is killed in front of Alicia Von Helsing at a festival in New York's Little Italy, then a politician is shot while making a speech. In each case, the same camera crew is on hand. Once again Alicia plays amateur sleuth. †††

MATHIS, EDWARD. *From a High Place*. 1985. A great job for a first novel. Texas private eye Dan Roman goes back to his hometown where he is hired by his former high school English teacher to discover who pushed her husband off a cliff. In so doing, Roman wraps up a lot of loose ends from bygone days. ††††

MAVITY, NANCY BARR. *The Fate of Jane McKenzie.* 1933. When a rich and famous woman disappears into thin air, the whole world speculates about her fate. But only California newspaper reporter Peter Piper (yes, that's really his name), who appears in most of Mavity's books, holds the clues to the mystery. Things get complicated when the mystery turns out to be murder. †††

MAXWELL, A. E. *Just Another Day in Paradise.* 1985. A private-eye story which crosses over into the spy world as yet another California private eye tries to keep some computer nonsense from falling into the hands of the Russians. ††

MEREDITH, D. R. *The Sheriff and the Panhandle Murders.* 1984. Sheriff Charles Matthews and his one deputy have their hands full with a case of murder at a small-town Texas festival. There is lots of local color. The story is told with a light touch, as though Charlotte Macleod had written a Texas-based mystery. †††

MEYER, LYNN. *Paperback Thriller.* 1975. One of the most engaging opening chapters imaginable. Dr. Sarah Chayse, psychiatrist, reading an "airport" book on her way home to Boston from a conference, finds that her own offices and her files figure prominently in the thriller. Chayse is a well-drawn character, and we eagerly enter into her search for the truth. But when the mystery is uncovered, it is a bit too weak for such a promising opening. ††

MILLAR, MARGARET. This Canadian-born writer sets her tales of bizarre passions against a California backdrop. Millar, a Mystery Writers of America Grand Master, is the wife of the late Ross Macdonald, and the author of twenty-five novels. These books are not detective fiction, but psychological suspense, usually with a mysterious twist or two.

The Devil Loves Me. 1942. One of the author's weakest books. She tries a straight, English country-house mystery set in the U.S. at a society wedding. A bridesmaid is poisoned just before the ceremony, and then her brother is murdered. The book grinds along, peopled by far too many characters and too much plot. All the graceful, insightful, realistic touches of Millar at her best are missing here. ††

Beast in View. 1955. Helen Clarvoe, a reclusive heiress, is tormented by anonymous threats. She suspects that her brother's ex-wife, Evelyn, is the culprit, and enlists the aid of her lawyer to track down Evelyn. In the course of his search, the lawyer becomes convinced that Evelyn is mad, but he is in for a surprise. This study of madness is superbly executed. †††††

A Stranger in My Grave. 1960. The premise of this one is fascinating. Daisy Harken dreams of her own tombstone with the dates clearly engraved on it. But according to the dream, Daisy has been dead for years. She becomes obsessed with finding the meaning of the date on the grave, and uncovers a trail to murder as she delves into the past. ††††

How Like an Angel. 1962. Down on his luck, and broke from gambling, Joe Quinn finds himself seeking charity from a group of California cultists. One of the faithful, Sister Blessing, asks him to locate a man for her in the world outside the commune. Quinn agrees to the simple favor, but it becomes more complicated when he hears that the man has died mysteriously. The trail of murder and deceit leads Quinn back to the cult. The author creates an eerily believable atmosphere for this tricky story. †††††

The Fiend. 1964. Charlie Gowen is a grown man who has a strong identification with children that has been known to get him into trouble. Few people look upon his interest as innocent and, when little Jessie Brant disappears, Charlie Gowen finds himself the prime suspect. But there is more brewing beneath the surface of this sleepy California town than meets the eye. The author has a devastating way of exposing the hypocrisy in everyday life, and draws you skillfully into this sad, tense tale. ††††

Mermaid. 1982. A beautiful, but simple-minded young woman disappears, and her wealthy older brother hires Tom to find her. The plot is simple, but the author's talent for characterization is at full throttle here. †††

MILLER, GEOFFREY. *The Black Glove*. 1981. The story opens with promise as Terry Traven, owner of the Black Mask Detective Agency—named for the magazine—is hired to find a rich man's son. Traven is Californian, quirky and interesting, but the story is a bit leaden. ††

MILLER, WADE. *Deadly Weapon*. 1946. A good hard-boiled cop story in which San Diego detective Walter James investigates murder in a strip joint. †††

MILLER, WADE. *Fatal Step*. 1948. San Diego private eye Max Thursday is hired to clear the name of a dead Chinese boy. The trail leads to an amusement park and a masked killer named "Bandage Head." ††††

MILLER, WADE. *Calamity Fair*. 1950. Private eye Max Thursday gets involved with fast society women, dirty pictures, and blackmail. Too much like a Chandler story for my taste. ††

MINER, VALERIE. *Murder in the English Department*. 1983. A very promising work in which Dr. Nan Weaver discovers the body of a fellow teacher at Berkeley and finds herself brought to trial for murder. Good characterization and family subplots keep the tension up. †††

MOORE, BARBARA. *The Doberman Wore Black*. 1983. A good read for animal lovers. Gordon Christy is a Vail, Colorado, veterinarian, and the story abounds with animals as Christy turns amateur detective and tries to solve the murder of a beautiful woman. †††

MORLEY, CHRISTOPHER. *The Haunted Bookshop.* 1919. A great and gentle classic about a Brooklyn used-bookstore, and its opinionated owner, and the bad guys who want to use it for evil purposes. A wonderful story. †††††

MORSE, L. A. *The Big Enchilada.* 1982. An updating of Chandler's *Big Sleep* has Los Angeles detective Sam Hunter up to his elbows in X-rated home movies, heroine, and beautiful girls. †††

MORSE, L. A. *Sleaze.* 1985. A tough private-eye novel about blackmailing the editor of a porn magazine. As usual in novels of this type, things are seldom what they seem. Morse's detective, Sam Hunter, is so tough that, by comparison, Spillane's Mike Hammer comes off sounding like a Broadway chorus boy. This is not for the squeamish; there is a high body count and the ending is a stunner. †††

MULKEEN, THOMAS P. *Honor Thy Godfather.* 1972. Private eye Clem Talbot shoots a man in self-defense, then gets rid of the body, but the Mafia has other ideas. They want it back. †††

MULLER, MARCIA. *The Tree of Death.* 1983. Elena Oliverez, curator of the Museum of Mexican Arts in Santa Barbara, is suspected of murder when the fat, loathsome director of the museum is found crushed beneath a gaudy thing called the Tree of Life. Since her beginning with *Edwin of the Iron Shoes*, Marcia Muller has never disappointed me with a novel. She is always a good read.
†††

MURRAY, WILLIAM. *Tip on a Dead Crab.* 1984. Shifty Anderson, a magician on vacation, and Jay Fox, an obsessive race handicapper, get involved in a horse-race scam at California's Del Mar racetrack. This book has a lot of style and the horse racing scenes seem authentic. †††

MURRAY, WILLIAM. *The Hard Knocker's Luck.* 1985. This second adventure of magician, horse player Shifty Anderson has everything from an unhappily married clairvoyant beauty (if she's clairvoyant, how come she's unhappily married?), and a racehorse that has seen better days, to a go-go dancer appropriately named "Boom-Boom" who winds up dead in a fire. †††

N

NASH, JAY ROBERT. *A Crime Story.* 1981. A good Chicago-based, hard-boiled story in which the governor's son is murdered, and it is up to Jack Journey, tough crime reporter, to get to the bottom of it. †††

NIELSEN, HELEN. A highly successful, prolific suspense writer, much of whose work was done in the 1950s. Among suspense writers, her work still shows a plotting quality much above average.

The Woman on the Roof. 1954. A woman recently released from a mental institution becomes involved in murder at her brother's bungalow. †††

Seven Days Before Dying. 1956. A judge, who has given the death sentence to a young punk, begins to receive death threats himself. †††

Verdict Suspended. 1964. The coroner's jury returns a verdict of homicide in the death of Jaime Dodson's sister. Under drugs, at the hospital, Jaime confesses to killing his sister, although no one can believe it. †††

NOLAN, WILLIAM F. *The Black Mask Boys.* 1985. A collection of short stories by Hammett, Chandler, Gardner, McCoy, Daly, Nebel, Whitfield, and Cain. †††††

O

O'CORK, SHANNON. *Sports Freak.* 1980. Woman photographer T. T. Baldwin investigates the murder of an NFL quarterback on the field. ††††

OGAN, GEORGE. *To Kill a Judge.* 1981. A standard private-eye novel with an outstanding New Orleans setting, which the author uses well as his Cajun detective attempts to find the murderer of a prominent judge. ††

O'MARIE, CAROL ANNE. *Novena For Murder.* 1984. Seventy-five-year-old, retired nun Sister Mary Helen makes a warm and engaging detective as she investigates the murder of a history professor. †††

P

PALMER, STUART. He's best known for his eccentric spinster detective Hildegarde Withers—played to perfection in the movies by Edna May Oliver. He also wrote other mysteries and nearly forty screenplays, many of which were also mysteries.

The Green Ace. 1950. A young man is stopped by the police, a body is found in his backseat, and he is convicted of murder. While he awaits execution, he makes out a will leaving all his money to the police lieutenant who handled his case. The lieutenant learns of this when Hildegarde Withers, schoolteacher and hard-boiled private eye, stops by. She determines to clear the man in the few days left before his execution. The opening paragraphs bear comparison with the opening of Chandler's short story "Red Wind." †††

Cold Poison. 1954. With her sidekick, the patient Inspector Oscar Piper, Miss Withers leaves her Manhattan territory for the wilds of Hollywood, where she closes in on a poisoner who wants to put a studio out of business. †††

Rook Takes Knight. 1968. Los Angeles crime journalist Howie Rook is another of Palmer's series characters. Here he acts as champion for a beautiful woman accused of the hit-and-run murder of her vicious husband. The tone is light, aiming for zany and almost making it. ††

PAPAZOGLOU, ORANIA. *Sweet, Savage Death.* 1984. Patience McKenna, a prominent romance writer, plays amateur detective when murder becomes the ultimate put-down at a conference for romance writers. Very bright and well done. An impressive debut. ††††

PARETSKY, SARA. *Deadlock.* 1984. Female private eye V. I. Warshawski investigates the murder of her cousin "Boom Boom" Warshawski, a famous hockey player. Good writing. †††

PARETSKY, SARA. *Killing Orders.* 1985. A lively tale as female private eye V. I. Warshawski is hired to investigate the theft of millions from a Dominican priory. There's plenty of action here, from someone trying to blind V. I. with acid, to murder. ††††

PARKER, ROBERT B. Unquestionably America's fastest rising detective writer. His Spenser series keeps adding more and more fans from among non-mystery readers. Spenser is such a lively, vital character that men and women alike would enjoy sitting down and having a beer with him. Parker's Boston settings are so real that you feel as though you're walking the streets with him. His descriptions of food and drink make your mouth water, and his humor is crisp and keen. The only knock on his work is that his plots are a bit light for a writer of his talent, but nobody's perfect.

The Godwulf Manuscript. 1974. A promising debut for Spenser which deals with a university and a rare manuscript. †††

God Save the Child. 1974. A good second novel in which Spenser is hired to find a missing teenage boy. It is memorable for the introduction of Susan Silverman, Spenser's lady friend. †††

Mortal Stakes. 1975. Spenser is hired to find out if a major-league pitcher is throwing games. ††

Promised Land. 1976. In this story, Parker comes into his own, exploring the social themes of modern life which began in *God Save the Child.* This time Spenser is hired to find a runaway wife—a typical plot, but Parker uses it to his advantage by exploring the difficulties of staying married, rather than following in the footsteps of the too often imitated Chandler and Ross Macdonald. †††

The Judas Goat. 1978. Spenser takes a tax-deductible vacation to London and Montreal. †

Looking for Rachel Wallace. 1980. Spenser is at his best as bodyguard to a radical, lesbian, feminist writer. One of the best of the series. ††††

Early Autumn. 1981. Although there is very little mystery here, this is one of the best of the series. Spenser is hired to bring back a teenage boy kidnapped by one of his parents in a divorce squabble. ††††

A *Savage Place.* 1981. Spenser is hired as bodyguard to a woman television reporter in a plot that is more John D. MacDonald than Parker. ††

Ceremony. 1982. Spenser straightens out a teenage girl who has drifted into prostitution. †

The Widening Gyre. 1983. Spenser helps out a senator's wife who has problems with sex, drugs, and blackmail. †

Valediction. 1984. Susan Silverman leaves Spenser for greener pastures. ††

PATTERSON, RICHARD NORTH. *The Lasko Tangent.* 1979. A well-written story in which U.S. attorney Christopher Paget is given the assignment to investigate William Lasko in a case involving some heavy-duty blackmail. ††††

PATTERSON, RICHARD NORTH. *The Outside Man.* 1981. A disappointing attempt at southern gothic by a novelist with little eye for atmosphere. The plot is average. A young lawyer tries to get to the bottom of the death of a client in a town full of secrets. ††

PATTERSON, RICHARD NORTH. *Private Screening.* 1985. A complex novel of terror and assassination as a beautiful rock star and an aggressive trial lawyer are thrown together by two separate, bizarre terrorist events. †††

PAUL, RAYMOND. A great new asset to the mystery field. Combining history and fiction, he brings to life New York City in the 1830s with a clarity that is mind-boggling.

The Thomas Street Horror. 1982. A Jack the Ripper type of story, and a good read. ††††

Tragedy at Tiverton. 1984. A leisurely retelling of the story of Ephraim Avery, the first minister in American history to stand trial for murder. Irish lawyer Lon Quincannon is a terrific character here. †††††

PEEPLES, SAMUEL. *The Man Who Died Twice.* 1976. The story of a present-day Los Angeles cop who is shot. When he wakes up, he finds himself in the Hollywood of the 1920s, and *in the body of* William Desmond Taylor, a real-life director who was murdered in 1922, in one of the most famous murder cases in American history. An excellent blend of fact and fiction. ††††

PENTECOST, HUGH. The author of several highly readable series, the best of which features Pierre Chambrun, the manager of the Hotel Beaumont in New York. All the murders take place at the hotel. Other noteworthy series and their heroes include Julian Quist, a New York public relations man; Uncle George, a retired county attorney in New England; and John Jerico, a somewhat bizarre character.

The Cannibal Who Overate. 1962. The rich sadist Aubrey Moon is staying at the Hotel Beaumont, and it is up to Pierre Chambrun to protect him from the killer who is stalking him. ††††

The Homicidal Horse. 1979. Julian Quist investigates the death of Judith Cameron, apparently caused by a kick from an over-age racehorse—only she is found to have a bullet in the brain. ††

Remember to Kill Me. 1984. Pierre Chambrun is once again knee-deep in problems as hoodlums from a rock concert invade the Beaumont, a guest is shot outside the penthouse, and four guests are taken prisoner by a group of terrorists. †††

Murder Sweet and Sour. 1985. A kidnapper is on the loose in the New England village of Lakeview, and he is out to hurt "Uncle George" Crowder, former county attorney, through his family. ††

The Party Killer. 1985. Julian Quist is in charge of public relations for a new hotel, owned by a famous comedian, who invites a number of enemies as well as his four ex-wives to the opening. During the night there is an explosion, which leaves two people dead, and Julian Quist on the trail of the killer. †††

PETIEVICH, GERALD. *The Quality of the Informant.* 1985. A well-written chase novel between a thug and a T-man with stops in Los Angeles, Houston, San Diego, and Ensanada. ††††

PHILBRICK, W.R. *Shadow Kills.* 1985. Wheelchair-bound mystery writer Jack Hawkins finds his books are being used as the inspiration for a series of murders. ✝✝✝

PHILLIPS, EDWARD. *Death Is Relative.* 1984. A wickedly funny novel of murder among the aged. Great fun but not the book for you if you are going through a mid-life crisis. ✝✝✝

PICKARD, NANCY. *Say No to Murder.* 1985. When Jennifer Cain and the Port Frederick Civic Foundation are blamed for teenage suicide by a distraught father, she doesn't take him seriously. Then he dies in a fiery crash trying to ruin a civic project, and the wrong person is arrested. ✝✝✝✝

PINES, PAUL. *The Tin Angel.* 1983. New York nightclub owner Pablo Waitz investigates the murder of his partner. There may have been drugs involved. There is some very good writing in this gritty atmospheric story. ✝✝✝

PLATT, KEN. Platt's hard-boiled series features private eye Max Roper. His plots are refreshingly gimmicky and show a lot of humor in their creation.

The Pushbutton Butterfly. 1970. Max Roper goes to Berkeley to find the missing daughter of a millionaire industrialist. ✝✝✝

The Kissing Gourami. 1970. Max Roper investigates the death of a woman who was *eaten* by her designer dress. ✝✝✝

The Princess Stakes Murder. 1973. Max goes to the track to meet a jockey, but when he arrives he finds the jockey dead. ✝✝✝

The Giant Kill. 1974. Roper is forced to act as middleman in an attempt to fix the NBA playoffs. ✝✝✝

The Body Beautiful Murder. 1976. Max Roper investigates the murder of a "Mr. America" type, who died while posing. A good read. ✝✝✝

POWELL, RICHARD. Although much of his work is the straight, *film-noir*, tough guy kind of novel written by the likes of John D. MacDonald, his best work is the warmly humorous Arab and Andy Blake series. They are husband and wife, cut from the Nick and Nora Charles cloth, but they are funnier.

Lay That Pistol Down. 1945. My favorite Richard Powell novel. Andy Blake, home on leave from the War Department, goes with his beautiful, gun-loving wife to an auction where she buys a gun which marks her for trouble. Very warm, tough-guy tone, and funny. †††† †

On the Hook. 1950. Pete Cameron sets out to locate a third of a million dollars hidden somewhere on Florida's Shark River, but the bad guys don't want him to find it. ††

A Shot in the Dark. 1952. One of the author's most famous works. Everything is going from bad to worse for Johnny Edwards. First his girlfriend leaves him, then he goes broke, and finally his best friend is murdered. But Johnny rises above all that as he works to find the killer. ††††

Say It with Bullets. 1953. After two attempts on his life, Bill decides his would-be killer is one of five friends scattered around the country. He takes a package bus trip which takes him to all the places where they live. Things are going smoothly until he discovers the tour guide is the beautiful daughter of his old football coach. †††

Masterpiece in Murder. 1955. Two beautiful packages—one blonde, one brunette—lead a quiet art dealer down the garden path of forgery and fraud. †††

POWERS, ELIZABETH. *All That Glitters.* 1981. Amateur detective Viera Kolarova investigates the murder of her boss's wife. Good, lively writing, and an interesting setting in the New York world of diamonds. †††

POWERS, ELIZABETH. *On Account of Murder.* 1984. Viera Kolarova once again proves to be hazardous to the business world, as she discovers the body of her blackmailing boss in an ad agency. †††

PRATHER, RICHARD. Shell Scott is one of my favorites of the 1950s and 1960s hard-boiled school. They are well-written, well-plotted, humorous, tongue-in-cheek stories. Dean Martin should have played Scott instead of Matt Helm in the movies.

The Trojan Hearse. 1964. The plot is a bit muddled in this one. Somehow it concerns an election, a nude woman in a psychiatrist's office, a dead singing idol, and a ruthless talent agent. Best of all, there is the title. ††

Dead Man's Walk. 1965. Shell goes to Verde Island in the Caribbean to investigate what turns out to be three murders all involving voodoo. This is a good one. †††

The Kubla Khan Caper. 1966. One of the funniest of the series. Scott is called in when a series of murders plague the opening of a posh Palm Desert hotel. †††

PRONZINI, BILL.   When you see the name Pronzini on the spine of a book, it can cover a lot of territory. It can mean his excellent hard-boiled series featuring the "Nameless" detective, an anthology he has compiled on some particular subject, an edge-of-the-seat thriller, or a book of criticism on the mystery. Pronzini is truly a man of many hats where the mystery is concerned, and he wears them all well.

The Snatch.   1971. "Nameless" is hired to deliver the ransom money in a kidnapping case and to recover the kid.   †††

Panic.   1972. A chase novel with Jack Lennox being hunted in a desert wilderness by two hired killers. Sooner or later, all of Jack's options are gone, and he has to fight back.   †††

The Vanished.   1973. Elaine Kavanaugh hires "Nameless" to find her fiancé, a retired soldier who disappears after being in San Francisco only a few hours.   ††††

Blowback.   1977. The best of the "Nameless" series as an old pal calls on him to stop violence at a fishing camp.   ††††

Hoodwink.   1981. One of the best of the "Nameless" series. An old pulp writer is being accused of plagiarism by a mysterious blackmailer who has to be one of a number of old writers at a San Francisco pulp convention. He turns to "Nameless" for help.   †††

Gun in Cheek.   1982. A classic collection of the worst writing ever to appear in the mystery. It is funny as hell, and a wonderful subject for a book. Pronzini handles it beautifully. This book is hard to find and it is a must for collectors. If you find a copy, buy it at almost any price.   †††††

Quicksilver.   1984. "Nameless" is getting ready to take on a partner. The weekend before the partnership is to begin, he is hired by a bitchy Japanese woman to find out who is sending her mysterious gifts of expensive jewelry. The search has barely begun when he finds one of her former lovers hacked to death with a Samurai sword.   ††††

PROPPER, MILTON.   *The Boudoir Murder.* 1931. A young woman calls the Philadelphia train station asking that a man be paged. While waiting for the man to pick up the phone, the woman is killed. The call is traced and detective Tommy Rankin sets out to solve this well-plotted mystery.   ††††

PROPPER, MILTON.   *One Murdered: Two Dead.* 1936. A burglar is captured in a wealthy Philadelphia suburb. When he is taken back to the scene of the crime, the mistress of the house is found murdered. Detective Tommy Rankin is not satisfied the burglar is the killer and begins to investigate the dead woman's unhappy marriage. ††††

PUZO, MARIO. *The Godfather.* 1969. If there is anyone out there who hasn't read this—the greatest book ever written about the Mafia—then get busy and read it—or I may make you an offer... †††††

Q

QUEEN, ELLERY. Words cannot express the debt of gratitude which the American reading public owes to the two cousins, Manfred B. Lee and Frederic Dannay, for their creation of Ellery Queen.

The Roman Hat Mystery. 1929. The first Ellery Queen novel. Ellery solves a case of murder in the theater, although this time, rather than onstage or backstage, the murder is in the audience. †††††

The Chinese Orange Mystery. 1934. One of the trickiest of the early Queen novels. Ellery deals with a locked-room mystery whose solution lies in what today can only be described as a "quaint piece of deduction." †††††

The Spanish Cape Mystery. 1935. A very good one, in which Ellery solves the murder of a male prostitute whose body was found nude except for a long, dark cape. A good country-house setting. ††††

The Four of Hearts. 1938. One of the Hollywood stories, and a bit weaker than many of the others. Ellery works his way through an overdose of drugs. †††

Calamity Town. 1942. Generally thought to be the best Ellery Queen novel. Ellery goes to the quiet New England town of Wrightsville to work on a novel, and discovers the eastern version of the corrupt-town novel. Possibly inspired by the successes of Hammett and Chandler, possibly not, but it is still an American masterpiece. †††††

Cat of Many Tails. 1949. Although we have had the psycho killer for quite a long while, this is still an excellent early example of the psycho novel. Ellery, in the heat of a New York summer, tries to catch a killer who is garroting people with a silk cord. †††††

The Scarlet Letters. 1953. Concerned about the marriage of fellow novelist Dick Lawrence and his wife, Martha, Ellery loans them Nikki Porter, his trusted secretary, to keep an eye on things. But even this is not enough, as murder rears its ugly head in this well-written 1950s novel which shows the influence of Erle Stanley Gardner. †††

The Player on the Other Side. 1963. Once again Ellery takes on a psycho. This time it is a very elegant psycho with flawless manners. †††

A Fine and Private Place. 1971. The last Ellery Queen novel. Unfortunately, Manfred Lee died before this one was published. †††

The Tragedy of X, The Tragedy of Y, The Tragedy of Z, and *Drury Lane's Last Case.* Between 1932 and 1933, under the name of Barnaby Ross, Queen wrote four novels featuring a retired Shakespearean actor named Drury Lane. While interesting and readable, they are nowhere near as good as the Queen series.

QUENTIN, PATRICK. A pseudonym used by four authors in various combinations. Some were British, some American, but all lived in the United States. They wrote several series with both British and American settings, but the name is most often associated with a series about Peter Duluth, a theatrical producer who gets mixed up with quite a few murders. This series eventually gave way to one about Lieutenant Trant of the New York Police Department, originally published under the name of Q. Patrick.

A Puzzle for Fools. 1936. In the first of the Peter Duluth novels, the alcoholic producer checks into a sanitarium to dry out and give his nerves a rest. But the place proves to be no asylum because there's an insane killer terrorizing it. Duluth has to pull himself together and—with the help of his kindly doctor and a pretty fellow patient—discover which of the maniacs in the place is also a murderer. †††

Puzzle for Players. 1938. Duluth's theatrical comeback is threatened by a mysterious curse that seems to haunt his new theater. Members of the cast start turning up dead before the curtain call. This book makes nice use of the character's Broadway background. ††††

Puzzle for Puppets. 1944. Set in San Francisco, this mystery takes place while Duluth is on leave from patriotic service in the Navy. When a man wearing his clothes commits a bloody crime, Duluth must turn sleuth to clear his name. The setting is Chinatown with a 1940s flavor. †††

Puzzle for Wantons. 1945. In a Wild West version of the traditional English country-house mystery, Peter and Iris Duluth spend a weekend at a playgirl's house near Lake Tahoe. There is a strange cast: a cowboy, a countess, a socialite, a femme fatale, and a killer. It's not the best book in the series, but the character sketches are pointed and funny. †††

Puzzle for Fiends. 1946. Having transferred his activities from Broadway to Hollywood, Peter Duluth wakes up one day after an auto accident surrounded by people who claim that he's really millionaire Gordon Friend. Even Gordon's beautiful wife agrees. Peter is sure that he is not Gordon, but he doesn't have a clue as to his real identity. †††

Puzzle for Pilgrims. 1947. A beautiful blonde is killed in Mexico while Peter Duluth is there, trying to get over his breakup with Iris, who left him for another man. It's a crime of passion—and the killer may be Iris. Passions of all sorts break loose in this moody and emotional but well-paced mystery.   ††††

The Follower. 1950. The author again uses a Mexican setting in this non-series novel. Mark Liddon's wife turns up missing and her ex-fiancé turns up dead. Mark tries to find her, and gets involved with a squalid criminal underground of vice and drug smuggling. Despite the mystery and action, this remains basically a love story.   †††

My Son, The Murderer. 1954. Peter Duluth's brother and nephew are the main characters in this murder mystery, which is investigated by Trant of the New York Police Department. The emphasis is on the emotions of the characters, but Trant provides a needed element of no-nonsense police activity. A father strives to prove his son innocent of murder—even though he secretly begins to believe him guilty.   ††††

R

RAFFERTY, S. S. *Cork of the Colonies.* 1984. One of the most intriguing collections of short stories I've come across in a long time. Each of the thirteen stories is set in a different American colony as Cork investigates everything from piracy to voodoo and shipwrecks. Great fun.   †††

RANDISI, ROBERT. A hard-working writer who has had a lot of success with a crossover series called the "Gunsmith," a western series featuring certain elements of the mystery. He also has written several mysteries, all of which are very enjoyable.

The Disappearance of Penny. 1980. A rich horse owner hires detective Henry Po to find his missing daughter. The racetrack atmosphere is so good that you can smell horse sweat.   †††

The Steinway Collection. 1983. There's no piano here. The Steinway collection is a collection of pulp magazines which are stolen, and Miles Jacoby is hired to find them.   †††

RAWSON, CLAYTON. Although he only wrote a handful of mysteries, I feel that Clayton Rawson is the best locked-room writer ever to put pen to paper. Better than Ellery Queen, Agatha Christie, or John Dickson Carr. As a serious student of magic, he understood the mechanics of misdirection better than his peers, and that is all a locked-room mystery is—a trick of misdirection.

Death from a Tophat. 1938. Merlini investigates *two* locked-room murders, based on a change-of-time gimmick. Beautifully handled, a true classic. †††††

Footprints on the Ceiling. 1939. Merlini investigates murder in a haunted house on an island. There is even a touch of humor here along with a couple of inside jokes. ✝✝✝✝

The Headless Body. 1940. The circus provides the background for Merlini's investigation of a decapitated corpse. ✝✝✝✝

No Coffin for the Corpse. 1942. Merlini pursues a ghost while he puts together a stage show. ✝✝✝✝

REEVE, ARTHUR. The creator of the scientific detective Craig Kennedy, who for a time was extremely popular in the U.S. and in Great Britain. The height of scientific chic in a white lab coat, Kennedy used his combination of gadgetry and psychoanalysis in the service of the U.S. government and the New York Police Department.

Gold of the Gods. 1915. The theft of an ancient Peruvian dagger piques Craig Kennedy's curiosity and draws him into a case with a New England setting and a south-of-the-border flavor. He sorts out a bundle of confusing clues to clarify a case of blackmail and double-dealing, and solves the mystery of the lost treasure of the Incas. ✝✝✝

The Ear in the Wall. 1916. White slavery and civic corruption—what a combination! Craig Kennedy, with the help of his reporter sidekick, the New York City District Attorney, and gadgets like his "detectascope," cleans up the city and saves a maiden from the fate worse than death. ✝✝✝

The Treasure Train. 1917. Twelve short stories that take Craig Kennedy all over the criminal map, from industrial espionage, and third-world revolutions, to diamond heists. ✝✝✝

REEVES. ROBERT. *Doubting Thomas.* 1985. A promising debut in which a young, seedy, likable professor wins big on a horse bet, and finds himself hip-deep in murder and organized crime. He wanders through the Boston combat zone, a seamy nudist camp, and is hired and harassed by a literature-loving gangster. ✝✝✝

RENO, MARIE R. *Final Proof.* 1976. Marcia Richardson, the editor-in-chief of a book club, is found shot to death at her typewriter. Her friend and fellow editor Karen Lindstrom plays amateur sleuth in a well-written little novel. ✝✝✝

RESNICOW, HERBERT. *The Gold Deadline.* 1984. The second adventure for Alexander Gold and his tall wife, Norma. Alexander investigates a murder in the ballet when a Russian tour will be canceled if he does not come up with the murderer within seventy-two hours. ✝✝✝

REYNOLDS, WILLIAM J. *The Nebraska Quotient*. 1984. A bright debut in which an Omaha investigator turned writer finds himself involved in murder, porno, and politics. †††

RHODES, VIVIAN. *Groomed for Murder*. 1983. The story of the murder of a California hairdresser, handled nicely by a Nick and Nora Charles type of detective team. †††

RICH, VIRGINIA. Her mysteries are just plain fun. They are warm, witty, and deal in food (always a favorite topic among mystery readers). What more can you ask of a mystery than that?

The Cooking School Murders. 1982. Mrs. Eugenia Potter investigates a murder committed with the French boning knife from a cooking class. ††††

The Baked Bean Supper Murders. 1983. After the baked-bean supper at North-cott Harbor, Maine, Mrs. Eugenia Potter's friends start to die mysteriously. She must stop the killer before she becomes the next target. †††

RIFKIN, SHEPARD. *The Murderer Vine*. 1970. The story of a New York private eye who is hired to kill five southern racists, who are responsible for the death of a powerful man's son during a voter-registration drive. The pacing is good, the sex and violence used well, but the ending is weak. ††

RINEHART, MARY ROBERTS. One of the greats. Her appeal is greater to women than men.

The Man in Lower Ten. 1909. Attorney Lawrence Blakely gets mixed up in an out-of-the-ordinary case when a murdered man is found in his Pullman booth. Before that mystery can be solved, the train crashes, Blakely falls in love, important legal papers are stolen, and events move quickly to a logical, if surprising conclusion. †††

The Red Lamp. 1925. In one of Rinehart's best books, a college professor and his family spend a summer at their new seaside home, where a series of baffling crimes directs suspicion against the innocent academic. Even more baffling is the ghostly red light that heralds every crime. There's a strong flavor of the supernatural, but the narrator is most matter-of-fact and the case is solved logically. ††††

The Bat. 1926. This is the novel based on the play of the same name by Rinehart and Avery Hopwood, which in turn was based on Rinehart's book *The Circular Staircase* (1908). The Bat is a mysterious super-criminal, and Detective Anderson is his nemesis. The two meet in a lonely country home, where everyone knows that the Bat is one of the party—but which one? This is one of the books that earned Rinehart her reputation for a hysterical style and dime-novel special effects, but it's tightly plotted and exciting in spite of these drawbacks. ††††

The Great Mistake. 1940. A young orphan, taken into the home of a generous, fabulously wealthy older woman, is disturbed by rumors about her patron's handsome son and by the social and sexual tensions of their small town. She soon has more to worry about, though, when a series of killings appears to point to her as the next victim. †††

Haunted Lady. 1942. Nurse Hilda Adams, Rinehart's only series character, appears in a handful of novels, of which this is the best. The police call her "Miss Pinkerton," because she's an excellent amateur detective. In this case, she signs on to take care of an old lady, and solves a tragic family mystery. †††

The Swimming Pool. 1952. Longer and more psychological complex than most of her other books, this is an ambitious tale of romance, suspense, and murder, all within the framework of a wealthy family's slow disintegration. Although it moves slowly, it contains some of Rinehart's best and most convincing writing. †††

ROBINSON, ABBY. *The Dick and Jane.* 1985. Jane, the heroine, is hired to take some photos for a real private eye and in the process, meets some zany, and not so zany characters. ††

ROGERS, JOEL TOWNSLEY. *The Red Right Hand.* 1945. An American classic of a night of terror told by a doctor. His female patient and her boyfriend pick up a hitchhiker, who kills the boyfriend and cuts off his right hand. You won't put this one down. †††††

ROOSEVELT, ELLIOTT. *Murder and the First Lady.* 1984. I started out expecting little from this mystery by FDR's son, in which Eleanor tries to clear a girl on her staff from murder charges. But I really enjoyed it a lot. ††††

ROSENBAUM, RON. *Murder at Elaine's.* 1978. In the tradition of Ellery Queen, darkness falls on Elaine's, the famous New York watering hole, a shot rings out, and a media power named Foster is dead. Enter Guy Davenport, reporter, as the detective. †††

ROSTEN, LEO. *King Silky.* 1980. An absolutely awful novel by the author of *Captain Newman, M.D.* From the jumble of what passes for a plot, it appears the author takes a rather condescending view of the mystery field. †

S

SADLER, BARRY, WITH ARR, BILLY. *Nashville with a Bullet.* 1981. A pleasant read if you know anything about Nashville. The plot is light and predictable, complete with evil managers, rising young songwriters, beautiful women, and murder. ††

SAUTER, ERIC. *Hunter.* 1983. The story of a Travis McGee look-alike who lives on an island in the Delaware River. The girlfriend of a friend wants him to find her missing boyfriend. †††

SCHERF, MARGARET. *The Banker's Bones.* 1968. A young secretary, accompanying her boss to a conference in Phoenix, is swept up in a storm of violence and murder. Dr. Grace Severance, newly retired from her profession of teaching anatomy, finds herself using her skills once more as both the banker and the bank's money are missing, with the girl as a suspect. †††

SCHERF, MARGARET. *The Beaded Banana.* 1978. Dr. Severance, living quietly in Montana, is called by a friend, who tells her three people are going to be killed because of criminal intervention in the battle for gambling to be put on the ballot. The friend is murdered right after the call, and soon Montana legislators begin to die. ††

SCHORR, MARK. *Diamond Rock.* 1985. Red Diamond, a comic cliché of hardboiled characteristics, is having problems with a woman who claims to be his ex-wife, and he finds himself in the world of rock music. ††

SCHULTZ, BENJAMIN. *Embrace the Wolf.* 1985. Private eye Leo Haggerty is hired to find two girls who were kidnapped five years earlier. ††

SHELDON, WALTER J. *Rites of Murder: A Bishop Burdock Mystery.* 1984. Bishop Paul Burdock, a suitably idiosyncratic cleric, investigates the murder of a hooker who is a friend of his ex-con chauffeur. ††

SHERBURNE, JAMES. *Death's Pale Horse.* 1980. A well-told tale in which 1890s bad-boy reporter Paddy Moretti tries to clear Isaac Murphy, the first black jockey ever to ride at Saratoga, of murder. I like James Sherburne a lot. Read any of the Paddy Moretti series you can find. ††††

SHERRY, EDNA. *Sudden Fear.* 1948. Myra Hudson, a New York playwright, finds out someone is trying to kill her, but because of her own morbid fear of losing face, cannot tell anyone about it. She devises a brilliant counterattack, which succeeds beautifully, but which leads to an incredible twist in the climax. A classic in the psychological suspense field. †††††

SHUBIN, SEYMOUR. *The Captain.* 1982. A retired cop is living in an old-age home where a series of killings are taking place. He knows who, but doesn't want them stopped. Why? †††

SILER, JACK. *Triangles of Fire.* 1984. The story of a California arsonist and the private detective who is tracking him down. Even though the hero is a private eye, the technical nature of the crimes brings it close to being a police procedural. ††

SILVER, VICTORIA. *Death of a Harvard Freshman*. 1984. When Russell Bernard, Harvard freshman and black activist, is found beaten, shot, stabbed, and drowned, Lauren Adler, another Harvard freshman, senses a similarity between his death and the death of Rasputin. From that slender clue, she surmises that the murderer is a member of her Russian history class. †††

SIMON, ROGER. *The Big Fix*. 1973. Moses Wine, a 1970s hippie-style Sam Spade, finds himself involved in political sabotage, a Satanist cult, and a mad bomber, all in scenic California. This one is a lot of fun. †††

SIMON, ROGER. *California Roll*. 1985. Moses Wine takes a job as the head of security for a go-go computer company. He begins getting threatening notes on his computer after an Oriental gentleman is killed in a confrontation over counterfeit computers. †††

SINCLAIR, MURRAY. *Only in L.A.* 1982. Hothead Ben Crandel sets out to free his son and dog from kidnappers when the cops fail. ††

SINCLAIR, ROBERT B. *The Eleventh Hour*. 1950. A perfect crime novel in which the bitchy wife of an unsuccessful writer is murdered. Did he, or didn't he? †††

SINGER, SHELLY. *Samson's Deal*. 1983. A good story of an ex-Chicago cop who moves to Oakland where he investigates the murder of a professor's wife. What really works here is the well-written relationship between detective Jake Samson and his lesbian, poker buddy Rosie. †††

SMITH, CHARLES MERRILL. Author of a series featuring Reverend C. P. Randollph, a Protestant minister and ex-pro football player. Randollph proves that sexiness is no detriment in creating a successful cleric/amateur detective.

Reverend Randollph and the Wages of Sin. 1974. The nude body of a woman who has embezzled ten million dollars from the church is found in the choir room. The Reverend gets help from a good-looking newspaperwoman. †††

Reverend Randollph and the Fall from Grace, Inc. 1978. Reverend Randollph investigates one of the top money earners in the religion field to see if his motives are pure. But before long, there is a box of poisoned bonbons and a double murder. †††

Reverend Randollph and the Unholy Bible. 1983. The Reverend goes to visit a recluse living in a house full of trash, only to find he has been murdered. Investigation shows the old man was rich and had a Bible rare enough to kill for. †††

SMITH, J. C. S. *Jacoby's First Case*. 1980. His first case should have been called "cases," as private eye Quentin Jacoby, a retired transit cop, investigates drugs, race-fixing, organized crime, and a mad slasher. †††

SMITH, J. C. S. *Nightcap*. 1984. Private eye Quentin Jacoby tackles a food murder. As security officer for a posh restaurant, he investigates the colorful murder of its equally colorful owner. †††

SMITH, JULIE. *The Sourdough Wars*. 1984. Attorney Rebecca Schwartz investigates murder within the San Francisco baking community. Well written, witty, and fun. A good read for Susan Isaacs' fans. †††

SMITH, JULIE. *True Life Adventure*. 1985. Unfortunately the hero, ghostwriter Paul McDonald, comes across just a bit too feminine to work. This would have been a good story if the lead character had been a woman. ††

SMITH, KAY NOLTE. *Elegy for a Soprano*. 1985. Dinah Mitchell, the widow of a police detective, and an orphan, sees an obituary for an opera star with the same name as her long-lost mother. The opera star was murdered. Dinah investigates in an excellent read. ††††

SMITH, MARTIN. *Gypsy in Amber*. 1971. Among some stolen items in a Cadillac are the mutilated parts of a dead woman. Gypsy, antique dealer Roman Grey sets out to bring in the killer for ruining his day. †††

SMITH, MARTIN. *Canto for a Gypsy*. 1972. Antique dealer and gypsy Roman Grey is picked to guard the royal crown of Hungary during an exhibition at St. Patrick's Cathedral. While guarding it from those who would take it, he uncovers a century's old secret about the crown. ††††

SPENCER, ROSS H. *The Dada Caper*. 1978. The first in a series of private-eye novels featuring Chance Purdue. Often *very* funny, the stories are set in a style which resembles poetic meter. Unfortunately, the style is much stronger than the content. ††

SPENCER, ROSS H. *Echoes of Zero*. 1981. When his best friend is murdered, and his girlfriend (the most likely suspect) is suddenly acquitted, reporter Rip Deston sets out to find the killer. ††

SPENCER, ROSS H. *The Missing Bishop*. 1985. A breezy Chicago private-eye novel that is very long on style, but short on substance as "Buzz" Deckerd searches for another missing person. ††

SPILLANE, MICKEY. One of the greatest hard-boiled writers ever to put pen to paper. He is most remembered for his creation of Mike Hammer, the tough guy against whom all tough guys are measured, but he also wrote a series featuring a secret agent named Tiger Mann, and several non-series books. In person, he is a great guy, outgoing as hell, and every bit as much fun to spend an afternoon drinking beer with, as you would imagine from his many television appearances. He is a true superstar in the mystery field and he wears it as well as an old, battered trenchcoat.

I, The Jury. 1948. A shocker in its time. Many a teenager secretly read his father's copy for the steamy scenes which, by today's standards, are somewhat tame. Still, it is a true classic in the field. Mike Hammer sets out to find a friend's killer, and runs into a white-slave ring, a set of twin sisters with different ideas, and a beautiful female psychiatrist. †††††

My Gun Is Quick. 1950. Mike Hammer meets a red-haired hooker with a heart of gold, only she's killed before their relationship can develop into something deep and meaningful, and Mike gets his pound of flesh from the bad guys. †††††

The Deep. 1961. "Deep" is an undercover cop who returns to his old neighborhood to avenge a friend's death. A perfect book to read before your high school reunion. †††

The Girl Hunters. 1962. Mike Hammer battles international spies, a killer, and a bad-news blonde. ††††

Day of the Guns. 1964. Secret agent Tiger Mann is in a New York nightclub when there enters a dead ringer for Rondine Lund, a wartime lover who shot Tiger and left him for dead. The story revolves around two questions: Is it really Rondine, and is she the villain? ††††

Bloody Sunrise. 1965. Tiger has to postpone his marriage to track down a missing Soviet skier, who is the mistress of a high-ranking defector from Russia. †††

The Death Dealers. 1965. Tiger Mann is called in to break up a death plot against the king of an oil-rich Mideast state. †††

The By-Pass Control. 1966. Tiger Mann tangles with another beautiful woman, Camille Hunt, in this tale about a secret By-Pass Control which has been added to America's ICBM program. †††

The Body Lovers. 1967. Mike Hammer investigates a very sophisticated sex ring filled with luscious beauties. ††††

Tomorrow I Die. 1984. A collection of previously released short stories, a novella, and the script for Mike Hammer's screen test, which is a lark to read. ††††

STAGGE, JONATHAN. *The Scarlet Circle.* 1936. On their way to the local New England inn, Dr. Westlake's daughter sees an eerie light out on the dunes. When they investigate, it turns out to be a Chinese lantern next to a half-filled grave. A good read. ††††

STAGGE, JONATHAN. *The Stars Spell Death.* 1939. When Dr. Westlake's car stalls, he walks through the woods in search of a gas station. On his way, he finds a wrecked car with a body in it. The body is wearing Westlake's clothes and carrying his mail. ††††

STEIN, AARON MARC. A gentleman and a scholar in the nicest sense.

The Rolling Heads. 1979. While on an engineering assignment, Matt Eridge finds himself the target of the affections of a beautiful young woman and the object of her boyfriend's wrath. †††

A Body for a Buddy. 1981. Matt Eridge goes to his college reunion. After a get-acquainted party he and his roommate find a dead woman in their room. ††

STEPHENS, REED. *The Man Who Risked His Partner.* 1984. I didn't finish this one. Ginny Fistoulari and Mick Axbrewder are hired as bodyguards. Mick is the narrator, and Ginny is a tough woman with one hand, and Mick's boss. ††

STEVENS, SHANE. *By Reason of Insanity.* 1979. The story of Thomas Bishop, a psycho on the loose, and investigative reporter Adam Kenton, the man who is on his trail. An excellent novel. ††††

STEWARD, DWIGHT. *The Acupuncture Murders.* 1973. Deaf amateur detective Sampson Trehune goes to an acupuncturist for a treatment, but the patient in front of him dies on the table. Was it murder? †††

STOUT, REX. One of America's finest mystery writers. The exploits of Nero Wolfe, the fat man who loves orchids, and his wisecracking Dr. Watson, Archie Goodwin, have pleased millions upon millions of fans over the past fifty years. As a writer, Stout had one gift which was outstanding—the power to erase the reader's mind. Even after years of reading, I still cannot remember which of the Nero Wolfe stories I've read, so I cheerfully read them again.

Fer-de-Lance. 1934. The first Nero Wolfe story. A young woman hires Wolfe to find her missing brother, who turns up dead. †††††

The League of Frightened Men. 1935. One of my favorites. A group of men hire Wolfe to stop a former friend from killing them all. †††††

Some Buried Caesar. 1938. Motoring to an orchid show with Archie as his chauffeur, Wolfe is involved in an auto accident. While the car is being repaired, he rests at a millionaire's farm where he finds murder and a most unlikely murder weapon—a $45,000 champion bull.   ††††

Black Orchids. 1942. One of the best. Wolfe wants to own the very rare black orchid—enough to involve himself in some very shady dealings.   †††††

Arnold Zeck stories:

Between 1948 and 1950 Stout created a super-villain named Arnold Zeck for Wolfe to battle. These stories are all excellent, and they should be read in order. *And Be a Villain* (1948), *The Second Confession* (1949), *In the Best of Families* (1950).

The Black Mountain. 1954. This one is great for two reasons: Wolfe leaves his house, and this is the only story which describes Wolfe's childhood and background.   †††††

The Mother Hunt. 1963. Wolfe and Archie wind up baby-sitting for a child left on their doorstep.   ††††

The Doorbell Rang. 1965. Possibly Stout's finest work. After a young woman comes to Wolfe claiming she is being harassed by the FBI, Wolfe and Archie decide to take on J. Edgar Hoover's finest.   †††††

Stout also wrote a few mysteries which do not feature Nero and Archie.

The Hand in the Glove. 1937. Dol Bonner is a female private eye.   ††

The Sound of Murder. 1941. This novel features Alphabet Hicks, a disbarred lawyer, as the detective.   ††

The Broken Vase. 1941. Tecumseh Fox is the detective.   †††

STRAHAN, KAY CLEAVER. *Footprints.* 1929. Lynn MacDonald appeared in all seven of Strahan's novels. In this one, set in Oregon, she gets involved in a small-town family murder, with roots in a long-buried family secret. The book requires careful reading because important clues are buried in a collection of old letters.   †††

STRIBLING, T. S. *Clues of the Caribbees.* 1929. Dr. Poggioli, a professor from Ohio State, takes a sabbatical in the Caribbean, and this collection of tales contains his adventures in Curaçao, Haiti, Martinique, Barbados, and Trinidad. ††††

SWARTHOUT, GLENDON. *Skeletons.* 1979. A complex story in which a divorced, children's writer from New York is convinced by his ex-wife to go to New Mexico to solve the murder of her grandfather, which occurred in 1916. Plot and action are both good here, but the thing I liked best is the well-drawn lead character and his ex-wife. ††††

T

TAPPLY, WILLIAM G. Author of a Boston-based series featuring lawyer Brady Coyne.

Death at Charity's Point. 1984. A wealthy woman asks Brady Coyne to investigate the drowning death of her son. At first it appears to be suicide, but further investigation proves it to be murder. †††

The Dutch Blue Error. 1984. A wealthy man who is a client of Brady Coyne enlists his aid in clearing up a scam involving a rare stamp. †††

Follow the Sharks. 1985. A somewhat disappointing third novel. The story of the kidnapping of a washed-up baseball pitcher. All the elements are there, but attorney Brady Coyne is very flat, and the story could have used a bit more work. ††

TAYLOR, L. A. *Shed Light on Death.* 1985. A nicely told tale in which J. J. Jamison, his wife, Karen, and an obnoxious scholar named Cameron Rogers go to rural Minnesota to investigate reports of a UFO landing. Once there, Rogers is murdered, and it was most certainly done by earthlings who are intent on making J. J. and Karen next. †††

TAYLOR, PHOEBE ATWOOD. The essential New England mystery writer. Writers like Charlotte Macleod, Lucille Kallen, Jane Langton, and J. S. Borthwick owe their roots directly to Phoebe Atwood Taylor. Her most popular series featured Asey Mayo, a homespun New Englander who is a plainspoken, but shrewd, jack-of-all-trades. She also wrote a series featuring Leonidas Witherall, but it is not as good as the Asey Mayo series.

The Mystery of the Cape Cod Tavern. 1934. Asey Mayo investigates the murder of the owner of a famous New England inn. There are a lot of suspects and some interesting gadgetry in this classic, lighthearted mystery. †††††

Octagon House. 1937. A new, unflattering mural of the leading citizens of the Cape Cod community and a hundred-pound block of ambergris lead Asey Mayo into one of his best stories. ††††

The Cut Direct. 1938. Leonidas Witherall wakes up beneath a parked car, then only a few hours later he wakes up in a strange house with a dead body.
††††

Proof of the Pudding. 1945. The finger of suspicion points to Asey Mayo when a young woman's body is found on the beach. ††††

TEILHET, D. L. *The Crimson Hair Murders.* 1936. A novel from the golden age of the Thirties. The detective, Baron Von Kaz, seems a little outdated by today's standards, yet the story holds up well. There are only a few suspects, and the guilt is cast first on one and then on another. The author is able to pull a final rabbit out of the hat in a solution that is surprising for the time. †††

THOMPSON, GENE. *Murder Mystery.* 1980. Attorney Dade Cooley tries to get to the bottom of the mystery in the death of a wealthy art collector when she is crushed by her Rolls-Royce. †††

THOMPSON, GENE. *Nobody Cared for Kate.* 1983. Someone kills the very sick Kate Mulvaney on a trip through France. Attorney Dade Cooley searches for the motive and finds it involves a huge ruby. †††

THOMPSON, JIM. A master of bleak crime novels dealing with twisted souls. He is a powerful writer in the tradition of James M. Cain and Cornell Woolrich. He is not the person to read when you are feeling a bit unstable.

The Killer Inside Me. 1952. A first person novel of a psychopath that is absolutely chilling. Brilliantly done. A masterpiece. †††††

A Hell of a Woman. 1954. A brilliant example of the fact that the sides of a love triangle are seldom equal. †††††

The Getaway. 1959. A relatively straightforward crime novel about a Bonnie and Clyde type of couple. ††††

Pop. 1280. 1964. A masterpiece of corruption. A corrupt man in a corrupt town. †††††

THOMPSON, THOMAS. A powerhouse in both fiction and the true-crime field.

Blood and Money. 1976. The true story of the murder of Texas socialite Joan Robinson Hill, her husband's trial, and his subsequent murder. ††††

Serpentine. 1979. The true story of Charles Sobhraj, the legendary criminal from the Middle East. ††††

Celebrity. 1982. A work of fiction about three young men who are involved in a high school murder, and what happens to their lives afterward. ††††

THOMSON, DAVID. *Suspects.* 1985. An unusual find in which the author gives short but interesting biographies of over eighty famous movie characters, such as Jake Gittis from *Chinatown,* Walter Neff from *Double Indemnity,* and Roman Miguel Vargas from *Touch of Evil.* A must for movie fans. ††††

THORNBURG, NEWTON. *Dreamland.* 1983. I really enjoyed this engaging story of a drifter, who picks up a young female hitchhiker on his way to Los Angeles to meet his private-eye-father, and the team that the drifter and the kid make. ††††

TONE, TEONA. *Full Cry.* 1985. A well-written story set in turn-of-the-century Virginia. It is steeplechase time, and a senator's son is killed by wire strung across the top of a jump to trip his horse as he goes over. The detective is Kyra Keaton McMasters, another senator's wife and former private eye. It is handled with a light touch, but it's a satisfying read. †††

TRAIN, ARTHUR. Known for his true-crime books, but also the author of a series featuring lawyer-investigator Ephraim Tutt.

True Stories of Crime. 1908. His treatment is emotional and reads more like late Victorian fiction than dry fact, but the eleven cases recounted are true. The author is clearly more interested in the human and moralistic elements of each story than in pure detection. †††

The Confessions of Artemas Quibble. 1911. In a Dickensian put-on of his profession, Train created a quick-thinking, rule-bending shyster of a New York lawyer, the hero of these comic cases of legal misadventure. Today he'd be chasing ambulances. If you like a good-natured rogue, you'll enjoy this book. ††††

By Advice of Counsel. 1921. Ephraim Tutt appeared in many short stories by Train. This volume contains seven of them. Tutt is Quibble's opposite, the exemplar of lawyerly virtue. He is wise, just, and scrupulously aboveboard. Needless to say, he's not as entertaining as Quibble. ††††

TRAUBEL, HELEN. *The Metropolitan Opera Murders.* 1951. Wagnerian soprano and mystery fan Traubel wrote herself into her novel as Elsa Vaughn, the Brunhilde who solves a complicated case of murder at the Met. It's a competent mystery even if you're not an opera lover, and a treat if you are. †††

TRUMAN, MARGARET. Harry's daughter clearly knows her way around Washington, and her series of books about Capitol crimes is full of details about restaurants, scenery, and government operations. Her plots tend toward the lurid and melodramatic, but her characters are well drawn and her observations on our cherished institutions and the people who run them are sharp.

Murder in the White House. 1980. It's tough at the top, as the secretary of state discovers when he has his throat cut in the White House. It's even tougher for the president, who has to ride out an investigation that unearths a twenty-year-old scandal. Sex and politics mix, with a surprising twist at the end. †††

Murder on Capitol Hill. 1981. When Caldwell is stabbed with an icepick at his own testimonial dinner, a young lawyer named Lydia James tries to track down his killer. She rakes up an old crime and a sordid connection with a powerful religious cult, proving that the first families of the land are also sometimes the worst families. †††

Murder in the Supreme Court. 1982. Abortion, blackmail, the CIA, adultery— all are involved in the murder of a supreme court clerk. A police officer and a woman from the Justice Department collaborate to solve the crime. †††

Murder in the Smithsonian. 1983. This book has less politics and more murder mystery. It involves an international art scandal and a transatlantic romance.
†††

Murder on Embassy Row. 1984. Truman writes with authority and élan of such matters as embassy parties and consular carryings-on. This is her wittiest book. ††††

• *Some novels to read before burning your draft card, Diner's Club card, or fishing license:*

THE CHANCELLOR MANUSCRIPT by Robert Ludlum
THE FIFTH HORSEMAN by Larry Collins and Dominique LaPierre
GORKY PARK by Martin Cruz Smith
MISSION M.I.A. by J. C. Pollock
SEVEN DAYS IN MAY by Fletcher Knebel and Charles W. Bailey II

TWAIN, MARK. The creator of Tom Sawyer, Huck Finn, and a host of other characters that have delighted us for almost a century.

Pudd'nhead Wilson. 1894. Mystery connoisseurs love this one for the trial in which a young lawyer educates a courtroom full of bumpkins about fingerprints. †††††

Tom Sawyer, Detective.   1896. A seriously dedicated fan of either Twain or the early detective story might enjoy this lighthearted adventure. Tom and Huck solve a mystery and collect a reward.   ††

U

UPTON, ROBERT.   *Fade Out*. 1984. Ambrose McGriffin, a San Francisco private detective, invades Hollywood seeking to find the reason for a Hollywood producer's one-way walk into the sea, and finds the roots of murder stretch all the way back to Bronx childhoods. Wry humor, but shallow characterization.   ††

V

VACHSS, ANDREW H.   *Flood*. 1985. An excellent hard-boiled novel in which New York private eye Burke is hired by Flood, an attractive, but not beautiful, female karate expert with a checkered past, to find the "Cobra," a baby-raper responsible for the death of her best friend. Burke is a great character, and there is some really good writing in this story. A "must read" for Crumley fans. ††††

VALIN, JONATHAN.   A promising follower of the Chandler-Macdonald school of the western detective story. Most of the series is set in Cincinnati, and features private eye Harry Stoner.

The Lime Pit.   1980. A promising debut in which Harry Stoner tries to help a teenage hooker out of a one-way trip to a starring role in a snuff movie.   †††

Final Notice.   1980. A nicely written story in which Stoner tries to find out who is mutilating pictures of women in books at the library. What seems at first a petty, almost laughable crime, leads to a psycho and murder.   ††††

Dead Letter.   1981. Harry Stoner is hired by a college professor to recover a document stolen from him by his daughter. The author relies too much on the conventions of Ross Macdonald to make this one noteworthy.   ††

Day of Wrath.   1982. Still firmly in his Ross Macdonald period, the author weaves a tale of a missing runaway girl and a guru.   †

Natural Causes.   1983. Stoner journeys to California trying to find the killer of the head writer for a soap opera. Overall, the best of the series.   ††††

VAN DINE, S. S.   Author of the Philo Vance series, and more importantly, the founder of the eastern style of American detective stories. As such, he is one of the most important American detective writers; the quality of his work ranks right up there with Hammett and Chandler. Philo Vance is the original of the 1930s suave, dilettante detective, armed only with a pencil-thin mustache and a lightening quip.

The Benson Murder Case.   1926. Philo Vance's first case allows him to explode not one but five successive police theories, until at last he reveals the murderer of Alvin Benson, the stockbroker everyone loved to hate.   ††††

The Canary Murder Case.   1927. A former Follies girl and Broadway singer is mysteriously strangled in her luxurious apartment. Is her death just one more in a series of gangland nightclub murders? Or is it a more subtle crime? And how was it committed in a locked room? Vance is at his keen-eyed best as he probes the depths of domestic and financial intrigue.   †††††

The Greene Murder Case.   1928. The best of the Philo Vance stories. He solves four murders in a true 1920s suspense classic.   †††††

The Bishop Murder Case.   1929. Philo Vance's work on a new translation of Menander is once again rudely interrupted—this time by a series of crimes set to Mother Goose rhymes. His love-hate relationship with New York D.A. John Markham and the homicide bureau continues.   ††††

The Scarab Murder Case.   1930. Egyptology runs rampant as Philo Vance traps the murderer of a wealthy art collector. Just what *is* inside that granite sarcophagus in Dr. Bliss's private museum? Vance knows before the lid is lifted.   ††††

VANVOOREN, MONIQUE.   *Night Sanctuary.* 1981. A page-turner in the Jackie Susanne mold, complete with murder galore, blackmail, and kinky sex, as three women of the rich and famous all fall in love with the same Russian ballet star. Take a couple of Midols, put your hair in curlers, and crawl into bed with this one.   †††

W

WALKER, WALTER.   *A Dime to Dance By.* 1984. A well-written, corrupt-town novel set in New England. Although the author digresses quite a bit from his story, I found myself caught up in it, and read this rather lengthy story in one sitting.   ††††

WALKER, WALTER.   *The Two Dude Defense.* 1985. Although it is well written, I was disappointed in Walker's second novel. It was pure California private eye, with a series of murders growing out of a simple assignment.   †††

WARGA, WAYNE. *Hardcover.* 1985. This first novel starts off promisingly with California book dealer Jeffrey Dean playing detective over two Steinbeck first editions with forged autographs. But from there it falls off a bit, with a plot about Libyan terrorists. Still, the author shows promise, and he will certainly bear watching in the future. ††

WATSON, CLARISSA. *The Fourth Stage of Gainsborough Brown.* 1977. Persis Willum, a well-drawn female amateur detective, sets out to solve the murder of Gainsborough Brown, a famous artist and ass, in a breezy enjoyable read. †††

WAUGH, HILLARY. A first-rate American mystery and suspense writer perhaps best known for his police procedurals, but also the author of a great number of good private-eye stories.

If I Live to Dine. 1947. Private eye Sheridan Wesley is hired by a beautiful woman to find out which of her dinner guests wants to kill her. †††

Hope to Die. 1948. A woman hires Sheridan Wesley to find her missing husband. Then she fires him, but not before the New York Police Department homicide squad takes an interest in the missing man's many aliases. †††

A Rag and a Bone. 1954. The title has to do with the re-creation of a mutilated woman's face by a young detective in an attempt to learn her identity. †††

The Case of the Brunette Bombshell. 1956. Cop Eddie Chavez goes to the scene of a murder where he discovers an earring under the body, an earring which belongs to the woman he is in love with—his brother's wife. †††

The Eighth Mrs. Bluebeard. 1958. The excellent story of a woman who marries a known wife-killer, using herself as bait to see him brought to justice. ††††

The Missing Man. 1964. A police procedural in which Chief Fred Fellows solves the murder of a young woman by slowly fitting together the bits and pieces of evidence until he identifies the killer, a man who still proves elusive. ††††

WEBB, MARTHA G. *Darling Corey's Dead.* 1984. An ingeniously plotted novel in which postal inspector Allen Conyers teams up with policewoman Cheryl Burroughs to track down a criminal mastermind who is running a check-cashing racket through Texas, Arkansas, and Louisiana. Good plotting and good locale work. †††

WEBB, MARTHA G. *White Male Running.* 1985. A novel of current race relations in small-town Texas, where a prominent black attorney finds himself threatened because of a forty-year-old incident, and two white cops join in to help him. †††

WENDER, THEODORA. *Knight Must Fall.* 1985. A woman English professor investigates the murder of the stuffy president of a traditional college, which is trying to move into the 1980s. Not a bad beginning. The author would seem to be a fan of Amanda Cross. She has humor, and the book is lively, even if it is a bit short. †††

WEST, JOHN B. His "Rocky Steele" private-eye series is closer to Spillane than Chandler. Rocky is a good lead character, and the plotting is okay, but the writing is a touch weak.

Cobra Venom. 1959. Rocky and his beautiful secretary, Vicky, reel in a body on a fishing trip and become involved in a mystery which leads them into the world of smuggling and espionage. †

An Eye for an Eye. 1959. My favorite of the "Rocky Steele" series. The writing is less wooden, and the emotions are more convincing as Rocky is hired by a beautiful woman. They have one passionate evening and then she is killed. ††

Never Kill a Cop. 1961. Rocky is brought in for questioning when the cops find a body in the trunk of his Cadillac—a body with no face. †

WHITFIELD, RAOUL. One of the early pioneers in the field of the hard-boiled detective story.

Green Ice. 1930. His best and best-known story. The hero is Mal Ourney, just out of Sing Sing but still in trouble. People start dying around him, and his attempt to track down an underworld leader gets him mixed up with some hot emeralds, a tough-talking cop, a few ruthless killers, and a slightly shopworn "frail." †††††

Death in a Bowl. 1931. The conductor at the Hollywood Bowl is shot on stage, and it is up to private eye Ben Jardin to sort through the Hollywood types who could be involved. †††

The Virgin Kills. 1932. An assortment of oddball guests are on board a millionaire's yacht, *The Virgin*, as it sails for the Poughkeepsie Regatta. Murder is also on board. †††

WILKINSON, SANDRA. *Death on Call.* 1984. Hospitals are depressing places, but Riverside Hospital in Cambridge, Massachusetts, is even more so after someone puts a dead woman down the laundry chute. As assistant administrator Rosemary Cleveland tries to get some answers, the corpses come fast and furiously. †††

WILLIAMS, CHARLES. *The Sailcloth Shroud.* 1960. Wendell Baxter made a habit of dying—or so it seemed. Even though Captain Stuart Rogers, skipper of the charterboat *Topaz*, is sure he had buried him at sea, the two men who showed up also claiming to have seen Baxter dead made him wonder. A good read for John D. MacDonald fans. †††

WILLIAMS, CHARLES. *Aground.* 1960. A yacht disappears. Involved are the woman who owns it, an ex-charter captain, and two thugs connected with its disappearance. †††

WILLIAMS, CHARLES. *Dead Calm.* 1963. The couple from *Aground*, now married, come across a sinking ship on their honeymoon. There is one man on board, a young man who has had to bury his wife and another couple, who all died of food poisoning. †††

WILTZ, CHRIS. *The Killing Circle.* 1981. New Orleans private eye Neal Rafferty investigates the murder of a rare book dealer. I could have forgiven the lifeless characters, if only the author had done more with the atmosphere. ††

WOLF, GARY. *Who Censored Roger Rabbit?* 1981. A bizarre novel in which private eye Eddie Valient is hired by a *cartoon character* (that's right, a cartoon character) to find out who is trying to buy out his contract. I won't say any more. Just read it, and you'll see for yourself. †††

WOOLRICH, CORNELL. To read Woolrich is to take a walk on the wild side. His books exude desperation and doom. His characters are solitary obsessives. No one has done a better job of creating powerful atmospheres of fear and suspense, using the seamy underbelly of city life as a setting. Woolrich wrote a couple of "literary" novels and put in a stint as a Hollywood screenwriter before finding his niche in the pulp magazines.

The Bride Wore Black. 1940. This was the first of Woolrich's "Black" series, which helped to shape the *film-noir* movies of the 1940s. It's a study in the psychology of obsession, in which the tiniest detail assumes portentous importance. A young woman stalks and kills five men and is, in turn, stalked by a detective. The surprise ending is so well written that we can forgive Woolrich for pulling it out of his hat. †††††

The Black Curtain. 1941. Frank Townsend recovers from three years of amnesia. Whose life did he live during those three years? It's a classic plot, and this is the classic treatment of it. Half a dozen radio, television, and movie versions have been made, but read the book anyway. †††††

Black Alibi. 1942. The third "Black" book has an unusual setting for Woolrich: a South American city menaced by a killer jaguar. Or is the jaguar really a human killer? In the book's best scene, a woman is stalked by the unseen beast. †††

The Phantom Lady.   1942. This book is a countdown to the execution day for a man convicted of murdering his wife. He swears he has an alibi—he spent the evening with a woman. The trouble is that he doesn't know who or where she is, so his two friends try to find her. A well-paced book with a sardonic moral at the end.   †††

The Black Angel.   1942. A pretty girl called Angel Face becomes a destroying angel as she tries to prove her husband innocent of the murder of his mistress. This book is a case history of love going crazy, with an ironic twist.   †††††

Waltz into Darkness.   1947. In a long novel of sexual obsession touched with black humor, Woolrich tells of a man who meets his mail-order bride and gets more than he bargained for. It's the old story of an upright gentleman enslaved by a shady lady, with overtones of magic and madness. It is set in the 1880s, one of the author's few ventures into period pieces, and a highly successful one.   ††††

Rendezvous in Black.   1948. One of the all-time greatest suspense thrillers. The dialogue may be dated, but you'll be hooked by the atmosphere of terror and the brutally simple plot: a man, whose fiancée is killed in a bizarre accident, hunts down the people responsible and vows to destroy not them, but the person each of them loves the most.   †††††

XYZ

ZACHARY, HUGH.   *Murder in White.* 1981. Corpses start to pile up at Bellamy Hospital as Sheriff Watson tries to stop a killer somewhere in the halls.   †††

THE
ENGLISH
MYSTERY

T HANK GOD THERE WILL ALWAYS BE
an England—or, more properly put, the British Isles—with its rainy
weather, drafty country houses, cozy pubs, afternoon tea, awful food,
overgrown golf courses, royal scandals, fine beers, whiskeys, gins, tweeds,
woolens, pipes, Burberrys, and most important of all—English mysteries.

For those of us bound by time and economic constraints, it is only
through the time-honored English mystery that we can enjoy the afore-
mentioned pleasures in their proper surroundings, or drop by the "local"
to rub elbows with the vicar, the major, and the innkeeper, flirt with the
village bitch, gossip with the old ladies, and examine footprints in the
flowerbed with the inspector.

In truth, no one really cares who did it. What we are interested in is
the opportunity to return to the simplicity, sanity, and serenity of the
English countryside. If you disagree, you can prove me wrong by simply
naming five well-known, or even reasonably well-known, English mystery
novels which take place in Liverpool, Manchester, or Birmingham.

Since the death of Agatha Christie, the plots have become somewhat
routine. Either the village bitch or the village busybody is killed. Gone
are the clever, quirky plots of Christie, Carr, Marsh, and Blake, or, before
them, Sir Arthur Conan Doyle. Unlike American mysteries, politics or
social change *never* plays a part in the plot of an English mystery. There
is never a mention of striking workers, social unrest, unemployment, or
the Irish situation, and thank God. For the British, in their wisdom,
understand that the mystery story, for its readers, is a dream—a good,
cozy dream, with just enough bad thrown in to make it interesting. And

109

that's the way it should be. If it has become somewhat routine, remember there is comfort in routine.

Even though England's first superstar, Sherlock Holmes, was an ultra-glamorous private detective, the private eye has very little place in the English mystery. Most heroes are police officials with titles like chief detective superintendent. They are solid, colorless, family men with a strong sense of values and a touch of the working man about them. They usually smoke a pipe, never drink too much, and above all, never have sexual relations with any of the other characters in the story.

The balance of the crimes are solved by gifted amateurs. These are the colorful heroes of the English mystery, drawing from the ranks of lords and members of parliament, elderly spinsters, Oxford dons, the clergy, and even more specialized pursuits in life such as antique dealers, poachers, gun dealers, booksellers, and mystics. Rest assured there is someone for every taste.

The amateurs, dating mainly from 1920, with Agatha Christie's introduction of Hercule Poirot in *The Mysterious Affair at Styles,* pretty well ruled the scene until the 1960s. They solved the house party, theater, and campus murders. They were the ones who called the suspects into the room and, after a clever explanation, pointed to the guilty party—who always then confessed.

In the 1960s, the amateur began to give ground to the chief detective superintendent as written by the likes of Michael Gilbert, P. D. James, Kenneth Giles, Alan Hunter, and Patricia Moyes. Many of these border on the police procedural, so if you don't find them here, check that section.

However, I am pleased to report, the amateur, though depleted in numbers, is still alive and well. Some of the more notable amateur detectives in current series are Simon Brett's Charles Paris, Jonathan Gash's Lovejoy, Frank Parrish's Dan Mallett, Antonia Fraser's Jemima Shore, and Tim Heald's Simon Bogner.

The most unique plotting today must surely go to Peter Dickinson. There is simply no one like him. And the greatest sleight-of-hand must surely go to Dame Agatha Christie, the creator of Hercule Poirot, one of the great murderers of our time. Murderer, did you say? That's right, murderer. For over fifty years every time the man got on a boat or train, or went to a house party, someone was killed. The fact that he was a master at shifting the blame does not alter the truth, for when his career is looked at from an overview, there can be no other explanation. I rest my case.

A

AIRD, CATHERINE. Solid is the word that best describes her writing. These are good, solid, satisfying, English countryside mysteries, which feature Inspector Sloan, and never disappoint her readers.

A Most Contagious Game. 1967. This is not an Inspector Sloan story, but one in which Thomas Harding buys an English country house. During renovations he discovers a sliding panel with a skeleton hidden behind it. Naturally the people in the village know more than they are saying.   †††

Henrietta Who? 1968. Inspector Sloan is trying to solve the routine hit-and-run death of Grace Jenkins. Routine, that is, until her daughter, Henrietta, discovers that Grace was not her real mother. Henrietta and Sloan must find the answers to Grace's death before the killer decides to strike again.   †††

The Stately Home Murder. 1969. A light, well-written story in which a body is found in a suit of armor at Ornum House, the showcase home of an Earl. The tone reminds me a bit of *Arsenic and Old Lace*, as Sloan tries to make sense of the lighthearted madness in my favorite Aird story.   ††††

ALLAN, STELLA. *An Inside Job.* 1978. A love affair with a cad leads Sheila into trouble when she agrees to help her lover pull a corporate swindle. Murder once again proves the course of illicit love affairs seldom runs smooth.   †††

ALLEN, MICHAEL. *Spence at the Blue Bazaar.* 1979. Chief Superintendent Spence investigates the murder of a beautiful stripper in a tale with some rather sordid overtones for an English mystery.   †††

ALLEN, MICHAEL. *Spence at Marlby Manor.* 1982. A series of unfortunate accidents to Lady Dinnister point to something more sinister. However, when Spence investigates, things take an unexpected turn. ††

ALLINGHAM, MARGERY. One of the most highly regarded of the English mystery writers, ranking right up there with Christie, Sayers, and Marsh. Most of her stories feature Albert Campion, who began as a con man/detective and wound up as one of Scotland Yard's trusted advisers. Her plots are a bit farfetched, but she always manages to pull them off to everyone's satisfaction.

The Crime at Black Dudley. 1929. Allingham takes the country house murder to task in this lighthearted debut of Campion. His character is somewhat unresolved here, being part good guy, part bad guy, but it is still a brilliant debut. ††††

Mystery Mile. 1930. Campion goes up against a kingpin of crime, rumored to be more than a century old, in this story which proves to be more of a backdrop for a crop of interesting characters than a brilliantly plotted mystery. †††

Sweet Danger. 1933. This story begins with a very funny scene of triple imposture at a hotel on the French Riviera and goes on to a fake treasure hunt that becomes real. The book is lighthearted but tightly plotted. Campion meets his future wife. ††††

Death of a Ghost. 1934. It is the art world's turn, as an artist, dead for eighteen years, "reappears" at a showing of his work. †††

Flowers for the Judge. 1936. A wealthy publisher is killed and suspicion is focused on his nephew who is a friend of Campion's. In solving the first murder, Campion also clears up a second, which has been on the books for twenty years. ††††

Dancers in Mourning. 1937. Campion and the murderer of a beautiful woman are trapped on a country estate. The basis of this story is passion, not greed or general evil, and its tone is more emotional than usual for Allingham. †††

Traitor's Purse. 1941. On a top-secret government mission, Campion struggles to overcome amnesia and stay one step ahead of the police. In this novel, Campion is more sober and less frivolous than before. †††

Pearls Before Swine. 1945. In wartime London, Campion finds a corpse in his bedroom and then, to his dismay, that the chief suspect is an old friend. The city under siege makes for good atmosphere. †††

More Work for the Undertaker. 1948. Campion is the least eccentric person in the story as he investigates the multiple poisonings in a very odd literary household. ††††

The Tiger in the Smoke. 1952. Universally hailed as a classic, rich with atmosphere, suspense, and haunting images, it is Allingham at her most grotesque and her most serious. The "tiger" is a criminal madman. The "smoke" is foggy London. It is Campion's greatest adventure. ††††††

AMES, DELANO. I've never read one of his Juan Llorca mysteries, but I'm very fond of his Jane Hamish and Dagobert Brown novels. They are the British Nick and Nora Charles, with a touch of Crispin thrown in.

She Shall Have Murder. 1949. Jane and Dagobert, as boyfriend and girlfriend, solve the murder of an old lady, who was a client of the law firm Jane works for. A great, lighthearted romp. I loved it. ††††

Corpse Diplomatique. 1950. Jane and Dagobert, now married, vacation in the south of France where murder takes place in their hotel. †††

Murder, Maestro, Please. 1952. Vacationing again, this time in the Pyrenees, Jane and Dagobert are shot at by a sniper. This serves as the opening for a story filled with the most whimsical characters of the series. ††††

For Old Crime's Sake. 1959. Jane and Dagobert win a contest for a cruise to a Mediterranean island where murder robs some of the other prize winners of their good time—but not Jane and Dagobert. †††

AMIS, KINGSLEY. *The Green Man.* 1969. Maurice Allington owns the Green Man, a pub haunted by the ghost of Dr. Thomas Underhill, a 17th-century villain who takes an unpleasant interest in the pub and its inhabitants. Allington is a fabulous, three-dimensional lead character as full of quirks and foibles as Babbitt, and *is* the story, rather than a participant in a larger story. ††††

ANDERSON, J. R. L. *A Sprig of Sea Lavender.* 1978. Piet Deventer of Scotland Yard investigates the murder of a young woman found dead on a train, with a fortune in artworks in a portfolio next to her. The only clue is a sprig of sea lavender. The trail leads to the seaside in an excellent read. ††††

ANDERSON, JAMES. *The Affair of the Blood-Stained Egg Cosy.* 1975. A beautifully written, funny-as-hell, 1930s country-house mystery with everything you can imagine in the story, ranging from a rogue with a secret identity, to beautiful women, to sliding secret panels, and murder among the eccentrics. I can't recommend this one highly enough. It is a "must read." ††††

ANDERSON, JAMES. *The Affair of the Mutilated Mink Coat.* 1981. Not as good as the first one, but this second of James Anderson's parodies on the 1930s country-house mystery is still worth a long, loving read. When you read him, there is a touch of Wodehouse in the air. †††

ASHFORD, JEFFREY.   A writer of suspenseful, realistic mysteries with British settings and likable, ordinary characters. These books concern themselves as much with the psychology of these characters—generally misunderstood innocents—as with criminal incidents.

Three Layers of Guilt.   1975. Harry Miles gets caught up in the machinery of the law, and it looks bad for him. But what if he's innocent and can't prove it? Murder, suspense, and a little romance in a rural setting.   ††

Hostage to Death.   1977. An ordinary man is caught in an extraordinary moral dilemma. In the aftermath of a bank robbery, bank employee Bill Steen becomes an unwitting partner of the robbers, and has a chance to profit from their mistakes. Tension is nicely built up, and the characterization gives plausibility to an otherwise shaky plot.   †††

The Anger of Fear.   1978. A naive, young detective constable grapples with problems of loyalty and betrayal within the police force. Assigned to investigate the kidnapping of a sheik's son from boarding school, he is gradually and inexorably drawn into a web of incriminating circumstances.   †††

B

BABSON, MARIAN.   She specializes in well-put-together mysteries in traditional English settings. Her tales are usually told in the first person by likable young characters with an inclination to laugh at themselves.

The Twelve Deaths of Christmas.   1979. Death strikes in a rooming house, full of angst-ridden youth. It's true what they say about holidays being the most depressing time of the year.   †††

Dangerous to Know.   1980. Tom Paige is the managing editor of the London *Evening Record*, a sleazy newspaper specializing in scandal to boost failing circulation. But having his reporters murdered one by one is a bit much, even for such a muckraking paper.   †††

Bejewelled Death.   1981. Her most lighthearted effort to date. A young woman, carrying a hatbox full of valuable family jewelry from Connecticut to London, finds her quiet transatlantic trip full of perils she had never expected.   †††

Death Warmed Up.   1982. A culinary mystery which centers around the adventures of a young woman whose catering service unwittingly dishes up disaster at one affair after another. It features a very clever kitchen murder.   ††††

A Fool for Murder.   1983. The mystery in this classic case of country-house poisoning is handled well, but the real fun is the incessant family squabbling.

An ill-assorted crew of relations and hangers-on are already on bad terms, but when the seventy-year-old, newly knighted head of the family returns from America with a seventeen-year-old wife, things heat up.   ††††

BAILEY, H. C.   *This Is Mr. Fortune.* 1938. A collection of "Reggie Fortune" short stories. Although Reggie Fortune was one of England's most popular detectives for many years, I find him dull reading.   ††

BALL, BRIAN.   *Death of a Low-Handicap Man.* 1974. A good golfing mystery in which the local bobby is playing a round when the murder occurs.   †††

BALL, BRIAN.   *Montenegrin Gold.* 1974. Bad people will do anything to get their hands on the war diary of a deceased British agent, as his son tries to keep it from them.   †††

BARNARD, ROBERT.   One of the best English mystery writers on the scene in recent years. With the exception of Superintendent Perry Trethowan, who appears in three books, Barnard doesn't have a series character.

A *Little Local Murder.*   1976. The village bitch is murdered when an international radio show comes to the village of Twytching. Not one of my favorites.   †††

Death of a Mystery Writer.   1978. A story of missing manuscripts, murder, literary dirty dealings, and familial hard feelings.   †††

Death of a Literary Widow.   1979. A complex story dealing with forgeries, people turning up alive who are supposed to be dead, and literary hoaxes. As usual Barnard gets in his licks about academics.   †††

Death of a Perfect Mother.   1981. Inspector McHale investigates the murder of the village bitch. An interesting and amusing story for anyone who has ever fantasized about killing his/her parents.   †††

Death by Sheer Torture.   1981. My favorite of Barnard's books. Inspector Perry Trethowan is ordered to investigate the death of his father, who died in spangled tights on a torture machine, presumably for sexual purposes. Good plotting. Very funny. Fine example of first person narrative.   ††††

Death and the Princess.   1982. Perry Trethowan is called in when the friends of Princess Helena, a distant member of the royal family, start to turn up dead.   †††

The Case of the Missing Bronte.   1983. An old lady shows Perry Trethowan what appears to be an unpublished manuscript by Emily Bronte, and they almost die because of it.   ††††

BEEDING, FRANCIS. Although most of the Beeding novels were more adventure than mystery, I am including them here because of his classic *Death Walks in Eastrepps.*

The Five Flamboys. 1929. This story combines elements of Edgar Wallace and John Buchan, as John Butler of the League of Nations finds a body in Scotland, and becomes involved with Colonel Alastair Granby of British Intelligence in a fast-moving kidnapping story of a prince. ††††

Death Walks in Eastrepps. 1931. One of the masterpieces of mystery writing. Robert Eldridge returns home on the train from London at the same time Mary Hewitt is murdered, and he is the suspect. †††††

The Three Fishers. 1931. Ronald Briercliffe, cashiered from the British army, is recruited into British Intelligence and sent to France to replace a murdered agent. His task is to find out how an adventurer fits into the plans for the Nazification of Germany. Remember this one was written before Hitler actually came to power. †††

The One Sane Man. 1934. The League of Nations is threatened by a villain who is attempting to control the world's economics by successfully manipulating the weather. †††

The Twelve Disguises. 1945. The war is beginning to turn in favor of the Allies, but the Germans still hold France. Colonel Granby, who stayed behind when his French counterpart was killed, now has to make his way back to England with the Nazis in hot pursuit. How he succeeds is told with dash and humor, using methods suggested by the book's title. ††††

BELL, JOSEPHINE. *No Escape.* 1965. On his way home from work, Dr. Tim Long rescues a young woman from the Thames only to become involved in the nightmare of illegal drugs. Light reading, but interesting. †††

BELL, JOSEPHINE. *A Question of Inheritance.* 1980. A crib death and a police investigation of a violent crime twenty years later bring amateur detective Philip Bennet and his aunt into the game in a well-written English mystery. ††††

BELLAIRS, GEORGE. His series character, Inspector Littlejohn of Scotland Yard, eventually made it to chief superintendent. Like Patricia Moyes's Henry Tibbett, Littlejohn is usually accompanied by his pleasant wife.

Devious Murder. 1973. Littlejohn is walking the dog when he discovers the corpse of a notorious cat burglar. Criminal or not, the victim deserves a thorough murder investigation, which brings Littlejohn into contact with a variety of colorful and dangerous characters. ††††

All Roads to Sospel. 1974. A British travel group is stranded in France when the tour conductor is shot, and the bus driver is accused of the murder. Luckily, Inspector Littlejohn is holidaying nearby and is on hand, both to interpret for the annoyed tourists and to solve a baffling double crime. †††

Fear Round About. 1975. Bellairs makes good use of an effective setting: an isolated mansion in a deserted village that was once a leper's colony. Approaching retirement, Littlejohn is invited to work for a disagreeable recluse, but his prospective employer is killed before Littlejohn shows up for the interview. †††

BELLOC LOWNDES, MARIE. An early pioneer in the suspense field.

The Chink in the Armor. 1912. A naive, wealthy, beautiful, young English widow traveling alone in France makes the acquaintance of a mysterious nobleman. The novel successfully builds a portrait of her waiting for a crime to happen. Despite its dated sentimentality, it is an interesting look at a mystery told mainly from the point of view of a completely unaware victim. ††

The Lodger. 1913. Although the killer is called the Avenger, he is obviously modeled on Jack the Ripper, and the book clearly demonstrates the author's theory about Jack's identity. A classic suspense story. †††††

BENTLEY, E. C. He wrote *Trent's Last Case* as an entry in a contest which he did not win, but it went on to become one of the masterpieces of the field.

Trent's Last Case. 1913. The fun of this book lies in the fact that Bentley's shrewd, suave, likable investigator, Philip Trent, gets everything right but the motive for the murder of a wealthy financier. A love story parallels the murder investigation, and there too we watch Trent leap to the wrong conclusion. The tone of this classic is light, the plot adroit, and the surprise ending ever so smooth. †††††

Trent's Own Case. 1936. Bentley collaborated with Herbert Warner Allen on this one. The case is Trent's own in two senses: he's both the suspect and the solver. An old man—a philanthropist—is murdered. If Trent didn't do it, then Trent's best friend must have. ††††

Trent Intervenes. 1938. In twelve stories Trent demonstrates his encyclopedic erudition, his canny deductive powers, and his wit. He seems a bit like Lord Peter Wimsey throughout. †††

BERCKMAN, EVELYN. *Lament for Four Brides.* 1959. A romantic suspense story in which English archaeologist Melanie Baird agrees to investigate a medieval crypt at a monastery run by the evil Baron de Lanthelme. ††

BERKLEY, ANTHONY. The author of a number of zany, tongue-in-cheek mysteries from the 1920s and 1930s.

The Poisoned Chocolates Case. 1929. A classic mystery in which, one by one, the six members of the Crime Circle offer their solutions to an unsolved murder. A man has received a box of chocolates at his club. He gives them to a friend, who in turn gives them to his wife, and the wife is poisoned. ✝✝✝✝✝

The Piccadilly Murder. 1929. The mild-mannered Mr. Chitterwick is not only the chief witness for the prosecution in a murder case, but he is also the investigator for the defense. In the process he is able to find out who poisoned the old lady in the Piccadilly Palace. ✝✝✝

Trial and Error. 1937. A terminally ill man decides to murder someone evil, but an innocent man is accused of the crime. The well-meaning killer tries to prove his guilt (aided by Ambrose Chitterwick), and hires a lawyer to prosecute himself. ✝✝✝✝

BIRMINGHAM, MAISIE. *Sleep in a Ditch.* 1978. Kate Weatherby, deputy director of a London settlement, is drawn into a mystery concerning the relationship between her husband and a dead junkie, whose body is found on her doorstep. Kate is a good character. ✝✝✝

BLACK, LIONEL. His stories of Kate and Henry Theobald are nice English updates of Elizabeth Daly. The mysteries are light, well-drawn stories with a touch of humor and warmth.

Death Has Green Fingers. 1971. Kate investigates the murder of a rose breeder whose rare blue rose has vanished with his death. ✝✝✝

A Healthy Way to Die. 1976. My favorite. Kate checks into a fat farm to do a story and finds murder to be an unpleasant way to lose weight. ✝✝✝

The Penny Murders. 1979. A locked-room mystery in which Kate tries to figure who could have caused the death of Miles Cabral in his sealed townhouse.
✝✝✝

The Eve of the Wedding. 1980. Kate and Henry attend an English wedding which has German customs and a German ghost. There is murder at a prewedding party. ✝✝✝

BLACKSTOCK, CHARITY. An English suspense writer whose work is more closely associated with the gothic novel than with the normal English country mystery.

Dewey Death. 1958. This well-known English mystery deals with murder and libraries (namely the Inter-Libraries Dispatch), and heroine Barbara Smith. The idea was good, I found the writing and the pace of the story to be jerky. †††

Witches' Sabbath. 1961. Tamar Brown, an occult writer, finds herself accused of robbing the grave of a dead witch. ††

The English Wife. 1964. A gothic mystery in which a wife stands by her husband accused of murder. ††

BLAKE, NICHOLAS. A first-rate English mystery writer whose works have that same timeless quality of Christie and Marsh. Good indoor amateur-detective work.

A *Question of Proof.* 1935. The first Nigel Strangeways story. He investigates murder at a boys' school. Good atmosphere and well plotted. A terrific debut.
††††

Thou Shell of Death. 1936. My favorite. A terrific story in which Nigel Strangeways meets his future wife, Georgia, at a country house party in which the host is murdered. A very strong piece of plotting. †††††

There's Trouble Brewing. 1937. A novel of murder, beer, and pubs. I like all three. †††

The Beast Must Die. 1938. Many college mystery courses use this finely told tale of a father who stalks his son's killer as a course text. Unfortunately Strangeways plays a rather reduced role here. †††††

The Smiler with a Knife. 1939. Blake introduces more political overtones on the eve of WWII as Strangeways and his wife, Georgia, investigate fascists in Devonshire. †††

Malice in Wonderland. 1940. Someone is playing practical jokes at a summer camp—jokes which prove very sinister. Strangeways investigates. The premise is good, but the execution is not up to his better novels. †††

The Corpse in the Snowman. 1941. One of Blake's best. This is a house-party murder set in the dead of winter, and the corpse turns up—you guessed it—in the snowman. ††††

Minute for Murder. 1947. Set in WWII England, Nigel investigates the poisoning of a war hero's girlfriend who was having an affair with the hero's brother-in-law. ††††

End of Chapter. 1957. Strangeways investigates murder in the publishing business. The setting and Strangeways's role strongly reminds me of Sayers's *Murder Must Advertise.* †††

The Widow's Cruise. 1959. Nigel—now a widower—and his girlfriend, Claire Massinger, investigate the murder of one of two women twins during a cruise to the Greek islands. Unfortunately it is far too transparent. †††

BOWICK, DOROTHY MULLER. *A Tapestry of Death.* 1973. This one leans more toward suspense than mystery, as lovely Diana Marshall finds herself the target of an evil French scientist, who has supposedly found the secret of youth and beauty. †††

BRAHMS, CARYL, AND SIMON, S. J. *A Bullet in the Ballet.* 1937. A classic both in the mystery field and in the field of English humor, as Victor Stroganoff investigates the murder of dancer Anton Palook before he can even take his curtain calls. In addition to the humor, the story also shows the tremendous knowledge of the ballet possessed by Caryl Brahms. †††††

BRAMAH, ERNEST. *Best Max Carrados Detective Stories.* 1972. An excellent reprint of a collection of short stories involving the Edwardian blind detective Max Carrados. ††††

BRAND, CHRISTIANNA. One of the greats. No more need be said. If you haven't read her, you should.

Death in High Heels. 1941. Probably her most lighthearted mystery. The setting is a London dress shop, and the characters, affectionately satirized, are pretty models, eccentric designers, salespeople, and a puppyish detective. Even with its light touch, it is a satisfying read. ††††

Green for Danger. 1944. A classic in which Inspector Cockrill investigates the mysterious deaths of several patients, who died in the operating room of a hospital in war-torn England. The Inspector fades into the background, letting the suspects present this cleverly done mystery. †††††

Cat and Mouse. 1950. Brand's witty, grisly modern gothic appears predictable until the plot begins to take on twists and turns. Every clue is there, but the solution will surprise you. The Welsh scenery adds just the right touch, too. ††††

Fog of Doubt. 1952. Young Rosie Evans is pregnant, and rather than keeping quiet about it, she shoots off her mouth to everyone in sight. When Roland Vernet, the suspected cad turns up and is murdered, all are suspect. The author hides her most important clue in plain sight and pulls off a satisfyingly tricky ending. ††††

Tour de Force. 1955. Similar to Blake's *Widow's Cruise.* Cockrill is on a Mediterrean holiday when a woman in the group is murdered. The twist here is that the misguided local police fix on Cockrill as the chief suspect. †††

BRANSTON, FRANK. *An Up and Coming Man.* 1977. Tommy Tompkins, hard-boiled scoundrel and reporter for the *Ridley Guardian,* finds himself in hot water with the public and his own newspaper, when a man he is about to expose in an article kills himself. Good reading for would-be reporters. †††

BRETT, SIMON. My all-time favorite for theater murders. His hero, down-at-the-heels Charles Paris, is a well-drawn masterpiece with just the right amount of intellect, blind luck, and angst to make him an addiction.

Cast in Order of Disappearance. 1975. The first and weakest Charles Paris story After reading it, I almost didn't read a second one, so give this one a miss until you are well into the series. ††

So Much Blood. 1977. My favorite of the series. The humor and the plotting is the best here as Paris goes to Edinburgh to do a one-man show. ††††

Star Trap. 1977. Charles Paris is hired to protect a prima donna from a killer. A very interesting study of an actor's ego. †††

An Amateur Corpse. 1978. Charles lends a hand to an amateur production and a beautiful starlet is killed. In this one he seems a bit like Rumpole with his resolute individuality. †††

A Comedian Dies. 1979. This time the leading man in a variety show literally does what the title suggests, and it is up to Charles to find out who and why. †††

The Dead Side of the Mike. 1980. Clearly the best of the series. Charles is hired by BBC radio to do a series. A young studio manager is found dead, her wrists slashed. When Charles finds that she was involved with a shady record producer, who also committed suicide, he begins to investigate. The real interest here is generated by Brett's strong inside knowledge of the workings of the BBC. ††††

BROWNE, DOUGLAS G. *Too Many Cousins.* 1946. This excellent story of six cousins, who one by one go to their deaths in mysterious ways, predates the more popular *List of Adrian Messenger* by MacDonald by several years. Extremely well done. †††††

BRUCE, LEO. Author of two series: Sergeant Beef, a village policeman turned private eye, and Carolus Deene, a gentleman detective. The Beef books are better known today.

Case for Three Detectives. 1936. The first Beef story and a lot of fun if you're up on your British detectives. Beef outsmarts three flashy rivals: Lord Plimsoll, Monsieur Picon, and Monsignor Smith, thinly disguised parodies of his rivals in detective fiction. ††††

Case Without a Corpse. 1937. A man announces that he is a murderer and then commits suicide, but no victim is found. Is it murder or a hoax? The class-conscious byplay between Beef and the narrator adds humor. †††

Case with Ropes and Rings. 1940. Beef and his chronicler spend a lot of time in pubs in this one. It makes for thirsty reading as they investigate the death of a student. Was it suicide or murder? †††

Case for Sergeant Beef. 1947. Beef and the narrator develop rival theories about the victim of a so-called "perfect" murder. It's a nice touch to have the narrator working on his own, while continuing to present Beef's side of the story. †††

Jack on the Gallows Tree. 1960. Carolus Deene, the erudite, independently wealthy schoolmaster and amateur detective, is sent to quiet Buddington-on-the-Hill, the least criminal place imaginable, to recover from the nervous strain of solving a previous crime. Here he has to bring to justice a maniac who gets his kicks by strangling old ladies. ††††

Crack of Doom. 1963. One of Bruce's best novels as Carolus Deene matches wits with a killer in a seaside resort town in winter. Unlike *Albert Park*, there is humor here and deft characterization, especially in the description of the barmaids. ††††

Death in Albert Park. 1964. A modern Jack the Ripper invades a quiet London neighborhood. Carolus Deene sets out to catch the killer in a very atmospheric novel totally void of humor. ††††

BURLEY, W. J. *Death in the Willow Pattern.* 1969. A terrific story in which Dr. Henry Pym and his secretary, Susan, are invited to a manor house in the country to look over some old manuscripts. But the real reason for the invite is that the current baronet is receiving threatening letters accusing him of involvement in the disappearance of two young women, because an ancestor of his had been involved in a similar crime two centuries earlier. ††††

BURLEY, W. J. *Wycliffe and the Beales.* 1983. Inspector Wycliffe investigates the death of Bunny Necombe, a local handyman, but the story gets so bogged down in the comings and goings of the Beales family that it becomes tedious. Not one of his better books. ††

BUSH, CHRISTOPHER. All but two of his over sixty mysteries are about, or narrated by, Ludovic Travers, an amateur detective who helps out Scotland Yard in seemingly unsolvable cases.

The Case of the Tudor Queen. 1938. A scandalous double suicide—an actress and her elderly handyman—turns out to be a particularly devious, almost perfect, murder. †††

The Case of the Second Chance. 1947. The long arm of coincidence stretches across several years to link an unsolved murder and a baffling case of blackmail. The setting is wartime London and the suspects all actors. †††

BUTLER, GWENDOLINE. *The Doll Dead.* 1958. An early Inspector Coffin novel in which the theme is a threat to a well-drawn five-year-old girl. †††

BUTLER, GWENDOLINE. *A Coffin from the Past.* 1970. Detective Coffin investigates the murder of a member of parliament and his secretary with overtones which stretch back to a series of murders committed in 1820 in the same house. The pacing of the story is jerky, marred with flashback scenes at irregular intervals, and a plot too ambitious for a book this short. ††

BUTTERWORTH, MICHAEL. *The Soundless Scream.* 1967. A bit thin for a satisfying psychological suspense novel as a pretty young woman goes on holiday, only to find her psychiatrist murdered under her window. ††

BYRD, ELIZABETH. *Rest Without Peace.* 1974. The author turns the grisly work of Burke and Hare, body snatchers and murderers par excellence, into a novel of a Victorian nightmare that makes you glad you were born in the 20th century. ††††

BYRD, ELIZABETH. *The Search for Maggie Hare.* 1976. In the follow-up to *Rest Without Peace,* an orphan, Dorothea, sees a newspaper photo of Maggie Hare and decides she could be her mother. Curiosity takes hold, and she has to find out, but at an awesome price in this novel of Victorian depravity. †††

BYROM, JAMES. *Take Only as Directed.* 1959. A doctor finds himself in trouble when he fakes a murder alibi for a girl from his past, and he is caught in the middle between blackmailers and Scotland Yard. †††

C

CANDY, EDWARD. A first-rate English mystery writer whose only drawback is his lack of a series character. However, his ingenious plots and humor more than make up for it.

Bones of Contention. 1954. The director of the Museum of Pathological Conditions in Childhood is murdered shortly after a skeleton arrives in a steamer trunk. Then a second murder occurs, and the museum members have their hands full.   ††††

Which Doctor? 1954. When a brilliant prig of a doctor is found murdered, and a nine-year-old boy is missing from his bed, Professor Fabian Honeychurch investigates and uncovers a can of worms, which includes blackmail, narcotics, adultery, and all sorts of other good stuff at the hospital.   †††

Words for Murder Perhaps. 1971. Gregory Roberts is a mama's boy who teaches crime fiction to old ladies and is suspected of a series of murders beginning with the death of a professor of Egyptology.   †††

CARMICHAEL, HARRY. Author of more than forty novels about the team of insurance investigator Piper, and crime reporter Quinn. The stories are filled with meticulous clue planting, methodical investigations, and careful plotting.

Naked to the Grave. 1972. The brutal murder of a lovely young housewife leads Piper and Quinn into a nest of dirty secrets in tidy Hampstead: adultery, gambling, and more murder.   †††

Too Late for Tears. 1973. Piper and Quinn investigate the particularly horrible shooting of a writer in a lonely country cottage. It looks like suicide, but could it be murder? The two investigators painstakingly bring the truth to light. ††††

CARR, JOHN DICKSON. A master of the locked-room mystery. Best known for his characters: Dr. Gideon Fell and Sir Henry Merrivale. If plot and atmosphere are his strong points, character and conversation are his downfalls. Still, he is one of the greats. It will be a long while before we will see his like pass before us again.

The Mad Hatter Mystery. 1933. A city-wide series of pranks by a mysterious character called the Mad Hatter culminates in a crossbow murder at the Tower of London. Essentially the solution is a matter of timing and alibi breaking.
†††

The Blind Barber. 1934. Fell solves this complicated case of shipboard theft without moving from his chair in his study. This book is generally regarded as Carr's most madcap mystery, and while there are some funny scenes, the story and the detection are very strong. †††††

Death Watch. 1935. This is one of those books in which too many of the characters speak in elliptical sentence fragments, and no one ever knows what is going on. However, it does have an unusual murder weapon and a houseful of eccentrics. †††

The Three Coffins. 1935. This book contains Carr's famous "locked-room lecture," in which Fell enumerates the possibilities for "impossible" murder. It is Carr at his best. †††††

The Arabian Nights Murder. 1936. A practical joke takes a grim turn when the victim is murdered in a museum of antiquities. Carr's attempt to create a sexpot doesn't work too well, but the rest of the story is fun. †††††

Four False Weapons. 1937. French sleuth Henri Bencolin comes out of retirement to solve the murder of a beautiful woman in a Paris villa. The first problem is to determine how she died—by poison, bullet, or blade? †††

The Burning Court. 1937. This book reads like an experiment in both style and subject matter. It's structured like a trial, from indictment to verdict, and it's a cross between criminal deduction, a vampire story, and a tale of domestic intrigue. †††

To Wake the Dead. 1938. Mystery writer Christopher Kent tries to win a bet by swindling a hotel but finds himself in a room with a murdered woman. She just happens to be the wife of his cousin, who just happens to have been murdered in the exact same way two weeks earlier. †††††

The Problem of the Wire Cage. 1939. Fell investigates a murder in which the victim was killed on a wet, clay tennis court with no footprints around. †††††

The Skeleton in the Clock. 1948. Henry Merrivale gets involved with a psychic researcher who wants to look for ghosts in the execution shed of an old prison. Along the way, a twenty-year-old "supernatural" murder, some anonymous letters, and a new murder enter the picture. †††††

CARVIC, HERON. *Picture Miss Seaton.* 1968. On her way home from seeing *Carmen*, Miss Seaton stumbles across a murder. Naturally, she decides to give Scotland Yard a hand. †††††

CARVIC, HERON. *Odds on Miss Seaton.* 1975. Scotland Yard once again uses the services of amateur sleuth and full-time busybody Miss Seaton. This time it is to clean up gambling irregularities, but Miss Seaton, with all her charm, manages to take a simple task and make it much more complex. A "must read" for fans of Dorothy Gilman's Mrs. Polifax. †††

CAUDWELL, SARAH. *Thus Was Adonis Murdered.* 1981. A clever, skillfully plotted first novel in the understated bizarre tradition of Edmund Crispin, featuring hilariously eccentric characters. Without leaving London, the narrator matter of factly solves a locked-room murder in Venice. ††††

CAUDWELL, SARAH. *The Shortest Way to Hades.* 1984. Featuring the same pleasantly pedantic characters as in her first novel, the author gives us a second just as skillfully told. The professor and his friends become involved in the legal—and criminal—affairs of a huge inheritance. ††††

CHALMERS, STEPHEN. *Blood on the Heather.* 1932. This tale of domestic drama, murder, and classic police investigation is a true period piece. It features a Scottish castle, a plethora of baffling clues, and an old-fashioned melodramatic style, which adds to the fun, which includes Rob Roy's pocketknife and sunken treasure. ††††

CHESTERTON, G. K. Chesterton's detective, Father Brown, is one of the best characters *ever* to appear in detective fiction. The tone of the stories (all short stories, there are no novels) sometimes resembles that of the Sherlock Holmes series, but Chesterton takes it one step further by exploring the emotional makeup of his characters. This psychological aspect marked a distinct change and elevation in the art of the mystery story. *The Innocence of Father Brown*, 1911, †††††; *The Wisdom of Father Brown*, 1914, †††††; *The Incredulity of Father Brown*, 1926, ††††; *The Secret of Father Brown*, 1927, ††††; *The Scandal of Father Brown*, 1935, ††††.

The Man Who Was Thursday. 1908. Gabriel Syme, part-time detective, goes up against the Supreme Council of Seven, a group of anarchists, in a story so close to fantasy that it must have been a knockout in its day. †††††

CHRISTIE, AGATHA. Her settings are routine, her characters wooden, but she is probably the greatest of all mystery writers. In her ever so tricky plots, appearances always are deceiving and the solutions dazzling. Once you are a Christie addict, the eighty-odd mysteries that she wrote will seem far too few. She had three series detectives, most notably the bald Belgian, Hercule Poirot, the elderly spinster, Miss Marple, and the flapper couple, Tommy and Tuppence. The Poirot mysteries are generally the most ingenious.

The Mysterious Affair at Styles. 1920. Narrated by Hastings, Poirot's own Dr. Watson, this was Christie's first mystery. Poirot looks into the poisoning death of the wealthy mistress of a country house. A disinherited stepson is the likely suspect, but Poirot realizes that timing is the crucial element in catching a clever suspect. †††††

The Secret Adversary. 1922. A search for a missing girl leads Tommy and Tuppence into romance, adventure, and espionage. Christie dedicated this book to "all those who had monotonous lives," and while Tommy and Tuppence are not exactly a sizzling pair, they do have some fun in this one. So will you.

††††

The Mousetrap. 1925. This classic story was turned into the longest running play in history. A group of people are stranded by snow in a remote guest house, and one of them is murdered. Police Inspector Trotter suggests an old grudge is involved, and the murderer is identified in the nick of time.   †††††

The Murder of Roger Ackroyd. 1926. Arguably Christie's most famous book. The village doctor narrates this account of Hercule Poirot's sleuthing to find the killer of the widow Ferrars and her fiancé, wealthy Roger Ackroyd. There are greedy suspects galore, but opportunity is everything, and the solution is great.   †††††

Murder on the Orient Express. 1934. My favorite Christie story. The murder of the wealthy and worried Mr. Ratchett in his compartment on the famous train seems insoluble. All aboard have alibis. But Poirot reveals an almost perfect crime.   †††††

The ABC Murders. 1936. A homicidal maniac has killed an Asher in Andover, a Barnard in Bexhill, and a Clarke in Churston, all towns on the same train line. Poirot must find him before he murders his way through the whole alphabet. A brilliant plot.   †††††

And Then There Were None. 1939. Ten people, all with nasty secrets, are summoned to an island by an unknown host. One by one they are murdered, and their terror mounts as each suspects the other. I won't say any more, except this is one of the greatest of the great.   †††††

What Mrs. McGillicuddy Saw. 1957. Elspeth McGillicuddy sees a woman strangled through the window of a passing train, but no one can find the body. Only her friend Jane Marple believes her. This one is filled with the misdirection and mistaken identities that Christie used so well.   ††††

Halloween Party. 1969. Ariadne Oliver, Christie's apple-munching alter ego, appears in this tale of a child drowned while bobbing for apples. Mrs. Oliver enlists her friend Poirot, who finds that love and money are, as usual, involved. Most notable here is the way in which Christie hides her most important clues in plain sight.   ††††

Curtain. 1975. Published posthumously, this final case of Poirot's brings him back to Styles, the scene of his first case. Several apparently unrelated deaths occur here, including the great detective's own. It would seem that he had failed, but had he?   ††††

Sleeping Murder. 1976. Miss Marple also has a last case. She comes to the aid of young Gwenda Reed, who has moved into a new house and dredged up an old murder. This novel depends on some of Christie's time-honored tricks, but it is stale. †††

CLARK, DOUGLAS. Not one of my favorites, but everyone else seems to like him, so I'm including him.

Sick to Death. 1971. Inspectors Masters and Green investigate murder by diabetic coma. Nice touch for a different murder method. †††

Dread and Water. 1976. Scotland Yard steps in to investigate murder in a secret research facility. †††

Golden Rain. 1980. In spite of what the title may suggest, this is merely an adequate novel about murder at a girls' school. ††

The Longest Pleasure. 1981. Scotland Yard Superintendent Masters investigates an outbreak of botulism. †††

CLARKE, ANNA. *Game Set and Danger.* 1981. A psychological suspense novel in which two women—former tennis rivals—now find themselves again facing each other across the net, and with each volley the negative emotions of competitive athletics lead them closer and closer to death as the match point. ††

CLINTON-BADDELEY, V. C. *Death's Bright Dart.* 1967. The weakest of the Dr. Davie novels. A young up-and-coming professor is killed by a dart from a blowgun as he gets up to speak at a conference. The author did not bother to create either a setting or characters for the story. There is little or no description of the locale, and the characters—of which there are far too many—are nothing more than names and academic credentials. ††

CLINTON-BADDELEY, V. C. *To Study a Long Silence.* 1972. Clinton-Baddeley's last novel. Dr. Davie investigates the murder of a young student-actor. †††

CODY, LIZA. A promising young English mystery writer whose detective, Anna Lee, closely resembles P. D. James's Cordelia Gray.

Dupe. 1981. A promising debut in which Anna Lee, private investigator, is hired by parents to investigate the auto accident in which their daughter died. †††

Bad Company. 1983. Anna Lee is hired to watch the wife and daughter of a client, but there is a kidnapping, with Anna as one of the victims. †††

Stalker. 1984. Some say third time is the charm. This time it wasn't. The author missed the mark with this missing persons story, which involves the poaching business. Anna Lee is still a strong, vibrant character, but the story is far too short and reads almost like an outline, with page upon page of meaningless dialogue and little else.   ††

COLLINS, WILKIE. Possibly the first of the "big book" writers in the mystery field, making major impact with complex, atmospheric plots with social relevance. Even with all this depth, his stories are fast paced and still highly readable today.

Basil. 1852. A story notorious in its time for its plot which involved a young gentleman and his infatuation with a shopgirl. It's a tale of violence, vengeance, and elements of the fantastic.   †††

The Woman in White. 1860. The story of an heiress imprisoned and defrauded by her husband and his henchmen. One of the earliest gothic novels.   †††††

The Moonstone. 1868. Collins's most famous novel. Sergeant Cuff is called in after a priceless diamond mysteriously disappears. Like many of his fictional descendants, Cuff bungles the job, leaving the mystery to be solved by a gifted amateur, the rakish young hero.   †††††

CONNINGTON, J. J. He wrote crime and adventure novels in which outlandish plot situations and over-sized villains rub elbows with the British gentry.

Grim Vengeance. 1929. Sir Clinton Driffield steps in to save English womanhood from the unspeakable horrors of white slavery in Argentina.   †††

Gold Brick Island. 1933. Sir Clinton does not appear in this adventure of secret passages, coded messages, and mysterious foreigners on a small Scottish island, with the lost treasure of the Armada thrown in. The story starts off strongly, but quickly loses its punch.   †

COPPER, BASIL. *The Curse of the Fleers.* 1976. A wonderful pastiche of the gothic novel, complete with midnight chases, an escaped ape, an impossible murder, a hooded killer, and a hidden treasure. An excellent novel from all aspects.   ††††

CREASEY, JOHN. The most prolific of all mystery writers, writing under at least a half-dozen pen names. Since these names are so familiar I have decided to list three of them here.

As J. J. Marric:

Gideon's Week. 1956. An escaped convict goes after the wife who turned him in. She's as good as dead unless Commander Gideon of Scotland Yard can capture him first. †††††

Gideon's March. 1962. Gideon is in charge of security for a four-nation summit meeting in London. He has plenty of headaches as everyone from pickpockets to psychopaths is waiting to greet the visiting heads of state. †††

As Kyle Hunt:

To Kill a Killer. 1960. A tense well-plotted story of a madman determined to murder his already dead wife. ††

As Anthony Morton:

The Baron on Board. 1964. John Mannering, known as the Baron, was once a master jewel thief. He is still in the jewelry game, but as a dealer and consultant. Despite his moral reformation, he gets involved in a messy case of murder and missing crown jewels. †††

As John Creasey:

The Toff Proceeds. 1941. The Toff is the Honorable Richard Rollinson, gentleman-adventurer, friend of Scotland Yard and foe of the underworld. His collection of souvenirs rivals the Yard's Black Museum. In this case, he tangles with murder in a country-house setting. Invited for a weekend of sports, he soon finds that all is not quite cricket with the two beautiful look-alikes and the huge inheritance. ††

The Toff Goes to Market. 1942. Black market, that is, in this wartime novel of profiteering and murder. Rollinson's suave valet, Jolly, and his refined derring-do make this, and some of the other Toff novels, resemble Dorothy Sayer's Lord Peter Wimsey books. The Toff, though, is not quite so elevated, and his cases are considerably grittier. †††

The Toff and the Deadly Parson. 1944. The East End of London is a sordid test of faith for the Reverend Kemp, but with the help of the local pugilists, the Toff keeps him on the straight and narrow, while dodging flying fists. ††

The League of Dark Men. 1947. Department Z, top-secret British counter-intelligence office, must outwit the sinister Council of Three before it starts WWIII. ††

The Toff at the Fair. 1954. The Toff has it all: money, good looks, the works—everything but the respect of his family. But he learns that murder can be a family affair, as he tries to extricate his relatives from a morass of drugs and blackmail. †††

The Toff and the Fallen Angels. 1970. Still dapper after all these years, the Toff places the life of his own niece, Angela, on the line to put an end to a series of horrific incidents at a home for unwed mothers. To his credit, he does so without excessive moralizing. †††

CRISPIN, EDMUND. My favorite English mystery writer of them all. My only complaint is that he did not write more of his urbane, witty, well-plotted tales featuring his Oxford don, amateur detective Gervase Fen.

Holy Disorders. 1945. A perfect example of the modern British detective novel. Murder and witchcraft run riot in an English cathedral town, as Fen finds the solution to the murder of a number of church organists in his usual witty way. †††††

The Moving Toyshop. 1946. A poet goes on a toot and breaks into a toyshop, where he discovers a body. The next morning he goes back sober only to find the toyshop has become a grocery store, and the body is gone. He turns to Gervase Fen for help, and this story rapidly becomes one of the great classics of the field. †††††

Swan Song. 1947. A locked-dressing-room murder in which opera star Edwin Shorthouse is done in. Fen is even more fun than usual because of Crispin's funny asides about the world of opera. ††††

Love Lies Bleeding. 1948. A beautiful missing student, missing poisons from the science lab, and the murder of two professors bring Fen into the case. ††††

Buried for Pleasure. 1949. At the top of his form, Crispin has Fen running for parliament in a hysterical novel filled with energy, fun, and murder. My favorite of all the Crispin novels. †††††

Frequent Hearses. 1950. Fen is a consultant on a film about the life of Alexander Pope when first a bit player dies, then a cameraman. The climax has an especially good setting. ††††

Beware of the Trains. 1953. A collection of sixteen short stories which Crispin felt were not worthy of novel length, all featuring Gervase Fen. †††

The Case of the Gilded Fly. 1954. Although published later, this is the first Gervase Fen story, written during Crispin's college days. While still a good read, it is a typical theater story, in which the beautiful leading lady of a repertory company visiting Oxford is murdered, and Fen investigates. †††

CROFTS, FREEMAN WILLS.   He wrote a host of mysteries featuring Inspector (later Superintendent) French, a dogged meticulous investigator, who never accepts anything at face value. With Crofts we are talking about intricate plotting.

Inspector French's Greatest Case.   1924. Contrary to what you might think, from the title, this is French's first appearance. He's confronted with an open safe, a missing fortune in diamonds, a murdered witness, and an unbreakable alibi.   †††

The Cheyne Mystery.   1926. Maxwell Cheyne is invited to lunch by a stranger, who drugs him. When he wakes, he finds his house has been burgled. Angry, Cheyne seeks revenge, which leads him on a merry chase with a beautiful woman by his side and against gentlemanly adversaries. However, he ultimately winds up over his head and has to call for help from Inspector French in this warm mannerly mystery.   †††

The Sea Mystery.   1928. A decomposed body, found in the sea off the Welsh coast, leads French to Cornwall and then back to London in a case of mistaken identity, marital infidelity, and murder. One nice touch is that logic is helped out by luck.   ††

The Loss of the Jane Vosper.   1936. An insurance inquiry into the loss of a ship evolves into a murder case. The opening chapter, in which the ship sinks in the mid-Atlantic, creates a sense of drama and urgency which counterbalances the lengthy land-locked investigation.   †††

Fear Comes to Chalfont.   1942. Julia Elton marries a man she does not love, and comes to live in the house of Chalfont with an assortment of his relatives. If moderate unhappiness can be said to run smoothly, then Julia's life does— until a guest's emerald is missing, and one thing leads to another. Very slow moving.   ††

CURRINGTON, O. J.   *A Bad Night's Work.* 1974. A novel of the British underworld in which Jack and Alfie, a couple of top-notch safecrackers, join forces with a gang to pull off a big job, but things start to go sour for them.   †††

D

DALE, CELIA. *The Deception.* 1979. The perfect couple next door—only the husband comes home to find his wife murdered, and Detective Simpson and Inspector Hogarth discover the mysterious disappearance of the son years ago and begin to put two and two together. †††

DAVEY, JOCELYN. *Murder in Paradise.* 1982. Ambrose Usher, Oxford don, in another cerebral mystery involving a diverse set of characters on a Caribbean island. The host is supposed to be blown away by a bomb, but the killer gets the wrong person. †††

DAVIES, L. P. A writer of novels with science-fiction overtones. His books are serious, even grim, in tone, with fast-moving plots which often involve amnesia or the fear of insanity.

The Paper Dolls. 1964. An eerie story in which a British schoolmaster suspects foul play in the death of a student. He suspects a mysterious thirteen-year-old—that's all I'm telling. ††††

Who Is Lewis Pinder? 1965. A classic in the field. A tour de force in plotting about an amnesia victim with a one-in-a-million birthmark, which identifies him as *four* separate men, all of whom have been dead for twenty years.
†††††

The White Room. 1969. Can scientific indoctrination—brainwashing—turn a respectable industrialist into a crazed killer? And if so, which is the real man? Davies has some sardonic fun with the notion of identity in this ingenious thriller. †††

The Shadow Before. 1970. Another tale of psychological suspense in which a dull pharmacist and a prosperous investor seem to be the same person. He wonders whether one of his existences is only a dream, and which one. What at first appears to be a purely intellectual mystery turns into a clever crime story. †††

Give Me Back Myself. 1971. A friendless immigrant is duped into impersonating a reclusive millionaire in a robbery and smuggling conspiracy. Everyone around him thinks he's lost his memory. He fears he may lose his sanity. The book is well written with believable characters and a satisfying conclusion.
††††

Assignment Abacus. 1975. Big business seems to attract Davies with suggestions of chicanery and conspiracy. In this story, a rising young executive tries to uncover a security leak in his corporation and finds himself, pumped full of LSD, having hallucinations in a lonely house on the Scottish moors. He must crack a top-secret code in order to survive. †††

The Land of Leys. 1979. An elderly woman in a quiet, wealthy suburb is apparently the victim of a satanic cult. Gradually the evil influence spreads through the community, bringing death and destruction, until the climactic battle between white and black magic—which may be only psychological suggestion, stage props, and old-fashioned criminality. †††

DELVING, MICHAEL. Author of a series of mysteries featuring Dave Cannon, an American antique dealer married to a British girl. Like Jonathan Gash, Delving makes good use of antiques to add color and motive to his plots.

Smiling, the Boy Fell Dead. 1967. On his first trip to England, Cannon plays the innocent abroad. He meets his future wife, fills in for an absent player in a very funny game of cricket, and gets blamed for the murder of a village boy. To clear himself, he has to solve a mystery involving murder, suicide, morphine peddling, and a rare manuscript. †††

The Devil Finds Work. 1969. Dave Cannon and his partner have the opportunity to purchase the private papers of a notorious satanist. But someone's out to commit murder and gives Cannon a hell of a scare. †††

Die Like a Man. 1970. Set in Wales, this book has a pretty improbable plot and set of motives, but suspense and a tight pace pull it off. Cannon comes into possession of the Holy Grail—maybe—and finds himself in the unpleasant position of being a man on the run against a townful of friends, who turn out to be enemies. †††

Bored to Death. 1975. Best of the series. The action takes place in a village on the river Severn, and a massive tidal bore is a key plot element. At the heart of the mystery is an ancient silver coffer, which raises questions of ownership, dispossession, and belonging, that go far beyond this one case. It's thoughtful, well plotted, and even a little moving. ††††

DEWHURST, EILEEN. *Drink This.* 1980. A novel with a title like this and a lot of pub scenes immediately caught my eye. It turned out to be worth it. Inspector Carter goes to the village of Bunington, supposedly on holiday, but in reality checking up on the wife of a bank robber. However, there is more going on in the sleepy village than that. †††

DEXTER, COLIN.   *Last Seen Wearing.* 1976. Two years after the death of Valerie Taylor, a schoolgirl, Chief Inspector Morse is asked to reopen the case. He is reluctant to bother, until an acquaintance of Valerie's is found murdered. A solid, English countryside mystery.   †††

DICKENS, CHARLES.   Yes, the author of *Great Expectations* and *Oliver.Twist* even wrote a couple of mysteries in his time. Personally, I wouldn't give you two cents for either of them. Even though I recognize his impact on Literature, reading him is like taking unpleasant medicine.

Bleak House.   1853. Dickens's most brooding work. This complex tale of blackmail and murder features Inspector Bucket, and is the story of a generations-long court case, and its effect on the families involved.   †††

The Mystery of Edwin Drood.   1870. Dickens didn't finish writing this story, and I didn't finish reading it. It is a straight mystery with a villain, a disappearance, and a disguise.   ††

DICKINSON, PETER.   A true one-of-a-kind stylist in the English mystery field. There is no one even vaguely like him. The closest description of his work I can give is to say that he is the Kurt Vonnegut of mystery writers.

The Glass-Sided Ant's Nest.   1968. Dickinson's first mystery novel. Superintendent Pibble investigates the murder of the chief of a tribe of New Guinea aborigines, which has moved intact to London. Black magic, sacrifices, and offbeat sexual practices keep this one moving.   ††††

The Old English Peep Show.   1969. Pibble investigates a case of death by lion in an old English estate converted into a safari park. His ability to sniff out deception and skullduggery leads him to a terrifying confrontation with the truth—and the lion.   ††††

The Poison Oracle.   1974. In this bizarre thriller set in an Arab emirate, an English scientist is trying to teach a chimpanzee to communicate. But when the chimp is the sole witness to murder, giving evidence strains its new skill to the limit.   ††††

King and Joker.   1976. A practical joke played on the British royal family is no laughing matter for the palace security force, and when a series of jokes grows progressively more grisly, the very survival of England's monarchy is threatened. Dickinson creates an interesting alternate history in which England is ruled by Victor II, descended from Edward VII.   †††

Walking Dead.   1977. Science again mingles with mystery in Dickinson's tale of voodoo and zombies on a Caribbean island. As always, political corruption is rampant and revolution just around the corner. A naive, young English lab technician is the hero. ††††

The Last Houseparty. 1982. One of his best, using a crime in the 1930s at one of the Countess of Snailwood's parties as the focal point for a satiric, disturbing investigation in the present. ††††

DOYLE, ARTHUR CONAN. See **Holmes, Sherlock.**

DRUMMOND, JUNE. *Drop Dead.* 1974. Sergeant Lockval is summoned to a department store where a young woman is perched on a ledge, threatening suicide. To save her he must dig into her complex past, and he doesn't have much time. †††

DRUMMOND, JUNE. *Slowly the Poison.* 1975. Delicate Alice Frobisher, widow of ne'er-do-well Hugh, comes to South Africa to live with her in-laws, only to find herself suspected of murdering her young husband. The stiff-necked society of the 1920s in South Africa makes an ideal background for this well-written and engaging book. ††††

DRUMMOND, JUNE. *Funeral Urn.* 1976. Margot Wooten, recently released from a sanitarium, discovers an old gravestone in an English village that intrigues her. She is a botanist and recognizes that the plants on the gravestone indicate the dead woman was a poisoner. Driven by curiosity, she begins to investigate the dead woman only to find the usual village secrets and hatreds. The weakness is the main character who is a tiresome pain in the ass. ††

DUNNETT, ALASTAIR. *No Thanks to the Duke.* 1978. The title in no way refers to John Wayne. Instead a terminally ill rugby player is tapped to foil a kidnapping involving the royal family and ending in a chase on the Scottish moors. ††

• *Some novels to read when your guru offers you a cut-rate vacation package to the East:*

THE DECEIVERS by John Masters
FLASHMAN by George MacDonald Fraser
THE PERSIAN PRICE by Evelyn Anthony
THE QUEEN'S MESSENGER by W. R. Duncan
THE ROSE OF TIBET by Lionel Davidson

DUNNETT, DOROTHY.   A top-flight historical writer who also writes mysteries for relaxation. Her stories feature Johnson Johnson, an artist, and his yacht, *Dolly*. They are well plotted and filled with humor that will make you laugh out loud.

Dolly and the Singing Bird.   1968. Dunnett's debut in which Johnson Johnson becomes involved with a Russian singer and a web of espionage.   †††

Dolly and the Cookie Bird.   1970. A young English girl, refusing to believe her father committed suicide, turns the exotic island of Ibiza upside down as she breezes through a maze of double-crossing, industrial espionage, violent death, and people who are not what they appear, to a rousing climax during the macabre rites of the island's native Holy Week.   ††††

Dolly and the Starry Bird.   1973. Johnson Johnson and *Dolly* lead a group of astronomers on a tour across Italy and Sicily while seeking the source of the transmission of industrial and nuclear secrets to unfriendly hands.   ††††

Dolly and the Bird of Paradise.   1984. The narrator is a Scots-born flower child who has become a celebrity make-up artist despite seemingly insurmountable handicaps. She becomes involved with Johnson Johnson in a sometimes deadly, sometimes hilarious, romp across the Atlantic Ocean and various Caribbean islands in pursuit of drug smugglers, who use murder and piracy to gain their ends.   †††††

DU MAURIER, DAPHNE.   One of the classics of the field. If you haven't read her, you should.

Jamaica Inn.   1936. A compelling, evocative historical mystery set in 17th-century Cornwall, concerning a young woman who goes to live with relatives in a lonely inn on the seacoast. She finds few guests at the inn, but plenty of secrets—especially about the unusually large number of profitable shipwrecks on the nearby coast. Du Maurier creates a brooding atmosphere of tension and suspense, with a subtle erotic charge.   ††††

Rebecca.   1938. One of the great romantic mysteries of all times. It has every-thing: the new young wife, the troubled older husband, the disturbingly hostile servants, the deadly secret in the past that everyone but the heroine knows about, an oppressive sense of danger, an eerie setting, and a pace that accelerates to a shocking conclusion.   †††††

The Scapegoat.   1957. Two men, look-alikes who meet by chance, decide to swap lives. To the lonely, bitter man who winds up with the French chateau and the beautiful wife it seems ideal, until he discovers why.   ††††

The House on the Strand. 1969. A man experimenting with a hallucinogenic drug discovers that the "visions" he's been having are really glimpses into time— he is seeing events that took place several centuries ago. He becomes addicted to being a "peeping tom" of the past, falls in love, and eventually witnesses a horrible crime that he seems powerless to prevent. ††††

DURBRIDGE, FRANCIS. *A Game of Murder.* 1975. A golfing murder. Harry Dawson dies when a flyaway ball hits him on the head, and his paranoid son— who happens to be a Scotland Yard inspector—decides it's murder. There's more, but I found just that little bit to be breathtaking. ††

E

ERSKINE, MARGARET. She has been writing mysteries starring Inspector Septimus Finch of London's Metropolitan Police for more than forty years. Although some editions of her books package them as gothics, they're not. They are nicely written straightforward English mysteries.

Old Mrs. Ommaney Is Dead. 1955. Finch is called to the remote village of Hammerford to investigate a murder—before it happens. The plot involves a black-sheep uncle, an amnesiac acquaintance who may be the heroine's first husband, an old lady's unpopular will, and more. †††

The Woman at Belguardo. 1961. Bland, beer-drinking Inspector Finch unravels the case of the beautiful young adultress savagely murdered just before her divorce was due to become final. ††††

No. 9 Belmont Square. 1963. The setting is a London boarding house; the characters are a collection of half-crazy pensioners; the prize in the game of murder is a famous lost diamond. Finch not only solves the case, but becomes involved with a strange and likable group of people, none of whom is what he or she seems. †††

The Family at Tammerton. 1965. In an Agatha Christie-like plot, Nurse Louise Morton is first summoned from London to seaside Tammerton Hall, then warned away by telegram. Of course, she shows up at the hall anyway, and becomes the target of a murderer. Luckily, Inspector Finch is on hand. ††††

F

FERGUSON, JOHN. *Death Comes to Perigord.* 1931. Set in the Channel Islands, this little known mystery is what Dickens would have written had he lived in the 20th century. Opening with the emotional cries of an old woman who believes herself wronged by a wealthy moneylender, the scene shifts to the disappearance of the moneylender, and introduces a host of detectives—amateur, private, and police—all in one story. †††

FERRARS, E. X.   A writer of well-crafted, traditional British mysteries who also publishes romantic suspense novels under the name of Elizabeth Ferrars, so watch out what you are getting when you pick up one of hers.

Hunt the Tortoise.   1950. The theme of this one is "You can't go home again," as a female journalist probes into the disturbing changes that have taken place in her favorite prewar French hotel. A Riviera setting adds color, and murder and romance spice up Celia Kent's vacation. ††

Skeleton Staff.   1969. Arriving in Madeira to look after her sick sister, Camilla Carey finds Roberta strangely changed. Something sinister is happening in their remote house. Will Camilla live long enough to find out what? ††

Foot in the Grave.   1973. The disappearance of a guest's shoes soon turns into a complicated murder case that tries the patience of a crowded, weekend house party. Lots of red herrings and a good surprise ending. ††††

Experiment with Death.   1981. Although a murder takes place and is duly investigated, this book is really about the relationships, healthy and otherwise, among members of a small research institution. †††

FITT, MARY.   *Death and the Pleasant Voice.* 1946. When Jake Seaborne's car breaks down on a lonely, rainy road, he goes to the nearby manor house where he is greeted with all the enthusiasm normally reserved for a traveling salesman, stopping over at a farmhouse belonging to a suspicious farmer and a host of beautiful daughters. †††

FLEMING, JOAN.   Author of a number of mysteries ranging from strict detection to psychological thrillers. Her setting for the most part is contemporary England, but she has written some which feature a Turkish detective or 19th-century London.

Malice Matrimonial.   1959. A lonely young drifter suddenly acquires a beautiful Italian wife, a wealthy mother-in-law, and an inheritance. But when his wife disappears mysteriously, he has nothing but trouble. He tries to investigate from London to Rome, but every new twist and turn of the case makes him look guiltier. ††††

Young Man, I Think You're Dying.   1970. This book is the portrait of a snot-nosed, scumbag, juvenile delinquent named Joe Bogey, and his criminal mentor, Sledge. †††

Be a Good Boy. 1971. Young Gideon only wants to open a pizza stand in a resort town, but before he can blackmail the necessary funds out of his former boss, he finds himself made into a hero for saving a drowning child, and then into a prime murder suspect. This book manages to be heartwarming, even with a cast of scummy characters. †††

The Day of the Donkey Derby. 1978. An unusual suspense novel laced with humor. This is the story of Dr. Tom Lavenham. In a single day, his quiet, country life is shaken up by the revelation that his son is marrying a Chinese girl, the discovery of a dead girl at a patient's house, and a kidnapping. ††††

FLETCHER, J. S. *The Middle Temple Murders.* 1918. Woodrow Wilson's admiration for this book made Fletcher famous in the United States. Unfortunately, most of his other books are pretty awful. This one involves a young newspaperman, who reluctantly discovers that some of his acquaintances are involved in the murder of an unidentified man. The style is a bit Sherlockian. ††††

FORESTER, C. S. The author of the Hornblower series of sea sagas also wrote two very good psychological mysteries, well worth reading.

Payment Deferred. 1942. This, the more famous of the two, deals with a financially troubled man driven to murder by his plight, and the nightmare that develops around him as he lives with the results of his work, buried in the garden behind his house. †††††

Plain Murder. 1954. Morris, the psycho, and two friends are caught swindling the firm they work for. To keep things under wraps, they kill their discoverer, then Morris decides to kill his two accomplices. Everyone has a relative like Morris. †††

FRANCIS, DICK. English jockey turned author, and a first rate author at that. His stories deal with various aspects of the horse world. Sometimes it is racing, but often it is something behind the scenes and much more interesting than someone trying simply to fix a horse race. He has no series character.

Nerve. 1964. Atmospherically this is Francis's most eerie novel, with a claustrophic kidnapping scene that will stick with you for a long time. ††††

For Kicks. 1965. A very good story in which Daniel Rake, a successful breeder, poses as a stable hand to sniff out a horse-doping ring. ††††

Flying Finish. 1966. This book is similar in style to Gavin Lyall. Transport pilot Harry Gray finds that he is flying more than horses out of England. ††††

Enquiry. 1969. This is the closest Francis ever came to a Chandler-Macdonald type of plot. Kelly Hughes is framed for fixing a horse race. As he tries to get to the bottom of it, he finds a crazy woman, lots of money, and jealousy. †††

Bonecrack. 1971. Neil Griffon is just trying to run the stable after his father's death, but thugs invading the racing game won't leave him alone.   ††††

Slayride. 1973. Racing investigator David Cleveland goes to Norway to try to solve the disappearance of a jockey. This one reads very much like the work of Gavin Lyall.   ††††

High Stakes. 1975. A good one. Steven Scott, wealthy inventor and horse dealer, becomes the victim of a crooked trainer.   ††††

In the Frame. 1976. One of my favorites. Artist Charles Todd comes to the aid of his cousin when his house is burglarized and his wife killed. The only Francis novel which doesn't deal directly with horses.   ††††

Twice Shy. 1982. Francis's most ambitious novel to date. A great job of interweaving two stories in which two brothers both encounter the same villain years apart.   †††††

Banker. 1984. A young investment banker arranges to buy a champion racehorse only to find that he has bought a pig in a poke instead.   ††††

The Danger. 1984. An action-filled novel in which Andrew Douglas sets out to capture Giuseppe-Peter, a kidnapper who preys on people associated with the world of horse racing.   †††

FRASER, ANTONIA. Although she is the author of several important biographies, including *Mary Queen of Scots*, Fraser is better known as the creator of Jemima Shore, British television reporter and mystery heroine.

Quiet As a Nun. 1977. Murder takes place at Jemima's old convent school, and the victim is an old school chum, now an heiress and a nun. In her first investigation, Jemima reveals herself as shrewd, fashionable, and competent, with a complicated inner life. Fortunately, the mystery is strong enough to carry the story.   ††††

The Wild Island. 1978. A holiday in the Scottish highlands turns into a case of mystery and romance. Jemima gets involved with a strange aristocratic family, and also gets involved in a dangerous, tragic love affair. The setting is Fraser's best and is also part of the mystery plot.   ††††

A Splash of Red. 1981. Jemima is staying in the posh new flat of her friend, Chloe Fontaine, when Chloe disappears. Jemima's reason for being there is downright neurotic, but as long as she's on the spot she's able—after a few false starts—to clear up the murder mystery. ††††

Jemima Shore Investigates. 1983. Introduced by Fraser, who contributes a biographical essay about Jemima, the volume contains seven short-story versions of episodes from the Thames Television series. †††

Oxford Blood. 1985. Social comedy and satire mix with mystery in this tale of genteel crime. Jemima is supposed to be making a TV documentary about upper-crust Oxford students, but winds up investigating a case of murder. ††††

FRASER, JAMES. *Death in a Pheasant's Eye.* 1971. Inspector Bill Aveyard investigates a series of unrelated crimes ranging from the theft of the squire's pheasants to murder. However, a thread begins to appear which links them together. †††

FREEMAN, R. AUSTIN. An important early 20th-century contributor to the development of the mystery novel. Freeman is given credit for the invention of the inverted story as well as the invention of the scientific detective with his creation of Dr. Thorndyke.

Mr. Pottermack's Oversight. 1930. An early and classic example of the inverted detective story, in which the question is not "whodunit" but "how to catch 'em." A must for fans of the *Columbo* television series. †††††

The Penrose Mystery. 1936. It is enough to say that the publication of this novel caused a *new* archeological dig. ††††

The Stoneware Monkey. 1938. Written late in Freeman's life, this novel shows more than a touch of humor as the author pokes fun at the world of antiques. Beautifully written. †††††

G

GARVE, ANDREW. A very versatile English writer, whose work at first glance seems to be on a level with Creasey, but on closer inspection proves to be far superior. Sometimes his stories are straight mysteries, sometimes thrillers from the Household mold, but either way, they are like good bourbon, they go down so smooth that you never even feel the bite.

No Tears for Hilda. 1950. After a date with a young nurse, George Lambert arrives home to find the house filled with gas, and his wife dead—an apparent suicide. The police investigate and there is evidence of foul play. Lambert is arrested. It is up to his friend Max Easterbrook to clear his name. †††

A Hole in the Ground.   1952. A young member of parliament discovers a series of caves on his ancestral estate, which end up under an atomic plant nearby. He enlists the aid of a young man from his district to help him explore. That's when the trouble begins.   ††

The Cuckoo Line Affair.   1953. My favorite Garve novel. Through an indiscretion on a train, an absent-minded father finds himself suspected of murder. It is up to his kids to clear him. A very satisfying English mystery.   ††††

The Galloway Case.   1958. A short but sweet story of a young reporter who meets a beautiful girl on a Jersey holiday. He goes to her hotel, but she has checked out. He moves heaven and earth to find her. When he does, he learns that her father, a famous author, has been convicted of murder stemming from a plagiarism scandal. Before love can bloom, he must first prove her father's innocence.   ††

A Hero for Leanda.   1958. A good read about a solo navigator whose boat goes down, leaving him penniless. A legendary millionaire hires him to take a yacht to a small island and smuggle out an exiled revolutionary. His only crew member is Leanda, a beautiful woman with a huge streak of bitch.   †††

The Far Sands.   1960. The story of identical female twins, one of whom is accused of murder. Not one of Garve's best.   ††

The Ashes of Loda.   1964. On holiday from his Moscow assignment, foreign correspondent Tim Quainton meets a beautiful woman of Polish extraction at a cocktail party and falls in love with her. Quite by chance, he discovers her father was tried in absentia in Russia as a war criminal. It causes a strain in their relationship. Back in Russia, Quainton sets out to clear his future father-in-law only to find himself in big trouble—life-threatening trouble.   †††

Home to Roost.   1976. This is Garve at his best. The story is a first-person narrative told by mystery writer Walter Haines, whose beautiful wife is stolen by a virile actor. When the actor is murdered, Haines confesses, but did he really do it?   ††††

Counterstroke.   1978. Out-of-work actor Bob Farrow learns of the kidnapping of the wife of the British Minister of Export Promotion. Part of the ransom is the release of a convict named Tom Lacey. Farrow offers to impersonate Lacey for a price.   †††

GASH, JONATHAN.   One of the bright lights to appear on the mystery horizon in the past ten years. His detective—Lovejoy—is an antique dealer, but an antique dealer like you've never seen. He's a right bastard, who is always bedding down the ladies or trying to close a deal, and in personality seems more like J. P. Donleavy's Ginger Man than a genteel antiques dealer. The plots are all the same—Lovejoy, murder, antiques, and the ladies. None are remarkable, but he is still one of my favorites because he's so darn much fun.

The Judas Pair. 1977. Lovejoy is asked to locate a famous set of dueling pistols called the Judas Pair. Well told with a great ending. ††††

Gold by Gemini. 1978. This time Lovejoy is searching for gold coins from Caesar's legions. †††

The Sleepers of Erin. 1983. This time Lovejoy combines Ireland, phony antiques, and murder. †††

The Gondola Scam. 1984. Lovejoy gets involved in a scheme to steal Venetian antiques and replace them with reproductions. Not one of the best. The Italian locale does not lend itself to Gash's narrative style. ††

GILBERT, ANTHONY. *Riddle of a Lady.* 1956. One of the better Arthur Crook stories. It involves a young woman, a missing husband now dead, and a complex love triangle. The plot is good and the characters sharply drawn. †††

GILBERT, ANTHONY. *A Nice Little Killing.* 1973. A disagreeable story with the improbable opening of a bar owner turning to Arthur Crook to help him to get rid of a customer at closing time—an annoying young woman who quickly turns out to be more trouble than she's worth to both Arthur Crook *and* the reader. †

GILBERT, MICHAEL. One of the very best. If he has ever written a bad book, I don't know it. He doesn't rely on series characters, although some characters do reappear from time to time. His style is somber. I've often thought he might be an inspiration to P. D. James, since her work resembles his somewhat in tone.

Smallbone Deceased. 1950. Many feel this is Gilbert's masterpiece, but I strongly disagree. This story of the search for the missing Mr. Smallbone (whose body turns up stuffed in a deed box in a legal office) has a weak premise, a weak gimmick, and proceeds far too long without a hero. †††

Death Has Deep Roots. 1951. Gilbert's background as an attorney is evident in this novel, which consists mostly of courtroom scenes that are both detailed and interesting. A French girl is on trial for the murder of her lover. Ah, those French! †††

The Danger Within. 1952. Very similar to *The Great Escape.* A group of British officers are ready to break out of a POW camp when they discover a traitor among them. †††

Fear to Tread. 1953. Inspector Hazlerigg steps in when a proper schoolmaster takes on a slick gang of black marketeers and thieves. ††††

Blood and Judgment. 1959. A woman's murdered body is found in London. Detective Sergeant Petrella discovers who she is—an escaped convict's wife. All that remains is to discover who did it and why. †††

The 92nd Tiger. 1973. This novel illustrates Gilbert's ability to write just about any kind of mystery and do it well. It's a slightly satiric tale about a British actor who plays the TV superhero, the Tiger. Hired during a lull in his career to impress an Arabian politician's entourage, he gets mixed up in real-life adventures wilder than any he has played on the screen. ††††

The Night of the Twelfth. 1976. This psychological suspense thriller concerns the police investigation of a series of brutal torture-killings at a boys' school. The presence of an ambassador's son at the school adds the problem of political terrorism. It's a serious book about an ugly subject, but well written and shot through with Gilbert's characteristic sanity and good humor. ††††

The Killing of Katie Steelstock. 1980. Television personality Katie Steelstock is killed when she returns to her rural hometown for a visit. Superintendent Charlie Knott begins to untangle the knot that was Katie's life. ††††

End-Game. 1982. A great story of lovers who split up, and each goes his own way: he, toward drink and desperation; she, toward riches. But there is an undercurrent which keeps drawing them back together—an evil undercurrent. Don't miss this one. ††††

Mr. Calder and Mr. Behrens. 1982. An excellent collection of short stories by a master. Some of the stories are quite violent and do not necessarily hinge on detection gimmicks as Calder and Behrens go about their business for the government. ††††

The Black Seraphim. 1984. An overworked, overwrought psychologist vacations in a small cathedral town. His nerves are so bad that he has nightmares about poison, but his much-needed rest turns into a nightmare of poisonous church politics. It's a good mystery and—if you let yourself take the canonical subject seriously—a moving novel. ††††

The Long Journey Home. 1985. One of his best. The hero, dissatisfied with the performance of the plane he is on, leaves it to roam around Italy, helping farmers repair their tractors. A sudden, tragic incident puts his life in jeopardy. From then on it's a race to see if the Mafia, the Union Coru of France, or the multinational corporation, to whom he has sold his business, will manage to kill him before he gets the goods on them. ††††

GILES, KENNETH. *Death Cracks a Bottle.* 1969. James and Honeybody investigate who in the Heavan family of wine merchants killed the firm's manager with a bottle of vermouth. ††††

GILES, KENNETH. *Murder Pluperfect.* 1970. A nice treatment of the murder-in-the-past and murder-in-the-present story as Inspector James and Sergeant Honeybody try to clear the name of a long-dead woman, accused of murdering her fiancé, and at the same time try to clear up a recent murder of a local from the small village. †††

GILES, KENNETH. A *File on Death.* 1973. Very funny as James and Honeybody seek to stop a political eccentric from revealing a state secret by proving a suicide on his estate was murder. That's when the fun begins as they get involved with a cast of characters who belong in the *Confederacy of Dunces.* ††††

GILES, KENNETH. A *Murderous Journey.* 1974. This time it is a British hard-boiled story as a widow hires a private eye to prove her husband's death was murder. †††

GILL, B. M. *Death Drop.* 1979. When twelve-year-old David Fleming dies in what looks like an accident, his father goes to his school seeking an explanation, only to receive the cold shoulder. As he looks deeper he discovers it was murder, but why would anyone want to kill a twelve-year-old? ††††

GILL, B. M. *Victims.* 1981. Someone is killing everyone close to Dr. Paul McKendrick. First there is his nurse, then his daughter, then his mistress. Naturally the doctor begins to get a bit edgy when they start dropping like flies. †††

GLOAG, JULIAN. *Sleeping Dogs Lie.* 1980. A wonderfully brooding novel which involves a psychiatrist and his beautiful wife in a Ross Macdonald type of story triggered by a student who comes to the psychiatrist because he has developed a fear of walking downstairs. ††††

GOSLING, PAULA. *The Zero Trap.* 1980. A planeload of people are hijacked to a snowy area somewhere in Scandinavia or Siberia. One of them is the daughter of NATO general who is codirecting delicate negotiations. As people begin to die violently, it becomes obvious that many in the group are not what they seem, and all are caught up in a deadly power game. †††

GOSLING, PAULA. *Solo Blues.* 1981. The author is in top form in this gripping tale of menace and revenge. A concert/jazz pianist becomes a prime suspect when an old love is murdered. To prove his innocence, he seeks the real killer, and both he and his new love find themselves the targets of a vengeful murderer. ††††

GOSLING, PAULA. *The Woman in Red*. 1984. A British career diplomat, shunted to the Costa Brava, is sent to help a fellow countryman charged with murder. He finds himself surrounded by eccentric expatriates, who are mixed up in drug dealing and art faking, and falls in love with an attractive widow, enmeshed in a milieu of mistaken identity and double-dealing that leads to a shattering denouement. †††

GRIBBLE, LEONARD, *The Grand Modena Murder*. 1930. Anthony Slade of the Criminal Investigation Department solves most of Gribble's many mysteries. In this one, he investigates the murder of a crooked financier who had an innocent daughter, an untrustworthy partner, and a few secrets. The setting is moderately high-society London. ††††

GRIERSON, EDWARD. *A Crime of One's Own*. 1969. Too much imagination gets Donald Maitland, bookstore owner, into trouble when he begins to suspect his customers are involved in a spy ring. He follows one home, later finding she has been murdered, and he is the chief suspect. I know a bookstore owner or two who are just like him—crazy as bedbugs. It's overexposure to the glue in the bindings that causes it. ††††

GRIMES, MARTHA. Ah, the hottest thing on the English mystery scene, and oddly enough she is an American. Her books, featuring Inspector Richard Jury and amateur detective Melrose Plant, are full of humor, complex plotting, and very heavy on atmosphere, filled with the kind of details that only an outsider can know another outsider will enjoy. She is a must. If you haven't read her— do.

The Old Fox Deceived. 1982. Inspector Jury and Melrose Plant team up to solve the murder of a beautiful woman in a stark, image-evoking, Twelfth Night costume. ††††

The Anodyne Necklace. 1983. A young girl, playing her violin for change, is brutally beaten in a London Underground station. Miles away, in the village of Littlebourne, a woman is found murdered in the woods, her fingers severed. Inspector Jury works in London and Melrose Plant in Littlebourne as they piece together the connection between the crimes. ††††

The Dirty Duck. 1984. The scene is a famous pub in Stratford-on-Avon where a young woman has a drink and then moments later is found dead in a public toilet. It is again up to Plant and Jury to get to the bottom of things. †††

Jerusalem Inn. 1984. The setting is Christmas Eve in the English countryside. Grimes gathers a crowd of her recurring and delectable characters around the wassail bowl to solve the murders of a haunting beauty and a scheming, glamorous novelist. †††

H

HAMMOND, GERALD. *The Revenge Game.* 1981. When the canal overflows, residents of Newton-Lauder find a skeleton that turns out to be a missing canal employee. Keith Calder, local gun dealer, becomes involved over problems with the dead man's firearm license. Quite a bit of action. Keith Calder combines the qualities of Gash's antique dealer and Parrish's poacher.   †††

HARE, CYRIL. A cozy type of English mystery writer to curl up with on a rainy night when a low-key read is what you're after.

Tenant for Death. 1937. Inspector John Mallett gets involved in a convoluted story of murder, business chicanery, and romance. A good first novel, but not as good as Hare's later works.   †††

Death Is No Sportsman. 1938. Inspector Mallett is called to the village of Didford Magna, where trout fishing is a mania, to solve the murder of a businessman. Hare is beginning to get his plot under control, and his humor is starting to show.   †††

Suicide Excepted. 1939. The story of an apparent suicide at a hotel. Mallett doesn't appear until late in the story, but it is still well plotted with a good ending.   †††

Tragedy at Law. 1942. Some consider this to be Hare's best work. Attorney Francis Pettigrew is a suspect when someone tries to kill a judge because of his involvement in an auto accident. The plot has a lot of twists and turns. Hare pokes a bit of fun at the legal profession.   ††††

With a Bare Bodkin. 1946. Francis Pettigrew investigates violations of government regulations and murder in wartime England. The best part of this story is that Pettigrew meets his future wife here.   †††

The Wind Blows Death. 1949. The death of a violinist puts a sour note on the efforts of the local orchestra, and Francis Pettigrew must orchestrate the capture of the culprit.   ††††

An English Murder. 1951. An extremely clever, English country-house mystery, set in a snowbound Christmas season. The detective is neither Mallett nor Pettigrew, but is Dr. Wenceslaus Bottwink, an expert on English history. The plot hinges beautifully on both the literary and the legal.   ††††

Death Walks the Woods. 1954. Pettigrew investigates the murder of Miss Pink and has to wade through a lot of conflicting statements from the country locals. Not one of Hare's strongest.   †††

Untimely Death. 1958. Published after Hare's death, it is one of his weakest. Pettigrew and Mallett work together one last time as Pettigrew apparently returns to his second childhood.   † †

HART, GEORGE. *The Punch and Judy Murders.* 1977. A broken marriage and subsequent career failure drive John Richards to answer an ad from a rich woman needing a bodyguard, because of threats from her ex-husband. This leads to an extremely effective tour de force of murder and madness, played out in bright English seaside towns, with a local Punch and Judy show as a violent counterpoint. Well written, smashing denouement.   † † † † †

HASTINGS, MacDONALD. While Mr. Cork, the elderly insurance executive, is not quite a detective, and the stories are not quite mysteries, they have a great deal of suspense. I have always found them fun in a stuffy English sense.

Cork on the Water. 1951. Cork sorts through murder and fishing in Scotland in the first of the series.   † † †

Cork in the Doghouse. 1958. The female bulldog, which Cork finds himself owning, steals the story here and is the instrument for a great climax, unlike anything I have ever read in a mystery.   † † † †

Cork on Location. 1967. Cork pokes around the television business as he tries to recover missing jewels. Television is not Hastings's area.   † †

HEALD, TIM. An English writer with a sense of humor similar to Edmund Crispin. His hero, Simon Bognor of the Board of Trade, is a wonderful bumbling character, full of warmth and idiosyncracies.

Blue Blood Will Out. 1974. A country-house mystery with a zany cast of characters such as Lord Maidenhead and his nympho wife, gay eccentric Cosmo Green, and black eccentric Honeysuckle Johnson.   † † † †

Murder at Moose Jaw. 1981. Simon Bognor tries to unravel the murder of a wealthy man who died in his bath. Good story, but a weak ending.   † † †

HEYER, GEORGETTE. Best known for her Regency romances and historical novels, she also wrote a handful of entertaining mysteries set in England in the 1930s. They are good reads for Christie fans.

Why Shoot a Butler? 1933. Heyer takes one of the great, old mystery traditions and turns it around. Instead of "the butler did it," it is the butler who is done in. Barrister Frank Amberley, whose claim to fame is his rudeness, tries to find out why and comes up against a beautiful, but uncooperative witness.   † † †

The Unfinished Clue. 1934. A country-house murder in the best tradition. Detestable Sir Arthur is stabbed in his study with an oriental dagger, and everyone has at least one motive. Inspector Harding solves the case. ††††

Death in the Stocks. 1935. This lighthearted, almost farcical, book introduces Superintendent Hannasyde and Sergeant Hemingway, who feature in several of Heyer's mysteries. Here they investigate the murder of a man whose stabbed body is found in a set of picturesque village stocks. Along the way, they deal with flippant witnesses, a long-lost uncle suddenly returned from South America, and other traditional plot elements. Funny and fast. ††††

Behold, Here's Poison. 1936. Hannasyde looks into the murder of Gregory Matthews, a wealthy man who is thoroughly disliked. Not until the victim's sister is also poisoned does he uncover the ingenious and diabolical modus operandi of the killer. †††

No Wind of Blame. 1939. Sergeant Hemingway is promoted to inspector for this case, a typically bizarre house murder with the usual cast of eccentrics and unloved victim. Someone bagged poor Wally Carter during a shooting weekend, and Scotland Yard is faced with an embarrassment of riches: a wealthy widow, her two ardent suitors, the young girl Wally seduced and her left-wing brother, Wally's sleazy partner, and so on. †††

Duplicate Death. 1951. Duplicate bridge turns into duplicate death when a beautiful girl's suitor and then her mother are strangled within a week at card parties. Chief Inspector Hemingway investigates. †††

Detection Unlimited. 1953. It's the classic English village murder. An unpleasantly pushy newcomer to a staid little hamlet is killed during a garden party, and everyone from the squire to the village dotard takes a turn at playing detective. Chief Inspector Hemingway discovers that all the would-be detectives also make good suspects. †††

HIGHSMITH, PATRICIA. A suspense writer of the first order. Unlike most other suspense writers, she *has* a series character, although he only appears in a few of her books. He is Ripley, and his name is in the title of all the novels in which he appears.

Strangers on a Train. 1950. Although Raymond Chandler hated it (of course Chandler could not plot worth a damn, so who's he to talk?) this best-known work of Highsmith's is a classic in the field. Two strangers meet on a train, and each agrees to murder someone for the other, to provide the perfect alibi. †††††

The Talented Mr. Ripley. 1956. Tom Ripley, a young man of weak character, is hired by a wealthy couple to locate their son, Dickie, a onetime friend of Ripley's. The parents finance Ripley's search through Europe, where he finds Dickie easily enough. But he soon decides that he could make better use of Dickie's allowance than Dickie does. This decision leads him deep into crime. You won't be able to put this one down.   †††††

The Two Faces of January. 1964. A man's passing resemblance to his father compels Rydal Keener to help the man cover up the murder of a Greek policeman. Rydal and Chester MacFarlane, accompanied by Chester's sexy wife, Colette, then embark on an odyssey of escape and mutual psychological torment that leads again to murder.   ††††

Suspension of Mercy. 1965. While his wife is away, husband Sidney decides to play out the act of murdering a wife. The local busybody notices and Sidney is in trouble.   ††††

HILL, REGINALD. *Deadheads.* 1984. Dalziel and Pascoe investigate a string of seemingly accidental deaths associated with Patrick Aldermann. On the surface, the evidence seems to point to Aldermann's guilt, but Dalziel's wife becomes friends with Aldermann's wife, and the plot thickens—and a good plot it is, too.   ††††

HILTON, JAMES. *Was It Murder?* 1933. A very daring novel for its time, about murder in an English boarding school, by the author of *Goodbye Mr. Chips.*   †††††

HILTON, JOHN BUXTON. *The Green Frontier.* 1981. A clever, interesting mystery built around *Crucible*, a popular British television show specializing in exposé, and a secret which stretches back to the dark days of WWII.   †††

HOLMES, SHERLOCK. The only entry in the book listed by character, rather than author. Without a doubt, Sherlock Holmes and his faithful sidekick Dr. Watson are the best known characters in *all* of fiction. Millions of words have been written about him by far more eloquent people than me, so without further ado, here are a few juicy tidbits for those of you who yearn for hansom cabs and London by gaslight . . . and the sight of a tall gaunt man in a deerstalker.

DOYLE, SIR ARTHUR CONAN. *The Complete Sherlock Holmes.* Known as the "Canon" among dedicated fans, it is composed of four novels (A *Study in Scarlet, The Sign of the Four, The Hound of the Baskervilles, The Valley of Fear*) and fifty-six short stories broken down into five groups (*The Adventures of, The Memoirs of, The Return of, The Casebook of,* and *His Last Bow*). The best novel is *The Hound of the Baskervilles.* The best group of short stories is *The Adventures of Sherlock Holmes.*   †††††

ASIMOV, ISAAC; GREENBERG, MARTIN HARRY; AND WAUGH, CHARLES. *Sherlock Holmes Through Time and Space.* 1984. A collection of very far-out Sherlock Holmes short stories (i.e., Holmes, as a German shepherd, solves the murder of "A Scaletin Study"). Great fun. ††††

BARING-GOULD, W. S. *Sherlock Holmes of Baker Street.* 1962. A wonderful fictional biography of Sherlock Holmes. †††††

BARING-GOULD, W. S. *The Annotated Sherlock Holmes.* 1967. This two-volume set of the four novels and fifty-six short stories, complete with Baring-Gould's exhaustive research into the stories, is the last word in the works of Sir Arthur Conan Doyle. †††††

BAYER, ROBERT JOHN. *Some Notes on a Meeting at Chisholm.* 1947. An interesting pamphlet in which the author more or less successfully proves that Sherlock Holmes and Father Brown once collaborated on a case. †††

BELL, H. W. *Sherlock Holmes and Dr. Watson: The Chronology of Their Adventures.* 1984. A rare research piece recently reprinted in a small number of copies. Valuable to a collector in any edition, but to me, a nightmare of nit-picking with the date for this and the date for that. ††

BOUCHER, ANTHONY. *The Case of the Baker Street Irregulars.* 1940. On learning that Hollywood plans to cast an unworthy actor as Sherlock Holmes in the movie version of "The Adventure of the Speckled Band," the Baker Street Irregulars, New York's famous Sherlockian society, organizes a protest with funny and disastrous results. ††††

BOYER, RICHARD L. *The Giant Rat of Sumatra.* 1976. Boyer expands the obscure but intriguing reference to the giant rat in "The Adventure of the Sussex Vampire" with a very well-written Sherlock Holmes novel. The tone of Watson as the narrator is clear and good. ††††

CAPPS, DALE. *The World's Greatest Sherlock Holmes Quiz.* 1976. Test your knowledge of Sherlock with this rather too involved quiz. ††

CARR, JOHN DICKSON, AND DOYLE, ADRIAN CONAN. *The Exploits of Sherlock Holmes.* 1954. Carr worked with Doyle's son on this volume of *authorized* short stories. One of the best. ††††

CHRIST, JAY FINLEY. *An Irregular Chronology of Sherlock Holmes of Baker Street.* 1947. Any author who found his work subjected to the pompous, microscopic nit-picking of this work (for instance, the newspaper account says it was Tues., Mar. 4; Watson says Tues., Mar. 3; if it was Tues., Mar. 4, then it had to be 1885, not 1882, and so on) could only describe it as a real pain. †

CLAUSTON, J. STORER. *The Truthful Lady.* 1920. A pamphlet in which Dr. Watson consults Mr. Carrington on a matter of some delicacy. †

CUTTER, ROBERT A. *Sherlockian Studies: Seven Pieces of Sherlockiana.* 1947. A pamphlet-sized collection of Sherlockian musings by the Three Students of Long Island Sherlockian society. It includes a couple of poems, a quiz, a couple of very short stories, and some general commentary. ††

DERLETH, AUGUST. *The Solar Pons Stories* (various pub. dates). A series of eight to ten volumes of Sherlock Holmes pastiches featuring Solar Pons and Dr. Parker. After Derleth's death the series has continued with a couple of volumes by Basil Copper. The many volumes by Derleth as well as the few by Copper are great fun. Read and enjoy. †††

ESTLEMAN, LOREN D. *Sherlock Holmes vs. Dracula.* 1978. One of my favorites. Sherlock takes on the old count himself. †††

FISH, ROBERT L. *The Incredible Schlock Holmes*, 1966, and *The Memoirs of Schlock Holmes*, 1974. The play on Sherlock's name in no way indicates the quality of these parodies. Both †††

FISHER, CHARLES. *Some Unaccountable Exploits of Sherlock Holmes.* 1956. Absolutely hilarious. A great job of satirizing Holmes in this beautifully written pamphlet. ††††

GARDNER, JOHN. *The Return of Moriarty.* 1974. The other side is heard from as Professor Moriarty, having foiled Holmes at Reichenbach Falls, returns to London and his life of crime. This is not a Sherlock Holmes story. It is a Professor Moriarty story. †††

GARDNER, JOHN. *The Revenge of Moriarty.* 1975. Moriarty, now more insane than ever, vows revenge on the leaders of the European underworld and returns to seek that revenge. Again, this is not a Holmes story, but a Moriarty story. †††

HAINING, PETER. *The Sherlock Holmes Scrapbook.* 1974. A collection of essays related to Holmes and his times. The packaging of this work is more interesting than the content. A good volume for a beginning collector. ††††

HALL, ROBERT LEE. *Exit Sherlock Holmes.* 1977. Dr. Watson, on his deathbed, gives us Holmes's last adventure. While it is nowhere near as good as the worst story by Doyle, it still brought a lump to my throat. ††††

HARDWICK, MICHAEL. *Sherlock Holmes: My Life and Crimes.* 1984. The prologue sets a somewhat melancholy tone for these remembrances of Sherlock Holmes in this profusely illustrated volume. †††

HARRISON, MICHAEL. *In the Footsteps of Sherlock Holmes.* 1972. This is not a Holmes story, but rather an in-depth study of the London of Holmes's time. A fascinating piece of work. ††††

HARRISON, MICHAEL. *Cynological Mr. Holmes: Canonical Canines Considered, Dog-Lore and Dog-Love in the Sherlockian Saga.* 1985. The title is damn near as long as the pamphlet, but being a dog lover, one afternoon I settled down with it. For some reason, the first few pages put me off. But as I got more deeply into it, I enjoyed it. It turns out to be filled with a number of good dog stories. †††

HODEL, MICHAEL P., AND WRIGHT, SEAN M. *Enter the Lion.* 1979. A fantastic tale involving an 1875 attempt to overthrow the American government and restore the Confederacy under British rule, but Sherlock and Mycroft Holmes rush to the rescue. †††

JONES, KELVIN I. *Upon the Tracing of Footsteps.* 1983. Mr. Jones would have us believe this pamphlet was written by Holmes himself in the year 1878. We know better. Holmes could never have been this dull. †

JONES, KELVIN I. *Sherlock and Porlock: A Study of Literary Influences in the Sherlock Holmes Stories.* 1984. This thin volume is exactly what the title indicates, but it is not at all boring. Instead, by its very nature, I found that it intriguingly fleshed out the character of Holmes, centering more on the man than the influences. †††

JONES, KELVIN I. *The Making of Sherlock Holmes: An Investigation into the Forensic Methods of the World's First Consulting Detective in the Year 1881.* 1984. A highly readable and interesting volume on the state of the art of forensics and criminology in England at the time Conan Doyle began writing the Holmes stories. †††

KIMBALL, ELLIOTT. *Dr. John H. Watson at Netley.* (n.d.) In spite of the heavily documented source material in this pamphlet, the question is—who really cares whether Watson was at Netley? †

LANE, W. *Sherlock Holmes and the Wood Green Empire Mystery.* 1985. Watson lures Holmes out of retirement to solve the mystery of the murder of a Chinese magician, who died on stage while performing his act, which consisted of catching a live bullet in his teeth. Well done. ††††

LEHMANN, R. C. *The Return of Picklock Holes.* 1980. A collection of *very early* parodies of Sherlock reprinted from *Punch* magazine of 1903–1904. †††

LEWIS, ARTHUR. *Copper Beeches.* 1971. A delightful blend of fact and fiction in which the Sons of the Copper Beeches, Philadelphia's chapter of the Baker Street Irregulars, respond to a challenge by one of its members to use Sherlock's methods to solve a fictional crime. But the fictional crime soon changes from a game into something far more deadly. †††††

MCKEE, WILBUR K. *Sherlock Holmes Is Mr. Pickwick.* 1941. A not too re-markable pamphlet in which the author, for some unknown reason, attempts to prove Sherlock is Mr. Pickwick. †

MEYER, NICHOLAS. *The Seven-Percent Solution.* 1974. Sherlock goes Hol-lywood and goes through analysis to try and kick the cocaine habit. ††

MEYER, NICHOLAS. *The West End Horror.* 1976. Holmes rubs elbows with Oscar Wilde and George Bernard Shaw in one of the more boring of the Holmes stories. ††

MONTGOMERY, JAMES. *A Study in Pictures.* 1984. A study of the work of twenty-seven artists and their illustrations of Holmes. ††††

MORGAN, ROBERT S. *Spotlight on a Simple Case* The publication date is described as "The 105th year since the Master's birth and the 14th year of the Atomic Age, i.e. only a few years before Cyrano could have made his voyage to the moon." Need I say more, except to say that this one was a waste of my time. †

PARK, ORLANDO. *The Sherlock Holmes Encyclopedia.* 1962. Every little thing you ever wanted to know about the Holmes stories is contained in this simple alphabetical format. This is a backup book. Virtually no one could sit down and read it from cover to cover. ††††

SAFFRON, ROBERT. *The Demon Device.* 1979. It is 1917 and Sir Arthur Conan Doyle, the creator of Sherlock Holmes, undertakes a dangerous mission of espionage—to enter wartime Germany and discover the secret weapon which can tip the scales of victory in Germany's favor. ††

SAXBE, JESSIE M. E. *Joseph Bell, M.D., F.R.C.S., J.P., D.L., etc: An Ap-preciation by an Old Friend.* 1913. The story of Joseph Bell, who was Conan Doyle's real-life model for Holmes, by one who knew him well. A wonderful book about a remarkable man. Until a small recent reprint, it was somewhat rare. ††††

SHEPARD, MICHAEL. *Sherlock Holmes and the Case of Dr. Freud.* 1985. Not a story, but an essay based on a lecture. ††

SILVERSTEIN, ALBERT. *Sherlock Holmes and the French Connection.* 1983. A collection of essays celebrating the tenth anniversary of the Cornish Horrors, a Sherlockian fan club. †††

SMITH, D. O. *The Adventure of the Unseen Traveller.* 1983. A beautiful job. Sherlock and Dr. Watson investigate a murder on a train. †††††

SMITH, D. O. *The Adventure of the Zodiac Plate.* (n.d.) Holmes is hired by a famous surgeon to recover a valuable silver plate given to loan sharks by a gambling nephew. ††††

SMULLYAN, RAYMOND. *The Chess Mysteries of Sherlock Holmes.* 1979. A collection of fifty maddening chess problems set up as Sherlock Holmes short stories. ††††

STASHOWER, DANIEL. *The Adventure of the Ectoplasmic Man.* 1985. Sherlock comes to Houdini's rescue when the latter is jailed for espionage. †††

STEINBRUNNER, CHRIS, AND MICHAELS, NORMAN. *The Films of Sherlock Holmes.* 1978. A wonderful book, loaded with pictures, which details virtually every Sherlock Holmes film ever made from the 1900 *Sherlock Holmes Baffled* all the way to the *Seven-Percent Solution.* †††††

THOMAS, FRANK. *Sherlock Holmes and the Golden Bird.* 1979. Holmes and Watson try their hands at their version of the *Maltese Falcon* as they set out to find a jeweled bird. †††

THOMAS, FRANK. *Sherlock Holmes and the Sacred Sword.* 1980. A well-written and complex story involving the loss of the sword of Mohammad, and Sherlock's efforts to find it before holy war breaks out in the Middle East. †††

TROW, M. J. *The Supreme Adventure of Inspector Lestrade.* 1985. I was all set to dislike this one because it was another Sherlock Holmes vs. Jack the Ripper story, but I was very pleasantly surprised. Lestrade takes stage center, and the plot is larger than just Jack the Ripper. It is well told, with humor and good color. †††

WALSH, RAY. *The Mycroft Memoranda.* 1984. Another boring rehash of Sherlock and Jack the Ripper. Give us a break, three or four times is enough of Holmes vs. Jack. ††

WELLMAN, MANLY W., AND WELLMAN, WADE. *Sherlock Holmes's War of the Worlds.* 1975. Sherlock and Professor Challenger find themselves in the middle of H. G. Wells's *War of the Worlds,* the Martian invasion of earth. ††

WILLIAMSON, J. N., AND WILLIAMS, H. B. *Illustrious Client's Case-Book.* 1984 reprint. I have volumes I and III, but not II of this series, so I cannot comment on that one, but I and III are delightful collections of essays, poems, limericks, parodies, and quizzes written by the best of the Sherlockian scholars. A treat from start to finish. †††††

WOLFF, JULIAN. *Practical Handbook of Sherlockian Heraldry.* 1983. This one deserves an "A" for effort as the author turns up the family crest of virtually everyone associated with Sherlock Holmes. ††††

WOLFF, JULIAN. *The Sherlockian Atlas.* 1984. A collection of thirteen maps all pertaining to the Holmes stories. ††††

HOLT, HENRY. *The Midnight Mail.* 1931. Inspector Silver of Scotland Yard investigates an attempted strangling on the midnight mail train to London, in this tale of criminal gangs, jewel theft, and murder. It's a good old-fashioned story—part detection, part swashbuckling, part snappy romance. †††

HOWES, ROYCE. *Death on the Bridge.* 1935. One of several nautical mysteries by Howes, this is the story of multiple murder on a tramp steamer bound for New York out of Liverpool. The plot has enough holes to sink a ship, but the atmosphere has the real tang of the salt air. †††

HUBBARD, P. M. *High Tide.* 1970. Curtis, after serving a prison term for murder, is trying to build a new life for himself, but as he travels across England looking for the right place, he realizes he is being followed by people with murderous intentions. ††††

HUBBARD, P. M. *The Dancing Man.* 1971. A well-told tale of a man seeking information about his brother's death and encountering an odd group (probably the victims of too much inbreeding) near a Cistercian monastery. The "Dancing Man" is a pornographic carving. †††

HUBBARD, P. M. *Kill Claudio.* 1979. The murder of a friend of twenty years takes Ben Selby on a search which ultimately leads to "buried treasure" on a remote island. †††

HULL, RICHARD. *Keep It Quiet.* 1935. A story of murder in an English men's club. Very similar to Sayers's *Unpleasantness at the Bellona Club.* ††††

HUME, DAVID. *Dangerous Mr. Dell.* 1935. Mr. Dell is dangerous because he is a very good blackmailer. Operating in London theatrical circles and using petty criminals as operatives, he expands into the kidnapping business and runs afoul of the Cardbys, a spunky father-and-son detective team. †††

HUME, FERGUS. *The Mystery of a Hansom Cab.* 1886. The best-selling mystery of the 19th century, surpassing even Sherlock Holmes. The story of an Australian cabby who finds his passenger has been chloroformed to death. †††††

HUNTER, ALAN. The Inspector Gently stories are light English mysteries on a par with John Creasey. They are perfect when you are looking for something not too taxing.

Gently with the Innocents. 1970. Gently investigates the death of an old man and finds a treasure dating back to Innocent III at the heart of it. ††

Gently Through the Woods. 1974. The very strong opening of this story, in which Gently investigates the apparent suicide of a film director and a love triangle, will keep you turning the pages. My favorite of the Gently stories.

†††

The Unhanged Man. 1984. Inspector Gently investigates the shotgun murder of a judge. The only clue to the identity of the murderer is a fingerprint which belongs to a man sentenced by the judge and hanged twelve years earlier. Be sure to read the dedication in this one.

†††

HUTTON, JOHN. *Accidental Crimes.* 1983. A psychological suspense novel in which Conrad Nield, an inspector of schools and a victim of blackouts, finds himself the chief suspect in two bizarre sex slayings on the moors. Is he guilty or not?

††††

HYLAND, STANLEY. *Who Goes Hang.* 1958. A mummified body dressed in 19th-century clothes is discovered beneath Big Ben's bell chamber. When the police give up, Hubert Bligh, a member of parliament, takes up the investigation. Together with other members he begins to investigate the past in a nicely written mystery.

†††

HYLAND, STANLEY. *Green Grow the Tresses—O.* 1967. It looks like a simple but sordid murder to Detective Inspector Sugden when a girl, who has been linked to half the men in town, is found dead and nearly bald in a vat of boiling dye. But soon the mill town finds she was not the first, and Sugden is pressed by Scotland Yard, the British and American Air Forces, and the local head librarian before he finds himself putting the binding on a skintight solution to the murder.

†††††

I

INNES, MICHAEL. Author of a host of witty, erudite mysteries for the literary set. Low in action (sex or violence), they are not for everyone, but they are extremely well written and pristine examples of the days when books were more, if you get my meaning.

Hamlet Revenge!. 1937. Appleby sifts a colorful array of suspects and clues to solve the dramatic murder of a prominent peer in a ducal mansion. It's a country-house mystery all the way, with an atmosphere of refinement, and espionage, treason, greed, and madness as possible motives.

†††††

Lament for a Maker. 1938. In this complicated classic set in the wilds of Scotland, Innes eschews the remoter reaches of whimsy and delivers an atmospheric, psychologically disturbing mystery. For once, the constant literary allusions are integral to the plot, which springs from character rather than from fancy. The book's strength lies in the fact that it is told, not simply from Appleby's point of view, but by several other well-realized and grittier characters who counter Appleby's occasional preciousness. †††††

The Secret Vanguard. 1940. A classic situation: A young girl menaced by mysterious forces finds herself on the run. Whom can she trust? The most innocent-seeming stranger may be part of a conspiracy. Or is she mad? The setting is Scotland, the villains are Nazis, and Appleby—as in *Lament for a Maker*—works well as a peripheral character. The overall effect is fantastical, which somewhat diminishes the plot's paranoiac possibilities. ††

Appleby's End. 1945. Perhaps the giddiest of the Appleby books, this is the one in which our hero meets his future bride, the fey Judith, and her demented family. The bizarre adventures in which they embroil him are silly but very funny in a dry way. It's worth reading for the names of the villages alone. ††††

What Happened at Hazelwood. 1946. A baronet is murdered at midnight in the library of his country estate. The only problem is, he's so thoroughly detestable that everyone within reach had a motive. Festering family feuds and class consciousness don't make finding a solution any easier for Inspector Cadover. †††

One Man Show. 1952. The daring theft of a painting by a dead young artist leads Appleby through a farrago of espionage and murder, and gives Innes the chance to take some sardonic shots at the world of art dealers and critics. ††

Hare Sitting Up. 1959. In this, one of the most improbable and attenuated of the Appleby books, Sir John foils what appears to be a plot to wipe out the world with a lethal lab culture. †

Death by Water. 1968. Sir John discovers a corpse in a neighbor's gazebo and becomes involved with a frantic charity fete, an assortment of oddballs, and a legendary lost treasure. In short, the usual—with a little dilemma of etiquette and morality thrown in at the end. ††

Honeybath's Haven. 1977. Starring artist Charles Honeybath and a gaggle of oldsters, this thriller, set in an exclusive old-age home, features an ingenious method of murder. It's a lighthearted romp, tempered by the perspective of a man all too aware that he's aging. †††

The Ampersand Papers. 1978. An unusually fast-paced and concise Appleby adventure, mixing genealogy, speleology, the treasure of the Armada, a lost literary correspondence of incalculable value, and the death of an archivist. Did he fall, or was he pushed? †††

Sheiks and Adders. 1982. Appleby, in retirement, takes it upon himself to investigate the bow-and-arrow slaying of a guest at a costume ball at Drool Court.

Druids, snake collectors, and impetuous young lovers further complicate what proves to be an international crisis, but Sir John responds to all of them with urbanity and undiminished powers of observation and deduction. ††

ISLES, FRANCIS. *Malice Aforethought*. 1931. The only mystery in this suspenseful story is whether the main character, a murderous doctor, will get caught and how. It's a complicated tale of a selfish fool, a harsh harridan, and a nymphomaniac bitch, all of whom eventually get what they deserve. †††††

ISLES, FRANCIS. *Before the Fact*. 1932. The chilling story of a woman who gradually realizes that her husband of eight years is a murderer, and she's the victim. He may be the guilty one, but she becomes an accomplice. There may never have been a more concentrated, ruthless portrait of a born victim. ††††

J

JAMES, P. D. One of the hottest mystery writers working today. With the exception of *Innocent Blood*, all her books have either been about Inspector Adam Dalgliesh or private detective Cordelia Gray.

Cover Her Face. 1962. James's first book, and a more typical English mystery than her later works. Dalgliesh investigates the murder of a beautiful young woman who was many things to many people—all of them bad. †††

A Mind to Murder. 1963. Dalgliesh investigates the murder of the head of a psychiatric institute, who is stabbed with a chisel, and a phallic symbol is left near her body. Needless to say, the institute turns out to be a wild and crazy place. †††

Unnatural Causes. 1967. One of her most intriguing. Dalgliesh is called in when the body of a mystery writer is found in a floating dinghy. What gives this story a touch of color is that someone has chopped off the deceased's hands. ††††

Shroud for a Nightingale. 1971. It is murder in the hospital as someone kills a good nurse and a bad nurse. I was as curious about the motive as the identity of the killer. †††

An Unsuitable Job for a Woman. 1972. Although not her best-seller, it is far and away my favorite of James's novels. Cordelia Gray inherits a detective agency and investigates the apparent suicide of a young man, who went to his reward with a lipstick mark on his lips and the picture of a nude girl nearby. (It certainly beats being buried with your shield and dog.) ††††

The Black Tower. 1975. My least favorite of her works. Very slow moving. There is murder in a monastery nursing home to which Adam Dalgliesh is asked to come by an old priest. All the elements of a great mystery are here, but the author never makes you care one way or the other. †††

Death of an Expert Witness. 1977. Adam Dalgliesh investigates the murder of a scientist who emotionally resembled his lab rats. Nicely written with everything in place, but still I did not warm to any of the characters. ††††

Innocent Blood. 1980. On turning eighteen, Phillipa Palfrey, an adopted child, determines to find her natural parents. She learns that her mother has spent years in prison for murder, and is about to be set free. This is only the first in a series of shocks for Phillipa, whose search for identity leads her into a psychological maze with a violent but satisfying conclusion. ††††

The Skull Beneath the Skin. 1982. Cordelia Gray is hired by the husband of Clarissa Lake, a washed-up actress, as her bodyguard for a weekend production of the *Dutchess of Malfi* at an island off the coast of Dorset. She has been receiving death threats in the form of Shakespearian quotes. James's writing is flawless, but this story is totally unworthy of a novelist of her ability. That old nonsense of Shakespearian quotes has been used so many times it has cobwebs on it. †††

JEFFREYS, J. G. *A Wicked Way to Die.* 1973. The Regency Sherlock Holmes— Jeremy Sturrock of the Bow Street Runners—and his Watson—Maggsy, the clerk—investigate the locked-room murder of a wealthy young man found dead in an actress's dressing room. †††

JEFFREYS, J. G. *A Conspiracy of Poisons.* 1977. Beginning with the discovery of a poisoned prostitute, Jeremy Sturrock and Maggsy are drawn deeper and deeper into a Napoleonic plot which threatens England's safety. †††

JENKINS, CYRIL. *Message from Sirius.* 1961. Inspector Marc Island has his hands full as he investigates the murder of England's top rock singer. Offbeat and interesting. ††††

JON, MONTAGUE. *The Wallington Case.* 1981. A very nice updating of the *Paradine Case* in which a middle-aged barrister defends a beautiful woman accused of murdering her husband and becomes emotionally involved. A promising first novel. †††

K

KITCHIN, C. H. B. *Death of My Aunt.* 1929. Malcolm Warren, a penniless nephew in the Wodehouse mold, undertakes to solve the murder of his rich aunt. †††

KITCHIN, C. H. B. *Death of His Uncle.* 1939. A friend of Malcolm Warren, amateur detective and stockbroker, asks him to help find his uncle who has vanished on a trip to Cornwall. A well-told classic English mystery. ††††

KNOX, RONALD A. *The Footsteps at the Lock.* 1928. A wonderful story of two cousins—one about to receive a huge inheritance—who disappear on a canoe trip, and Miles Bredon, the insurance investigator sent to get to the bottom of things before his company has to pay off. †††††

L

LEMARCHAND, ELIZABETH. *Unhappy Returns.* 1977. The housekeeper of the recently deceased vicar shocks the village by announcing that a jeweled chalice has been stolen by someone in the village. When the old woman is killed, Inspector Tom Pollard takes on the job. ††††

LEMARCHAND, ELIZABETH. *Suddenly While Gardening.* 1978. Pollard, on holiday, investigates the discovery of a thoroughly modern skeleton in a Bronze-Age grave. †††

LEMARCHAND, ELIZABETH. *Change for the Worse.* 1980. Inspector Tom Pollard investigates the murder of the caretaker of a stately manor. Good solid job. †††

LEVI, PETER. *Grave Witness.* 1985. Ben Jonson, a professor of archaeology, is drawn into a web of greed, fraud, and murder by an elderly recluse, who has apparently discovered some ancient artifacts on his estate. Two murders follow, and the professor's life and that of his girlfriend are threatened. Matters are resolved on the Isle of Wight where a similar find has been made. †††

LEWIS, ROY. *Once Dying, Twice Dead.* 1984. A very episodic story of attorney Eric Ward who tackles problems ranging from a beaten newspaperman, to his wife's company, to an aging villain in France. Lewis is a victim of too much story for too little space. ††

LEWIS, ROY HARLEY.   *A Cracking of Spines.* 1981. A delightful mystery for bookstore owners. Matthew Coll, antiquarian bookseller, investigates a series of rare-book thefts.   †††

LORD, JEREMY.   *The Bannerman Case.* 1935. The Secret Service and Scotland Yard join forces to investigate the death of an inventor who was working on a top-secret weapon for the British government. It looks like an accident but turns out to be murder. A showgirl Mata Hari also appears in this explosive, if slightly dated, story.   †††

LOVESEY, PETER.   Author of the series of Victorian mysteries starring Sergeant Cribb and Constable Thackeray of Scotland Yard. Each Cribb book is well researched and shows it. They are first-rate jobs. Recently, Lovesey has also begun writing non-series mysteries as well. Each of these is as painstakingly researched as the Cribb stories.

Wobble to Death.   1970. A "wobble" is a six-day, endurance footrace. These torturous events were actually popular in England during the 1880s. In the wobble which forms the setting of the story, murder is afoot and serves to introduce Cribb and Thackeray.   ††††

The Detective Wore Silk Drawers.   1971. The seamy world of bare-knuckle boxing attracts Cribb's attention when a headless pugilist surfaces in the Thames. The police boxing champ goes undercover to bust a ring of crooked promoters.   ††††

Abracadaver.   1972. Someone's out to murder the scantily clad belles of London's low-life music halls, and Constable Thackeray poses as a stage-door Johnny to trap the killer. As in many of Lovesey's books, when the villain's motive is finally revealed, it doesn't bear the closest scrutiny, but the plotting and color are good enough to make up for it.   †††

Mad Hatter's Holiday.   1973. Brighton, seaside resort of high society, attracts all kinds of people, including a recluse whose hobby is spying on strangers through field glasses. When one of his subjects disappears, and a severed human hand is found in the crocodile cavern at the aquarium, he lends his services to Cribb and Thackeray.   †††

A Case of Spirits.   1975. The world of Victorian spiritualists and mediums afforded plenty of opportunity for mischief. In this case, mischief leads to murder, and Cribb and Thackeray try to pierce the veil of mysticism to find a killer, who is very much of this world.   ††††

Swing Swing Together.   1976. Jerome K. Jerome's best-seller *Three Men in a Boat* inspired a host of imitative punters to throng the waterways of England during the summer following Jack the Ripper's murders. Cribb and Thackeray, along with a brawny rural constable and an adventurous young woman, take to the water to trace a trio of boat-borne killers.   †††

Keystone. 1983. An English variety actor winds up acting as a Keystone Cop for Mack Sennett, Hollywood's king of comedy in the early years of filmdom. He mingles with the likes of Fatty Arbuckle and Mabel Normand as he spoons with a starlet and uses fledgling film technology to solve a murder.   †††

M

MacDONALD, PHILIP. Many feel he was one of the best English mystery writers from the 1930s and 1940s. That may be true, but the only one of his works which I feel still holds up today is *The List of Adrian Messenger*, which was written in 1959.

The Rasp. 1930. Anthony Gethryn investigates the murder of a millionaire. It is far too much like *Trent's Last Case* to make it memorable.   ††

The Mystery of the Dead Police. 1933. Gethryn tries to find a killer who is terrorizing the police force of Farnley by killing them off one at a time.   †††

Warrant for X. 1938. The story of a young man who overhears two women plotting a kidnapping in an English tearoom. It is paced so slowly that it can only be described as turgid. The young man who overhears the plot is a total ass. Don't bother.   †

The List of Adrian Messenger. 1959. In spite of his resurrection of the "shopping list" clue, used so poorly in *Warrant for X*, this is MacDonald's masterpiece. A list of ten names—all murdered. By whom and for what reason keeps you turning the pages.   †††††

McGINLEY, PATRICK. *Bogmail.* 1978. In a comic Irish mystery worthy of Kingsley Amis or Peter Ustinov, Roarty, a pub owner, kills his teenage daughter's lover, drops the body into a bog, and returns to his pub, only to find he is the object of a blackmailer's attentions. A very fine read.   ††††

MacKENZIE, DONALD. His Raven stories are an English version of Travis McGee, with Raven, the ex-cop, living on a houseboat in the Thames. While they have nowhere near the quality of the Travis McGee stories, they still have a certain charm that makes them fun to read.

Raven Settles the Score. 1978. Raven runs into an old enemy while rescuing a damsel from distress and gets a touch of revenge as well.   ††

Raven and the Paperhanger. 1980. Raven and his lady, Kristie, are enjoying Paris until they inadvertently get caught up in a forgery scheme in which General Chemical blue-chip securities are being counterfeited.   ††

MCNEILLY, WILFRED. *The Case of the Muckrakers.* 1967. All British mysteries are not cozy little affairs with an affable inspector. Here, a respectable publisher, Lord Salous, is being blackmailed by a sleazy magazine called "Keyhole." He hires private eye Sexton Blake to put it out of business. (Sexton Blake novels are also written by other writers such as W. Howard Baker and Ross Richards.) ††

MCSHANE, MARK. Author of short, strange novels which combine mystery with the occult and psychological suspense. Some of them also contain an element of sardonic humor. Despite his use of morbid atmospheric effects, McShane is a meticulous plotter who plays fair with the reader.

Seance on a Wet Afternoon. 1961. Clairvoyant Myra Savage plans a publicity stunt to pump up public faith in her powers. She will kidnap a little girl and then, at a seance, "reveal" the child's whereabouts. But when the girl is discovered murdered, Myra finds that she can't deny her true gift of second sight, which leads her to disaster. ††††

Night's End. 1966. Investigator Norman Pink is hired to find the murderer of a man stabbed behind the scenes at a traveling carnival in Scotland. Pink's matter-of-fact imperturbability contrasts well with the freakish set of suspects and the eerie atmosphere. †††

The Crimson Madness of Little Doom. 1967. Under a mounting campaign of anonymous letters, the dozen or so inhabitants of the isolated village of Little Doom begin to crack. Then they begin to die. McShane pulls off a tour de force of sorts—a book in which every character is somehow repulsive, but which compels interest by the twists and turns of plot alone. ††††

Ill Met by a Fish Shop in George Street. 1968. This may be the limit of the author's penchant for weird titles. In this story, a fugitive who has lived a blameless life in Australia for thirty years suddenly comes face to face with the one man who can destroy him. The two men stalk each other, and their confrontation has a sudden but believable surprise ending. †††

MALCOLM, JOHN. *A Back Room in Somers Town.* 1984. Art dealer Tim Simpson investigates the murder of a dealer and the theft of two modest paintings. I didn't care too much for the part set in Brazil, but I enjoyed the part set in London. The book has the flavor, but not quite the vitality, of Jonathan Gash. Still, a very good first effort. †††

MANN, JESSICA. *The Sting of Death.* 1978. Grebe Bay in Cornwall seems much like Martha's Vineyard as local preservationists battle local exploiters, and the natives argue with the artistic types—all in the spirit of harmony and good times—until a body is found in the bay. There, any resemblance to Martha's Vineyard ends. †††

MARSH, NGAIO. Although many have been described as the heir to Agatha Christie, Marsh is the one who truly deserves the title. Her Roderick Alleyn mysteries are cleverly plotted and strongly set—often at house parties or in the theater—in the best of the British mystery tradition.

A Man Lay Dead. 1934. Marsh's first mystery. A house-party murder. Not one of my favorites. †††

Enter a Murderer. 1935. Her best. It is murder at the Unicorn Theater, and as fine an example of a theater mystery as you will ever find. †††††

Overture to Death. 1936. One of my favorites. An excellent story of the murder of a pianist on stage. Good gimmicky murder weapon. ††††

Artists in Crime. 1938. Inspector Alleyn investigates a murder in an art colony and falls in love with his future wife. Shades of Dorothy Sayers's *Strong Poison*. ††††

Death at the Bar. 1940. Another of my favorites. Alleyn investigates the murder of a barrister in a pub. The murder weapon is a poisoned dart. ††††

Colour Scheme. 1943. Murder and espionage at a New Zealand resort. Unfortunately she spends far too much time on the set and characters. Alleyn doesn't get involved in the story until rather late. ††

Died in the Wool. 1945. A member of parliament is found dead in a bale of wool, and during the course of the investigation, we learn more about the sheep and wool business than I really wanted to know. ††††

Final Curtain. 1947. Another of her best. Agatha Troy, artist-wife of Inspector Alleyn, plays a large part in the story of the murder of an old duffer who was about to marry a chorus girl. †††††

False Scent. 1959. The murder method in this killing of the queen bitch of the theater is interesting, and if any victim ever deserved to die, it was she. †††

Dead Water. 1963. The worst of her books. Murder at a healing spring. There are visions, warts, and other manner of distasteful things in this one. †

Clutch of Constables. 1969. A cleverly plotted story in which Alleyn takes on "Jampot," a cunning, chameleonlike villain, during a cruise along the Thames. ††††

MASTERMAN, J. C. *An Oxford Tragedy.* 1933. A classic with a beautifully drawn Oxford setting, an interesting amateur detective—Professor Ernest Brendel—and a strongly told story of the murder of a tutor, whose body is found in the dean's lodgings. †††††

MEYNELL, LAWRENCE. *The House in Marsh Road.* 1960. It was the house that tormented author Arthur Engleton, tormented him until he began an affair with a beautiful woman, tormented him until he finally committed murder—or so he would have us believe. ††

MILNE, A. A. *The Red House Mystery.* 1922. The creator of Winnie the Pooh constructs a classic, English country-house puzzler. Mr. Mark Ablett, a nouveau riche bachelor, argues with and apparently murders his prodigal brother. Then he disappears. A weekend guest, Bill Beverly, joins forces with his friend, Anthony Gillingham, to search out the truth. The pair are clever and charming, although they have only the flimsiest of reasons for being on the scene. The twist in the solution is truly surprising and the reading breezy. †††††

MITCHELL, GLADYS. It's time people began to read Gladys Mitchell again, one of the true stylists of the field. Her novels, featurng Dame Beatrice Lestrange Bradley, are filled with superior plotting, the supernatural, and heavy suspense.

The Rising of the Moon. 1945. Two small boys see a person with a knife standing on a bridge in the moonlight. When a body is discovered, the boys decide to investigate, but encounter problems which call for Dame Beatrice's help. †††††

Watson's Choice. 1955. Dame Beatrice investigates murder committed at a Sherlock Holmes dinner. †††

Spotted Hemlock. 1958. Dame Beatrice investigates a murder caused by poisoning. The story includes a headless horseman. ††††

Winking at the Brim. 1974. An expedition in search of a Scottish lake monster provides the backdrop for murder and Dame Beatrice's investigation. †††

The Crozier Pharaohs. 1984. This time it is dog breeding which provides the interesting setting for murder and Dame Beatrice. †††

MORICE, ANNE. Like Simon Brett and Patrick Quentin, Morice sets her mysteries in the theater. While the theater murder is a limited field (it is always a cast member who is killed), she does it very well. Her detective is actress Tessa Crichton. With her taciturn policeman-husband and neurotic playwright-cousin, Tessa solves a series of well-told mysteries.

Scared to Death. 1977. A rich and domineering old lady claims to be haunted by a mysterious double. No one believes her—until she dies under strange circumstances. Tessa Crichton, in town for an arts festival, decodes the dead woman's diary and brings things to a successful conclusion. ††††

Murder in Outline. 1979. Tessa Crichton returns to her old school to judge a drama contest, but the real drama is offstage. The headmistress and some of the students are acting badly out of character, and someone improvises a murder. Tessa decides that school is no place for a grown-up. †††

Death in the Round. 1980. One of Morice's best, this is the story of a small, provincial theater company thrown into disarray by the death of its elderly patron. The plot is clever and surprising, the characters and their seedy secrets are well presented, and the story moves along briskly, with touches of suspense and wit. ††††

MORRISON, ARTHUR. *Best Martin Hewitt Detective Stories.* 1976. Modeled on Sherlock Holmes and taking place during the same period, Martin Hewitt was second in popularity only to Holmes himself. This collection includes the famous "Lenton Croft Robberies." †††††

MOYES, PATRICIA. Author of the charming Henry and Emmy Tibbett series. Although gentle in tone, she does not shy away from hard-hitting themes.

Down Among the Dead Men. 1961. Henry and Emmy, on holiday, investigate a drowning at an English seaside town. Good solid story. †††

Death on the Agenda. 1962. Henry strays and becomes involved in a liaison during a conference in Switzerland. Unable to account for his movements, he becomes a suspect in a murder. †††

Murder a la Mode. 1963. Henry and Emmy investigate murder in the high-fashion world. †††

Falling Star. 1964. An actor on a movie set in a railway station trips and falls beneath an oncoming train. What looks at first like an accident soon turns into a murder for Henry and Emmy. †††

Johnny Under Ground. 1965. This is a good one. Emmy Tibbett attends her twentieth RAF reunion and finds she was the last to see one of the old group, a heroic pilot, before his death. ††††

Murder Fantastical. 1967. The eccentric family plot smacks of Ngaio Marsh, but it is handled nicely as Henry and Emmy investigate a body in the driveway. †††

Death and the Dutch Uncle. 1968. The author manages to tie the pub murder of a small-time hood into African politics. I think she was reaching a bit, but it was still a good read. †††

Season of Snows and Sins. 1971. An excellent story of the murder of a ski instructor. All things point to his wife. There are love triangles and quadrangles galore. ††††

Who Is Simon Warwick. 1978. It's the old "who is the real heir" trick, as Henry and Emmy try to figure out who stands to gain from the dead millionaire's will. †††

Angel Death. 1980. On holiday in the Caribbean, Henry and Emmy investigate the disappearance of a boat and an old lady. †††

MURRAY, MAX. *The Voice of the Corpse.* 1948. A good example of the busybody murder, as once again the village gossip is done in by one or more of a cast of characters who seem to be taken from the game of "Clue." ††††

N

NASH, SIMON. Author of a series of mysteries that can be compared to Edmund Crispin's in their conscious eccentricity and their funny, malicious descriptions. Like Crispin's Fen, Nash's Adam Ludlow is an English scholar who helps Scotland Yard on murder cases.

Dead of a Counterplot. 1962. Adam Ludlow's favorite student is accused of an extra-curricular crime—the murder of a woman who happened to be the campus communist. In an antic, active investigation, Ludlow helps Inspector Montero find the real killer. ††††

Killed by Scandal. 1962. A suburban, amateur theatrical club mounts a production of Sheridan's "School for Scandal," with predictably awful results. Adam Ludlow is roped in to lecture but remains to detect, after a murdered body is discovered on stage in a show-stopping scene. †††

Death over Deep Water. 1963. Ludlow's path again crosses that of the Yard's Inspector Montero when a woman is poisoned on a Mediterranean cruise. The vacationing Ludlow has no lack of opportunities to display his cleverness and erudition. †††

Unhallowed Murder. 1966. The professor and the policeman once more join forces to investigate a pastoral murder, with clergymen and satanists as the chief suspects in the slaying of a London churchman. †††

O

OLIVER, ANTHONY. *The Pew Group.* 1980. Very much like Jonathan Gash in tone, as a zany group of heroes all race around England trying to recover a valuable antique. Inspector Webber is the designated hero, but not so much that he gets in the way of the story. ††††

OLIVER, ANTHONY. *The Property of a Lady.* 1983. A very nicely drawn story in which a young woman brings home a hitchhiker to live with her. The village of Flaxfield gets so flustered that they call in Inspector Webber, and then the fun begins. ††††

ORCZY, BARONESS. *The Scarlet Pimpernel.* 1905. One of the all-time classics. In a well-handled case of double identity, a decadent English aristocrat has a secret life as a masked avenger of the victims of the French Revolution. †††††

ORCZY, BARONESS. *The Old Man in the Corner.* 1909. The "old man" of the title helped define the term "armchair detective." He's an old man who sits in a tea shop, listens to cases, and solves them by pure deduction. This was the first—and best—of several volumes of short stories. They're notable for their foggy Holmesian settings and for their arrogant (perhaps even criminal, as one story hints) main character. If you'd rather have detail than drama, you'll like them. †††

P

PAGE, EMMA. *Last Walk Home.* 1982. A collection of blowflies buzzing around Rose Cottage triggers the postman's curiosity. Inside is the body of the beautiful schoolteacher, Janet Marshal. Her beauty and aloofness seem to have driven someone off the deep end. It is up to Chief Inspector Kelsey and Detective Sergeant Lambert to figure out who. †††

PARRISH, FRANK. Author of the Dan Mallett stories. Mallett is a poacher, a rather unusual type of hero, blue-collar in the truest sense of the word, with a touch of Lady Chatterly's young man thrown in for good measure.

Fire in the Barley. 1977. Dan Mallett turns reluctant hero when a strong-arm protection group threatens the balance of nature *and* life in his district. A terrific first novel. ††††

Bait on the Hook. 1983. Dan Mallett is topping the local babysitter at Medwell Old Hall when an intruder is murdered. Suspected of murder and blackmailed by the babysitter's young charge, Mallett has to find the killer. My favorite of the Mallett novels. ††††

Death in the Rain.   1984. Sakes alive, Dan Mallett, ne'er-do-well poacher, has a job! He is the weekly gardener for an old lady. When she is murdered, Dan is the main suspect, and well he should be, too.   ††

PENN, JOHN.   *An Ad for Murder.* 1982. A clever read in which a former army officer reads about his forthcoming death in a series of newspaper ads. As he investigates, he is drawn deeper and deeper into a maze of menace, murder, and misdirection as a pawn in a deadly double game.   ††††

PENN, JOHN.   *Mortal Term.* 1984. A well-plotted story in which detectives Thorne and Abbot are called in to investigate an attempted rape of a young hitchhiker by the head of a college, only to find there's more going on at the college than a simple molestation. Similar to Michael Gilbert.   ††††

PERRY, ANNE.   Author of a series of well-plotted mysteries based on the tension between the stiff-necked public propriety of the Victorian era and its lurid sexual underground. Her knowledge of the period seems as encyclopedic as that of Victorian authors themselves, and she offers the added dimension of likable characters.

The Cater Street Hangman.   1979. In this, Perry's first book, we meet Charlotte Ellison, the strong-minded, unmarried daughter of an upper-class Victorian family. Charlotte is resigned to the dreary life of an old maid when she encounters Inspector Thomas Pitt during Scotland Yard's investigation of a series of horrific stranglings. Despite opposition from her father, the two fall in love and solve the mystery.   ††††

Paragon Walk.   1981. Perry's best exposition of the conflict of appearance and reality has rape and murder rearing their ugly heads in Charlotte's sister's posh street. References to the newly popular vampire abound, as do images of death, creating a powerful, suffocatingly suspenseful atmosphere. Pitt's detective skills and Charlotte's social savvy trap a surprising killer.   †††††

Resurrection Row.   1982. From Gilbert and Sullivan to a series of gruesome grave robbings, this novel features a dead cabbie who's really a peer, blackmail, reform politics, and murder. As usual in Perry's novels, there's a final truth that's known but unprovable, and a moment where Pitt must take justice into his own hands.   ††††

Rutland Place.   1983. Charlotte's mother loses a locket with a sentimental photograph in it—or is it a compromising photograph? As she discovers undreamed-of things about her mother, Charlotte reveals a complicated case of incest, abortion, obsessive love, and murder.   †††

Bluegate Fields. 1984. Like all Perry's books, this one is named after a London neighborhood. Bluegate Fields is a port slum where the corpse of a young aristocrat washes up from the Thames sewers. Suspicion falls on a man whose only offense appears to be that he is unpopular with his socially superior employers. Pitt and Charlotte use their special combination of observation and intuition to track the real killer. †††

PETERS, ELLIS. Author of a series of novels about a 12th-century warrior-monk-detective named Brother Cadfael. They are well written, using just enough period details to keep the story moving and create a believable atmosphere, but not enough to carry them over into historical novels.

The Virgin in the Ice. 1982. It is the winter of 1139. Civil war rages in England, and a Benedictine monk shows up at Brother Cadfael's monastery looking for a missing young woman and her brother. At the abbey they know nothing. Shortly thereafter, the abbey receives word that another Benedictine monk has been ambushed. Brother Cadfael sets out through the winter snow to offer aid. As he returns to the abbey, he finds the boy alive, but the sister is dead, frozen in the ice of a stream. My favorite of the series. ††††

The Devil's Novice. 1983. Brother Cadfael solves the murder of the political envoy Peter Clemence. †††

Dead Man's Ransom. 1984. Brother Cadfael operates against a backdrop of the 12th-century civil war between King Stephen and the Empress Maud to solve the murder of a prisoner so that an exchange can be completed freeing the sheriff of Shropshire. ††††

PETERS, ELIZABETH. She blends highly accurate Egyptology, Victorian melodrama, and irony in her books about Amelia Peabody, amateur archaeologist. The settings—excavations in Egypt in the 1880s—are extremely well done, and the mysteries combine elements of myth, folklore, or the supernatural with realistic criminals and motives.

Crocodile on the Sandbank. 1975. The outspoken and unconventional Amelia inherits a fortune and arrives in Egypt where she conquers archaeologist Radcliffe Emerson. The villain in the piece is a murderous mummy. In unwrapping him, Amelia discovers that the past can sometimes haunt the present. ††††

The Curse of the Pharaohs. 1981. Death and disaster plague Lord Baskerville's excavation of an ancient tomb, and Amelia and Radcliffe are called in by the not too bereaved widow to clear up the mystery. As in the earlier book, much of the fun lies in the period flavor which Peters evokes and then parodies. †††

The Mummy Case. 1985. This book could be called *Son of Mummy*, as it's about equally devoted to the entertaining eccentricities of Amelia and Radcliffe's son, Rameses, and to their attempt to excavate a forbidden pyramid. Amelia is sidetracked by murder and other irregularities in the black-market antiquities trade. †††

PHILLIPS, STELLA. *Death in Sheep's Clothing.* 1971. An antiques mystery, but much more claustrophic than those of Jonathan Gash or Anthony Oliver. A somewhat disagreeable old lady is done in by someone equally disagreeable. Chief Inspector Matthew Furnival thinks the death is related to a missing Meissen statue of a man playing a fiddle. †††

PHILLPOTTS, EDEN. *The Red Redmaynes.* 1922. A blending of the gothic and the traditional detective novel, as American-in-England Peter Ganns, a snuff connoisseur, tackles evil inherent in the Redmaynes family at their gloomy Dartmoor home. ††††

PLAYER, ROBERT. *The Homicidal Colonel.* 1970. The story of a family as vicious as a pit bull in a feeding frenzy, with a fortune hanging in the balance. †††

PORTER, JOYCE. *Dover Two.* 1965. In the best and funniest of a series of books about Chief Inspector Wilfred Dover of New Scotland Yard, the irascible detective investigates the murder of "Sleeping Beauty"—a young woman who has been in a coma since a murder attempt months earlier. Clues are few and the case is a tough one, but even an open-and-shut case might prove difficult for Dover, who is distinguished chiefly by corpulence, ill temper, and incompetence. ††††

Q

QUEST, ERICA. *The October Cabaret.* 1979. American Tess Pennicott goes to England to take over her uncle's antiques shop. At first glance it appears the uncle died from diabetic coma. However, Tess soon thinks differently when she discovers insulin in the jacket he was wearing. Tess Pennicott is a very likable heroine. †††

QUEST, ERICA. *Design for Murder.* 1981. A very civilized little story in which Tracy Yorke, assistant to an interior designer, finds her boss dead. A fun, enjoyable read. †††

R

RADLEY, SHEILA. *Death in the Morning.* 1978. A promising debut, in which Chief Inspector Quantrill tracks down the killer of a young woman found floating in the river. It has a very good ending for a first novel. †††

RADLEY, SHEILA. *The Chief Inspector's Daughter*. 1980. The inspector's daughter, a typist for a beautiful romantic novelist, goes to work one morning, only to find her employer's raped and murdered body. The characters are somewhat indistinct physically, but well defined psychologically. †††

RENDELL, RUTH. A true long-ball hitter in the mystery field. She can do it all—characterization, atmosphere, and deft plotting. She alternates between novels featuring Inspector Wexford and psychological suspense novels filled with well-drawn, quirky ideas. She is a "must read," if you haven't already.

From Doon with Death. 1964. This was Rendell's first published mystery, and it introduces Inspector Wexford and his sidekick, Burden. Margaret Parsons disappears and then is found murdered. She is a plain, unimaginative woman, but she inspired a love that led to her death. The book hinges on a sleight of hand which is not as surprising now as it must have been in 1964. †††

To Fear a Painted Devil. 1965. Max Greenleaf, a country doctor, is drawn unwillingly into a case of murder when Patrick Selby dies mysteriously after a fight, and a family friend asks him to look into it. The murder method is ingenious, and the motive is unusual and creepy. †††

The Best Man to Die. 1969. Charlie Hatton, a cocky little braggart who dabbles in crime, is murdered the night before his best friend's wedding. Inspector Wexford gets his man, but the book is memorable for its depiction of a friendship that defies reason and transcends death. †††

A Guilty Thing Surprised. 1970. Sexual love, perverse and obsessive, is at the heart of this story. Wealthy and beautiful Elizabeth Nightingale is murdered, and Inspector Wexford and his sidekick Burden suspect her faithless husband. But the truth is bound up in a terrible secret from the past. The conclusion is one of her best. ††††

A Demon in My View. 1976. Two men with the commonplace surname of Johnson end up living in the same shabby rooming house. This believable coincidence sets off an explosive chain of events in this beautifully drawn psychological thriller. The character of Arthur Johnson, fussy bachelor and ruthless sexual maniac, is also unforgettable. ††††

A Judgement in Stone. 1977. Rendell's best. Eunice Parchman, a servant in an upper-middle-class household, massacres the entire family one night with the aid of a religiously zealous friend. Her motive for murder is surely unique in mystery literature. †††††

Make Death Love Me. 1979. The chain of circumstances that drags ordinary people into disaster is epitomized in this tale about Alan Groombridge, a middle-aged bank teller, who finds himself holding the loot after two punks bungle a bank robbery. ††††

Master of the Moor. 1982. Stephen Whalby is unable to satisfy the needs of his young wife, or the demands of his moody father, but on the moors near his home, he is master. That is, until he finds the dead body of a young girl, and his hiding place is exposed. †††††

An Unkindness of Ravens. 1985. A murder victim turns out to be a bigamist, and Inspector Wexford naturally suspects a jealous wife or two. But a feminist group of high school girls is shielding an attacker of local Lotharios, and Wexford suspects a connection. †††

• *Some novels to read when your own singing voice is starting to sound better and better to you:*

THE METROPOLITAN OPERA MURDERS by Helen Traubel
MURDER AT THE MET by David Black
THE OPERA HOUSE MURDERS by David Hanna
SERENADE by James M. Cain
SWAN SONG by Edmund Crispin

If you think that taking off your clothes might further increase your chance of success, read:

THE G-STRING MURDERS by Gypsy Rose Lee

ROBERTSON, ROBERT. *Landscape for Dead Dons.* 1956. Inspector Autumn travels to Oxford to find the vandals who shredded the original of Milton's *Paradise Lost,* and who it is feared will go after a newly discovered Chaucer manuscript. Truly excellent. †††††

ROSS, JONATHAN. *A Rattling of Old Bones.* 1979. When a small-time jewel thief stumbles across a body in a cupboard where it had been hidden some five years earlier, Inspector Rogers's troubles are just beginning. The identity of the woman is Judith Quint, a woman Inspector Rogers was rumored to be having an affair with at the time of her death. Good read. †††††

ROUDYBUSH, ALEXANDRA. *Blood Ties.* 1981. Far too much material for this short book. There are two rich female cousins, Felicia and Hilary. Hilary becomes a secret agent, Felicia a homebody. Entering into a second marriage Felicia finds herself in "ye olde gothic household" with the usual number of creepy things going on. ††

S

SAYERS, DOROTHY L. One of the true masters of the mystery, whose detective, Lord Peter Wimsey, has delighted readers for generations. As if it were not enough that her writing was flawless, her plotting brilliant, and her characters sharply drawn, this strong-willed woman—who physically bore a striking resemblance to Franklin D. Roosevelt in drag—also dealt with feminist social issues in her mysteries, which often gives them a contemporary theme as well as a timeless quality.

Whose Body? 1923. The first Peter Wimsey novel. A great debut. ††††

Clouds of Witness. 1927. Lord Peter's brother is accused of murdering their future brother-in-law. ††††

Unnatural Death. 1927. I found this one more interesting for the biographical notes on Lord Peter than for the story of murder which leads from rural England to fashionable London. ††††

The Unpleasantness at the Bellona Club. 1928. The weakest of the novels. Lord Peter investigates the murder of man found dead in his chair at his club. †††

The Documents in the Case. 1930. Written with Robert Eustace. This well-written novel of poisoning is not a Lord Peter story. ††††

Strong Poison. 1930. My favorite of the novels. Lord Peter meets and falls in love with Harriet Vane, a mystery writer accused of poisoning her lover. Brilliant plotting, a fabulous opening, and relevant social issues combine to make this a true masterpiece. †††††

Five Red Herrings. 1931. Lord Peter investigates the murder of an artist in Scotland. The setting and the trickiness of the plotting make this one a classic. †††††

The Nine Tailors. 1934. A classic which many feel is her best work. However, because of all the information about bells, I found it tougher going than the rest of the stories. †††††

Gaudy Night. 1936. The second novel to team up Lord Peter and Harriet Vane. A series of malevolent pranks leads to murder at an Oxford reunion. This one is a bit on the long side, but still excellent. ††††

Busman's Honeymoon. 1937. This novel features the now-married Lord Peter and Harriet Vane. On their honeymoon, the former owner of their estate is found dead in the basement. However, the most interesting aspect of the story is the sexual development of the new couple's married life. ††††

SHAW, HOWARD. *Killing No Murder.* 1972. Henry Carter, the new headmaster of a boys' school, is making a mess of things. Everyone in the school wants to get rid of him. Someone does, and Chief Detective Inspector Barnaby comes to investigate. †††

SHERWOOD, JOHN. *A Shot in the Arm.* 1982. An excellent story in which someone shoots one of the bigwigs at the BBC. But what makes it so good is the atmosphere and background of the BBC in 1937. Do yourself a favor and read this one. ††††

SHERWOOD, JOHN. *A Botanist at Bay.* 1985. Celia Grant, amateur detective, will undoubtedly draw a great number of fans, but I'm not one. I found this story of Celia's search through the wilds of New Zealand for the missing relative of a duchess to be unsatisfying. ††

SHEPERD, ERIC. *Murder in a Nunnery.* 1940. A well-told tale in which Chief Inspector Pearson finds himself feeling like a bull in a china shop as he investigates the murder of the Baroness Sliema, whose body has been found on the steps of the altar in the chapel of the Harrington Convent School. †††

SIMS, GEORGE. *The Sand Dollar.* 1969. Nicholas Howard, a middle-aged bookseller with a roving eye, turns a cold shoulder to his wife just before she is killed by a train. Nicholas finds himself in danger. However, who really gives a damn about what happens to a first-class ass like Nicholas, anyway? †

SIMS, GEORGE. *The End of the Web.* 1976. Again a story built around disagreeable people. This time, three sleazebag antique dealers find some papers and decide to turn to blackmail. But they are too incompetent to pull it off, and a nephew of one of them sets out to avenge the death of his worthless uncle. He should have left well enough alone. †

SMITH, SHELLEY. *The Cellar at No. 5.* 1954. This is one of those oppressive, claustrophobic tales of two old women living together and driving each other crazy. It makes a good argument for nursing homes. ††

SNOW, C. P. A master novelist turns his loving attention to the English mystery and shows what can be accomplished when one puts his mind to his work.

Death under Sail. 1932. Snow does one hell of a job with a simple plot—murder on board a boat with seven passengers. Beautifully told with a great lead character and a narrator who is full of wit and wisdom. †††††

SPRIGG, C. ST. JOHN. *The Six Queer Things.* 1937. There's more than one queer thing in this mystery. A confused young girl falls under the spell of a psychic medium, who is murdered during a seance. The first thing the police discover is that the murdered man was really a woman. The story goes on to include brainwashing, swindling, black magic, and more murder.   †††

STUBBS, JEAN. *The Painted Face.* 1974. Artist Nicholas Carradine hires Inspector Lintott to help him find his missing sister. Naturally they go to Paris. After all, where else would a young woman with any brains disappear to? †††

SYMONS, JULIAN. A fine British mystery writer who has turned out jewel after jewel throughout his career. If you haven't heard of him, it is probably because he has never developed a series character.

Bogue's Fortune. 1956. A young novelist finds himself in the way of a bunch of criminals looking for a buried treasure.   †††

The Belting Inheritance. 1965. A somewhat ordinary story about a rich family with four sons—two alive and two dead. While the living sons wait for their mother to die, word arrives that one of their brothers is alive.   †††

The Players in the Game. 1972. A chilling psychological suspense novel, inspired by actual crimes (the Moors Murders and the American Lonely Heart Murders), in which three thrill-seeking young women, through a newspaper ad, find themselves the prey of two psychos who call themselves "Dracula" and "Bonnie Parker."   ††††

The Plot Against Roger Rider. 1973. Roger and Geoffrey grew up together. Roger went on to become wildly successful, hiring Geoffrey as his clerk. Then Roger's wife begins an affair with Geoffrey. They all go on holiday together and Roger disappears. A great job.   †††††

A Three-Pipe Problem. 1975. Sheridan Hayes, a British television actor who portrays Sherlock Holmes, tries his hand at outwitting Scotland Yard as he attempts to solve a series of killings.   †††

The Detling Secret. 1982. Young love prevails as Dolly Detling marries Bernard Ross, a poor but bright member of parliament, and with the marriage comes murder, Fenians, anarchists, and a Christmas climax at the Detling country home.   ††††

The Tigers of Subtopia. 1982. An excellent collection of short stories, especially the one from which the title is taken, as four suburbanites decide they have had enough of gang violence in their neighborhood and take matters into their own hands.   ††††

T

TAYLOR, ANDREW. *Caroline Miniscule*. 1982. The story of a medieval script, a treasure of diamonds, and a graduate student turned amateur detective. Unfortunately, the author's irritating attempt at a stream-of-consciousness style doesn't work well with the story. † †

TEY, JOSEPHINE. The only complaint that can be made about Josephine Tey is that she died too soon. Her stories appeal more to women than men. Her detective, Inspector Alan Grant, is a forerunner of the somber, introspective detectives of Ruth Rendell and P. D. James.

Miss Pym Disposes. 1946. Not an Inspector Grant story, this book stars a retired schoolmistress turned amateur psychologist, who solves an improbable schoolgirl murder. It is Tey's weakest offering, though the academic setting is handled well. † † †

The Franchise Affair. 1948. Inspector Grant appears briefly in this tale, based on a real incident, of a young woman who claims to have been kidnapped, beaten, and otherwise mistreated by a pair of eccentric women. The climax, a skillful trial scene, deflects attention from a not too gripping romance. † † †

Brat Farrar. 1949. A story of impersonation of a missing heir, deception and murder. This book compensates for a predictable plot with good characterization and well-managed pacing. More a family drama than a real mystery, it does not feature Inspector Grant. † † †

To Love and Be Wise. 1950. A flamboyant American photographer stirs up a British artists' colony—sexually and otherwise—only to disappear under murderous circumstances. Inspector Grant penetrates one of the great disguises in mystery fiction to discover the surprising truth about Leslie Searle. † † † † †

The Daughter of Time. 1951. Some say this is the best mystery ever written. I don't agree, but I do feel it is a classic which stands alone in its greatness. The story never leaves a hospital bed, where Detective Grant, while recuperating, investigates whether the infamous Richard III really did kill the children. Tey's smooth, simple narrative style transforms her tremendous research into an easily digestible novel. † † † † †

The Singing Sands. 1952. Inspector Grant, suffering from a nervous breakdown, takes a holiday with relatives in Scotland where he becomes involved in the mystery of an anonymous murdered man and a scrap of haunting poetry. The plot is contrived, and the resolution somewhat melodramatic, but the Scottish scenes are nicely atmospheric, and the mystery has exotic, original overtones. † † †

THOMAS, DONALD. *Mad Hatter Summer.* 1983. A lot of work went into this Victorian period piece in which Lewis Carroll—of *Alice in Wonderland* fame—is blackmailed over his nude photos of young children, which somehow turn up in the porn market. It definitely deserves a read. ††††

TOURNEY, LEONARD. *Low Treason.* 1983. A jeweler's apprentice in 16th-century England disappears, and Matthew Stock, village constable, wants to find out why. Good Elizabethan setting. A "must read" for Ellis Peters fans. †††

TROY, SIMON. *Road to Rhuine.* 1952. Murder rears its ugly head in the atmospheric setting of the village of Rhuine as investigator Lee Vaughn looks into the death of Stuart Fabian. †††

TROY, SIMON. *Swift to Its Close.* 1969. Inspector Smith has to sort through the murderous pieces of a complex emotional affair which comes to a head on the opening night of the Seachurch Music Festival. It seems Grace and Doyle are recently divorced but working together on the festival. Meanwhile, Grace is messing around with a local married man who is not the soul of discretion, and Doyle is casting smoldering glances at his attractive housekeeper. From there, things start to get a bit crazy. ††††

U

UNDERWOOD, MICHAEL. *Crime upon Crime.* 1980. A small-time blackmailer takes on a powerful judge, who is a victim of his own weaknesses: gambling, drink, and certain sins of the flesh. †††

UNDERWOOD, MICHAEL. *Victim of Circumstance.* 1980. A well-written psychological novel in which John Ferndon, a teacher at an English boarding school, marries a French girl who hates England. He plots her murder but then is murdered himself. Very nicely done. †††

UNDERWOOD, MICHAEL. *Death in Camera.* 1984. Rosa Epton investigates the death of a judge in a well-plotted story with a strong ending. †††

V

VICKERS, ROY. *The Whispering Death.* 1947. A warmly told tale of a young man who steals jewels from his employer to ransom his girlfriend, who has been kidnapped by a vicious criminal known as "The Whisperer." It reads like a cross between Delano Ames and Edgar Wallace, but unfortunately it is a bit short. †††

VICKERS, ROY. *Murder Will Out*. (n.d.) A collection of short stories involving the Department of Dead Ends, a section of Scotland Yard where unsolved crimes end up. These are clever stories built around good gimmicks and well-drawn characters. Some have the feel of the old Alfred Hitchcock television show.
††††

W

WADE, HENRY. *The Duke of York's Steps*. 1929. When a man dies—apparently without human intervention—moments after being jostled by a stranger on the London landmark, the Duke of York's Steps, the police in charge must first determine whether a crime has been committed. Then, of course, they have to find the mysterious stranger. And then they have to build a case against him. Slow moving, but well planned and written. †††

WADE, HENRY. *The Hanging Captain*. (n.d.) In one of Wade's favorite plot situations, an apparent suicide turns out to be murder. The investigators are confronted with a plethora of refined suspects, all with impeccable motives, including a priest, a sheriff, and the dead man's widow. Once again Wade's process of detection is slow and steady. †††

WADE, HENRY. *A Dying Fall*. 1955. Did she fall or was she pushed? A woman tumbles down a flight of steps, and her death begins an investigation of blackmail and death among the sporting set. Characterization is excellent. Wade plays his cards close to his vest on this one, letting us see no more than the police see and reserving an ironic surprise for the end. ††††

WALLING, R. A. J. *A Corpse by Any Other Name*. 1943. The tone is Sherlock Holmesian as Farrar tells of his adventure with Tolefree when they leave wartime London and head for the coast to get a message from a man who survived a torpedo in the North Atlantic. †††

WALSH, MAURICE. *Nine Strings to Your Bow*. 1945. The murder of Mark Aiken still hangs over Peter Falkner, his nephew, who has finally been acquitted after three trials. It is up to Con Madden to wade through such diverse clues as the limping man and the missing fishing rod to get to the bottom of things.
††††

WARNER, MIGNON. *A Medium for Murder*. 1976. A good English country setting is the only thing I liked about this rather irritating story of a medium who, to clear her reputation, must solve an old murder. The first half of the story is all women sitting around gossiping, and the heroine doesn't even appear until around page 90. ††

WARNER, MIGNON. *Death in Time*. 1982. Poor, bitchy Cynthia Playford comes to a magicians' convention and gets herself murdered. A very promising opening, but that's as far as it goes. Once again Warner's detective, Mrs. Charles, appears late in the book, and I came away convinced that Mrs. Charles, as a character, does not work. ††

WATSON, COLIN. Watson draws Inspector Purbright and the Flaxborough police department with a comic touch, but that does not mean he doesn't take his stories seriously. Within the framework of often zany plots, he is able to make us develop feelings and care about the fates of his characters.

Coffin Scarcely Used. 1958. Six months after the death of the town councillor, his next-door neighbor, the publisher of the local newspaper, is found electrocuted—with a marshmallow in his mouth. Now that's news, and it means trouble for Inspector Purbright. ††††

Hopjoy Was Here. 1962. Inspector Purbright investigates the murder of Brian Hopjoy, who appears to have been a secret agent. But the story is stolen by Ross, a super secret agent, as Watson, not too subtly, puts Ian Fleming in his place. My favorite of the series. ††††

Just What the Doctor Ordered. 1969. Inspector Purbright investigates a series of sexual assaults on the women of Flaxborough which have been committed by an aged mugger. When the mugger dies, everything seems settled, but really, it's not. †††

Six Nuns and a Shotgun. 1975. There's talk in Flaxborough that six nuns from Philadelphia are going to be involved in some not very respectable dealings at the local country club. A professional killer may be involved. Inspector Purbright fears the worst. †††

WENTWORTH, PATRICIA. Author of the Miss Silver series. Miss Silver is a prime member of the old busybody set in the tradition of Miss Marple. The books are well written, and the fans totally devoted. My only complaint is that Miss Silver should have her cough seen to.

Miss Silver Intervenes. 1944. A woman's fiancé, a victim of amnesia, is restored to her. However, there is another woman who can't leave well enough alone and is murdered for her meddling. When the amnesia victim is suspected, Miss Silver comes to his aid. †††

She Came Back. 1945. A woman comes back from the dead to reclaim her husband and fortune. It is up to Miss Silver to determine if the woman is real or an imposter. ††††

The Listening Eye. 1955. A deaf woman at an art exhibition lip-reads a private conversation between two villains and is killed shortly after she takes her findings to Miss Silver. ††††

The Fingerprint. 1956. Another case of a distraught person picking up the murder weapon at the scene of the crime and becoming a suspect. Miss Silver to the rescue. †††

WHITE, ETHEL LINA. She wrote excellent, suspenseful thrillers, featuring resourceful young heroines, mysterious conspiracies, and well-realized description.

Fear Stalks the Village. 1932. The village in question is a tiny, peaceful, prosperous hamlet, full of contented villagers. The fear is brought about by a series of poison pen letters that inevitably prove fatal to their recipients. Joan Brook, the young companion to the lady of the manor, is the most likely candidate for the role of penwoman, so she determines to unmask the real culprit. The result is a satisfying mystery with gothic overtones. †††

The Spiral Staircase. 1933. A maid in an isolated country mansion is the target of a killer, who has already eliminated most of the young women in the area. In her attempt to protect herself, she discovers the murderer's identity, and the knowledge is fatal. The climax is a stormy night when Helen and the killer are alone in the locked house. No surprises, but good suspenseful writing. †††

Wax. 1935. Sonia Thompson, an ambitious young newspaperwoman, arrives in quiet Riverpool and stirs up interest in its old wax museum, now used mainly as a meeting place by illicit lovers. She's convinced that something else, something mysterious and dangerous, is happening at the museum, and she volunteers to spend a night alone at the museum to prove her point. A true classic which has influenced everyone from John Dickson Carr in *The Corpse in the Waxworks* to Don Knotts in *The Ghost and Mr. Chicken.* †††††

The Lady Vanishes. 1936. Perhaps White's best-known book. This is an Orient-Express mystery worthy of the company of Agatha Christie and Graham Greene. It tells the story of a carefree and careless young Englishwoman, returning from a holiday in Eastern Europe, who becomes enmeshed in the baffling case of her disappearing seatmate—a woman whom no one else on the train remembers seeing. The heroine's attempt to find her friend and prove her sanity is one long nightmare of helplessness, terror, and nerve. †††††

While She Sleeps. 1940. Miss Loveapple (a juicy tomato) has always prided herself on her extraordinary good luck. But her luck takes a turn for the worse when she is marked out as a killer's victim. Through a crazy but plausible series of circumstances, she not only escapes but remains ignorant of her plight. This lighthearted, tidy book is really a tongue-in-cheek parody of the creaky gothic genre. ††††

WHITE, T. H. *Darkness at Pemberly.* 1932. This book was published when White, later to become famous for his Arthurian novels, was an unknown author. It combines a locked-room murder in an academic setting, a ghoulish, suspenseful game of hide-and-seek in a rambling country house, and a refreshingly offhand romance. It's ingenious, fast moving, and atmospheric, and it will make you wish White had written more like it.   †††††

WILLIAMS, DAVID. *Unholy Writ.* 1976. An old aristocrat has second thoughts about selling the family mansion to a reactionary group and calls in his friend, London financier Mark Treasure, to stop the sale. From there we encounter murder, treachery, romance, and a valuable Shakespearean manuscript. Great fun.   ††††

WILLIAMS, DAVID. *Treasure Preserved.* 1983. Amateur detective Mark Treasure investigates the death of a local busybody, who was dead set on keeping Round House, an architecturally unique building, from being torn down.   †††

WINSLOW, PAULINE GLEN. *Death of an Angel.* 1975. This has a lot going on: a New York death of a young man named Angel, a trail which leads to London, ESP, and a zany bunch of kooks who serve as suspects for Superintendent Capricorn.   †††

WINSLOW, PAULINE GLEN. *The Witch Hill Murder.* 1977. On the eve of his wedding, Richard Brewster, the town clerk, is found murdered on the Witch Hill Road. Superintendent Merle Capricorn's investigation is made more difficult by the fact that the bride-to-be is an old friend.   ††††

WODEHOUSE, P. G. If you read British mysteries for their country-house atmosphere and humor, you'll love Wodehouse's classic tales of bumbling domestic intrigue. He was a gifted creator of comic characters and preposterous plots, but perhaps his greatest skill was his ability to turn a phrase, making the sublime ridiculous. Don't look for social realism, but keep a sharp eye out for satire—there's more to Wodehouse than mere buffoonery.

Leave It to Psmith. 1923. Psmith, one of Wodehouse's most engaging characters, is a young man who wants to make his way in the world. He decides to do it by stealing a diamond necklace from the formidable Lady Constance Keeble of Blandings Castle—for impeccable reasons, of course. Hilarious misunderstandings and good-natured jibes at the literary world ensue.   ††††

Carry on, Jeeves. 1925. A short-story collection introducing Wodehouse's most-popular series characters, the amiable nitwit Bertie Wooster and his valet, the erudite and resourceful Jeeves, in muddled romances, near escapes from matrimony, and close encounters of all kinds with that peril of perils—his aunt.   ††††

Meet Mr. Mulliner. 1927. My favorite of Wodehouse's books. Many feel the tales told by Mr. Mulliner in the Angler's Rest pub to be Wodehouse's best and funniest. Mulliner has a nephew for every occasion, and the most innocent observation by a patron of the bar (never identified by name, only by drink, such as "the Pint of Stout observed") invariably results in a recital of the exploits of Sacherverell, Lancelot, Wilfred, Clarence... †††††

Thank You, Jeeves. 1934. Bertie and Jeeves visit the lair of Bertie's Aunt Dahlia, where they become embroiled in the tangled affair of Gussie Fink-Nottle, the inebriated newt-fancier, and Madeline Bassett, a girl who thinks that rabbits are gnomes in attendance on the Fairy Queen. †††††

The Code of the Woosters. 1938. Essence of Wodehouse. The saga of Gussie and Madeline continues. While visiting Totleigh Towers, Bertie tangles with the menacing Roderick Spode, whose gimlet eye can open an oyster at twenty paces. With Jeeves's help, Bertie unearths Spode's guilty secret just in time to save the day. †††††

Full Moon. 1947. Blandings Castle and its inhabitants, headed by the eminently absent-minded Lord Emsworth, appear in a number of Wodehouse novels. In this one, cosmopolitan Uncle Galahad foils a brace of slavering aunts to unite sundered young lovers, one of whom, posing as Landseer, is commissioned to paint a portrait of the earl's prize pig. †††

WOODS, SARA. Her mysteries—set in London and small-town England—star Anthony Maitland, a barrister and amateur detective with a reputation for taking on difficult cases. His chief assets are his stubbornness, his ability to tell when someone is lying, his irreverent wit, and his young wife. These books are strong on deduction and often have good courtroom scenes.

Let's Choose Executioners. 1966. A well-crafted plot centers around the poisoning of a rich old lady. As is often the case, Maitland enters the case only after guilt has been fixed on the most likely suspect. No believer in half measures, he undertakes not only to get the girl acquitted but to clear her name by proving someone else committed the crime. ††††

The Case Is Altered. 1967. Maitland mingles with the world of film stars as he attempts to prove that a lovely starlet's fiancé didn't steal an emerald necklace. What he doesn't bargain for is mixing it up with a powerful gang of jewel thieves. †††

Knives Have Edges. 1968. This plot centers on an unusual and amoral woman, who involves Maitland in her murderous fantasy. As always, however, his instinct for the truth saves him from making a fool of himself. His relationship with his wife, Jenny, plays an especially strong part in this book. †††

Proceed to Judgment. 1979. Maitland is retained to defend a doctor accused of conspiring to murder his mistress's husband. ††

Most Grievous Murder.   1982. In an amusing change of scene, Maitland and Jenny visit New York City, where he investigates a political assassination at the U.N. There's more danger, action, and suspense than in many of Woods's books, and Third-World people and politics are humorously parodied.   ††††

XYZ

YORKE, MARGARET.   *Dead in the Morning.* 1970. Oxford don, Dr. Patrick Grant, investigates the murder of the local bitch. Rather ordinary plot.   †††

YORKE, MARGARET.   *No Medals for the Major.* 1974. A psychological suspense novel in which a retired major has tragic adjustment problems.   †††

YORKE, MARGARET.   *Intimate Kill.* 1985. A well-written, but not remarkable psychological suspense novel about a man on parole for killing his wife. He tries to clear his name.   †††

THE
THRILLER

$\mathbf{B}$ECAUSE THE THRILLER COVERS such a multitude of sins, it is the largest and most popular of the categories—at least over the past twenty-five years. Since the 1903 appearance of the first modern spy novel—Erskine Childers's *Riddle of the Sands*—the Thriller has undergone continual changes, and its characters have also had to change.

These changes have, for the most part, not been in the characters' physical or emotional makeup. The heroes are still resolute, strong-jawed, and handsome; the heroines are tall, long-haired, intrepid, and beautiful, with fantastic breasts (I wish just once a heroine would have normal breasts instead of always looking like the jutting front end of a 1958 Cadillac); and the villains are loathsome creatures with bottomless pits for souls and exteriors marked by either a reptilian iciness or some hideous physical defect.

No, the area of change has been much more external, but nonetheless still very essential to the Thriller novel. It is in the area of fashion, for the fashions of the time and place of the novel create an indelible image in the mind of the reader, and therefore become a strong aid in the author's ability to set the story.

The mainstay of the Thriller category is the spy story, a novel whose beginnings were never humble. The object of the spy novel, in its purest form, is for a character, operating under an assumed identity, to steal military or political secrets of an important and sensitive nature, and to get them back successfully to his own country before he is captured. Since these are not the sort of secrets left lying around for the cleaning woman to see, the spy must often operate at top levels of society, dangerously mixing political, social, and sexual intrigue all at the same time. For this, a tuxedo, or suitable evening wear for the ladies, is the order of the day. This held true from the days of Oppenheim and Wallace all the way to Ian Fleming.

Then along came John le Carré and changed all that with *The Spy Who Came in from the Cold*, along with other, mainly British writers like Len Deighton, Adam Hall, and Brian Freemantle. The objective is still the same—to steal the other fellow's secrets—but the clothes are quite different. The tuxedos and ball gowns are still there, but they are always above and out of reach of the bureaucratic clerks, who betray their country as much out of boredom and resentment with their own un-importance as from any heartfelt political ideology. They are drab, rum-pled people, whose fingernails need a good cleaning, and whose clothes always have the decidedly unromantic odor of failure about them.

For a time the most fashionable offshoot of the spy novel was the Nazi novel. Whether the setting was in the days of WWII or the present, and whether the objective was precious military secrets, high-level assassi-nation, art treasures, gold and jewelry, secret weapons, or merely Hitler's missing testicle, the Nazis were the fellows we loved to hate the most. Never in the history of mankind has a group gone to such lengths to glorify and make fashionable their own villainy as did the Third Reich with its jackboots, black SS uniforms, skull-and-crossbones, Iron Crosses, monocles, Prussian haircuts, dueling scars, and crimson armbands em-blazoned with that all-pervasive symbol of hatred—the swastika. Against such overwhelming visual images, our hero and his ever-present ladylove seemed surely doomed.

But the hero was never what we were interested in. It was the boys in black and boots, and what even more diabolical plot they could come up with this time. The plots ranged further and further afield from the beautiful simplicity of Higgins's *The Eagle Has Landed*, Forsythe's *Odessa File*, and Follett's *Eye of the Needle* until, in the end, they became stories of clones and clowns, and the public grew tired of them. But don't count them out yet. The Third Reich doesn't die easily.

Currently, the hot item is the terrorist novel, in which a small group of terrorists—almost always backed by an evil Mideastern power—attempts to mimic the six o'clock news by planting a nuclear device in a city, or holding something highly visible—like the Statue of Liberty, the Super Bowl, the Golden Gate Bridge, jetliners, or oceangoing vessels and every-one nearby—hostage until its demands are met. The demands always begin with some political mumbo jumbo and end with cold, hard cash—lots of it. And somehow, adding intensity, the U.S. and the USSR stand poised on the brink of nuclear war with the fate of the world in the balance.

Ski masks, camouflage fatigues, berets, and body odor are the uniform of the day for the terrorists, and once again it is civilian clothes for the hero and his girlfriend. But it is neither the hero nor the villains who are fashionable in these stories, it is the technology that the books glamorize. They feature in intimate, loving detail such things as death-ray lasers, high-tech computers, killer satellites, germ warfare, and, for the handy at home, instructions on how to build your very own atomic bomb.

Speaking of male sweat, there is nothing that gives you more, page per page, than the basic adventure novel and its country cousin, the mercenary novel.

Adventure novels are stories of men at work. Men, both hero and villain, wearing oil-spattered khakis, rain slickers, or hooded parkas. Men whose high-risk occupations   charter boat captains, pilots, explorers, smugglers, engineers, and dreamers—are almost story enough, but as an added bonus, there is usually an "Indiana Jones" type of treasure at the end of the rainbow. The action is fast and furious, whether you are in the desert in Bagley's *Flyaway*, or the frozen wasteland in Kyle's *Cage of Ice*, or in war-torn Ethopia in Smith's *Cry Wolf*; and the sex is minimal, for at the end of one of their hell-for-leather days, there's nothing left in these fellows except the need for a strong drink and a good night's sleep.

The mercenary novel is a totally male domain. The cast is always a group of lovable, battle-scarred rogues chosen for one last dangerous mission. It is one last time to don the old khakis and camouflage, made distinctly individual by a lucky scarf, a well-worn beret, or a tasteful earring, and to go out against the might of the Reich, or thousands of little fellows in black pajamas, or literally millions of half-naked, screaming, African natives covered in war paint.

Our side always wins, no matter what. If the mercenaries accomplish their mission and get back—fine. If not, that's okay too, because the world is ultimately a better place without men who are identified by names and descriptions like "Frenchie, he was good with a knife," or "Wet Willie Peter, a hundred and eighty pounds of explosive rage with a short fuse."

But as the last burst of machine-gun fire brings down one of those rogues I have lovingly followed through page after page of travail, I always feel a lump in my throat and a desire to raise my glass in salute.

A

ABBEY, EDWARD. *The Monkey Wrench Gang.* 1975. A hilarious story of a lunatic gang composed of a doctor, his girlfriend, a Vietnam vet, and a Mormon who set out to sabotage progress in the Southwest. Abbey's writing is crisp, colorful, and excellent. He makes a wonderful thriller out of the idea of ecological preservation.   ††††

ABRAHAMS, PETER. *The Fury of Rachel Monette.* 1980. A promising plot in which Rachel Monette sets out to rescue her kidnapped daughter and revenge her husband's death, but that's as far as it gets. It's easy to see Rachel was written by a man, for she is totally void of all female emotion. She might as well have been a female James Bond.   †

ABRAHAMS, PETER. *Tongues of Fire.* 1982. A readable but disappointing thriller about an Israeli so bent on revenge against the Arabs that he trains his son to become a leader of Islam in order to bring destruction from within.   ††

MEN'S ACTION SERIES.   These are the super-special-secret-agent/assassin/lover/fighter/wild-bull-rider stories which fill the revolving racks at all bus stations, grocery stores, drug stores, etc. Compared to mystery or adventure fiction on the whole, they are awful, but they have sold millions and millions and millions and. . . . So they must be doing something right.

AHERN, JERRY.   The Survivalist series. The first of the post WWIII series. John Thomas Rourke survives thanks to a hideout so fabulous that it makes the "Bat Cave" look like a low-rent motel without an ice machine. By the middle of the first book, the body count is over 140 million dead. I wondered what he was going to do for a climax, but he pulled one off worthy of "Mad Max."

The Nightmare Begins. 1981. The war over, America is partially destroyed, partially in the hands of the Russians, and partially in the hands of brigands. Rourke sets out to find his family and proves it is a big country out there. †††

ALBANY, JAMES. The SAS series. A WWII British commando series, with some pretty good writing.

Warrior Caste. 1982. The Germans and British both want a mysterious Englishman hiding in a French village. ††

BARKER, WADE. The Ninja Master series. Although only *Dragon Rising*, 1985, has hit the stands at the time of writing, it is easy to see this is going to be one of the very best of the action series. It combines a love of darkness, exotic people, places, and things, and a hatred of evil not seen since the days of the Shadow and the Green Hornet. Look for more of this one.

CARTER, NICK. There is no Nick Carter, just eight million ghostwriters and a succession of editors. He's changed from the old days of being a detective and now is just another superagent in the deadly game of espionage. But in spite of all his changes, his fans remain loyal. Give 'em hell, Nick.

The Human Time Bomb. 1969. This could be about anything from a madman's scheme to the unhappy results of overeating. I prefer the latter, but unfortunately it is about the former. †

DA CRUZ, DANIEL. The Jock Sargent series. Sargent is so macho—he's an ex-con, black belt, etc.—in so many absurd situations that I always think of Dean Martin when I read him.

Deep Kill. 1974. Sargent goes under water with three killers and a nymphomaniac. This one is just for laughs. †

DENNIS, RALPH. The Hardman series. This Atlanta-based, private-eye series is one of the best of the men's action series, keeping very much in the tradition of Mickey Spillane and Brett Halliday.

Atlanta Deathwatch. 1974. Murder is the name of the game when Hardman and his sidekick Hump Evans get involved with politicians, blondes, and the black mafia. †††

MARLOWE, DAN J.   The Drake series. As in Earl Drake, top-level thief and bank robber. The writing in this series is hard-boiled in tone and very similar to Brett Halliday's Mike Shayne series, but the plotting is closer to the "Man From Orgy."

Operation Flashpoint.   1970. Drake is blackmailed into helping the government rid itself of yet another group of Mideast terrorists.   †

MURPHY, WARREN.   The Digger series. A hard-boiled series about an insurance investigator. Nowhere near as good as the Destroyer series.

Fool's Flight.   1982. Digger investigates a plane crash with a passenger load of converts en route to a retreat headed by a religious weirdo.   ††

MURPHY, WARREN, AND SAPIR, RICHARD.   The Destroyer series. (Later written solely by Warren Murphy.) My personal favorite of all the action series. The plotting is so much better than every other series that it puts them all to shame. Remo Williams, aka the Destroyer, and his sidekick and martial arts instructor Chiun find themselves in stories incredible enough to rival any Saturday afternoon serial.

Chinese Puzzle.   1972. This is one of the more ordinary plots as the president calls for Remo and Chiun to stop a United States–Red China confrontation.
                    †††

Sweet Dreams.   1976. Remo and Chiun try to keep the Mafia and Hollywood from gaining control of a device which will let you watch your fantasies on television. This was before the VCR.   †††

PENDLETON, DON.   The Executioner series. The best-selling action series of them all. This is the one that began the whole craze. Sales to date are in the mega-millions with no end in sight. The early books (published by Pinnacle) pit Mack Bolan against organized crime. However, a change of publisher (to Gold Eagle) has broadened the scope of Bolan's anger to now include evil wherever it is found worldwide.

War Against the Mafia.   1969. This is the first of the series and details how Mack Bolan's father goes crazy, murders the Bolan family, and then commits suicide, and then how Mack, showing the same strain of instability as his father decides the Mafia is to blame. He begins a killing spree which lasts for many books.   †††

Tehran Wipeout.   1985. That old meanie, the Ayatollah Khomeini, is up to his dirty tricks, and Mack Bolan joins forces with the rebels to save the country. ††

SPENCER, RICK. The Viking Cipher series. Our hero, Eric Ivorsen, modeled on James Bond, tries to keep his father's work—some kind of mumbo jumbo about a global forecast—from falling into the hands of the bad guys. What makes this interesting is that Rick Spencer is a pretty good writer.

Icebound. 1983. Eric and the beautiful Maggie are one step ahead—or behind—an assassin and a master of crime. †††

STANTON, KEN. The Aquanauts series. It features Commander William Martin and the Secret Underwater Service. The quality of the writing is especially good for a men's action series, more like Alistair MacLean than the "Executioner."

Ten Seconds to Zero. 1970. The first of the series. Martin battles the Russians, who are destroying our submarines with a new underwater missile. †††

ALBRAND, MARTHA. Author of spy suspense thrillers in the Helen MacInnes mode, although she has also written mainstream fiction and at least one police procedural.

Without Orders. 1943. Charles Barrett wakes up in a hospital with no memory of how he got there. Everyone tells him his name is da Ponte. It's WWII, and he has to get out of this mess and get back to the front. ††

Remembered Anger. 1946. Paris, 1945. Chester Burton, an American intelligence officer, was reported dead a year ago. He's alive and on a secret mission, passing as a French POW—until he meets his former fiancée. Together they discover a Nazi plot to incriminate her new lover. †††

Desperate Moment. 1951. A man convicted of a murder he didn't commit escapes from a German prison to find the woman he loves and clear his name. The plot is melodramatic and convoluted, with a predictable but sensitive love triangle, and there are moments of real suspense. †††

Nightmare in Copenhagen. 1954. The detailed colorful Copenhagen setting is the best part of this espionage gothic, in which a young Danish woman and a stalwart American pursue and are pursued by a German spy ring. †††

A Call from Austria. 1963. An American in search of his brother, a missing mountaineer, gets sidetracked by romance and scared by attempts on his life. In the spirit of the plucky but ordinary guy who can rise to any challenge, he saves his brother and the Free World too. ††††

ALLBEURY, TED. A very fine English spy writer. His stories combine a good deal of action with well-designed plots—and he is prolific, too.

Snowball. 1974. An agent is sent to retrieve papers from the Russians which show the U.S. and Canada contemplated forgetting about England during WWII. †††

The Special Collection. 1977. A Communist plot begins in the closing days of WWII. Now, twenty-five years later, it raises its ugly head to cause industrial and social chaos in Britain. Only British agent Stephen Felinski can stop it.
††††

Moscow Quadrille. 1978. The title of this excellent spy novel comes from the four people—a Russian actor, a wife, a Russian beauty, and a British diplomat— who engage in a dance of betrayal and death set against a backdrop of contemporary Moscow. ††††

The Reaper. 1980. A woman filled with a desire for revenge against the Nazis single-handedly takes on the SS alumni organization, Odessa. This is for fans of Forsythe's *Odessa File.* †††

AMBLER, ERIC. A major contributor to the development of the modern, morally ambiguous novel of intrigue. In his books, survival, not patriotism, is the name of the game, and his sometimes unlikely heroes flounder in a murky world where good and evil aren't easily distinguishable.

Epitaph for a Spy. 1938. On the eve of WWII, a young teacher is seized by the French secret police and accused of spying. Showing the double and triple lives of spies and the hollowness at the core of those lives, Ambler breaks free forever of the Valentine Williams and Phillips Oppenheim stereotypes. †††

A Coffin for Dimitrios. 1939. In one of the great intrigue novels, a writer delves into the muddy past of a mysterious, international double-dealing spy. The writer of academic detective novels discovers the difference between fiction and reality when he becomes involved in murder. †††††

Journey into Fear. 1940. In the course of a simple business trip to Istanbul, Graham is marked for assassination by the agents of three countries. Unable to solve the situation by reasoning with it, he is forced to take action to stay alive. ††††

Passage of Arms. 1959. Set in the Far East, this is a tale of opium and munitions smuggling in which business means blackmail and treachery. A pair of amateur adventurers from Wilmington, Delaware, get caught up in the intrigue. Their view of the Far East gives Ambler a chance for some humor. ††††

The Light of Day. 1962. A straight crime novel with an international setting, concerning an attempt to steal the treasure of Istanbul's richest museum. It was made into a movie called *Topkapi.* †††

Dirty Story. 1967. Simpson, the star of *The Light of Day*, returns to tell his life story with engaging sleaziness. Ranging from pornography in Athens to politics in Africa, it's not a pretty story, but somebody has to live it. ††††

The Intercom Conspiracy. 1969. Charles Latimer, hero of *A Coffin for Dimitrios*, disappears while researching a book on NATO. The plot goes on to involve a right-wing conspiracy and two top spies who want to come in from the cold. Not one of his best works. ††

The Levanter. 1972. Howell, a Levanter who is Armenian, Lebanese, Greek Cypriot, Syrian, and even a bit British, is drawn into politics despite himself. Also not one of his best works. ††

The Care of Time. 1981. Robert Haliday, a ghostwriter who helps celebrities write their autobiographies, receives a letter from a terrorist, who insists that he collaborate on a book. A real gem, very much like Ross Thomas. ††††

ANDERS, K. T. *Legacy of Fear.* 1985. The cover on this paperback original smacked too much of a hard-boiled novel and probably hurt sales. The story is a well-written spy chase set in Paris with lots of local color. The believable heroine has her hands full. Hitchcock could have made a good movie out of this one. †††

ANDERSON, JAMES. *The Abolition of Death.* (n.d.) Similar in style to Desmond Cory's Johnny Fedora stories. Somewhat vague as to the "whys, wheres, and wherefores," assassin Mikael Petros must save the formula for everlasting life from the bad guys. ††

ANDRESS, LESLIE. *Caper.* 1980. Jannie Shean, author of caper novels, has her latest rejected because she has lost touch with what her editor perceives as the reality of crime, so she sets out to plot her own crime, using real people. But the crime gets out of hand, and what was funny turns deadly serious. ††††

ANTHONY, EVELYN. Usually likened to Helen MacInnes. Their novels are similar with suspenseful international settings, but Anthony's are more romantic and told from a feminine point of view. She is best at stories where hatred turns to love as the heroine finds her destiny in the arms of an enemy.

The Poellenberg Inheritance. 1972. The inheritance is a Cellini saltcellar, the action is cosmopolitan European, and the plot involves a beautiful young woman's search for her mysterious father. Along the way she encounters Nazis, a private detective, and decayed royalty. She and the detective are on opposite sides and a collision course toward love. ††††

Mission to Malaspiga. 1974. Moving through high-life settings in New York and Italy, including her ancestral gothic castle, Katherine di Malaspiga Dexter becomes embroiled in a family mystery and an ugly, drug-smuggling racket. The current head of the family, her sworn enemy, is tall, dark, and handsome. †††

The Persian Price. 1975. The neglected wife of an oil tycoon is the target of a gang of Iranian terrorists, who kidnap her for political reasons. Politics is less important to the plot than passion, as she is assaulted by one of her captors and falls in love with another. †††

The Janus Imperative. 1979. A mystery left over from the last days of the Third Reich surfaces in modern Paris. The plot isn't terribly logical, but it's colorful, featuring Nazis, gay lovers, assassins, and convents, as well as a political journalist (married) and a beautiful German woman (freshly widowed). Do they, or don't they? †††

The Defector. 1980. A defecting KGB agent and a highly placed female British intelligence agent fall in love; her mission is to get his wife out of Russia. The result is a complicated but satisfying mishmash of patriotism and passion, with some good action scenes. †††

The Avenue of the Dead. 1982. This sequel to *The Defector* isn't quite as good as its predecessor, but it has its moments. It takes British agent Davina Graham to Washington, D.C., and Mexico as she unravels a plot leaked to her old school friend, who has somehow discovered that the Russians are trying to take over the world. ††

ARCHER, JEFFREY. *Shall We Tell the President?* 1977. An updating of *Seven Days in May*. Ted Kennedy is president and there is a plot afoot which Special Agent Marc Andrews has six days to figure out. Not one of Archer's best efforts. ††

ARICHA, AMOS. A man enamored with assassins and terrorists.

Phoenix. 1979. The world's best assassin is hired to kill Moshe Dayan. ††

Hour of the Clown. (n.d.) His most ambitious work. Russia sends a load of terrorists to kill America's top men. †††

Journey Toward Death. (n.d.) Mossad agent Nimrod Eden becomes involved with a mystic as he tries to stop a group of assassins, who are leaving bodies from New York to California. ††

ARNOLD, WILLIAM. *China Gate.* 1983. A story based on American students in a Taiwan university who band together to fight Chinese and Formosan gangs. They build a financial empire by questionable means and get caught up in politics. †††

ASHFORD, JEFFREY. *A Sense of Loyalty.* 1984. A novel of industrial espionage set in the English auto industry. Unfortunately the book doesn't work because the author has so many plot devices he can't adequately explore even half of them in a novel of this somewhat short length. ††

B

BAGLEY, DESMOND. One of the absolute best thriller writers to ever put pen to paper. His recent passing will be long mourned by those addicted to adventure. His work bears a marked similarity to the early Maclean novels, except that in many cases they are much better researched.

The Golden Keel. 1963. An English shipbuilder, a South African ex-sergeant, his drunken co-conspirator, and an Italian contessa devise a scheme to recover the buried treasure of Mussolini. Stalked by a cunning soldier of fortune, their successful conclusion is even more hampered by a sudden Mediterranean storm. This one is about average for Bagley. ††††

The Spoilers. 1969. A group of daring men—a torpedo mechanic, a soldier of fortune, a con man, a psychologist, and a newspaperman—are recruited by Dr. Nicholas Warren to work on a film set in the colorful Iranian desert. The film, of course, is a decoy to cover the real reason for gathering together such a group. ††††

The Freedom Trap. 1971. Owen Stannard has to stop the Scarperers—a gang who specialize in prison breaks—and Slade—a recently sprung, Russian double agent—in a fast-moving, tense thriller. †††

Snow Tiger. 1975. A tense story which investigates the cause of an avalanche. There is an excellent court scene which is somewhat of a departure for Bagley. ††††

Flyaway. 1978. My favorite. A classic adventure novel in which Max Stafford, the head of Stafford Security Consultants, is feeling desk-bound with his success, so he decides to follow up on an employee who has left the firm under rather hurried circumstances. However, it becomes evident there is more to the man's departure than meets the eye. Stafford stays on the trail all the way to North Africa as the former employee searches for signs of his famous, missing aviator-father among the Tuaregs. You will learn more about life in the African desert than you ever wanted to know.   †††††

BAKER, IVON.   *Grave Doubt.* (n.d.) Our hero, made redundant by a Ministry of Defense economy move, is hired by an industrialist to investigate a buried airplane on his property in the south of England. When it turns out to be a WWII Heinkel bomber, he finds himself enmeshed in a web of treason, deception, and murder which involves his own former work.   †††

BARAK, MICHAEL.   *The Secret List of Heinrich Roehm.* 1976. The target is Middle East oil and the obliteration of Israel. Everything is set to go unless an agent and a beautiful woman can stop it.   ††

BARAK, MICHAEL.   *The Enigma.* 1978. Francis de Belvoir (known as the Baron) and a beautiful woman undertake to steal the German code machine from the Nazis. Sounds like a Dennis Wheatley story, only Wheatley does it better. ††

BARAK, MICHAEL.   *The Phantom Conspiracy.* 1980. Clint Craig, American author, discovers that Hermann Goering may not have committed suicide as history reports. Craig follows the twisted trail, which leads to the White House and a confrontation with the Arabs over oil.   †††

BARAK, MICHAEL.   *The Deadly Document.* 1980. A history student finds a fascinating letter and is murdered. The CIA gets involved.   ††

BARBOUR, ALAN G.   *Cliffhanger.* 1977. A history of the adventure serials of the old Saturday matinee days. The last word for serial buffs. Loaded with pictures. Terrific.   †††††

BARCLAY, IAN.   *The Crime Minister.* 1984. The world's best assassin, Richard Dartley, takes on Ali Osker, the world's biggest drug dealer, whose enterprise is backed by the Russians.   †††

BARLAY, STEPHEN.   *In the Company of Spies.* 1981. In the midst of Kennedy/Khrushchev confrontation in 1962, Helm Rust slips into Russia, hoping to free his father. Once there, he meets a beautiful woman who tries to take his mind off business.   †††

BASS, RONALD.   *Lime's Crisis.* 1982. The U.S. brings Harry Lime in from the cold to act as middleman in a global threat. I started to read it, but it didn't hold my attention enough to finish it. The author should have used a different name for his hero. Graham Greene already used it. †

BEACH, EDWARD L. *Cold Is the Sea.* 1978. A first-rate submarine novel from the *best* of all submarine writers. (He also wrote *Run Silent, Run Deep.*) The nuclear sub *Cushing*, on an Arctic mission, has a collision with an enemy vessel. Damaged, the sub has no choice but to await the inevitable showdown. ††††

BEATTY, DAVID. *The Temple Tree.* 1971. A plane crashes at a Sri Lankan airport, built on what is considered to be sacred ground. Hannaker, investigating the crash, becomes involved with the airline's chief pilot, an attractive stewardess, the owner of a communications company, and an inscrutable religious leader. Suspicious because the gold cargo does not show up in the wreckage, he tries to prevent a second crash which he is sure is coming. ††††

BENCHLEY, PETER. *Jaws.* 1974. The classic story of a great white shark terrorizing a New England community. †††††

BENCHLEY, PETER. *The Deep.* 1976. It is tough to follow a book like *Jaws*, but Benchley tried with this novel of romance and high adventure in the Carribbean in which a pair of honeymooners explore the ocean floor in search of treasure. ††††

BENCHLEY, PETER. *The Island.* 1979. Weaker than the others. A story of missing boats and island pirates who go back a ways in history. †††

BLACK, GAVIN. *You Want to Die, Johnny?* 1966. It is murder in Borneo as Paul Harris, English businessman, flies friends home. †††

BLACK, GAVIN. *The Cold Jungle.* 1969. Paul Harris comes home to London to buy ships, but his friend, the shipbuilder, is murdered. †††

BLEECK, OLIVER. *The Highbinders.* 1974. St. Ives finds himself in London trying to recover the St. Louis Sword, which has been stolen. †††

BLEECK, OLIVER. *No Questions Asked.* 1976. St. Ives, the professional go-between, acts as the middleman to recover a rare copy of Pliny's *Historia Naturalis*. †††

BOBKER, LEE J. *The Unicorn Group.* 1979. An elite group of U.S. espionage agents is being infiltrated and some agents are eliminated. Suspicion deepens that one of the group is behind the whole thing. A retired professor, who started the group, is brought in to match wits with the traitor in a deadly chess game which leads to a satisfying climax. ††††

BOBKER, LEE J. *Flight of a Dragon.* 1981. The second most powerful man in China is defecting to the West, and David Lincoln, an agent in place, is detailed to get him there safely. The intelligence centers of four great powers vie for control of Li Peng, while, unknown to them, the gears of oriental vengeance are slipping into place to satisfy an old enmity which dictates Peng's ritual death.   †††

BOWICK, DOROTHY MULLER. *Tapestry of Death.* 1973. A French scientist discovers the secret of youth, but with it goes horror and death as Diana Marshall blunders along in a mystery that is part gothic and part "had-I-but-known." ††

BRIERLY, DAVID. *Blood Group "O."* 1980. A standard terrorist novel, relieved by the constant violent action of the story. Cody is a female James Bond, employed irregularly by the French Sûreté. Here she is trying to stop the assassination of a foreign dignitary by the terrorist group self-named Blood Group "O." She has added incentive in that one of the leaders was responsible for the death of her lover.   †††

BROWNE, GERALD. *19 Purchase Street.* 1982. A well-written but farfetched novel about the Mafia becoming the pawns of the WASP business establishment in a money-laundering scheme. A good, fat beach book that doesn't require too much attention.   †††

BUCHAN, JOHN.   One of the masters in the espionage field. He brought the chase novel into its present form with his famous *Thirty-nine Steps.* His basic form has been followed ever since, by writers up to and including Ludlum. The man was great, there's no getting around it. He was simply great.

Prester John.   1910. A young Scotsman gets involved with rebellious natives and a fabulous hidden treasure in South Africa. The charismatic native leader is a powerful, unforgettable character.   ††††

The Thirty-nine Steps.   1915. A true classic in which Richard Hannay leads the police and a bevy of German spies on a wild-goose chase across the Scottish moors as he struggles to avert an international crisis. It's a bluff, no-nonsense adventure, and if it seems to rely a bit too heavily on coincidence, the fast pace and brisk dialogue cover any flaws.   †††††

Greenmantle.   1916. Hannay is again on the job for England. This time he's in Constantinople, trying to keep Turkey out of WWI and head off a fanatical holy war in the Near East.   ††††

The Power House.   1916. Similar to *The Thirty-nine Steps* in some ways, this book is also the story of one man against a vast, incredible conspiracy. Edward Leithen—not at all a man of action until forced to it—is the only one who has discovered the terrifying truth about a gentlemanly traitor. Leithen must lie low in London while he carries on an almost surrealistic battle of wits.   ††††

Mr. Standfast. 1919. Hannay again battles a German conspiracy in the early days of the war. With the American agent he met in *Greenmantle* and Peter Pienaar, a comrade from his days on the South African veldt, Hannay struggles against a sinister and formidable German mastermind. The trench warfare in France comes grimly alive. ††††

The Three Hostages. 1924. The war is over, and Hannay has returned to the quiet life of a country gentleman. But although the wars of nations have ended, crime endures. Hannay is called in to deal with a particularly ugly and dangerous kidnapper-extortionist. Good suspense and unusual characters. †††

John McNab. 1925. This offbeat adventure stars Edward Leithen. Three jaded professional men decide upon a spell of poaching in the Scottish highlands as the cure for their boredom, and they bag bigger game than originally planned. †††††

The Courts of Morning. 1929. In this too-long-overlooked adventure, characters from the Richard Hannay and Edward Leithen books meet in the mythical republic of Olifa. It's in South America, which one plainspoken Scot describes as "too big and too badly put together." The story combines action, mystery, romance, espionage, travelogue, and domestic comedy in a vivid, volatile setting. ††††

The Island of Sheep. 1936. In Richard Hannay's last adventure, he receives a mysterious message from a dying man and is forced to remember a long-forgotten episode thirty years ago in Africa. To fulfill an old pact, and to win a treasure, he goes to a desolate island, where he must forget how to be a gentleman and remember how to survive against a brutal enemy. †††

BUCKLEY, WILLIAM F., JR. Yes, *The* William F. Buckley, Jr., writes thrillers. Damn good ones in which Buckley puts aside his big words and just tells a straightforward story with style and humor. His hero is Blackford Oakes, a devil-may-care CIA man.

Saving the Queen. 1976. A solid beginning in which Oakes comes to the aid of the Queen of England—both physically and sexually. ††††

Stained Glass. 1978. Oakes finds himself in the middle of an attempt by Count Axel Wintergrin to reunify East and West Germany. †††

Who's on First? 1980. Oakes goes to Paris to kidnap a Russian scientist to tip the balance of power in the space race. †††

Marco Polo, If You Can. 1982. Oakes gets involved in the U-2 controversy. †††

BUTTERWORTH, MICHAEL. *The Man in the Sopwith Camel*. 1975. A very funny novel of a male mid-life crisis in which Ernest Kitteridge, a middle-aged bank clerk whose only escape is a fantasy involving a Sopwith Camel, sees his chance at romance and adventure when a recently promoted colleague dies during the celebration for his promotion. Ernest decides to impersonate him for embezzlement purposes, picking up a lady of the evening as a partner along the way. Similar to Graham Greene's *Travels with My Aunt*. †††

C

CAIDIN, MARTIN. *Aquarius Mission*. 1978. "Star Trek" of the deep. A team of scientists go in search of missing nuclear subs and find a civilization of amphibious people at the bottom of the sea. Imaginative and atmospheric. †††

CALLISON, BRIAN. *A Flock of Ships*. 1970. The merchant vessel *Cyclops* radios that it has been torpedoed and is sinking in the South Atlantic. This is in 1941. More than twenty-five years later, she is discovered in a landlocked harbor, and a document found aboard tells a story of war at sea, treason, heroism, and final victory in death. A superior read, a thriller from start to finish. ††††

CALVIN, HENRY. *It's Different Abroad*. 1963. The story of a young school-teacher who drives her new, red car into France only to be pursued by the bad guys. She is going to visit her sister, her brother-in-law, and their children. The interesting dynamic of the story is not the chase, but the relationship between the young single woman and her sister's family. †††

CAMPBELL, R. WRIGHT. *The Spy Who Sat and Waited*. 1975. A melancholy German spy, Willhelm Oerter, settles in Scotland after WWI, marries, and raises a family there. When Hitler comes to power, Will is pressed back into service and ordered to betray his new family and adopted homeland. Short on action and long on windy, poetic speeches and descriptions. ††

CANNING, VICTOR. A strong thriller writer whose work can best be described as a "bridge" between the early writers like John Buchan and the late writers like Ludlum. He's well deserving of a read.

Panther's Moon. 1948. One of the first espionage and adventure tales from a prolific and consistent master of the trade. Roger Quain, supervising the shipment of his uncle's circus panthers from Milan to Paris, finds himself trailing them through the Swiss Alps after a train accident. But there is something about the panthers that invites murder and leads to a deadly confrontation in the snow. ††††

The Limbo Line. 1963. A spy story which never gets off the ground about a retired British spy who comes out of retirement to stop the Russians from brainwashing refugees and taking them back to Russia. Not one of his best, but this was the "Spy Who Came in from the Cold" era, and everyone was trying his hand at it. ††††

The Rainbird Pattern. 1972. My favorite by far of all his work; it is more mystery than thriller. This is a split-level story with two people kidnapping prominent officials, while at the same time, an elderly woman is trying to bring the missing elements of her family together before she dies. There seems no connection, but, as a lovable and charismatic psychic and her jack-of-all-trades partner seek the whereabouts of a man who disappeared years ago, the suspense mounts and culminates in violence, with the author delivering an unexpected aftershock in the final pages. †††††

The Vanishing Point. 1982. This is not one of Canning's best. The contrived plot is about a carefree French artist found to be actually the scion of a titled English family. As an infant he was kidnapped by his nurse. After an amicable, but uncomfortable, reunion with his parents, he leaves with a gift which turns out to contain material that several intelligence groups are anxious to recover. ††

CAPUTO, PHILIP. *Horn of Africa.* 1980. An unwieldy, overly long mercenary novel about three men who are hired to train a primitive African tribe in the fine art of modern warfare. ††

CARNEY, DANIEL. *The Wild Geese.* 1977. The mercenary novel par excellence. Rafer Janders and his old comrade, Colonel Faulkner, scare up a team for one last mission into Africa, to rescue the kidnapped Congolese leader, Julius Limbani, and return him to England. The mission makes sense, the outlook of the soldiers is appropriately romantic and bleak, and there's bloodshed galore. ††††

CARROLL, JAMES. *Family Trade.* 1982. Set in the Kennedy era, it is the story of a Washington family connected with the CIA and British Intelligence, and the strains put upon the college-age son when his uncle defects to the Russians. An otherwise good story is weakened badly by a huge amount of padding in the middle in the form of useless past history. †††

CAVE, PETER. *Foxbat.* 1978. Based on a real incident, a Russian pilot, Mikhail Volgolsky, is recruited by the CIA to steal a record-breaking plane and fly it out of Russia. An exciting chase in the air climaxes this technical, no-nonsense military tale. †††

CHARTERIS, LESLIE. Author of the Saint series featuring Simon Templar, who is handsome, urbane, and good with his fists. The Saint isn't exactly on the side of the law, but he fights crime wherever he finds it. His most deadly weapon is his unfailing sense of style.

The Saint and the Tiger.   1929. The first Saint book is also the best. In a remote coastal village in England, Templar tracks a ruthless smuggler and meets his future wife. It's one of those cases in which the villain must be one of a limited and unlikely group of suspects, and the solution is nicely handled.   ††††

The Last Hero.   1930. The Saint may be outside the law, but he *is* a patriot, as he proves in this mix-up with a mad scientist and a warmongering European crown prince. It's melodramatic and sentimental, but fun.   †††

The Saint and Mr. Teal.   1933. Chief Inspector Teal of Scotland Yard is the Saint's friendly enemy. This case takes the Saint to the Left Bank of Paris and then to court as he and Teal together try to nail an evil Egyptian.   †††

The Saint Intervenes.   1934. A collection of fourteen short stories in which con men, pornographers, thieves, and murderers are all grist to the Saint's mill.   ††††

The Saint at the Thieves' Picnic.   1937. Set in Spain, this book opens with a rip-roaring fight as the Saint saves a girl from an attempted abduction. It's a case of "ticket, ticket, who's got the ticket?" as the Saint tries to recover a stolen, winning lottery ticket.   †††

Call for the Saint.   1947. The Saint and his wife, Pat, are in Chicago where he finds out that the deadly King of the Beggars is really a queen. He also gets involved with a gang of boxing promoters and knocks out their villainy in an incredible fight to the finish.   †††

The Saint on the Spanish Main.   1955. The Saint visits the sunny Caribbean and has six tongue-in-cheek adventures on six different islands. Charteris uses native characters, dialects, and folklore effectively in some of these stories.   ††††

Vendetta for the Saint.   1964. This was the first new Saint novel in twenty years. It's set in Naples and Sicily, where the Saint runs afoul of the Mafia, which interrupts his lunch to murder a fellow British tourist. Both the author and the character are aware of the passage of time since the first adventures, and he now moves a step slower.   †††

The Saint Abroad.   1969. Based on two television episodes, this book was approved, but not written by, Charteris. In the first tale, the Saint saves a woman from abduction and ends up helping her sell five priceless paintings. In the second, he travels to Nagawiland in the African tropics to protect a prime minister from blackmail.   †††

Catch the Saint.   1975. Another volume okayed by Charteris. This book delves into the Saint's past for pre-WWII experiences. It's successful, because the 1930s and 1940s suit the Saint's style better than current times.   †††

CHASE, JAMES HADLEY.   His work falls somewhere in that gray area between mystery and thrillers. Although he is British, his work is a far cry from your run-of-the-mill Agatha Christie or Sherlock Holmes stories; it is violent in nature and often centering around capers. His readers are the type of people who prefer thrillers to mysteries.

No Orchids for Miss Blandish.   1939. This is a classic—of a type. Some feel it is the most violent novel ever written. While I doubt it, it still remains a gut-wrenching story of the sadistic kidnapping of Miss Blandish, a young, beautiful heiress.   †††††

Well Now, My Pretty.   1967. Serge Maisky has his eye on the casino and its $2 million, when a beautiful, greedy, young woman and her weak husband get involved. Serge gets angry.   ††

Just a Matter of Time.   1972. Another kidnap story. This time the target is Alice Morley-Johnson, a wealthy, retired concert pianist who has a penchant for jewelry and attractive young men. The gang: a master forger, a loose woman, and a pretty boy. Sound sleazy?   ††

Hit Them Where It Hurts.   1984. Dirk Wallace is hired to find out who is blackmailing Mrs. Thorsen's daughter. It turns out organized crime is involved.   ††

CHEYNEY, PETER.   Author of several series of both detective and spy novels. Among the detectives were Slim Callaghan and Lemmy Caution. They are similar to Mickey Spillane's Mike Hammer. Today his spy series of "Dark" books is more often read.

Can Ladies Kill?   1938. Lemmy Caution is an FBI special agent who must have been hired in a year when the Bureau relaxed its requirements. He narrates this slangy story of smuggling in San Francisco and dalliance with a dazzling Chinese girl—who happens to be the number one suspect in a murder case.
                                                                                                                                      †††

It Couldn't Matter Less.   1941. Slim Callaghan is a much suaver version of Lemmy Caution, but equally deadly with a wisecrack and a punch in the nose. Between shots of Canadian Club and rounds of repartee, he solves the mystery of a missing young man. Even though the case involves drugs, secret codes, and exotic Russian émigrés, Callaghan probably wouldn't have touched it if the victim hadn't had the qualities that appeal to him most: a beautiful sister and a wealthy mother.   †††

Dark Wanton.   1948. Everard Peter Quayle, who appears in several books in this series, is a smooth and subtle British counterspy, middle-aged but by no means past his prime. In this story he pulls the strings in a complicated espionage plot involving a Spanish "lounge lizard," an agent out to make a spectacular comeback, and a dedicated virgin. ††††

Dark Bahama. 1950. This book's hero is Johnny Vallon, who works for Chennault Investigations. Also appearing is Ernest Guelvada, who works as an agent for the British government, but enjoys a little knife play on a freelance basis. The setting is a sensual isolated island in the Bahamas. †††

CHIU, TONY. *Realm Seven.* 1984. Andrea Matteson becomes concerned by her daughter's involvement in a Dungeons and Dragons type of game called "Realm." When the game's demands escalate to murder, Andrea must crisscross the country to locate the malevolent source of "Realm." Well written but you have to be practically a genius to understand the game as Chiu explains it.
†††

CLANCY, TOM. *The Hunt for Red October.* 1985. This first novel is a high-tech sea hunt involving the navies and intelligence services of the Soviet Union, England, and the U.S. The commander of the latest model Soviet submarine decides to defect to the West, and the search for him creates a global crisis.
††††

CLARK, ERIC. *China Run.* 1985. A low-key thriller in which the hero, an American engineer studying Chinese locomotives, is on the run through the People's Republic of China with a female Chinese government guide. A Russian defector has been found dead in the American's hotel room, and the chase is on to recover a top-secret file. A good read. ††††

COLES, MANNING. In addition to the celebrated *Drink to Yesterday* and *Toast to Tomorrow,* Coles wrote a number of other adventures featuring Tommy Hambledon, the glib, suave British hero.

They Tell No Tales. 1942. A bit longer than some of Coles's later offerings, this book features Tommy Hambledon as a straightforward police investigator in a murder case. The plotting is tight, the naval harbor setting done well, and the tone wry. †††

Green Hazard. 1945. Believed killed in a chemical explosion, Tommy Hambledon turns up in Nazi Germany, where he attempts to mess up the Reich's scientific research. †††

Not Negotiable. 1949. Tommy Hambledon cooperates with the Sûreté and holds passionate Frenchwomen at bay while tracking down a continental counterfeiting gang. ††

Now or Never. 1951. Hambledon returns to Germany to foil the machinations of a coven of born-again Nazis. Martin Bormann does a "walk-on." ††

Alias Uncle Hugo. 1952. In what is perhaps his most hilarious adventure, Hambledon dons a bewildering variety of disguises—beginning with Comrade Commissar Peskoff—in an attempt to rescue a young crown prince from Russia. †††

COLLINS, LARRY, AND LaPIERRE, DOMINQUE. *The Fifth Horseman.* 1980. Four years of research went into this chilling story of a terrorist group who plants a hydrogen bomb in New York City. To date, this is the best terrorist novel ever written. †††††

COOK, ROBIN. *Fever.* 1982. The author of *Coma* turns his hand to the medical-industrial complex, as Dr. Charles Martel tries to save his daughter's life. †††

COPPEL, ALFRED. *The Apocalypse Brigade.* 1981. Although this book had good sales, I couldn't finish it. To me, it was just another nuclear brinksmanship novel filled with Arabs, the CIA, a secret mercenary army, sex, and violence. †

CORNELISEN, ANN. *Any Four Women Could Rob the Bank of Italy.* 1983. A good caper novel written with humor and style in which four women do exactly as the title suggests. †††

CORY, DESMOND. *Undertow.* 1962. Johnny Fedora tries to outwit the Russians and find a sunken sub near Spain. Good James Bond type of story. †††

CORY, DESMOND. *Deadfall.* 1965. A well-told tale of complex relationships between a jewel thief, his mistress, and her homosexual husband, whose role proves even deeper as the book progresses, set against the backdrop of a heist in Spain. †††

CORY, DESMOND. *Mountainhead.* 1966. Johnny Fedora tangles with a mad Englishman in the Himalayas and an espionage plot that reaches all the way from London to Nepal. ††

COSGROVE, VINCENT. *The Hemingway Papers.* 1983. An excellent thriller based on a true incident when Hadley, Ernest Hemingway's first wife, left a suitcase containing all his work in progress on a Paris train. The suitcase was lost and Cosgrove builds an entertaining "what-if" thriller around it that is a must for all Hemingway fans. ††††

CRICHTON, MICHAEL. *Congo.* 1980. One of the greatest thrillers I have ever read. It combines the Congo region of Africa, a gorilla with a six-hundred-word sign language vocabulary, a super-sophisticated computer company, and the lost city of Zinji from H. Rider Haggard. Great fun. †††††

CUNNINGHAM, JERE. *Hunter's Moon.* 1977. Just when you thought it was safe to go into the woods again, another group of hunters runs afoul of a pack of web-footed, inbred, no-neck hillbillies, hellbent on sodomy and murder. Sounds a bit like *Deliverance*, doesn't it? ††

CUSSLER, CLIVE. In order to give some other folks a chance I'm only reviewing one of Cussler's massive best sellers here, but he is a "must read." He never disappoints from the first page to the last.

Night Probe. 1981. Dirk Pitt, salvage expert, is brought in to locate a missing train and a missing boat in the hopes of finding a treaty between the U.S. and Canada and staving off world problems. ††††

D

DAVIDSON, LIONEL. *The Night of Wenceslaus.* 1960. A behind-the-Iron-Curtain thriller in which a bewildered amateur, in the Eric Ambler mold, is thrust into professional intrigue. It's sink or swim, and he swims—right into the arms of a burly Czech blonde. †††

DAVIDSON, LIONEL. *The Rose of Tibet.* 1962. A naive young artist *bicycles* into forbidden Tibet where he finds surprising passion and a fortune in gems. Written only a few years after the Chinese invasion of Tibet, *Rose* makes excellent use of the turbulent political background. A real classic in the field. †††††

DAVIDSON, LIONEL. *The Menorah Men.* 1966. Buried somewhere in Israel is a lost treasure, the central symbol of Judaism. The Israelis want to recover it. The Arabs want to destroy it. The Israelis have a brilliant young professor. The Arabs have an endless supply of terrorists. Lots of sex, and a good job of blending historic and contemporary violence. †††

DAVIS, BART. *Blind Prophet.* 1983. A science fiction crossover with a potential satellite war in outer space, triggered by yet another Soviet crop failure. Only shuttle pilot Christopher Leyland and the beautiful Dr. Arielle Simmons, computer scientist, can save the world. †††

DAVIS, PHIL. *Nemesis.* 1979. A world-takeover novel filled with the likes of Klaus Wagner, neo-Nazi, epileptic, psychopath; General Marley, retired general, manufacturer of atomic explosives, fanatic; Reverend Robert Carson, great spiritual leader, fascist, hemorrhoid sufferer. ††

DE BORCHRAVE, ARNAUD, AND MOSS, ROBERT. *The Spike.* 1981. An excellent but convoluted novel about worldwide intrigue and manipulation of the news. It makes you wonder if maybe there isn't more than a grain of truth to the story. ††††

DEIGHTON, LEN.   One of the best spy writers in the history of the field. His early works feature a nameless spy (played by Michael Caine and called Harry Palmer in the movies). After six taut, well-executed thrillers, Deighton abandoned his hero to pursue subjects in the thriller vein which were not as confining as a series. His work can best be described as "le Carré with action."

The Ipcress File.   1962. A brilliant debut in which Harry Palmer tries to stop a band of kidnappers who specialize in erasing the memory of scientists. †††††

Horse Under Water.   1963. Deighton strays dangerously close to James Bond territory in this story of Harry Palmer, a sunken sub, and a beautiful sexpot.
†††

Funeral in Berlin.   1964. Unquestionably a classic. Harry Palmer acts as a middleman in a Berlin exchange operation between the British and the Russians. In this masterpiece, Deighton captures the feeling of Berlin at the height of the 1960s Cold War better than anyone before or since.   †††††

The Billion Dollar Brain.   1965. Harry Palmer has to stop a mad Texan from taking over the world in this combination of James Bond and Dr. Strangelove.   †††

An Expensive Place to Die.   1967. Harry Palmer gets involved in passing phony information down the pipeline to the Russians. The best part of this story is the strong picture of Paris that Deighton paints.   ††††

Spy Story.   1974. Harry Palmer gets appointed to the Strategic War Games Center in London. After a flat tire, Palmer goes to his *old* apartment to make a phone call and finds all his possessions duplicated there.   ††††

SS–GB.   1978. An excellent novel about a murder investigation in Nazi-occupied England. The story works very well because Deighton uses just the right touch of atmosphere.   ††††

XPD.   1981. A Ludlum type of thriller in which Great Britain, America, Germany, and Russia are pitted against each other over some document signed a lifetime ago between Churchill and Hitler.   ††††

Berlin Game.   1983. A well-written novel about a mole in the heart of the British spy system. Unfortunately, it is marred by a disturbing similarity to le Carré's *Tinker, Tailor, Soldier, Spy.*   †††

Mexico Set.   1985. The sequel to *Berlin Game.* The traitor from *Berlin,* now safely in Russia, sets out to make trouble for Bernard Sampson.   ††††

DELANEY, LAURENCE. *The Triton Ultimatum.* 1977. A group of terrorists commandeer a Triton sub, loaded with Polaris missiles, and demand $4 billion in gold or the world goes up in flames. Can you imagine what $4 billion in gold weighs? †

DeMARIA, ROBERT. *Out-Break.* 1978. A disaster novel built around the outbreak of Legionnaires' disease. It's a yawner. †

DeMILLE, NELSON. *Cathedral.* 1981. It is St. Patrick's Day, and a group of IRA terrorists seize St. Patrick's Cathedral. Their demands—the release of all the prisoners from Ireland's Long Kesh prison, or it is the end of the Cathedral and the hostages inside. DeMille has worked hard to showcase the delicate Irish question in a well-written thriller. †††

DEMOUZON (NO FIRST NAME). *The First-Born of Egypt.* 1979. The most offbeat assassin novel I have ever come across. Marcel Ribot undertakes a series of little killings throughout Europe. The world does not hang in the balance. In fact nobody important is killed. It borders on the surreal. †††

DERBY, MARK. *Afraid in the Dark.* 1951. Patrick Derrey, broken in body and spirit after being tortured by Indonesian terrorists, is offered the job of finding and killing a Eurasian, Dr. Mengele-type, who caused the death of the wife of an English military man. Accompanied by his old sweetheart, Derrey travels to Malaya and finds himself in a death duel with his enemies, and also trapped by his claustrophobia in a thrilling and lethal climax. ††††

DERBY, MARK. *The Bad Step.* 1954. A burnt-out British agent finds himself hounded by a man he thought was dead. Forced to abandon a rest cure in England by a threat to the woman he loves, he returns to Singapore to hunt down his antagonist, even though he knows he is walking into a baited trap. †††

DERBY, MARK. *The Sunlit Ambush.* 1959. Dunster, footloose in Singapore, is drawn by his own grief into the orbit of a young brother and sister, who turn out to be the children of a murdered white rajah. He travels with them to the island of Selandar and finds he has been plunged into an atmosphere of terror and revolt. Supporting the children, Dunster once again finds a reason for living amid the violence. ††††

DEVERELL, WILLIAM. *High Crimes.* 1982. Two men and a woman set out to smuggle at least a trillion dollars worth of marijuana from Colombia to Canada and then to the U.S. There are two major flaws with the story: there is far too much information for the average reader about the drug business, and the narrator keeps shifting from third person to first person and back again. †

DEWAR, EVELYN. *Perfume of Arabia.* 1973. Mark Petersen is sent to Arabia to replace an oilman who has been killed in what seems to be an accident, but, when he arrives, he finds the man was murdered. It reads a bit like Desmond Bagley. †††

DiMONA, JOSEPH. *Last Man at Arlington*. 1973. On the tenth anniversary of Kennedy's death, a mysterious assassin begins to kill off six people on a list. A well-written variation of Christie's *ABC Murders*, or MacDonald's *List of Adrian Messenger*. ††††

DOLINER, ROY. *On the Edge*. 1978. The Astra File is missing from Roper International. Powerful men from the vice president of the U.S. on down want it recovered. All signs point to Jack Sullivan, an operative who is on the run in Manhattan. Very close—at least in concept—to *Six Days of the Condor*. †

DRISCOLL, PETER. *The Wilby Conspiracy*. 1972. In racially-torn South Africa, mining engineer Jim Keough finds himself and a black fugitive in a tense fight for life. ††††

DRUMMOND, IVOR. *The Necklace of Skulls*. 1977. Lady Jennifer Norrington, Cally, and Sandro attempt to break up a drug ring only to run afoul of the powerful Thug cult of the worshippers of the goddess Kali. The book is set in India. †††

• *Some novels to read while you are waiting for your divorce to become final: Ladies should read:*

THE EIGHTH MRS. BLUEBEARD by Hillary Waugh
A KISS BEFORE DYING by Ira Levin
STRONG POISON by Dorothy Sayers

Men should read:

SKELETONS by Glendon Swarthout
SLEEPING DOGS LIE by Julian Gloag
THE THIRD DEADLY SIN by Lawrence Sanders

DUKE, MADELINE. *The Bormann Receipt*. 1977. A fictionalized version of the author's attempts to get the family art treasures stolen by the Nazis returned to her. †††

DUNCAN, ROBERT L. *In the Blood*. 1984. Another slasher novel, only this one is a bit too weird. The killer is allergic to electricity and wears lead foil under his clothes. He does his dirty work with a special ax. ††

DUNCAN, W. R. *The Queen's Messenger.* 1982. Possibly the best novel of international espionage and adventure published in the last ten years. Moving from the conference rooms of Whitehall to 1980 Thailand, the story is almost impossible to put down as Gordon Clive seeks answers to the unprecedented disappearance of a Queen's messenger from a train in Mongolia.   †††††

DUNNE, COLIN. *Retrieval.* 1984. A no-nonsense, mercenary novel in which Peter Makins takes his crack team behind the Iron Curtain to rescue a young girl. As if this is not enough story, there's more. Repercussions caused by the mission reach from Bangkok to East Germany.   †††

DUNNING, LAWRENCE. *Taking Liberties.* 1981. A very average thriller about the Statue of Liberty, the Romanoff crown jewels, the CIA, and the KGB. The cast: a disillusioned spy, a ruthless killer, and you guessed it—a beautiful woman.   ††

E

EBERSOHN, WESSEL. *A Lonely Place to Die.* 1979. A very well-written first novel in which Yudel, a South African prison psychiatrist, is brought in to interview an insane prisoner accused of murder. From this simple beginning, the author skillfully takes us into the heart of a local gang, which resembles the KKK, and uses it to comment on the tense South African racial scene.   ††††

EGLETON, CLIVE. *A Piece of Resistance.* 1970. Part one of an excellent trilogy about David Garnett as he fights a losing war in Russian-occupied England. The other two volumes are *Last Post for a Partisan* and *The Judas Mandate.*
††††

EGLETON, CLIVE. *The Bormann Brief.* 1974. Written early in the Nazi craze, this is a strong story about a plot hatched between German General Gerhardt and British Intelligence agent Ashby to assassinate Martin Bormann.   †††

EGLETON, CLIVE. *Skirmish.* 1975. Secret agent McAlister is marked for assassination by the KGB. When the attempt fails and an Arab sheik is killed by mistake, McAlister turns the tables with the aid of a child who just happened to photograph the assassin in the act.   †††

ELDER, MARK. *The Prometheus Operation.* 1980. Nazi spy Stephen Roebling is operating in WWII America and on Erika Huntingdon, a beautiful Washington socialite and Nazi agent. It is agent Greg Allison's job to track him down.   ††

ELLIOTT, RICHARD.   *The Sword of Allah*. 1984. It is 1991, and the Arabs have finally gained control of a satellite with more deadly capabilities than merely conveying cable television signals. Guess who it is trained on . . .   †††

ERDMAN, PAUL.   A one-of-a-kind thriller writer who uses international finance as the backdrop for his well-written books.

The Billion Dollar Sure Thing.   1973. A great plot which combines the best safecracker in Europe, a group of international bankers, a beautiful French-woman, and a young American financial wizard, as Russia waits in the wings to profit from a huge, American, financial faux pas.   ††††

The Crash of '79.   1976. A dated, wheeler-dealer, stock-market novel with global implications.   ††

The Last Days of America.   1981. The Russians are in Poland. The U.S. is slipping. Frank Rogers, president of a California aerospace company, goes to Switzerland with a suitcase full of money to bribe all the right people.   †††

ERDSTEIN, ERICH, WITH BEAN, BARBARA.   *Inside the Fourth Reich*. 1977. In these memoirs, the author would have us believe he did such incredible things as tricking the Germans into scuttling the Graf Spee, sharing a prison cell with Aristotle Onassis, and stalking Martin Bormann. Judge for yourself.   †

ERWIN, CAROL, WITH MILLER, FLOYD.   *The Orderly Disorderly House*. 1960. The true story of a modern madam, her adventures, and customers who included "Legs" Diamond and "Pretty Boy" Floyd.   †††

EVANS, JONATHAN.   *Misfire*. 1980. A thriller built around the workings of an actual German-owned company—although the name was changed for the book—which offers spy satellites for sale. There the truth ends and the fiction begins as the KGB and CIA mount a joint operation to infiltrate the company.   †††

EVANS, JONATHAN.   *The Solitary Man*. 1980. Hugo Hartman, a man of many faces, is a survivor of Bergen-Belsen, a CIA agent, and a KGB agent. He wants out and wants revenge on the Nazi tormentor from the camp who is now living in New York.   †††

EVANS, PETER.   *The Englishman's Daughter*. 1983. Sort of the "Jackie Collins" of thrillers as a sophisticated, Soviet espionage expert, a ruthless KGB official, a film director, a sexy playboy, an English monetarist, and—at the heart of it all—the Englishman's daughter all cast smoldering glances at one another.   †††

F

FALKIRK, RICHARD. *Blackstone.* 1973. A real swashbuckler in which Blackstone, the handsome, dashing, pride of the Bow Street Runners, must stop a kidnapping attempt against the soon-to-be-queen Victoria. Great fun. †††

FALKIRK, RICHARD. *Blackstone's Fancy.* 1973. Blackstone is called in to put an end to bare-knuckle fighting. †††

FARAGO, LADISLAS. *The Game of the Foxes.* 1971. The true history of Nazi spying in England and America before WWII. Painstakingly researched and beautifully written. †††††

FERGUSON, NANCY. *Black Coral.* 1985. A romantic suspense novel set in the Caribbean in which two lovers become the target of a killer. Similar to Benchley's *The Deep.* ††

FINNEY, JACK. He may be best remembered for *Invasion of the Body Snatchers*, but he also wrote a couple of offbeat, brilliant books which offer clever plotting, atmosphere, action, intellectual pleasure, and real characters.

Time and Again. 1970. Simon Morley is an ordinary advertising artist who gets tapped for an incredible adventure that's half fantasy, half science. He travels back in time to the New York of 1882. He's supposed to be an observer, but what happens if he tampers with the course of history? And what happens if he falls in love with a girl who was dead before he was born? A thoughtful, exciting, and very moving story. †††††

Marion's Wall. (n.d.) Marion Marsh was a wild, beautiful Hollywood starlet who died in the 1920s, so wild, in fact, that even death could not hold her, and fifty years later she's back, offering a devil's bargain to the man who may give her the career she was cheated out of. A funny romance—and a gold mine for film buffs. ††††

FISH, ROBERT L. *Pursuit.* 1978. The story of Helmut Von Schraeder, a Nazi death-camp monster, who, after the war, becomes Benjamin Grossman, Israeli hero and military leader, waiting for just the right moment to kick off yet another fiendish Nazi plot. †††

FISH, ROBERT L. *The Gold of Troy.* 1980. Another case of "button, button, who's got the button." This time it is Nazi gold, and the Germans think the Russians have it, the Russians think the CIA has it, but no. The question is: who does have it? †††

FLANNERY, SEAN. *The Trinity Factor.* 1981. Two Soviet agents, Alek and Jada, in the closing days of WWII, leave a bewildering trail of false clues as they cross the U.S. toward the top-secret installation at Los Alamos and the atomic bomb. ††††

FLANNERY, SEAN. *The Hollow Men.* 1982. Sonja, formerly of the CIA, persuades Wallace Mahoney to come out of retirement and help uncover the identity of a mole in Mossad, the Israeli intelligence organization. †††

FLANNERY, SEAN. *False Prophets.* 1983. Wallace Mahoney, CIA operative, is killed on an Israeli airliner. His son John vows vengeance on those responsible. But is Wallace really dead, or is it all part of something larger? †††

FLANNERY, SEAN. *Broken Idols.* 1985. Wallace Mahoney is back, and his son John is at his side. This time General Sir Robert Marshall and NATO's top-secret Genesis plan are missing. ††††

FLEMING, IAN. What can you say about James Bond, except that in him Fleming created the most identifiable character in mystery fiction since Sherlock Holmes? However, his enduring popularity is due more to luck than to Fleming's writing skill. Initially, he was catapulted to superstardom on the coattails of a remark made by John F. Kennedy about his own personal reading taste, and he has remained there because of the twenty-years-worth of great movies made from Bond adventures.

Casino Royale. 1953. The first Bond story. It is more interesting for that reason than for its plot in which Bond pursues beautiful women and the high life of a casino to break the power of corrupt Communist LeChiffre. †††

Live and Let Die. 1954. Bond takes on one of SPECTRE's biggies in one of the weakest of the series. ††

Moonraker. 1956. Because of a simple matter of cheating at cards, "M" asks Bond to investigate Hugo Drax, a man single-handedly financing a rocket that could destroy Europe. ††

From Russia with Love. 1957. SPECTRE sets out to steal a Russian code machine and blame it on England, but Bond gums things up in one of the best of the series, complete with hair-raising experiences on the Orient Express. ††††

Dr. No. 1958. When Bond tries to determine the fate of a missing agent in the West Indies, he runs up against Dr. No, a scientist bent on stopping the American space program. A good plot, especially for its time. †††

For Your Eyes Only. 1960. A collection of Bond short stories. Hardly worth the effort. †

Goldfinger. 1960. One of the best of the series. Fleming was at the height of his plotting ability in this story of Auric Goldfinger's attempt to take over Fort Knox. This is the one with Pussy Galore. ††††

Thunderball. 1961. Another good one, Ernst Blofeld holds the world to ransom with nuclear bombs from a crashed British bomber. †††

The Spy Who Loved Me. 1962. A woman tells what it is like to be in love with James Bond. Boring, in a word. †

On Her Majesty's Secret Service. 1963. Bond falls in love with a beautiful woman while once again trying to stop Blofeld. This time it's in the Alps. ††

You Only Live Twice. 1964. Blofeld again, now in Japan. My, how that Blofeld gets around. †

Diamonds Are Forever. 1965. Ernst Blofeld has been stealing South African diamonds. Bond goes to Amsterdam and to Las Vegas, where Blofeld is using the casino of a Howard Hughes type as his headquarters, to stop him before he can use these diamonds in a laser satellite that would give him world control. †††

Man with the Golden Gun. 1965. After being brainwashed by the Russians and dry-cleaned by the British, Bond goes to Jamaica to lay waste yet another enemy of the crown. †††

Octopussy. 1966. Some old Bond short stories reprinted from magazines like *Playboy.* †

FLICK, CARL. *The Danziger Transcript.* 1971. The story of a hard-hitting foreign correspondent, who may be an enemy agent. The answer lies in a tape recording called the Danziger Transcript. †††

FOLLETT, KEN. *The Eye of the Needle.* 1978. The story of a Nazi spy who is desperately trying to get out of England with information about the Allies D-Day plans. But that's not the real story; it is merely character establishment for the leading man. The real story occurs when the spy gets to a windswept island off the coast. There he becomes involved in a love triangle with a beautiful woman and her crippled husband in a gothic tale of romance that shows the influence of both *Wuthering Heights* and *Lady Chatterley's Lover.* This is a perfect story in every respect and deserves to be read and reread by men and women alike. †††††

FOLLETT, KEN. *The Key to Rebecca.* 1980. The WWII story of a spy and his attempt to steal the British North Africa plans and get them to Rommel. Good action and a well-told story. ††††

FOLLETT, KEN. *The Man from St. Petersburg.* 1982. A rehash of *The Eye of the Needle,* only this time it is set in WWI, and nowhere near as strong. †††

FORBES, COLIN. *Tramp in Armor.* 1969. The German panzers are rolling across France, and a British tank and its crew are stranded behind enemy lines. This is the suspenseful saga of a resourceful sergeant leading his mates through many harrowing encounters to join the withdrawal from Dunkirk. A nonstop thriller. ††††

FORBES, COLIN. *Target Five.* 1972. The Arctic wastes and the northern seas lend added atmosphere to this tug-of-war between the Soviets and a Canadian-American intelligence team over a Russian scientist trying to defect with details of his country's submarine deployment. ††††

FORBES, COLIN. *Double Jeopardy.* 1982. About every third book, Forbes decides to write a thriller that is short on subtlety but long on action. A neo-Nazi group is creating havoc in a Bavarian election campaign, or is it? Four Western leaders are boarding a train to meet at a summit, and one of them is to be killed, but which one? The English agents Tweed and Martel are delegated to untangle the web of intrigue, and the suspense mounts as fast as the body count. †††

FORESTER, C. S. The dean of all writers of swashbuckling seadog stories. His ten novels featuring Hornblower, who begins as a midshipman and works his way up to lord, are the finest sea stories ever written.

Ship of the Line. 1938. It is a race against time for Captain Hornblower and the men of the battleship *Sutherland* as they try to stop Napoleon's navy in a classic sea story. †††††

Commodore Hornblower. 1945. Hornblower returns to the sea, this time the Baltic, to fight Napoleon again. But just when things are looking up, one of his men creates an international incident by pointing a gun at the czar. ††††

Lieutenant Hornblower. 1952. The young Hornblower and his fellow officers find themselves at the mercy of a maniacal captain who is about to hang all of them for mutiny. Hornblower subdues the captain, blows up a fort in Haiti, and saves the day. ††††

Hornblower and the Hotspur. 1962. Commander Hornblower executes a raid on a French naval station in a desperate attempt to stop Napoleon's invasion of England. ††††

FORREST, ANTHONY. *Captain Justice.* 1981. The story of an English spy in the Napoleonic wars sent to France to locate another spy who has the crucial plans to stop Napoleon. A not so well done updating of the *Scarlet Pimpernel.* It could have used more atmosphere. ††

FORSYTH, FREDERICK. One of the greats. How can you argue with a career which has given us *The Day of the Jackal, The Odessa File,* and *The Dogs of War?* The mystery field owes him a huge debt.

The Day of the Jackal. 1971. The story of an assassin whose mission is to kill Charles de Gaulle. Flawlessly told. It is the grandfather of the assassin novel.

†††††

The Odessa File. 1972. The best Nazi resurgence novel ever written. Until the publication of this book, most of the world didn't even know ODESSA existed, but as Forsyth's hero, a young German journalist, traces the diary of a dead man, who had spent years in a concentration camp, not only do we become aware of the existence of the organization, but we get a clear picture of its operation as well.

†††††

The Dogs of War. 1974. The story of a small group of mercenaries hired to add muscle to the African situation. One of the best ever written. †††††

The Devil's Alternative. 1979. After a long vacation from writing, Forsyth returned to the scene with this story of the hijacking of a supertanker and a world on the brink of nuclear destruction. Unfortunately, it seems as if Forsyth spent his vacation reading Ludlum, for this story is not nearly as clear as his earlier work.

†††

No Comebacks. 1982. A collection of short stories, all of which are well written, but one—"There Are No Snakes in Ireland"—is especially good. ††††

The Fourth Protocol. 1984. Better than *The Devil's Alternative,* but still not as good as his earlier work. The most interesting thing about this complex plot about Russian dirty-dealings in England is that it has no designated hero. ††††

FOX, PETER. *Mantis.* 1980. The author, a mathematics professor, makes a dazzling debut in this foreign-intrigue tale with interesting plot twists and turns. Five people with high security clearances are killed, and the preliminary evidence links the Israelis to the murders. The two top troubleshooters in MI6 trace the real killers to a supposedly charitable scientific trust, which leads to an exciting climax.

†††††

FRASER, GEORGE MACDONALD. He is the man for you if you like your adventure stories bawdy, funny, and historically accurate, but he ain't for everyone. He's a little too good for that.

Flashman. 1969. The first volume of the Flashman Papers picks up the story of our hero, Harry Flashman, after he is expelled from Rugby in the 1830s. Despite his arrogant cowardice, he becomes a soldier and even a hero of the war in Afghanistan; despite his perpetual lechery, he marries one of his conquests and may even love her. Fraser's descriptions of Flashman's encounters with the great and not so great personages of the era—including the queen—are sardonic, lively, and based on much thorough research. But the best part of the book is old Flashy himself: sleazy to the core, but unrepentantly honest about it.

†††††

Royal Flash. 1970. Flashman's bad judgment and perpetual horniness get him mixed up with Lola Montez, Otto von Bismarck, and a shady episode in European politics. Flashy impersonates a prince, but blood will out. ††††

Flashman's Lady. 1977. The best of the series so far. Our hero (in spite of his cowardly nature) battles a variety of lechers and savages in Borneo and Madagascar to save the honor of his long-suffering wife, Elspeth. †††††

Flashman and the Redskins. 1982. Flashy's up to his old tricks in the New World: lying, cheating, wenching, and generally having fun on the frontier. He meets General Custer, Wild Bill Hickok, and Geronimo—and what he has to say about them wasn't in your sixth-grade history book. ††††

Mr. American. (n.d.) This book is something different for Fraser, and it is terrific. A straight mystery-adventure story, set in the late Victorian years, it's about an American who comes to England, hires a valet, buys a country house, falls in love, and tries to become a typical English gentleman—until a secret from his mysterious western past surfaces dramatically. It's a compelling story that will make you hope for a sequel. †††††

The Pyrates. 1985. Fraser's most tongue-in-cheek book is both an homage to and a parody of the great adventure stories that were made into Errol Flynn and Tyrone Power pictures. It's a wonderful example of how to love something and make fun of it at the same time. Flashman is not in this one. ††††

FREEMANTLE, BRIAN. *Charlie M.* 1977. One of the best spy novels ever written. Charlie Muffin, a British spy, finds himself shot at and missed and then shit at and hit by his own employers in this truly excellent novel of double crosses in the spy game. A "must read" for fans of le Carré or Deighton.

†††††

FREEMANTLE, BRIAN. *Here Comes Charlie M.* 1978. From the way Freemantle plotted *Charlie M*, he didn't intend to write a sequel. When he did, it was necessary to go back and clear up some loose ends from the first book. That's what he does here, and it is nowhere near as good. †††

FREEMANTLE, BRIAN, *The Inscrutable Charlie Muffin.* 1979. Charlie is not a spy anymore. Now he has something to do with insurance. Exactly *what* is what makes him inscrutable. †††

FREEMANTLE, BRIAN, *Charlie Muffin, USA.* 1980. Still in insurance, Charlie comes to the U.S. and winds up in the middle between the FBI and the Mafia in a story that reads more like Ross Thomas than Brian Freemantle. †††

FREEMANTLE, BRIAN. *The Lost American.* 1984. A spy tale of ambition and avarice in which a young British MI6 agent stationed in Moscow decides to humiliate his Moscow CIA counterpart by stealing his wife and taking all the credit for an important defection success. Well plotted and well told. †††

FULLER, JACK. *Convergence.* 1982. There is a mole in the organization. It can only be one of two people: Harper or Birch, the man he trained. It is up to Harper to prove it is Birch. †††

FULLER, JACK. *Fragments.* 1984. A *Thin-Red-Line* type of story about a group of marines in Vietnam. †††

FURST, ALAN. *Your Day in the Barrel.* 1976. The title comes from an old joke and serves to introduce Roger Levin, a nice, New York, Jewish boy who falls in with bad friends, fast women, and dirty talk. †††

FURST, ALAN. *The Paris Drop.* 1980. Lots of fun. Levin is hustled into going to Paris to deliver money to a secret Israeli organization, and along the way he meets some great villains. ††††

FURST, ALAN. *Shadow Trade.* 1983. Metro Data Research specializes in the use of "body doubles" for blackmail purposes. Everything was going along fine until they agreed to substantiate the death of an international hit man. Nowhere near as good as his earlier work. ††

G

GALLICO, PAUL. *The Poseidon Adventure.* 1969. Between the movie and the huge popularity of the novel, almost everyone is familiar with the exciting story of the sinking of the *Poseidon.* If you haven't read it, you should. ††††

GANN, ERNEST K. One of the great thriller writers of our time. Gann was a professional pilot, and his stories of the air ring with the sincerity of Dick Francis's writing about horses.

The High and the Mighty. 1953. One of the most essential flying novels ever written. Past the point of no return, things start to go wrong on a flight from Hawaii to San Francisco. Can they make it? This plot has been done and redone many times since 1953, but the only two which come close are Nevil Shute's *No Highway* and Arthur Hailey's *Airport.* †††††

Soldier of Fortune. 1954. Combining romance and adventure against the colorful backdrop of Hong Kong, Gann has an American expatriate renegade pilot give a beautiful woman a hand in locating her missing husband.   ††††

Fate Is the Hunter. 1961. A forerunner of Tom Wolfe's *The Right Stuff*. Gann turns to nonfiction to chronicle the true life-and-death adventures of pilots. The quarry is man, and·fate is the hunter.   ††††

GARBO, NORMAN. *Spy.* 1980. A well-written spy novel with a nice plot twist. Richard Burke, the usual jaded spy, wants out, so he has plastic surgery to change his face enough to allow him to live a normal life. His service wants him dead, and the only clue to his new identity is four patients in the hospital at the same time: an actress, a prizefighter, a female executive, and a writer.   ††††

GARBO, NORMAN. *Turner's Wife.* 1983. When Turner's wife, a beautiful, former radio personality, dies of a heart attack at a party, her husband suspects the KGB, the president, and almost everyone else except the Lone Ranger. ††

GARDNER, JOHN. An interesting and versatile adventure writer whose work covers the field ranging from the bumbling Boysie Oakes, to Professor Moriarty (see the Sherlock Holmes section), and a new crop of James Bond stories. Of all his work, the Oakes stories are the best.

The Liquidator. 1964. The first Oakes story and a zany classic. The British Secret Service finds Oakes holding a smoking gun and standing over a body. Sure they have found a steely-eyed killer they press him into service as their "Liquidator." The only problem is Oakes is a coward, and his whole future depends on his figuring out unique ways around it.   †††††

Understrike. 1965. With his reputation now firmly established, Boysie is feared by both the Russians and the British so much that the Russians bring in a double for him, and the world has to contend with *two* Boysies.   ††††

Amber Nine. 1966. Boysie treads dangerously close to the Man from Orgy territory as he takes on a girls' school devoted to the manly arts of murder and mayhem—with a little seduction thrown in for good measure.   †††

The Werewolf Trace. 1977. Another time-release dose of madness from our favorite bad guys—those boys in black who brought us WWII. Not a Boysie Oakes story.   †††

The Dancing Dodo. 1978. A well-plotted thriller in which a wrecked plane from WWII, filled with six bodies, is found in an English marsh. It falls to RAF Commander David Dobson to sort things out, and to avoid becoming a victim, too.   †††

License Renewed. 1981. The first of Gardner's James Bond stories. Although well-written, this story of Bond and the evil Scottish Laird of Murcaldy misses the mark. †††

For Special Services. 1981. Much better than *License Renewed.* Bond and Cedar, the daughter of Felix Leiter, take on SPECTRE and a Texas tycoon. More like Fleming. †††

Icebreaker. 1983. I was all set to dislike this story of Bond joining forces with the KGB, the CIA, and Mossad to stamp out a neo-Nazi group whose head-quarters is in arctic Russia. But when I got into it, I enjoyed it. †††

Role of Honor. 1984. Bond resigns from the service, and it appears that he is an agent for SPECTRE. †††

GARFIELD, BRIAN. Although best known for the popular *Death Wish*, Garfield has produced other work which has not received the notice it deserves.

Hopscotch. 1975. An excellent novel about American agent Miles Kendig who doesn't want to be retired from the field, so he takes matters into his own hands in a thriller which combines both humor and tension. ††††

Recoil. 1977. Everyone knows that the witness protection program (giving someone a new identity if he will testify) doesn't work too well. The villains can always find you if they want to. Garfield takes this premise and turns it into a tense thriller. †††

The Paladin. 1980. The story of Christopher Robin, an agent who rubs elbows with the biggies of WWII. A bit like Dennis Wheatley. †††

GARNER, WILLIAM. A first-rate but overlooked thriller writer. He deserves better. Give him a read.

Overkill. 1966. Michael Jagger, a British agent shunted aside, answers an advertisement which seems to promise some action. It leads him into a wild world of chemical and nuclear weaponry, where his life is threatened by a mad botanist and La Macchina, which may or may not be human. †††

The Us or Them War. 1969. Jagger has been reinstated and is thrown by his boss, the Master, into the middle of a struggle among England, Russia, and the U.S. to get control of a new nonnuclear weapon, which could change the balance of world power. Garner's mastery of satire in dealing with the world of espionage begins to show here. ††††

A *Big Enough Wreath*.   1975. In this book the author handles a mélange of unusual characters: a scientist with a secret, whose 115-year-old father is the world's richest man; a teenage computer genius, who upset the "Star Wars" surveillance plan of a Chinese general; and a dedicated assassin, whom Jagger is ordered to stop. Garner is at his satirical best as he guides the reader through a series of executions and zany chases to a final tongue-in-cheek scene which punctures the BBC balloon.   †††††

The Mobius Trip.   1979. A star-crossed hero, an out-of-this-world villain, and a devilish conspiracy are the ingredients in this story of high-tech, computer sabotage. The takeover of the firm, which has sensitive ties to British intelligence, a seemingly unrelated murder in France, and the shadowy presence of the man called Worthington lead the reader through a maze of dark villainy, the roots of which go back to the beginning of time.   †††††

Think Big, Think Dirty.   1984. Garner is once again back in the world of British Intelligence with a tale of Russian defection and disinformation, and the West— with Britain and the U.S. as uneasy allies—seeking to foil a KGB plot to plant yet another mole in England. A tricky plot, less dependent on gimmicks and more on character, leads to a satisfactory conclusion, and—as is usual with this writer—an ironic one.   ††††

GEDDES, PAUL.   *Codename Hangman*. 1977. There is evil at the heart of a terrorist, bombing, drug-running ring in England. It is up to a retired agent to get to the bottom of it.   †††

GETHIN, DAVID.   *Wyatt*. 1983. In what appears to be the first of a series, the hero is drawn into a web of treason and conspiracy by the detention of an MI5 executive accused of selling secrets to Libya. Wyatt, formerly of the Special Services and now the head of a multi-national corporation, helps to bring the affair to a timely conclusion.   †††

GIFFORD, THOMAS.   One of my favorites. With the exception of *The Man from Lisbon*, his work has been flawless. His thrillers keep you on the edge of your seat, and his mysteries are well plotted and tricky as hell.

The Wind Chill Factor.   1975. John Cooper receives a telegram from his brother and heads home to Minnesota only to find his brother murdered for a box of old Nazi documents left to the town library by his grandfather. An auspicious debut for a new thriller writer.   ††††

The Cavanaugh Quest.   1976. This beautifully written "clue" mystery begins with a suicide in the lobby of a country club and then leaves bodies strewn everywhere.   †††††

The Man from Lisbon. 1977. A caper novel and a disappointment compared with Gifford's other work. ††

The Glendower Legacy. 1978. A good chase novel that moves up and down the East Coast like a roller coaster as the KGB and CIA try to figure out if George Washington was really a traitor. ††††

GILMAN, DOROTHY. Her heroine, Mrs. Pollifax, is a widow from New Brunswick, New Jersey, who lives quietly, making cookies for the garden club and reading the *Times*, except on those occasions when she is called upon to be a secret agent.

The Amazing Mrs. Pollifax. 1970. Istanbul is the scene, and the job is to rescue a beautiful female agent who wishes to defect to the West. Mrs. Pollifax gamely travels in gypsy caravans, outsmarts evil spies, flies a helicopter, and in general has a great time. ††††

The Elusive Mrs. Pollifax. 1971. This time the irrepressible Mrs. P. must tear herself away from the night-blooming cereus plant, budding on her fire escape, to smuggle passports into Bulgaria inside her hat. But that's only the beginning. Once there, she participates in an explosive prison break and dupes a famous general. †††

The Clairvoyant Countess. 1975. Madame Karitska, an impoverished countess who is also a psychic, helps the police to solve the murder of a young girl. The mystery is passably good, but it doesn't seem quite cricket for a detective to be psychic. The whole idea is for the detective to make conclusions from the clues at hand. ††

Mrs. Pollifax on Safari. 1976. Aristotle, the notorious assassin for hire, has the president of Zambia as his next target. He is known to be meeting his prospective employers on an African safari. Mrs. Pollifax, posing as the average tourist in a disguise that comes naturally, is instructed to take photos of all her fellow travelers on safari, so that the elusive assassin can be identified. With the wild animals, the African bush, and a mysterious villain, this is a lively romp for Mrs. P. ††††

Mrs. Pollifax on the China Station. 1983. Once again everyone's favorite old lady, Mrs. Pollifax, joins forces with the CIA. This time she goes to China with the usual hilarious results. †††

GOLDMAN, WILLIAM. *Marathon Man.* 1974. A thriller of incredible tension. After you read it, you will never feel the same about your dentist. ††††

GRADY, JAMES. *Six Days of the Condor* (aka *Three Days of the Condor*). 1974. I didn't think this novel of an unwilling fugitive from his employer, the CIA, was anywhere nearly as good as the movie. ††

GRANGER, BILL. *Schism.* 1981. The second "November Man" novel, in which Father Leo Tunney, an American missionary, stumbles out of the jungles of Cambodia only to find the CIA, the KGB, the Vatican secret service, and a security force from a New York bank have decided that he's a threat to life in the fast lane. †††

GRANGER, BILL. *The British Cross.* 1983. Although written in the brooding style of early Len Deighton, I found this story of Devereaux and his trip to Eastern Europe to clear up the mystery of Raoul Wallenberg, WWII hero, to be slow reading. ††

GREATOREX, WILFRED. *Three Potato, Four.* 1976. Agent Calder has to find out if the Russian Pavel—a man with a fortune in diamonds and perpetual horniness—is a great defector or a double agent. ††

GREEN, WILLIAM M. *See How They Run.* 1976. A well-written, fast-paced thriller in which a character strongly resembling J. Edgar Hoover is killed by the old exploding-cigarette trick. It falls to Tobin, his live-in confidante, to protect his precious files, which contain proof of the dirty dealings of the high-and-mighty. †††

GREENE, GRAHAM. I can sum up Graham Greene's work in one sentence. It's a goddam shame that he has never received the Nobel Prize.

This Gun for Hire. 1936. Raven, a killer with a harelip, is turned in by his employer, Mr. Cholmondeley. Raven escapes and seeks revenge. In flight, he comes into contact with Anne, a young actress who is the girlfriend of Mather, the cop who is after him. A brilliantly written psychological novel, loaded with confusing emotions, sharply drawn characters, and tons of atmosphere. †††††

The Confidential Agent. 1939. "D"—we never learn his name—is a spy, not glamorous like James Bond, but emotionless and empty. He moves in and out of ordinary life but is never engaged with it. He is both hunter and hunted, and both roles are fundamentally dull. The book ends on a faint note that change may be possible. †††

The Power and the Glory. 1940. Set in sweaty and shabby Mexico, this is a struggle for salvation by a whiskey priest—or, rather, tequila in this case—who gets mixed up in the treacherous politics of a notoriously unstable country. ††††

The Ministry of Fear. 1943. In the middle of WWII, Arthur Rowe, previously accused of murdering his wife, buys a cake at a charity bazaar and finds himself tangled up with a conspiracy, a manhunt, and a locked-room murder. A true classic with a great ending. †††††

The Heart of the Matter. 1948. Scobie is a policeman with a miserable post in West Africa. In this tale of love, loyalty, war, and colonialism, he has a chance to redeem a lifetime of mediocrity. ††††

The Third Man. 1950. Greene's fascination with our inability to know our fellowman, even our closest friends, continues in this short novel. An American writer comes to postwar Vienna to clear up the mystery surrounding the death of his boyhood friend, Harry Lime. A classic. †††††

The Quiet American. 1955. This is the story of young Alden Pyle, a fresh-faced Harvard graduate in Indochina on a State Department mission, told by a weary and wise English war correspondent. ††††

Our Man in Havana. 1958. This account of a British agent in Cuba pretending to be a vacuum-cleaner salesman—or maybe it's a vacuum-cleaner salesman pretending to be a spy—is Greene's funniest book. In it he makes fun of diplomats, politicians, spies, and even people who read spy thrillers. †††††

Travels with My Aunt. 1969. The sudden appearance of a bizarre old woman, claiming to be his aunt, uproots a middle-aged bank clerk and introduces him to smuggling, strange parts of the world, bribery, corruption, adventure, and love. A dry, witty, moving story. ††††

The Honorary Consul. 1973. This fat book is about a political kidnapping, based on a ludicrous misunderstanding of a meaningless diplomatic title, in backwater Argentina. In a world filled with terrorism and absurdity, love is just another mistake, and second-best is more than any Greene character expects to get. †††

GUILD, NICHOLAS. *The Berlin Warning.* 1984. Karen Windemere and David Steadman, a suspiciously modern couple, operate in tandem in this odd WWII story where the British are the bad guys. Say what you will about the Nazis, but they *do* make better villains. Still Karen and David are a likable pair, and the tale is crisply, if not compellingly, told. †††

GURR, DAVID, *A Woman Called Scylla.* 1981. A great story in which a Canadian newspaper woman seeks the answer to her mother's death during WWII while on a mission for Churchill. Following a trail of bodies across Europe, the daughter becomes involved in a cover-up of deep treason, which, if made public, would shake the British security world to its foundations. †††††

H

HAGGARD, WILLIAM. He can best be described as the bridge between Eric Ambler's anti-heroes and Ian Fleming's James Bond, both in time and mood. His hero is the suave, sexy, understated Colonel Russell who starts out as the head of Security Executive, a diplomatic intelligence branch of the British government, but as the years pass, he is forced to retire, working only as the situation requires.

Venetian Blind. 1959. Russell doesn't occupy center stage in this early story of a mysterious, powerful industrialist who may be a spy, but Haggard's understated style and urbane tone is already in evidence. †✝

The Arena. 1961. The arena for this high-level espionage game is a rundown bank threatened with a takeover by a mysterious new firm. The problem is, the old bank's only real asset is a piece of top-secret technology. Russell probes beneath the surface of London's financial community and finds plenty of action. †††

The High Wire. 1963. Like le Carré's Smiley, Russell has a Soviet opposite number. His name is Victor, and he's the spirit behind an espionage attempt that must be foiled without rocking the diplomatic boat. An inconsequential romance between two pawns doesn't distract attention from the main game. †††

The Antagonists. 1964. A Communist scientist visiting London turns into a bon vivant and becomes the target for some not so subtle espionage attempts. Russell is up against an amateur brainwasher and a cut-rate Mata Hari, whose very incompetence makes them dangerous. This is one of his funniest and most fast-paced. ††††

The Powder Barrel. 1965. A little Arab sheikdom—a crust of sand on top of a fortune in oil—is the powder barrel ready to explode in this Middle-Eastern thriller. Russell has to handle princesses, potentates, and assassins, but it's all in a day's work. †††

Too Many Enemies. 1971. The Arabs and the Israelis are each lobbying for support in parliament on the eve of war. A South African millionaire and the prime minister get involved, and the result is blackmail. Only Russell can smooth things over. †††

The Notch on the Knife. 1973. Many years after their wartime association, Russell meets an old friend—now premier of a small Balkan country. Together they desperately try to avert a Communist takeover in this smooth, reflective thriller. Its tone is somber, but it is Haggard's best work. ††††

Poison People. 1978. Now retired, Russell is hired by a parliamentary friend to bust an Asian heroin ring. His dangerous mission takes him to deadly Delhi and a confrontation with an inscrutable oriental master criminal.   ✝✝✝

Visa to Limbo. 1978. Visiting Tel Aviv on purely innocent personal business, Russell is hijacked and threatened with bombs. He also confronts an old flame for rekindling purposes.   ✝✝✝

HALE, JOHN. *The Whistle Blower.* 1984. When Bob Jones, a clerk with British Intelligence, dies in what appears to be an accident, his father—a strong, plodding man named Frank—decides to investigate on his own. The writing is excellent, very much like Graham Greene at his best, but unfortunately the plot is a touch too ambitious for a medium-length novel.   ✝✝✝

HALL, ADAM. One of the most important of the British, Cold War, spy novelists. His work ranks right up there with John le Carré and Len Deighton, the main difference being that he has more action—much more—than either of them.

The Quiller Memorandum. 1965. A classic. The debut of Quiller, who is sent to Berlin to stop the Nazis from trying again in the 1960s. Sure, you've read this same story over and over, but trust me, this is one of the best.   ✝✝✝✝✝

The Striker Portfolio. 1969. Quiller goes back to Germany again to try to find out what is behind the numerous crashes of the "Widowmaker," the supersonic backbone of the new Luftwaffe. In addition to the strong plot, there is a great cast of eccentric characters.   ✝✝✝✝

The Tango Briefing. 1973. Quiller is sent to the Sahara to recover the contents of a crashed plane, but he is hardly under way before his cover is blown, and it becomes a deadly race between the ever-cool Quiller and agents from several other nations, set against the colorful backdrop of heat and sun in the Sahara.   ✝✝✝✝

The Mandarin Cypher. 1975. Nobody bothers to tell Quiller that his little trip to Hong Kong is going to be anything but usual, until bodies start to turn up, and it looks as though Quiller will be next.   ✝✝✝✝

The Scorpion Signal. 1980. Quiller is thrust into the middle between a British operative, driven mad by KGB torture, and his target for assassination, a world leader whose death would trigger WWIII.   ✝✝✝✝

HALLAHAN, WILLIAM H. *The Trade.* 1981. Colin Thomas, an arms merchant, seeks to avenge a friend's death, and to learn the meaning of his last words, "the doomsday book." He uncovers a German plan to destroy Russia and must decide what to do with this explosive information. Swiftly changing locales, a good love story, and lots of action give a lot of zip to this story of an outrageous plot to alter the balance of world power.   †††††

HAMILTON, DONALD. His Matt Helm series can be best described as the "American James Bond." The series is very well written and shows influences of the classic, hard-boiled detective school, but unfortunately Dean Martin portrayed Helm in the movies in a buffoonish slapstick manner and created a regrettable image in the public's mind. Forget about the movies and read the series.

The Silencers. 1962. Helm is sent to Juarez to bring back a female agent who has possibly defected. Before he can accomplish his mission, she is killed, and her sister has the information. Helm has no choice but to bring her along in the search for a battered old church and a date with death.   †††

The Ravagers. 1964. Once again Helm is sent to protect a beautiful woman, this time in Canada. Along the way, he stumbles across the body of an agent whose face has been eaten away with acid.   †††

The Devastators. 1965. One of the best of the series. Helm is sent to the wilds of Scotland when the body of the mission's third agent is discovered. The cause of death—bubonic plague. Together with a beautiful American spy and a beautiful Russian—who hates him—Helm has to crack the hideout of the mad scientific genuis behind it all.   †††

The Interlopers. 1969. Matt takes over another man's identity, fiancée, and fate, as decoy for an assassin.   ††

HARCOURT, PALMA. *Climate for Conspiracy.* 1974. Harcourt's first novel. The Russians intend to split Canada away from the West, and a young British ambassador is to be the scapegoat.   ††

HARCOURT, PALMA. *A Fair Exchange.* 1975. A nice turnabout on a gothic plot as Derek Allmourn, first secretary of the British Embassy in Washington, marries the daughter of a senator. After a terrible accident and subsequent posting to Oslo, Derek begins to have second thoughts about his wife.   †††

HARCOURT, PALMA. *Shadows of Doubt.* 1983. A high-ranking Russian wants to defect to the British. To sweeten the deal he has important papers, but are they real or a clever Russian trick to put the members of NATO at each other's throats?   ††

HARRINGTON, WILLIAM. *The English Lady.* 1982. The story of an English woman pilot who hobnobs with all the high-ranking Nazis. Although it was nicely written, I didn't like it at all. The story never made me believe, or want to.   ††

HARRIS, RICHARD. *Honor Bound.* 1982. This relentlessly grim tale has its share of thrills, but don't read it if you're feeling depressed. Thomas Hasker, a successful New York lawyer, seeks the truth about the suicide of a judge, who was his friend and mentor. Before this story of greed and insanity is over, Hasker has become both witness and participant in murder.   †††

HARRIS, THOMAS. *Black Sunday.* 1975. A massive best-seller in which a terrorist group raises hell at the Super Bowl. A very satisfying read.   ††††

HART-DAVIS, DUFF. *The Heights of Rimring.* 1982. An impressive first novel by a career foreign correspondent. Moving from the English forest lands to the mountains of Nepal, a retired Special Services operative sets out on a dangerous mission to rescue an American general lying wounded in the monastery of Rimring, with the Russians and Chinese snapping at his heels.   †††††

HARTLEY, NORMAN. *The Viking Process.* 1976. A TV newsman who is an expert on terrorism narrates this chilling tale of his capture by a group of radicals. By blackmailing him with threats to his wife, they force him to cooperate in helping them. His wife's act of courage frees him to strike back. For all its futuristic jargon and trappings, this is a book with a heart.   ††††

HARVESTER, SIMON. *Unsung Road.* 1961. Dorian Silk, troubleshooter for British Intelligence, is sent to Iran to break up a Russian plot against the shah. Hampered by the British agent in place, Silk wends his way through the maze of assumed identities of the other players in the game, solves two murders, and adds to the body count on his own.   ††††

HARVESTER, SIMON. *Forgotten Road.* 1962. Harvester's thrillers take the reader to various exotic locales in the Mid and Far East. Here Silk is sent to India's Hindu Kush to find out why a British agent has disappeared. With his usual aplomb, Silk brings a solution to the problem in an area where the British and Russians have played a deadly game for a century.   †††

HARVESTER, SIMON. *Nameless Road.* 1974. Sent into China to bring out a beleaguered agent, Silk is dropped by parachute into Inner Mongolia, an area which is terra incognita to the rest of the world. Hundreds of miles from where he should be, he battles the natives and Russian agents to get on with his original mission.   †††

HEAL, ANTHONY. *Man in the Middle.* 1980. A very ordinary thriller in which a secret, English security group takes a derelict and turns him into a super-killer. The characters are flat, but the action is good.   ††

HEATTER, BASIL. *The London Gun.* 1984. It's those darn Nazis again. This time it is the closing days of WWII, and Hitler, knowing the end is near, puts monstrous plans into effect to wipe out London. ††

HIGGINS, JACK. With the exception of *The Eagle Has Landed*, I'm not a great fan of Jack Higgins. He is prolific, churning them out by the dozens, and his output shows a general lack of quality, which would be remedied if he would just slow down.

East of Desolation. 1968. One of Higgins's early adventure stories. It is an exciting mixture of murder, sabotage, and grand larceny. The protagonist, an ex-war pilot, flies the mean skies as a fading movie star seeks to finance his final fling at fame by unconventional means. ††††

The Eagle Has Landed. 1975. I read this one in a New Orleans hotel, and, let me tell you, it takes a hell of a book to distract me from the diversions offered in the southern city of dreams. It is the story of a Nazi plot to kidnap Churchill as the war in Europe begins to go against the Germans. The suspense builds as the crack commando unit assigned to the job moves nearer and nearer to the wartime leader, while Churchill's protectors, with history on their side, help in the ironic ending. †††††

HONE, JOSEPH. *The Oxford Gambit.* 1977. A longtime British security official receives a letter. After reading it, he walks out of his home and disappears. Peter Marlow is assigned to find out whether he has defected when a brother agent is murdered. The trail leads from England through much of Europe, with the tragic ending bringing Marlow back to where it all began. A cerebral thriller. ††††

HONE, JOSEPH. *The Valley of the Fox.* 1980. Marlow is back, retired and writing his memoirs. An attempt to kill him backfires, and his wife is killed instead, leaving him in charge of an autistic stepdaughter. Forced to hide, he flees into an English forest, and there wages a battle for survival. He is helped by a reclusive heiress who is obviously on the edge of insanity. †††

HOUSEHOLD, GEOFFREY. One of the greats. Many of today's thriller writers could—and should—take lessons from him on how to make the most of the cleanly told and plotted novel.

Rogue Male. 1939. The classic story of a famous big-game hunter who decides to undertake the ultimate hunt—to assassinate Hitler in his own lair. When the attempt fails, the hunter becomes the hunted. A "must read." †††††

Watcher in the Shadows. 1960. Even though *Rogue Male* is Household's most famous book, I prefer this one. Similar to *Rogue* in plot, two master hunters— this time from WWII intelligence—go after each other in a duel in the dark

English countryside some ten years after VE-Day. I would go so far as to say this is the greatest chase novel ever written. †††††

Red Anger. 1975. A young English clerk fakes his own suicide, only to turn up as a Romanian refugee from a Russian trawler. From there he is recruited to hunt down a traitor, but soon he and the traitor are on the run together, fugitives from everyone. †††

The Last Two Weeks of Georges Rivac. 1978. Georges Rivac unfortunately agrees to carry some brochures from France to England. It is too late when Georges realizes that he has been used as a courier to smuggle military secrets. He must get this information to the right person, but as murders begin to occur, who is the right person? †††

Rogue Justice. 1982. The sequel to *Rogue Male* is not bad as sequels go. Our hunter returns to Germany for a second try at assassinating Hitler. †††

HOYT, RICHARD. *Cool Running.* 1984. *Rolling Stone* reporter Jim Quint is the agreeable, devil-may-care hero of this doomsday thriller. A nuclear bomb is set to go off in Manhattan—nothing unusual there—but the events, dialogue, and joie de vivre of the hero are definitely different. An outrageous, fun read that satirizes the genre, but still manages to give you a good story. Those of you who don't take doomsday too seriously will love it. ††††

HUNTER, JACK D. *The Blue Max.* 1964. The powerful story of a WWI German fighter pilot, his battles, his loves, and his cocktails. Excellent read. ††††

HUNTER, JACK D. *Spies, Inc.* 1969. The cover says, "A novel of industrial espionage in Pennsylvania, Delaware, and Maryland," and that's where you should stop. Don't bother to open the cover. †

HUNTER, STEPHEN. *The Master Sniper.* 1980. A basic retelling of *The Day of the Jackal*, with the closing days of WWII as the backdrop. The SS trains the ultimate assassin to perform one last dirty deed before the Third Reich collapses. The author's skillful buildup of tension which leads to the climax is so good that he makes an otherwise weak ending seem even weaker. †††

HUNTER, STEPHEN. *The Spanish Gambit.* 1985. Hunter's early books did well, but look for this one to really escalate his career. The time: 1937. The scene: the Spanish Civil War. Three men battle it out against this rich backdrop to keep the Communists from subverting Britain from within. ††††

HYDE, CHRISTOPHER. *The Tenth Crusade.* 1983. Phil Kirkland finds his girl and then loses her again to the world of religious cults, TV evangelists, terrorists, and other lunatics. †††

HYDE, CHRISTOPHER. *The Red Fox.* 1985. An international thriller filled with brooding menace. A search for a missing businessman leads Richard Thone from Pennsylvania to Halifax, Montreal, and Paris, illegally into Russia, and then home to the solution of a personal mystery and the possible answer to a famous historical puzzle.   ††††

I

INNES, HAMMOND. He specializes in sinewy tales of adventure in the far corners of the earth, where men are men and women are scarce. His heroes are loners, often tormented with troubled pasts, but always strong and resourceful. Innes does his legwork well. He never sends a character anywhere he hasn't been himself, a policy which is reflected in the power, richness, and accuracy of his settings.

The Angry Mountain. 1950. A business trip to Italy suddenly forces Dick Farrell to relive his nightmare experiences in a WWII prison camp. But the unsolved mysteries of his war years are no more explosive than Vesuvius, which broods over the novel. The human conflicts take a backseat to the big eruption at the book's climax.   ††

Campbell's Kingdom. 1952. Violence and revenge surround Bruce Wetheral's attempt to claim an inheritance of oil deposits seven thousand feet up in the forbidding Canadian Rockies. He battles all comers—a powerful industrial giant, outstandingly bad weather, even a fatal illness—to clear his grandfather's name.   ††

The Land God Gave to Cain. 1958. A young man in England claims that a radio message has been received from Canada—from a geological expedition long given up for dead. Then it's on to a grueling journey into the wilderness of Labrador, murders ancient and modern, a fortune in gold, and a punchy surprise ending.   ††††

Atlantic Fury. 1962. The setting is a top-secret weapons installation in the Hebrides islands. The main character is the stormy north Atlantic Ocean. As in many of Innes's novels, the narrator's murky family history somehow dovetails with present-day intrigue.   ††

The Strode Venturer. 1965. One of the best. Geoffrey Bailey confronts sharp boardroom politics and violent mysteries of the sea in his search for the elusive heir to the shipping empire that ruined his family. At the book's heart is a strange island in the Indian Ocean and a treasure waiting for anyone strong and clever enough to win it.   ††††

The Big Footprints. 1977. A terrifying mass stampede of elephants is the tour de force of this book about ivory poaching in East Africa. Innes did his homework on this one, and neither the breadth of his research on the Lake Rudolph area, nor the strength of his belief in the need for wildlife conservation get in the way of a powerful story of man against man, and nature against both of them. †††

Solomon's Seal. 1980. Old family strife, valuable stamps, political insurrection, and romance are the chief ingredients of this thriller set in steamy New Guinea. The woman is stronger and the man more fallible than in some earlier Innes stories. †††

IRVING, CLIFFORD, AND BURKHOLZ, HERBERT. *The Death Freak.* 1978. A truly great story about two master arms makers—one Russian, one American—both with the same girl friend, and both wanting to retire. The only problem is they know too much, so their employers want them dead. Their only hope is to look out for each other. †††††

J

JACKS, OLIVER. *Autumn Heroes.* 1977. A mercenary story in which a group of six lovable rogues are sadistically trained beyond normal human endurance for one purpose—to go into the desert and rescue Princess Anne from a group of diabolical kidnappers. ††

JENKINS, GEOFFREY. A teller of tales of incredible high adventure. He ranks up there right along with MacLean, Bagley, Kyle, and Lyall. Unlike the others, his tales usually—but not always—center on the sea.

A Twist of Sand. 1960. A retired, WWII submarine commander goes back to the pitiless waters of the southwest African coast after the war to rediscover an island bequeathed to him by his dying grandfather. He is caught up in a search for a rare beetle whose presence would indicate untold riches, and a variety of villains are after him. ††††

A Grue of Ice. 1962. The scene is the Antarctic as a former Royal Navy officer, aided by a stalwart Tristan da Cunha islander, seeks an island which practically everyone says doesn't exist, but which he had sighted during the war. He is kidnapped by an English millionaire, with a metal face and a beautiful daughter, and it all leads to a heart-stopping climax in uncharted waters. †††

The River of Diamonds. 1964. Returning to the "Skeleton Coast" for this taut thriller, the author takes the reader at breakneck pace through an obstacle race of underwater death traps. The hero exposes a secret, locked away since the war, in his attempt to solve the mystery behind an explorer's disappearance. All is complicated by an ex-Nazi ostensibly searching for his missing brother. The title gives you a clue as to what they are really after. ††††

The Hollow Sea. 1971. Once again the author builds a suspense-adventure tale around the unusual and awesome power of the waters of the sea. The hero's father and grandfather were lost in an air crash and a sunken ship in the same area, although a half century apart, and both mysteries are solved in a harrowing and almost incredible ending.   †††

A Cleft of Stars. 1974. A slam-bang thriller about the search for the other half of the fabulous Cullinan diamond, buried in the tomb of a long-dead African tribal king, climaxed by a killer cyclone at the confluence of two great South African rivers. Once again, the author nearly makes the unbelievable believable, but not quite.   †††

A Ravel of Waters. 1981. Using the cruise of a high-tech sailing vessel as a backdrop, the author spins a prophetic thriller of a militant Argentinian's effort to take over the Falkland Islands, abetted by the presence of a mysterious Soviet Antarctic base, and complicated further by the actions of the British and U.S. intelligence forces.   ††††

JEPSON, SELWYN. *The Angry Millionaire.* 1968. The heir to the controlling interest in a big financial house couldn't care less about the business. That is until his aunt convinces him to take a minor job, and he finds hints of a takeover plot involving top management, then he builds himself a team to turn the tables. This is a romantic suspense story which is hard to put down.   ††††

JOHNSON, STANLEY. *The Doomsday Deposit.* 1980. An adventure story in which plutonium deposits are found just inside the Russian border. The Reds don't know it, so we decide to reroute the border to give the deposits to the Chinese.   ††

JOHNSON, WILLIAM OSCAR. *The Zero Factor.* 1980. The title indicates that no president elected in a zero year has ever left office alive. But there's more: Cuban expatriates bent on vengeance and big bucks, and a slick assassin named LeBombardier.   †††

JONES, DENNIS. *Rubicon One.* 1983. A nuclear brinksmanship novel with the U.S. and the USSR at each other's throats.   †††

JONES, JAMES. *A Touch of Danger.* 1973. The author of *From Here to Eternity* tries his hand at the thriller field with disappointing results. The place: Tsatsos, a Greek island. The hero: a tough-guy expatriate. The plot: a mixture of loose ends hardly worth mentioning.   ††

K

KAPLAN, HOWARD. *The Chopin Express*. 1978. A nice job of plotting. A chase novel set against the backdrop of Russia's secret—or not so secret—war against the Soviet Jews. †††

KAYE, M. M. The author of flamboyant, fat, best-selling historical novels like *The Far Pavilions* has also written a series of mysteries with exotic settings. Originally published in the 1950s, they have been reissued with new titles. The formula is simple: a beautiful young woman is involved in a nasty murder with a strong silent man on hand to solve the mystery and save her life.

Death in Cyprus. 1956. Shipboard scandal and murder for starters, and then a deadly holiday in the sunny Mediterranean for a naive, young English heiress. Kaye uses humor and eccentric characters to break the tension. †††

Death in Kenya. 1958. An English girl's visit to the family ranch in Kenya is complicated by romances old and new, a series of meaningless but menacing practical jokes, and finally murder. The mystery holds water, the setting is exciting, and the characters rise above the limitations of their stereotypes. ††††

Death in Zanzibar. 1959. This is one of those books where the plot hinges on an improbably ingenious murder device. But then, this kind of book isn't meant to stand up to logic. It's worth reading for its color and fast pace. †††

KELLY, JOHN. *The Wooden Wolf.* 1976. A WWII flying story in which John Croft—aka the "Wooden Wolf"—takes off in his Havilland Mosquito to bomb Hitler's train as it moves through Bavaria. †††

KENNEDY, ADAM. *Debt of Honor*. 1981. Two plane crashes—each seemingly an accident—are the catalyst that propels Gabe Treptow into the Senate and into the line of fire from a group of dangerous men with dreams of high places. †††

KENRICK, TONY. A first-rate author of both high-tension thrillers and humorous ones. I prefer the humorous ones, which can be favorably compared to the novels of Donald Westlake.

Stealing Lillian. 1975. An absolutely hilarious novel about the U.S. Immigration trying to flush out a terrorist group by using a small-time con man, a Bloomingdale's decorator, and a nine-year-old brat. My favorite Kenrick novel, and a classic in the comedy-caper field. †††††

The Night-Time Guy. 1979. Not for people who are afraid of the dark. Two groups—the bad guys and the worse guys—are after Max Ellis, and they want his eyes—literally. ††††

The 81st Site. 1980. Toward the end of WWII the Nazis built eighty-one sites from which to launch V-1 bombs on London. The Allies discovered and destroyed eighty of them. Guess what's going to happen with the remaining one? †††

KERRIGAN, JOHN. *The Phoenix Assault.* 1980. In the closing days of WWII, the British and the Americans field a team to rush into the dying Third Reich to keep Martin Bormann from making a deal with the Russians. ††

KIRK, MICHAEL, *Dragonship.* 1977. A well-plotted story about the sinking of the cargo ship *Velella.* As Andrew Laird, insurance investigator, looks into it, he discovers it is far from routine. There was sabotage, and apparently a priceless full-scale replica of a Viking longship was destroyed in the sinking. His troubles multiply when a terrorist group later takes credit for the sinking and the subsequent murders. ††††

KIRST, HANS HELLMUT. Although best known for his series of novels featuring Gunner Asch, he also wrote a couple of thrillers well worth reading.

The Night of the Generals. 1964. The story of a psycho German general who gets his kicks out of killing women Jack-the-Ripper style, and the man who wants to bring him in regardless of the cost. Brilliant characterization and a truly great idea combine to make this a classic. †††††

The Nights of the Long Knives. 1975. Years later—long after the end of WWII—Hitler's hand-picked death squad rears its ugly head. †††

KLEIN, EDWARD. *The Parachutists.* 1981. Near the end of WWII, the OSS recruits Alex Albright to parachute into Germany, kill Adolph Eichmann, and free a half million Hungarian Jews. A mighty tall order for one man—and for one book. ††

KNEBEL, FLETCHER. *Poker Game.* 1983. Doug Perry is a poker player, who must play for very high stakes in this story of computer espionage. The characters are likable and the writing of high quality, but all the technological information drags the story down. I expected better from one of the authors of *Seven Days in May.* ††

KNEBEL, FLETCHER, AND BAILEY, CHARLES W., II. *Seven Days in May.* 1962. The story of an attempt at a military coup in the U.S. A blockbuster. A giant. A classic. One of the absolute best ever written. †††††

KYLE, DUNCAN. Another first-rate thriller writer in the vein of Bagley, MacLean, and Jenkins.

A Cage of Ice. 1971. A misaddressed package from a dead Russian scientist and an assassination attempt on a British surgeon set the groundworks for a deadly confrontation in the Arctic. ††††

Terror's Cradle. 1974. A journalist is run out of Las Vegas by threats on his life. His girlfriend disappears with vital microfilm, and they find themselves on the run in the Shetlands, hunted both by air and sea. †††

The Stalking Point. 1982. It is shortly after the outbreak of WWII, and Roosevelt and Churchill are to meet secretly in the north Atlantic. However, the Germans find out and plot to sabotage the conference and kill the Allied leaders. British and U.S. military intelligence engage the enemy in a deadly game of move and countermove. †††

The King's Commissar. 1984. One of the truly different foreign-intrigue novels in recent years. This story shuttles between 1915 Russia and 1980 England. A dead man leads the septuagenarian director of a bank founded by the legendary Basil Zaharoff through a multi-layered mystery backward in time to the Russian Revolution, and the author makes it work. †††††

L

LAMBERT, DEREK. *The Golden Express.* 1984. Hermann Goering, the greedy rascal, wants all the gold in the Bank of England. Doesn't everyone? ††

LAMBERT, DEREK. *The Judas Code.* 1984. Did Churchill pit Hitler and Stalin against each other to spare England from invasion? Of course he did, and it was with the Judas Code. †††

LATHAM, AARON. *Orchids for Mother.* 1977. A nicely done, nasty little novel about a duel for control of the top levels of the CIA. The author has some fun with some of the more idiotic real-life pranks of the CIA. †††

LE CARRÉ, JOHN. The man who revolutionized thriller writing, bringing to it a sense of style not seen since the early days of Eric Ambler. His books feature little or no violence or sex, concentrating instead on the drab, easily overlooked people who gravitate to the spy game. I think of them as bureaucratic novels, with clerks rather than swashbucklers as heroes.

Call for the Dead. 1962. George Smiley plays detective when a British civil servant apparently commits suicide. The story has a couple of interesting clues, but otherwise is nowhere near as good as his later work. †††

Murder of Quality. 1962. George Smiley plays detective again in a straightforward mystery, which is interesting only because it is the author's first attempt at the type of commentary on the British social system, which elevates his later work to such a pinnacle. ††

The Spy Who Came in from the Cold. 1963. This is the one which turned le Carré into a superstar. It is the story of Alex Leamus, the spy out in the cold, but it could just as easily been *Death of a Salesman*, since it is a novel about a man on the road who works for a heartless bureaucratic organization.   †††††

The Looking Glass War. 1965. An attempt to continue with the success he enjoyed in *Spy Who Came in from the Cold* in which le Carré again deals with agents in the field. Nowhere near as good.   †††

Small Town in Germany. 1968. The low point in le Carré's spy writing.   ††

The Naive and Sentimental Lover. 1971. Le Carré's one try at a non-espionage novel. Unfortunately, it isn't very good.   ††

Tinker, Tailor, Soldier, Spy. 1974. Le Carré's masterpiece. George Smiley attempts to ferret out a mole in the British Intelligence organization.   †††††

The Honorable Schoolboy. 1977. The second in what is now known as the Smiley trilogy. It takes up where *Tinker, Tailor* leaves off, and in concept and execution is a much more ambitious book, but this expansion of concept makes it extremely difficult to follow.   ††††

Smiley's People. 1980. The last and worst part of the Smiley trilogy. Le Carré, obviously tiring of Smiley, pits him one last time against his age-old enemy, Karla.   †††

The Little Drummer Girl. 1984. Back in form and filled with enthusiasm, le Carré tackles the point-counterpoint world of Middle Eastern terrorists. A thoroughly excellent read.   ††††

LECOMBER, BRIAN. *Turn Killer.* 1978. A stunt pilot investigates the death of a colleague in a crash and is almost killed himself. Holland finds himself the target of French criminals and a Mafia godfather, who are after something they consider worth millions. The hero and a beautiful companion are chased from the Mediterrean to the Caribbean in a wild thriller that stamps Lecomber as a welcome newcomer to adventure ranks.   ††††

LECOMBER, BRIAN. *Dead Weight.* 1979. Another flying story with an alcoholic pilot trying to redeem himself after a sojourn in prison for drug smuggling. He is caught up in a plot to transport stolen gold for a shady West Indian businessman and an ex-Nazi, with the CIA breathing down his neck.   †††

LEE, JOHN. *The Ninth Man.* 1976. A German assassin, sent by Hitler to murder Roosevelt, very nearly succeeds. America in wartime makes an interesting background as the assassin makes his way to the president. Very effective climax.   †††

LEE, JOHN. *The Thirteenth Hour.* 1978. Plenty of action in this retelling of the fall of the German high command in WWII. Captain Henry Bascomb finds himself pursuing an escaping Adolph Hitler when everyone else wants to believe that the Führer is dead. †††

LEHMAN, ERNEST. *The French Atlantic Affair.* 1977. One hundred and seventy-four terrorists take over a luxury liner in mid ocean. They want money, lots of money. But there is a new wrinkle, the terrorists are not identifiable among the 2,800 other passengers. ††††

LEVIN, IRA. *The Boys from Brazil.* 1976. One of the most imaginative of the Nazi resurgence novels ever written, as the good guys try to stop the remnants of the SS from unleashing a Hitler clone on the world. Now we know how the Führer spent all those long nights in his bunker. †††††

LIEBERMAN, HERBERT. *The Climate of Hell.* 1978. The fact that the fate of Dr. Josef Mengele is officially settled does not deprive this story of its impact. It is written with great conviction. Dr. Gregor Gregori, "Angel of Death" of Auschwitz, is still alive and operating in Paraguay. Ian Asher, a young Israeli soldier known to be mentally ill, does not believe reports of Gregori's death. He hunts the doctor down and imposes a punishment designed to fit the man's crimes. †††

LITTELL, ROBERT. *The Defection of A. J. Lewinter.* 1973. A masterpiece of double cross, triple cross, and even quadruple cross, as an American scientist defects to Russia, carrying with him information of the highest order. The question is—Is he for real, or not? This is a complex one. †††††

LITTELL, ROBERT. *The Amateur.* 1981. An unpretentious thriller similar in plot to *Marathon Man* or *Six Days of the Condor.* †††

LITVINOFF, EMANUEL. *Falls the Shadow.* 1983. A much better than average Nazi novel, centering around the cold-blooded murder of an Israeli businessman. Both the victim and the killer are former concentration camp inmates, but is either really what he seems? ††††

LOCKHART, ROBIN BRUCE. *Reilly: Ace of Spies.* 1967. The true story of the extraordinary adventures of Sidney Reilly, Britain's greatest spy ever, his career beginning at the close of the 19th century and ending finally in Bolshevik Russia in 1925. Fascinating, truly fascinating. ††††

LONDON, JACK, AND FISH, ROBERT L. *The Assassination Bureau, Ltd.* 1963. London's last book, finished after his death by Fish. The hilarious story of a woman who hires an English murder syndicate to kill its own leader. A great lesson in the rules of British fair play. ††††

LUARD, NICHOLAS. *The Orion Line.* 1977. A Ludlum type of thriller bridging the gap between WWII and the present. I finished it, but it left me cold. ††

LUDLUM, ROBERT.   A giant in the business. A hard worker, who puts his heart into his complex novels of paranoia that make you believe the bastards really are out to get you. His early work was outstanding, but his later work has slipped somewhat, due in large part to the greater and greater length of his books. They are just becoming too unwieldy. I don't think this is entirely his fault. Since the field has become glutted with people imitating him, to keep ahead of the pack he has had to reach more and more.

The Scarlatti Inheritance.   1971. His first book, and still one of the best of the Nazi novels ever done.   ††††

The Osterman Weekend.   1972. A group of friends gather at a suburban New Jersey home for a quiet weekend reunion. However, one or more of the group is involved in dirty dealings, as the author demonstrates in this version of "Ten Little Indians."   †††

The Matlock Paper.   1973. My personal favorite of his books. The story of a college professor drawn into discovering who is behind a drug ring at a New England college. I couldn't put it down.   ††††

The Rhineman Exchange.   1974. It is back to the Nazis again as David Spaulding and Jane Cameron are caught in the midst of global intrigue in a world at war.   ††††

The Gemini Contenders.   1976. A complex novel that includes everything from WWII Nazis to 1970s treachery.   †††

The Chancellor Manuscript.   1977. Ludlum's masterpiece. A fascinating, very complex story about the death of J. Edgar Hoover. He did a fine job on this one.   ††††

The Matarese Circle.   1979. The two best James Bond-type spies (one American, one Russian) must team up to stop the Matarese, an international group of killers.   †††

The Bourne Identity.   1980. A man with amnesia becomes the target for assassins.   †††

LYALL, GAVIN.   A fine English thriller writer in the mold of MacLean. His prose is very lean, without a wasted word, and his stories are beautifully crafted.

The Wrong Side of the Sky.   1961. A nail-biter about the search for valuable cargo lost with the disappearance of the aircraft carrying it. An intrepid flyer with an offbeat sense of humor picks his way among the mine fields of double and triple cross in an adventure tale from a master of the game.   ††††

The Most Dangerous Game. 1963. A double-barreled tale of international espionage set against a backdrop of Finland near the Russian border. Lyall's hero follows the trail of a suspected double agent, who uses murder to achieve his ends. He is hampered in his quest by a jaded big-game hunter, who is obsessed with capping his career by participating in "the most dangerous game"—man hunting man. ††††

Midnight Plus One. 1965. With an industrial empire at stake, one of the best of Lyall's four-letter-surnamed protagonists goes back to his WWII haunts to take on some of his French Resistance comrades in a deadly chase. ††††

Shooting Script. 1966. A flyer in need of money is hired by a film company to participate in a movie that is being produced and acted in by an aging actor in the John Wayne mold. He soon finds the film is a screen for Latin-American revolutionary activity, and the suspense builds, brick by brick, to one of the author's sardonic endings. ††††

Venus with Pistol. 1969. One of Lyall's real-life enthusiasms is the study of guns. In this international potboiler, he mixes this lore with the underground world of art thievery. The protagonist has been chosen by the villains for his slightly shady reputation, which in this caper proves to be more skin-deep than real. †††

Blame the Dead. 1973. A security specialist, his pride stung by the murder of his client in the south of France, follows a deadly trail of marine sabotage and international intrigue to the snowy mountains of Norway where he finds his search complicated by a beautiful woman. †††

M

MCAULIFFE, FRANK. The author of three truly excellent collections of short stories about a coldhearted British professional killer named Augustus Mandrell, and cut from the same cloth as James Bond. The titles are *Rather a Vicious Gentleman*, *For Murder I Charge More*, and *Of All the Bloody Cheek*.

MCCRUM, ROBERT. *In the Secret State.* 1980. An excellent novel of computer chicanery in British Intelligence as a small group of men gather more and more data, on the theory that knowledge is power. Frank Strange is swept up in the events and must either sink or swim. ††††

MCCUTCHAN, PHILIP. *Gibraltar Road.* 1960. Another Bond look-alike series. Commander Shaw tries to avoid disaster on Gibraltar as a nuclear power plant runs amok, and the scientist who can straighten it out has disappeared. ††

MCGARRITY, MARK. *A Passing Advantage.* 1980. General Mike Mackey, a mad military man, seizes the opportunity to best the Russians at the Elbe, if only for a moment, but his action sets off a domino-chain of events beyond his control.   ††

MCGHEE, EDWARD, AND MOORE, ROBIN.   *The Chinese Ultimatum*. 1976. Too much story for one book. Some of the episodes are Russia and China go to war, Germany reunites, Japan once again joins forces with Germany, England and France turn tail and run, etc., etc., etc.   ††

MACINNES, HELEN.   Like Eric Ambler, she writes of international espionage and suspense. Also, like Ambler, she often uses naive heroes who stumble into the intelligence underworld and have to prove that they can survive. But where Ambler dwells on the ambiguity of it all, she creates clear-cut good guys and bad guys.

Above Suspicion.   1941. Her first book, and still one of her best. Richard and Frances Myles, an Oxford don and his wife, who may be modeled on the author and her husband, literary critic Gilbert Highet, are sent to Nazi Germany by the British Foreign Office just before the war. They're supposed to track down a missing British spy.   ††††

Assignment in Brittany.   1942. This wartime adventure is really about people trying to get on with their lives in the middle of a cataclysm. A British soldier parachutes into a tiny French village to impersonate a wounded French soldier and keep an eye on German troop movements. He has to fool the man's friends, his family, and his fiancée. It's a war story, a love story, and a good mystery.
                                                                      †††

I and My True Love.   1953. In an updating of the Romeo and Juliet business, this novel sympathetically portrays the star-crossed love affair of a Czechoslovakian diplomat and an American woman. More than any of her other books, it shows the author's feelings about ideological conflicts, and the way they affect individuals.   †††

The Venetian Affair.   1963. The author enjoys introducing young Americans to the corrupt intricacy of the Old World. In the process, characters like Bill Fenner, the hero of this novel, exchange idealism for courage. Set in Paris, Switzerland, and Venice, this is a story about Soviet plots under the cover of peace talks. The villain is an unmistakably repulsive terrorist.   ††††

The Double Image.   1966. This story begins when an American in Paris meets a former professor, who has just seen a dead Nazi walking the streets. The American becomes part of a team of intelligence agents from all countries, who converge on Mykonos to penetrate a Nazi-Fascist-Communist multiple identity.   †††††

The Salzburg Connection.   1968. In a book that opens and closes with an echo of WWII, a young American on a business trip gets involved in espionage, murder, and the mystery of Nazi secrets hidden in a mountain lake. He also gets involved with not one, but two women. †††

The Snare of the Hunter. 1974. An American writer, who fell in love with a Czech girl years ago, joins a group of amateur agents in smuggling her into Austria. The pace is brisk and the characters well drawn, but the plot isn't quite up to her usual standards. ††

Agent in Place. 1976. This book is an inside look at a society within society: the brother- and sisterhood of intelligence agents, who have their own rules and passions. It suggests that two spies, of any two countries, have more in common than two fellow countrymen. Action ranges from New York to the French Riviera, as a hidden agent is forced into the open by misguided idealism. †††

The Hidden Target. 1980. An especially strong sense of place permeates this book, which opens in an old German church and moves to Istanbul, Iran, and London. A young woman is drawn into international intrigue and, pretending to be someone she isn't, travels with a group of people who also aren't what they seem. †††

Cloak of Darkness. 1982. Sequel to *The Hidden Target*, this book picks up the story of Nina and Bob Renwick, counter-terrorists who are marked for assassination by a secret organization bent on world conquest. †††

MacKENZIE, COMPTON. *Water on the Brain.* 1933. A warm, wonderful adventure in which Major Blenkinsop, of the British Secret Service, restores the King of Mendacia to his throne, encountering both beautiful and weird characters along the way. ††††

MacKINNON, ALLAN. *House of Darkness.* 1947. In a fast-moving adventure that starts in Cairo, passes through London into the wilds of the Scottish highlands, and winds up in an elegant townhouse, young Colin Ogilvie encounters a murderous traitor, a threat to national security posing as a religious movement, and a disarming blonde. He manages to take them all in stride—he has fun and so do the readers. ††††

MacLEAN, ALISTAIR. From his debut with *The H.M.S. Ulysses* (written from start to finish in only ten weeks), MacLean has been a force to be reckoned with in the thriller field. His first seven or eight are excellent, but alas, his later work has slipped somewhat. He still gives you MacLean word for word, but some of the zing is gone because his plots have become routine, only the setting changes, but the basic elements remain the same from story to story.

South by Java Head. 1958. Coming on the heels of his success with *The H.M.S. Ulysses*, MacLean decides to try it again—this time with the Japanese—as the last boat slips out of Singapore after its fall. It's a good read, but nowhere nearly as good as his first. †††

Night Without End. 1960. Dr. Peter Mason, IGY scientist in Greenland, watches as an airliner crash-lands nearby. He goes to help and becomes involved with secret agents and death.   †††

The Golden Rendezvous. 1962. John Carter, chief officer on the S.S. *Campari*, becomes involved with a secret atomic weapon and a beautiful woman, as the ship chugs on toward its date with destiny.   †††

Ice Station Zebra. 1963. A British meteorological team is trapped at the North Pole. A U.S. nuclear submarine is dispatched to rescue them, becomes involved in a full-scale, Cold War espionage operation. A classic.   †††††

Puppet on a Chain. 1969. An Interpol agent and two lovely assistants go to Holland to break up a drug ring in MacLean's most exotic novel. There are moments where the action has erotic overtones similar to Tryon's *Harvest Home*. My favorite MacLean novel.   †††††

Bear Island. 1971. The *Morning Rose*, an arctic trawler, brings Marlowe, the ship's doctor, and a movie crew to Bear Island, an island north of the Arctic Circle, for filming. Someone among them is a murderer, who has already killed three people on the voyage and will not hesitate to do it again. This is MacLean at his best.   †††††

The Golden Gate. 1976. The president of the U.S. is taken hostage on the Golden Gate Bridge, and the bridge is set to explode unless a huge ransom is paid. This is one of MacLean's weakest novels.   ††

MCLENDON, JAMES. *Eddie Macon's Run.* 1980. A chase novel involving a lovable escaped convict, a mean, dirty, vicious cop, and a hundred miles of hot Texas desert.   ††

MACPHERSON, MALCOLM. *Protégé.* 1980. Another weak Nazi resurgence novel. This time Admiral Canaris leaves behind a legacy of twenty-one handpicked sickos to carry on the Führer's work forty years later.   ††

MCQUINN, DONALD E. *Wake in Darkness.* 1981. The scene is Manila and Glen Drager of the CIA finds himself in the middle when one of his couriers is killed, and his boss—his control—goes crazy.   †††

MCQUINN, DONALD E. *Shadow of Lies.* 1985. A very well-written novel about a Russian spy ready to score a coup in the Silicon Valley when his superiors force him to take an amateur into his network. In our corner, we have the usual broken shell of a man who is obsessed with capturing the spy. But he doesn't detract from the overall excellence of the story.   ††††

MAGDALEN, L. L. *In Search of Anderson.* 1982. Derek Flaye, a cog in England's security apparatus, is hailed by an old schoolmaster by a name not his own. In his efforts to find out why, a Philby-like situation develops in which the old saw "where there's smoke, there's fire" proves that smoke can also act as a screen, hiding the true identity of Jamie Anderson. †††††

MARKHAM, ROBERT. *Colonel Sun.* 1968. Written after Fleming's death. "M" is captured and only one man can save him—007. ††

MARKSTEIN, GEORGE. *Chance Awakening.* 1977. Michael Golly, a Russian mole posing as a London businessman, gets the go-ahead signal he has been dreading for so many years. A well-written psychological novel of trust and mistrust. †††

MARLOWE, DEREK. *A Dandy in Aspic.* 1966. An excellent, Cold War spy novel, in the mold of Len Deighton and Adam Hall, about a double agent working both sides of the England/Russia fence. ††††

MARLOWE, STEPHEN. *The Valkyrie Encounter.* 1978. Another plot to kill Hitler. This time it is the Germans who are going to kill him, and the Allies who want him kept alive. ††

MARSLAND, AMY. *Cache-Cache.* 1980. The American wife of a French businessman realizes that her husband and his shadowy connections are trying to kill her. After two attempts fail, she flees to the south of France and the protection of former comrades in the Resistance movement. This is a solid chase story, with menace, violence, and romance leading to a successful climax. †††

MARTIN, TREVOR. *The Terminal Transfer.* 1984. A quasi-caper novel without the lightheartedness of that genre. Jordon Freeling, a math whiz, figures out a way to transfer corporate money to his own accounts and, when he is arrested, is able to bargain his way out of it with government agents. Lots of background masks a pretty thin story. ††

MARTIN, WILLIAM. *Nerve Ending.* 1984. A complicated plot, too slow in getting started. A kidney-transplant recipient decides to look into the accidental death of the TV executive who was his donor. The plot involves a conspiracy through television to exert mind control. Well written, but too slow. ††

MASON, VAN WYCK. *The Gracious Lily Affair.* 1957. Colonel North, of British Intelligence, is vacationing in Bermuda when a plane explodes nearby, a spearfishing trip proves deadly, and a beautiful oriental seductress plys her trade on him. You don't have to hit him over the head to let him know something is going on. †††

MASTERS, JOHN. *Night Runners of Bengal.* (n.d.) The author begins his long saga of the Savage family, with Colonel Rodney Savage caught up in the looming

Sepoy rebellion of 1857. When it breaks, Savage sees his wife killed, and flees with his son and an Englishwoman on a danger-filled trek of hundreds of miles across India.   ††††

MASTERS, JOHN. *The Deceivers.* (n.d.) Based on true happenings in India during the latter part of the 19th century, this tells the story of William Savage who seeks the answer to the disappearance of merchants' caravans. Disguised as a native, he uncovers one of the great mass murders in history, perpetrated by the followers of a Hindu goddess of death.   ††††

MASTERS, JOHN. *Bhowani Junction.* (n.d.) Twilight approaches for the British Raj as the Mahatma's policy of peaceful resistance takes hold in India. A 20th-century Rodney Savage fights a rearguard action on behalf of the British Empire, while falling in love with an Indian girl, who is torn between her sense of patriotic duty and her doomed love for a hated Englishman.   †††

MATHER, ARTHUR. *The Mind Breaker.* 1980. A group of terrorists hold the president's mind hostage. The only way I would read any further is if they hold *my* mind hostage.   †

MATHER, BERKELY. *The Achilles Affair.* 1958. The first half of this book deals with the heroism, the double-dealing, and the cynicism of war, as two English officers slog through the Balkans with partisan groups whose hatred for the Nazis is equaled by that for each other. Twelve years later, the two meet again against the background of the Greek-Turkish struggle for Cyprus, and Soviet interference in Lebanon.   †††

MATHER, BERKELY. *The Pass Beyond Kashmir.* 1960. The author introduces Idwal Rees, based in Bombay as a free-lance troubleshooter, and his Pathan servant, Safaraz. The two lead an expedition to recover papers buried years before, giving the location of a rich oil field near the Northwest frontier. Along the way they battle the area natives, a renegade Englishman, and a half-mad soldier of fortune, who wants the information for the Russians. An American scientist and his attractive assistant reluctantly help Rees accomplish his mission.   ††††

MATHER, BERKELY. *The Pagoda Tree.* 1979. This is a panoramic novel describing the adventures of Ross Stafford, who leaves England in 1850 to rescue his brother sent to Australia as a convict. From there, Ross joins the East India Company, and is swept into the middle of an Opium War in China and the Sepoy mutiny of 1856 in India.   †††

MAXIM, JOHN. *Abel, Baker, Charley.* 1983. A well-written story of a mad-dog assassin on the loose, with the Mafia, the FBI, the CIA, a beautiful woman, and heaven-knows-who-else after him.   †††

• *Some novels to read during Christmas:*

AN ENGLISH MURDER by Cyril Hare
A HOLIDAY FOR MURDER by Agatha Christie
REST YE MERRY by Charlotte MacLeod
TIED UP IN TINSEL by Ngaio Marsh
THE TWELVE DEATHS OF CHRISTMAS by Marion Babson

MAYO, JAMES.   *Hammerhead.* 1964. One of the best of the James Bond takeoffs. Charles Hood, intrepid hero, takes on Hammerhead, super-villain.   †††

MILLAR, JEFF.   *Private Sector.* 1979. John Harland and Molly Rice are live-in lovers and reporters for competing TV networks. They have assignments that end up being part of the same story—a corporate plan to take over the government through the use of energy sources. When one of them dies in pursuit of the truth, the other picks up the trail. A believable romance and a plot unraveled with authority make this an enjoyable read.   †††

MONTALBANO, WILLIAM D., AND HIAASEN, CARL.   A *Death in China.* 1984. Two American professors in Peking—one old, one young—find themselves looking down the wrong end of the Communist gun because of what they know about real crimes against the state.   ††††

MORRELL, DAVID.   *First Blood.* 1972. The famous Rambo—hippie, Vietnam vet, Medal of Honor winner, and former Green Beret—decides to take on an entire Kentucky town when the sheriff asks him to leave.   †††

MORRELL, DAVID.   *Testament.* 1975. There's far too much blood and gore in this chase novel about Reuben Bourne and his family being pursued by the usual socio-political weirdos. This one is not for sensitive people.   †

MUNRO, JAMES.   Author of a superior series on the order of James Bond, featuring John Craig. They are among the best of the 1960s high-action spy novels. I have read three of the series: *Die Rich Die Happy, The Man Who Sold Death,* and *The Money That Money Can't Buy.* I recommend all three.

MURPHY, CHRISTOPHER.   *Scream at the Sea.* 1982. This is a page-turner which strains the limits of credibility but is difficult to put down. Britain's western Highlands are the locale, in the few times anyone sets foot on solid ground. A high-performance amphibian plane, an F-4 Phantom jet and a disabled British nuclear submarine are essential to the plot, which finds a likable hero and a highly capable heroine mixed up in murder and intrigue.   †††

MURPHY, WALTER F. *The Roman Enigma*. 1981. Roberto Rovere, an American agent, is dispatched to Rome to steal Ultra, the German WWII code machine, only to be betrayed to the SS by our very own OSS. ††

MURPHY, WARREN, AND COCHRAN, MOLLY. *Grandmaster*. 1984. Murphy, the author of the successful "Destroyer" series, collaborated with his wife to produce this huge best-seller built around secret agents and the martial arts.
††††

MYKEL, A. W. *The Wind Chime Legacy*. 1980. A computerized weapons system and a Nazi revival are both at issue here. Justin Chaple, secret agent and trained assassin, goes from hunter to hunted and finds betrayal at every turn. Mykel writes well and with more authority than most about the netherworld of secret agents. ††††

MYKEL, A. W. *The Salamandra Glass*. 1983. Michael Gladieux, a trained killer from Vietnam, finds his father murdered, with a note accusing him of being a Nazi collaborator. There the chase begins in what is a good read. ††††

N

NEWCOMB, KERRY, AND SCHAEFER, FRANK. *Pandora Man*. 1979. Terrorists kidnap the president-elect with the idea of substituting their own man. Only one man can stop them. †

NEWHAFER, RICHARD. *Seven Days to Glory*. 1973. Matt Keane and Raul Garcia, a couple of hot-shot flyboys, hire out to make the difference in a Bay-of-Pigs type of Cuban coup. ††

NICHOLSON, MICHAEL. *The Partridge Kite*. 1978. A series of terrorist actions, ranging from the bombing of a bank and the theft of millions, to the bombing of an offshore oil rig in the North Sea, and the murder of a prominent union official, points toward the beginnings of a right-wing coup in England. †††

NICOLAYSEN, BRUCE. *Perilous Passage*. 1976. A Jewish family and a gruff-but-lovable Basque guide are being chased by the SS as they flee through the Pyrenees Mountains toward safety. ††

NIESEWAND, PETER. *Fallback*. 1982. A tense, well-written thriller in which an American computer expert must penetrate a Russian complex in the Ural Mountains before they launch the rockets which will signal the end of life as we know it. ††††

NIESEWAND, PETER. *Scimitar.* 1983. The CIA allows the Russians to kidnap back a Russian defector with important information. This puts two of America's best agents in the middle in a tense intelligence game, which they have no right to win. ††††

NOLAN, FREDERICK. *Brass Target.* 1974. The story of a plot to kill an American general named Campion, who is based on George Patton. A lot of real people do walk-ons in this decently plotted thriller. †††

O

O'BRINE, MANNING. *Mills.* 1969. The title character is a British agent who is designated by Whitehall to facilitate the defection of an ex-Nazi scientist from East Germany. Mills's bosses want the formula the scientist has developed, not knowing Mills has found out that the German helped in the wartime massacre of some of his comrades. After the demise of the scientist, everybody chases Mills to recover the formula. †††

O'BRINE, MANNING. *No Earth for Foxes.* 1974. Ray Pavane wants to leave MI6 to get married, but he is conned into one more job when he finds his old mentor, Mills, is making a Napoleonic return from exile to help break up a neo-Nazi outfit which seeks to revive Hitler's Third Reich. The Israelis, the Russians, and the Americans all get into the act. The author is at his best in manipulating a group of characters each of whom has his own ideas about teamwork. ††††

O'DONNELL, PETER. Forget sugar and spice—sex and violence are what Modesty Blaise is made of. If you think nothing becomes a legend more than guns, knives, and leather clothes, then here is your fantasy. Modesty Blaise started life as a cartoon strip in England, but she soon leaped to the silver screen and went on to star in a series of books. With her knife-throwing sidekick, Willie, Modesty fights and loves her way across the world. In terms of style, these books hit the point midway between Ian Fleming and Nick Carter. Their comic-strip roots live on in the fast-paced slam-bang action, the fantastic villains, and the lurid sexual posing, but there are moments of genuine humor.

Modesty Blaise. 1965. In her debut appearance, Modesty abandons the criminal network she heads for the even greater thrill of working for British Intelligence. †††

Sabre-Tooth. 1966. To save a child from a fate worse than death, Modesty and Willie take on a modern Genghis Khan and his corps of killers. Willie's verdict: "We should have stuck to crime." The real crisis comes when Willie betrays Modesty. The plot is comic-strip standard, but the characterizations are a bit deeper. †††

I, Lucifer.   1967. A madman plans a worldwide reign of terror, beginning with a series of utterly impossible death threats. The trouble is, he starts making good on the threats.   ††

A Taste for Death.   1969. Some of the focus shifts to Willie in this novel of a duel fought with a murderous giant in the broiling Sahara. Willie has fought this man before—and lost. A preposterous plot, but excellent combat scenes.   †††

The Impossible Virgin.   1971. A Soviet traitor tries to smuggle information out from behind the Iron Curtain, and danger interrupts Modesty's romantic idyll with a humanitarian doctor in Africa. But even more annoying than this coitus interruptus is the loss of Willie, pitched to his death by Modesty's archenemy. She's always eager to defy death herself, but this time she has an added motive—revenge.   ††

OLDEN, MARC.   *Giri.* 1982. A thoroughly satisfying thriller with revenge as its motive and martial arts as the backdrop. Martial-arts action scenes are very difficult to write because of the terminology and the unfamiliar movements, but the author handles this information beautifully, weaving it into the story until it becomes as interesting as the story itself.   ††††

OPPENHEIM, E. PHILLIPS.   *The Great Impersonation.* 1920. This is one of the classic espionage stories. Oppenheim wrote many popular thrillers and lived lavishly, sprinkling his stories with anecdotes about life among the rich and famous. In this, his most enduring tale, Sir Everard Dominey—a drunken, pathetic failure—disappears into the African jungle, only to emerge sometime later sober, pure-minded, and ready to go home and shoulder his responsibility. But is he really Sir Everard? Or is he Dominey's look-alike, a German officer and spy? Mixed in with the spy story is a juicy domestic mystery, replete with insanity, murder, and a ghost.   †††††

P

PATTERSON, JAMES.   *The Thomas Berryman Number.* 1976. The story of an assassin who sets out to kill the first black mayor of Nashville. Probably inspired by the Memphis slaying of Dr. Martin Luther King. Not a very good read.   †

PAUL, ELIOT.   *The Mysterious Mickey Finn.* 1939. An absolute classic as Homer Evans, American in Paris, tries to solve the disappearance of a millionaire. It has a wonderful description of Paris at its best and some very funny writing. Loads of excitement.   †††††

PEARSON, WILLIAM.   *Chessplayer.* 1984. Another in the growing series of "we have met the enemy and they are us" espionage thrillers. A taxi driver finds a briefcase filled with money, and this opens a Pandora's box which shakes the highest levels of U.S. and Soviet intelligence circles as one seeks to unmask and the other to protect "Chessplayer." ††††

PEEL, COLIN D. *Firestorm*. 1984. Harwood, an explosives expert, is called in to locate bombs which have been placed in the foundations of an oil rig. He is helped by the daughter of a man killed because he knew too much about the plans of a terrorist-controlled corporation, and the two face a fight for survival that culminates in an explosive finale in Sweden. ††

PENIAKOFF, VLADIMIR. *Popski's Private Army*. 1950. The true-life memoirs of a middle-aged businessman who established a guerrilla army which operated behind German lines during WWII. Fascinating. ††††

PERRY, RITCHIE. *The Fall Guy*. 1972. British Intelligence picks secret agent Philis to locate the source of the European cocaine trade. Good story with lots of action. †††

PERRY, RITCHIE. *A Hard Man to Kill*. 1973. The title describes Philis, Perry's series character, an English agent who survives because, as his boss says, he represents "cowardice plus a well-developed sense of self-preservation." Here he tracks an ex-Nazi who knows the identity of a double agent who has caused the exposure and deaths of agents on both sides. †††

PERRY, RITCHIE. *MacAllister*. 1984. Frank MacAllister seeks to track down the killer of his old friend and brother-in-law. The trail leads to Portugal, where the victim and his wife's family lived, and despite constant close brushes with death, he uncovers a diamond-smuggling scheme which leads to a violent climax. Unfortunately, not one of his best. ††

PERRY, ROLAND. *Program for a Puppet*. 1979. When a woman in Paris is killed while investigating computer smuggling, her boyfriend continues the investigation. He uncovers a plot in which an American company is supplying the KGB with computers which can alter the balance of power in the world. †††

PERRY, THOMAS. A rising young star in the thriller field. His work can best be likened to Ross Thomas's, his strongest points being his slightly eccentric characters and his humor.

The Butcher's Boy. 1982. An impressive debut. The story of an organized-crime hit man who is on a killing spree around the country, and the female treasury agent who discovers and chases him. ††††

Metzger's Dog. 1983. A wonderful rollicking tale of a lovable gang who blackmail the CIA, a cat, and a man-eating dog. A "must read" for animal lovers. ††††

Big Fish. 1985. While still very entertaining, this humorous novel of three people in an arms deal is not as good as either of his first two. †††

PERSICO, JOSEPH. *Spiderweb.* 1979. A poor job of execution on yet another Nazi terror rising from the ashes of the Third Reich. †

PHILBRICK, HERBERT A. *I Led Three Lives.* 1952. The most paranoid piece of claptrap to come out of the red-baiting 1950s. It spawned a popular TV show starring Richard Carlson, but even with Hollywood's tricks, nothing could make the true story of this glorified newsboy into a spy tale of any substance. †

PLUNKET, ROBERT. *My Search for Warren Harding.* 1983. The zany adventures of a Los Angeles history scholar as he tries to get his hands on a trunk filled with letters from Warren G. Harding. †††

POLLOCK, J. C. *Mission M.I.A.* 1982. A well-written mercenary novel in which Jack Callahan rounds up five ex-Green Berets to go back to Vietnam and free some POWs. It was nice to see us as the good guys for a change. ††††

POLLOCK, J. C. *Centrifuge.* 1984. A high-action thriller in which Vietnam vet Mike Slater becomes the target of both the CIA and the KGB because of a secret learned years ago in Vietnam. †††

PRICE, ANTHONY. The author of a series of very sophisticated thrillers featuring David Audley of British Intelligence. Price's work is hard to categorize except to say that it is completely unlike Ludlum's, or le Carré's either. He is his own man, a rare thing anymore.

The Labyrinth Makers. 1970. David Audley explores the mystery of a crashed plane with the dead pilot in it, found nearly twenty years later. Did the plane take off with a fortune in valuable jewels and art? If so, what happened to it? A well-organized plot with a satisfactory ending, not only for the reader but for Audley as well. ††††

Other Paths to Glory. 1974. Paul Mitchell, a young WWI historian, becomes the unsuccessful target of some person or persons who are plotting a deeper crime connected with a reenactment of the Battle of the Somme. Recruited by Audley and his associate, Jack Butler, Mitchell and a lovely French girl gamble their lives to stop a conspiracy which will rock the Western world. †††††

Our Man in Camelot. 1975. British Intelligence high-jinks in the historical diggings at the suspected site of King Arthur's stronghold, with David Audley creating the usual traitorous havoc and then helping to place the pieces back in their proper order. †††

War Game. 1976. The author evokes another historical era with the annual reenactment of a famous battle, but misses the mark this time with an inconsequential plot that limps to a ho-hum conclusion. ††

The '44 Vintage. 1978. With this book, the author goes back in time to Audley and Butler's first meeting on the battlefields of France, during the WWII days when the Germans were infiltrating the British army. The climax occurs in a historic French chateau. ††††

Tomorrow's Ghost. 1979. The widow of a murdered English agent is recruited to spy on Colonel Butler, whose appointment to a position of trust is being blocked by an old enemy, who casts aspersions on his loyalty. †††

Soldier No More. 1982. The author goes back to 1957 and the recruitment of David Audley for British Intelligence. Such disparate elements as a young officer working for the British and the Soviets, a Frenchman striving to foil an Algerian terror squad, a beautiful Israeli spy, and Audley himself making the moves with his fine touch, make for a slam-bang climax. ††††

PROCHNAU, WILLIAM. *Trinity's Child.* 1983. A doomsday thriller in which Russia shoots first, and we have to claw our way out of the rubble of our civilization. ††

Q

QUINNEL, A. J. *Man on Fire.* (n.d.) The story of a mercenary who is hired as a bodyguard for an Italian girl. The girl is kidnapped and killed. The rest is revenge. †††

R

REEMAN, DOUGLAS. One of the best sea-story writers to ever put pen to paper. His favorite plot deals with a virtuous first mate, an insane captain, a worn-out ship, and perils at every turn.

To Risks Unknown. 1969. John Crespin, the good first officer, has to battle both the enemy and his own psychotic, battle-weary captain. ††††

The Destroyers. 1975. Eight destroyers, all veterans from WWI, are pressed into service and sent to the icy north Atlantic on a death run. ††††

REVELLI, GEORGE. *Commander Amanda.* 1968. Originally published by Grove Press, this erotic series of adventures of Commander Amanda Nightingale at the hands of the Germans are very hot. Don't leave this one around for the kids to find. ††††

RHINEHART, LUKE. *Long Voyage Back.* 1983. WWIII has come to an end, and a small group aboard a trimaran in the Chesapeake Bay survive. But to continue to do so in a dying world will demand much of them. †††

RHODES, RUSSELL. *The Styx Complex*. 1977. The story of Ava Bardoff—one *bad* woman—who heads up an empire of torture and control by selling eternal youth, or the illusion of it. †††

RHODES, RUSSELL. *The Third Fury*. 1985. A load of hogwash about a former U.S. president disabling all U.S. weapons so they can't be used on us in the Middle East. Of course he's kidnapped by the KGB. Don't bother. †

ROBERTS, KENNETH. The greatest American historical adventure writer ever. His tales of early America are better than James Fenimore Cooper, and if you once read him, you'll have a lot of trouble settling down with a John Jakes novel afterward.

Arundel. 1930. The beginning of the Nathan family saga as the men of Arundel, Maine, join Benedict Arnold in his first expedition into Canada. You won't want to put it down once you start. In fact you'll want to save it to pass along to your children. †††††

Rabble in Arms. 1933. A five-star rating is too low for the greatest American historical adventure novel ever written. This is the second volume of the adventures of the Nathan family as they continue with Benedict Arnold in the Revolutionary War. After you read this, you will never think of Benedict Arnold in the same way. This meticulously researched story shows there is more than one side to history—even American history. †††††

Captain Caution. 1934. The further adventures of another generation of the men of Arundel, Maine, and especially the Nathan family, as they once again come to the aid of their country, this time in the War of 1812. ††††

Northwest Passage. 1936. The story of artist-to-be, young Langton Towne, who joins Rogers' Rangers after a drunken spree, and marches north toward Canada and the French and Indian War. Because he can write, he is ever in the company of the flamboyant Major Rogers. At the end of the war, Rogers steals Towne's girl and marries her. Towne goes to London to lick his wounds and paint, and once again his path crosses with Rogers, who is in London getting financing for an expedition to locate the Northwest Passage across the U.S. Unable to resist the charismatic Rogers, Towne once again dons buckskins and sets out with Rogers in search of adventure. †††††

Oliver Wiswell. 1940. The story of Yale undergrad Oliver Wiswell who, in the American Revolution, remained loyal to the British. Brilliantly told, the tale illuminates a side of American history not commonly regarded—that of the law-abiding citizens whose beliefs made them resist the bold undertaking of total revolution. †††††

ROBERTSON, CHARLES. *The Elijah Conspiracy*. 1980. A group of neo-Nazis and Palestinians murder, rape, and pillage with one objective in mind—bringing the world to its knees by an assassination at the Geneva Peace Convention. ††

ROBESON, KENNETH.   No thriller section would be complete without the works of Kenneth Robeson. His stories of Doc Savage and his band of merry men, and to a lesser degree, the stories of the Avenger, have delighted fans for over half a century. Selecting the best from the 200-or-so novels would be next to impossible, so I just picked a handful.

Doc Savage:

The Thousand-Headed Man.   1934. Indonesia is the scene as Doc and the boys search for the pagoda of the Thousand-Headed Man.   ††

The Squeaking Goblin.   1934. Doc takes on a campfire ghost story about an apparition of a frontiersman, complete with rifle, who is still killing people. ††

The Quest of Qui.   1935. Doc saves his band *and* New York City from an ancient Viking threat.   †††

The Yellow Cloud.   1939. Doc Savage investigates the disappearance of a secret navy plane, lost in a yellow cloud. It probably just strayed over Los Angeles on a smoggy day.   †††

The Avenger:

The Blood Ring.   1940. The Avenger investigates an Egyptian ring with a curse.   ††

The Death Machine.   1975. The Avenger gets the notion that the suicides of the people of San Francisco are being caused by a suicide machine.   †

ROHMER, SAX.   The insidious Dr. Fu Manchu is the epitome of the "Yellow Peril" that everyone felt in the early years of the century. I read somewhere that Rohmer allegedly based the evil doctor on a Chinese crime boss in Limehouse, but I don't believe it for a second. I'm sure he was inspired by an evil dentist who kept him in the chair too long and overcharged him. Whatever his origin, Fu Manchu appeared in dozens of books between his debut in 1913 and Rohmer's death in 1959.

The Insidious Dr. Fu Manchu.   1913. An evil Chinese criminal with plans for world domination can be stopped only by the staunch Sir Denis Nayland Smith. This book is full of deadly weapons from the inscrutable Orient, narrow escapes, and stiff upper lips.   †††

The Return of Dr. Fu Manchu.   1916. The gloating doctor prepares to administer a hideous torture to Nayland Smith. Can the detestable Fu Manchu be foiled? Can the world be saved?   †††

Daughter of Fu Manchu. 1931. The setting is Egypt, the danger is a coalition of murderous asiatic cultists, and the villainess is Fah Lo Suee, the doctor's daughter, a lethal opponent in a slinky dress. †††

The Mask of Fu Manchu. 1932. A stubborn British archaeologist digs up the golden relics of an ancient Persian prophet, and all hell breaks loose. A wave of religious fanaticism—engineered by the sinister doctor and his depraved daughter threatens to engulf civilization as we know it. †††

ROSS, ANGUS. *Ampurias Exchange.* 1977. A bomb planted in Farrow's trailer kills his girlfriend by mistake and is the opening for the part spy novel, part revenge drama, as Farrow's mission takes him to the Basque region of Spain. †††

ROSS, ANGUS. *The Hamburg Switch.* 1980. A first-rate spy novel in the tradition of the early Len Deighton. It is filled with excellent action scenes as British spy Farrow and his partner, MacKenzie, try to help a defecting East German laser expert. ††††

ROSS, ANGUS. *The Darlington Jaunt.* 1983. Farrow bulls his way through an international morass of treason, espionage, and terrorism in the town where the first locomotive was built, now the home of the prototype of the Challenger tank. ††

ROSS, FRANK. *The Shining Day.* 1981. An interesting premise. Willhelm Sommer, an unwilling civilian, in Nazi Germany (where else?), is recruited to change identities with a dead Englishman and return to England as a spy. The ruse is quickly discovered by the British but allowed to continue. Well-drawn characters that you can care about and a solid story distinguish this one. ††††

ROSS, PHILIP. *The Kreuzeck Coordinates.* 1985. A great opening scene of a shooting in a ski resort barroom sets the tone. An average guy, Ted Barstow, just wants to hit the slopes in the Alps, and have a little romance on the side. But instead he finds himself the target of international assassins. Ted proves resourceful in the crunch. †††

ROSS, ROBERT. *A French Finish.* 1977. A Harvard graduate and his girlfriend, looking to make a fast buck, enlist one of his ex-professors to set up a fake-antique-furniture scam. This quickly brings them to the attention of organized-crime bosses who already control this field. How they turn the tables on the villains and hit it rich is told wittily and leads to a satisfying conclusion. ††††

ROYCE, KENNETH. His hero, Spider, is an English ex-con who is also known as the XYY man because of an extra chromosome, which some feel leads young lads to crime. Spider is a fast-talking fellow reminiscent of Alfie.

The Concrete Boot. 1971. Spider is called in to identify his partner's body which has been fished out of the river. Spider knows who did it, and that he might be next.   †††

The Miniatures Frame. 1972. Spider is invited to sit on a board for prison reform. As he is being wined and dined, he recognizes some stolen objects in an industrialist's home and is tempted to come out of retirement.   †††

RUELL, PATRICK.   *Death Takes the Low Road.* 1974. The disappearance of the deputy registrar of her university causes Caroline Nevin to investigate and become involved in a wonderfully zany, English chase novel.   ††††

RUSSELL, MARTIN,   *Backlash.* 1981. Whom did he kill? When Albert, an accountant, calls a friend from the firm in the middle of the night, it is to confess that in a fit of passion he has killed a young woman. But the body turns out to be a middle-aged man. Well told and very funny.   ††††

S

SANDBERG, BERENT.   *Brass Diamonds.* 1980. The war in Cambodia has robbed Matt Eberhart of his wife and his manhood and left him with a badly injured young son. Just when it appears Matt is going down for the count, he gets the chance to redeem himself with a heroic act—a return to Cambodia for a load of diamonds—in this lively adventure novel.   ††

SANDERS, LEONARD.   *The Hamlet Warning.* 1976. A soldier of fortune and a CIA agent join to defuse the plan of the shadowy Hamlet Group and a psychotic scientist to hold the U.S. hostage by dropping an atom bomb on a Central American country. A nail-biter from start to incredible finish.   †††

SAPIR, RICHARD BEN.   *Spies.* 1984. Another in the spate of modern intrigue books which has its plot roots in WWII. A chance bit of intelligence opens a Pandora's box of traitorous past activity, which leads to a frantic cover-up and murder. Unfortunately, the characters are contrived and it is difficult to care about them.   ††

SAUL, JOHN RALSTON.   *The Birds of Prey.* 1977. A story of assassination and corruption with roots that go back to the hatred between the Free French and the Vichy faction in occupied France during WWII. Charles Stone, an Irish journalist, discovers the truth behind a tragic air crash and is pursued by forces who cannot allow the facts to become known.   †††

SCHWARTZ, ALAN.   *No Country for an Old Man.* 1980. Eric Newman, a professor and poet, Nick Burns, a CIA operative, and Odette Chavannes, a sexy, vulnerable French journalist, chase old Nazis through Europe and South America.   ††

SCOTT, CHRIS. *To Catch a Spy*. 1978. Like Philby, George Michael Stevens defects to Russia. A few months later his death is announced. It is up to journalist Bill Johnson to find out the truth about Stevens and his role in the Philby case. †††

• A *few novels to read when you are getting emotionally prepared to attend your college reunion:*

DEATH IN A TENURED POSITION by Amanda Cross
DEATH OF A HARVARD FRESHMAN by Victoria Silver
LANDSCAPE FOR DEAD DONS by Robert Robertson
THE LUCK RUNS OUT by Charlotte MacLeod
THE MOVING TOYSHOP by Edmund Crispin
MURDER IN THE ENGLISH DEPARTMENT by Valerie Miner

SCOTT, GAVIN. *A Flight of Lies*. 1980. Ronald Foster, a bumbling clerk in a British men's store, is a witness to a murder. Mistaking the killers for cops, he offers his assistance, which only makes matters worse. From there it is only a short but zany step to intrigue between British Intelligence and the KGB. †††

SCOTT, JUSTIN. *Normandie Triangle*. 1981. A Nazi saboteur, code-named the "Otter," sinks the passenger ship *Normandie* in New York harbor; but this is only the beginning, for the Otter has another, even more daring plan. †††

SCOTT, JUSTIN. *A Pride of Royals*. 1983. A dashing yachtsman is given the WWI mission of smuggling the czar out of Russia and past the Germans. †††

SELA, OWEN. *The Kirov Tapes*. 1973. A British agent and a Soviet trade official are found shot to death in a hotel room. Adrian Quimper finds tapes which indicate treason in the upper echelon of his own service. He follows the trail of the tapes through a jungle of double-dealing double agents to a solution that nearly causes his death. ††††

SELA, OWEN. *An Exchange of Eagles*. 1977. It is 1940, and to avoid the threat of WWII, a fantastic plot is hatched to kill both Hitler and Roosevelt. In spite of the slick packaging, this is not one of Sela's better novels. ††

SELIGSON, TOM. *Kidd*. 1983. A good plot idea about searching for Captain Kidd's buried treasure in New York City. However, the author is not quite up to the effort needed to pull it off. ††

SEYMOUR, GERALD. *In Honor Bound*. 1984. An English SAS man is given an assignment to parachute into Afghanistan to help the Mujahadin repel Russian gunship helicopters by providing them with heat-seeking missiles fired bazooka-style. An authentic-seeming picture of guerrilla warfare in defense of a homeland that has depended on the use of weapons of a bygone age against the modern war technology of the Russians.   † † †

SHAGAN, STEVE.   *The Circle.* 1982. A story of Korean corruption, murder, a U.S. deputy attorney general, and a beautiful woman. I can say no more about the plot, because there is no plot. Instead, the author, a skilled writer, has written three hundred pages of engaging action scenes which lead nowhere.   † †

SHARP, MARILYN.   *False Face.* 1984. A story of assassination at the highest levels of American government. The superhero of *Sunflower* is so hampered by the plot that it leads to the creation of a superheroine to help him out. Plenty of action.   † † †

SHELDON, SIDNEY.   *Bloodline.* 1977. The story of a young woman whose father is murdered and leaves her the controlling interest in the world's largest pharmaceutical company. There's a handsome man, plenty of kinky sex, and exotic locations.   † †

SHERMAN, DAN.   *The Prince of Berlin.* 1983. An excellent story of Harry Rose, the prince of spies in Cold War Berlin. Sherman concentrated on character and used the atmosphere to amplify character, and the result is a pleasant cross between Greene's *Third Man* and Ambler's *Coffin for Dimitrios.*   † † † †

SMALL, AUSTIN J.   *The Avenging Ray.* 1930. This is a little-known but enjoyable secret weapon story. There's an evil scientist, Carol Damian, who's building a Disintegrator Ray in a cave; there's a staunch bulldog Englishman, who'll risk his life to save his country; and of course, there's a beautiful girl. There's no logic or plausibility, but that doesn't matter much in this kind of book.   † † †

SMITH, JOHN.   *Skytrap.* 1984. An English charter pilot, whose license has been lifted because of alcoholism linked to a recent air crash, takes a job flying smuggled diamonds from South Africa to Tel Aviv. A good thriller with detailed flying lore, international characters, and exotic locales.   † † †

SMITH, WILBUR.   A South African writer who writes meaty novels of rip-roaring action and adventure, with both historical and contemporary settings. His military and geographical research is meticulous; and if his characters are larger than life, well, there's nothing wrong with the heroic approach.

The Dark of the Sun.   1965. A serious story of mercenaries in the Congo grappling with questions of honor. As in all his books, Smith's action scenes are unbeatable.   † † †

The Roar of Thunder.   1966. Set in turn-of-the-century South Africa, which comes vividly alive, this is the story of an adventurer and the passionate woman who hated (and, of course, loved) him. The Boer War is a fairly exciting background.   † † †

Shout at the Devil. 1968. This cross between *The African Queen* and *The Guns of Navarone* is based on the sinking of the German raider *Konigsberg* in the Rufiji River delta during WWI. It has adventure, romance, a vicious Hun villain, and a poacher with a heart of gold. One of Smith's best. ††††

The Eye of the Tiger. 1975. Possibly the greatest adventure novel ever written. Harry is a roguish, amoral hero with his own sense of humor. He's not really a superhero. He's just a man who loves his boat and gets involved in a murderous treasure hunt in the Indian Ocean. He knocks heads with some suitably sadistic villains and undergoes a romance with a few surprises. This is Smith's masterpiece. Whatever you do, don't miss it. †††††

Cry Wolf. 1976. A colorful, fast-moving tale of two hustlers and a beautiful girl. Caught in the tide of the Italian invasion of Ethiopia, they sell some ancient armored cars to the native forces but have to deliver them before they are paid. Once the job is done, however, things get worse. Very exciting, but still filled with humor. Smith used a delicate touch in the writing to keep the balance in this one. †††††

Hungry as the Sea. 1978. A saga of adventure at sea and in the world of corporate finance, marred only by the sickliness of its love story. The plot centers around marine salvage and has some of the author's best writing in the early pages, but about midway through it starts to break down a bit. ††††

The Delta Decision. 1979. This book, a departure from the author's usual style, is a save-the-world fantasy with an ironic conclusion, in which a mysterious mastermind organizes international terrorists. †††

Flight of the Falcon, 1980; Men of Men, 1981; and *The Angels Weep,* 1982. A three-volume saga of adventure and family strife in South Africa, beginning in 1868, at the heyday of the British empire. The Ballantyne dynasty—strong men and fiery women—interacts with people like Cecil Rhodes as it becomes involved in diamond mining, war, and racial strife. These books combine history with an element of somber prophecy and pose difficult questions about colonialism, race, and loyalty. †††

SPIKE, PAUL. *The Night Letter.* 1979. Hitler and Churchill have both come to the amazing conclusion that Roosevelt is the key to what is about to become WWII. To keep Roosevelt from using his power, Reinhard Heydrich launches a blackmail campaign based on Roosevelt's extramarital affair with his secretary. It is up to White House lackey Jack Jackson to handle the dirty laundry. ††

STEVENSON, WILLIAM. *A Man Called Intrepid.* 1976. The memoirs of William Stevenson, one of our best intelligence men and one of the controlling influences of the Allied intelligence network in WWII. It is fascinating. The author was right up at the top, and many of the people he dealt with were household names. †††††

STEWART, IAN. *The Peking Payoff*. 1975. The question is whether Hong Kong can remain a free territory, and involves delicate negotiations with the Chinese— negotiations which a splinter faction of the Chinese Communists want to upset. It is up to Hal Jurnberg to stop them.   †††

STEWART, MARY. Author of some of the best romantic suspense novels ever written. Although they could be reduced to a formula—vulnerable young her- oine, handsome and mysterious stranger who is both threatening and attractive, exotic setting, last-minute rescue from unprincipled villains—they also have excellent and unobtrusive characterization, a deft, almost literary style, and brilliant descriptive touches. Stewart has also written a series of novels set in Arthurian England.

Wildfire at Midnight.   1956. Folklore and a psychopath combine to create an atmosphere of murder and menace on the remote, wild Isle of Skye. There's an especially vivid mountain-climbing scene, and a nice, unusual twist to the romance.   †††

My Brother Michael.   1959. Antique treasure, a WWII criminal in hiding, and a case of mistaken identity make Camilla Haven's quiet holiday in Greece more exciting than she had expected. The setting—Delphi—is one of Stewart's best, and she cleverly mingles an ancient, a recent, and a modern mystery.   ††††

The Ivy Tree.   1961. A typical Stewart heroine—beautiful, resourceful, and lonely—attempts a dangerous impersonation. The plot twists and turns, and the romance is downplayed, but the suspense never falters. The Northumberland setting is less exotic than her usual locales but receives the same careful attention.   †††

The Moon-Spinners.   1962. On vacation in Crete, a young woman and her aunt stumble into a case of jewel robbery and murder. The action is fast paced and the characters engaging. Despite the suspense, this is essentially a cheerful, good-humored book.   †††

This Rough Magic.   1964. You may want to brush up on your Shakespeare before reading this one just to make sure you don't miss any of the clever allusions to *The Tempest*. The setting is Corfu; the plot is simple but satisfying; the heroine is Stewart's most likable ever; and all the ingredients are perfectly handled.   †††††

The Gabriel Hounds.   1967. Long before Lebanon became a fashionable setting for novels about terrorists, Stewart used it for a good old-fashioned story of greed, passion, and poison. As usual, Stewart throws in some comic relief, but there's a mournful, Arabian-nights quality about this story, set in a crumbling desert fortress where an eccentric old Englishwoman lives out her deluded last days.   ††††

STUART, ANTHONY. *The London Affair.* 1981. Vladimir Gull, the Russian-defector hero, begins an affair with a beautiful London journalist and is drawn into danger when he tries to solve the murder of her newspaper's publisher.

†††

T

TAYLOR, L. A. *Deadly Objectives.* 1984. This reads like a pleasant updating of an old Tom Swift novel, as J. J. Jamison, computer engineer whose hobby is UFOs, undertakes to recover a stolen piece of high-tech equipment.   ††

TAYLOR, ROGER. *Snatch.* 1981. A surprisingly good novel about terrorists kidnapping five of the contestants in the Miss World beauty contest. The strongest part of the story is the deft characterization of the beauty contestants.   †††

TEVIS, WALTER. *The Queen's Gambit.* 1983. The story of a young girl who discovers she is a child chess prodigy. While it is not a thriller in the usual sense, it will keep you on the edge of your seat pulling for her.   ††††

THOMAS, CRAIG. I've tried to read every one of his novels, but the only one I have been able to finish was *Firefox Down*. He is a good writer, but for some unknown reason, he never makes me care enough to read on.

Firefox Down. 1983. The sequel to *Firefox*. The entire story takes place in the air as Michael Grant still tries to evade the Russians and get their precious "Firefox" plane to our side.   †††

THOMAS, ROSS. My favorite thriller writer. An ex-newspaperman, Thomas approaches his familiar subjects of Washington political chicanery or labor-union dirty dealings with a touch of humor instead of paranoia. A marvelous writer— his opening scenes are the best in the business.

The Cold War Swap. 1966. The first McCorkle and Padillo story. In it they are Berlin saloon owners who find themselves caught in the middle between a U.S./Russia deal over two defectors. Excellent.   ††††

The Seersucker Whipsaw. 1967. Con man Clinton Shartelle engineers the election of a cannibal as president of a newly emerging African nation. Absolutely hilarious. My favorite Ross Thomas novel.   †††††

The Fools in Town Are on Our Side. 1970. Some feel this corrupt town novel is his best. I think it is his worst. Halfway through he completely abandons his story and goes for an entirely new line for no apparent reason.   ††

If You Can't Be Good. 1973. A Washington senator resigns and then refuses to help police solve the murder of his daughter. It is up to historian Decatur Lucas to get to the bottom of things. †††††

Chinaman's Chance. 1978. A revenge drama of the first order in which Quincy Durant and Artie Wu take on enough fun characters to fill five novels. This one almost brought Thomas the superstardom he so richly deserves. ††††

Briarpatch. 1984. Benjamin Dill, an investigator for a senate subcommittee, learns his sister, a homicide detective in his hometown, has been murdered. He returns home for the funeral and for justice in this brilliant "corrupt town" novel. Thomas makes the dead sister into a touching presence and creates a real sense of loss throughout the story. †††††

THOMPSON, STEVEN L. *Bismarck Cross.* 1985. A disappointing Ludlum-type thriller about the reunification of Germany for evil purposes. It's a good premise for a story, but it gets bogged down in detail early on and never gets off the ground. ††

THURSTON, ROBERT. *For the Silverfish.* 1985. Our hero, Rugger, is a New Jersey auto mechanic, an occupation that is refreshingly different. The fireworks begin when Rugger and his beautiful girlfriend go to a small Latin American country to repair a rare auto for the local dictator. †††

TINE, ROBERT. *Broken Eagle.* 1985. A crew from a downed bomber make their way on foot across what's left of post-nuclear-holocaust Russia. This dooms-day adventure yarn has the crew faced with the same problems of survival that all pioneers and explorers encounter, no matter what the time frame. †††

TOPOL, EDWARD, AND NAZANSKY, FRIDRIKH. *Deadly Games.* 1983. A cunning turnabout. This thriller was translated from the Russian. Igor Iosifovich, a special investigator in the public prosecutor's office, is assigned to find a missing journalist, who is a government favorite. The trail leads to a black market in drugs and a high-level cover-up. †††

TRENCH, JOHN. *Docken Dead.* 1953. The British army is testing a new anti-tank gun when one of the officers in charge is shot to death near the firing range. In the aftermath, the gun vanishes. Martin Cotterell, visiting museum curator, helps the police and the military solve the two crimes when the motives become tangled with the personal lives of several of the characters. ††††

TRENCH, JOHN. *What Rough Beast.* 1957. Martin Cotterell is back in a murder story involving an Anglican priest, his work with a youth club, and the sale of some rare books. In the midst of the book investigation, he is accused of the murder of his wife and is hounded by a police officer. Cotterell solves the crimes at great risk and personal damage to himself, but the story develops a little too slowly. †††

TRENHALE, JOHN. *The Man Called Kyril*. 1981. Kyril is the code name for Ivan Bucharensky, KGB superagent. Kyril's danger-fraught mission is to find the British mole in the KGB. ††††

TREVANIAN. The superstar of spy writers.

The Eiger Sanction. 1972. In his debut, Trevanian shows himself to be a master of the James Bond type of spy novel, as his protagonist, Jonathan Hemlock, is sent to Switzerland to climb the Eiger Mountain and kill one of the climbers with him. Literally a cliff-hanger. ††††

The Loo Sanction. 1973. In this second Jonathan Hemlock story, the author opens with one of the most chilling scenes I have ever read. In fact, I reread it a couple of times just to be sure I understood what was happening. From there, Jonathan Hemlock, secret agent and art expert, runs amok in an excellent story that has nothing to do with the Chinese, contrary to what the title may make you think. ††††

Shibumi. 1979. The author experiments in the ways of the Orient in the opening third of this one, and it is some of the best writing I have ever read. Unfortunately, the same cannot be said for the latter two-thirds. The middle part of the book is spent almost entirely in a cave and is quite boring, and the last part, the climax, is forced. †††

TRYON, THOMAS. *Harvest Home*. 1973. Ted and Beth Constantine and their daughter, Kate, are sophisticated New Yorkers who give up life in the Big Apple for an idyllic life in the New England village of Cornwall Coombe. Unfortunately, there is enough evil in the quaint village to make New York seem like a half hour with the Muppets. †††

TYLER, W. T. *The Shadow Cabinet*. 1984. A dazzling kaleidoscope of global manipulation in Washington's corridors of power. Haven Wilson finds himself in the middle of a struggle for control of a Washington "think tank," with a prestigious law firm, a Bible Belt senator, and a fundamentalist minister as the pawns in a struggle for power. The intrusion of the author's political leanings keeps this book from being as good as it should be. †††

UV

VANDERCOOK, JOHN W. *Murder in Haiti*. 1956. Bertram Lynch and Robert Deane are bodyguards on a financier's yacht as they search for pirate treasure. †††

VAN LUSTBADER, ERIC. *The Ninja*. 1980. The story of Nicholas Linnear, a modern-day Ninja—a Japanese warrior—and his nocturnal ramblings. ††††

VAN LUSTBADER, ERIC. *The Miko.* 1984. A female Ninja kills her instructor as a warm-up to taking on Nicholas Linnear in the sequel to *The Ninja.* ††††

VAUGHN, ROBERT. *The Fallen and the Free.* 1983. Marcel Garneau's Paris cafe becomes a French Resistance headquarters during WWII, while his brother, Georges, and his colleagues ready themselves to return from England and reclaim their country. †††

VON ELSNER, DON. One of my favorite time passers. He writes clean, crisp scenes full of life and humor. His locales are good, and his judo scenes well told. For bridge enthusiasts, his John Winkman series is a "must read."

Those Who Prey Together Slay Together. 1961. Good potboiler in which Colonel David Danning is hired to investigate a stock-takeover scheme involving an orange juice company. ††

The Ace of Spies. 1966. Jake Winkman is in Washington for a bridge tournament and finds a body in his hotel room. The FBI and the CIA move in squeezing Jake in the middle. ††

W

WAGER, WALTER. *Blue Leader.* 1979. The first of a series featuring Alison Gordon, a beautiful female private eye who smokes too much, drinks beer, swears, and packs a .357 magnum. In this story she gathers a group of out-of-work pilots and organizes a B-17 raid to knock out most of the world's heroin supply. The fault of this basic mercenary novel is not in the telling of the story, but in the lack of development of the lead character who is nothing more than a standard gumshoe, who happens to have fantastic breasts. ††

WALKER, DAVID. *Winter of Madness.* 1964. This is an adventure novel which almost defies definition. Part satire, part mystery, part fantasy, part science fiction, this story strews the Scots moorlands with dead bodies as Lord Duncatto tries to cope with an obsessed billionaire, international terrorists, willful women, and Tiger Clyde, a larger-than-life British agent assigned to the case because James Bond is busy elsewhere. †††††

WALLACE, EDGAR. One of the true giants of the thriller field. Wallace was so determined to succeed that he founded his own publishing company to get his first book into print. At the time of his death, he had cranked out nearly 200 novels, more than half of which deal with crime or mystery.

Jack O'Judgement. 1920. Stafford Kind, a refined police investigator, sets out to destroy Colonel Dan Boundary, one of Wallace's typical villains—an unctuous master criminal. Cocaine, gambling, show girls, and stage-door Johnnies add complications and color. †††

The Crimson Circle. 1922. This book is excellent Wallace: a psychic detective, a particularly devious master criminal, brave women and sturdy men, much rushing to and fro, and a dramatic climax. ††††

The Face in the Night. 1924. One of Wallace's favorite devices is the double life—the crook who is really a good guy, or vice versa. He uses it cleverly in this tale of a jewel thief and the rival detectives out to capture him. As always in Wallace, there's a rather forced romance, but it's less obtrusive than usual here. ††††

A King by Night. 1925. The central characters in this plot are a psychologist and an apparent madman, who claims to be the king of a country no one has ever heard of. The madman's niece attempts to find him, and she and her chums uncover a complicated case of fraud, impersonation, and murder. †††

The Door with Seven Locks. 1926. The hero of this novel is Dick Martin, a thief-catcher who is on fairly friendly terms with the better class of burglar. His romance with a wealthy, aristocratic girl parallels his investigation into a case of blackmail and murder. The criminal's creatures—half beast, half human—add a nice touch. †††

The Girl from Scotland Yard. 1926. This book is really about families good and bad. Wallace takes on illegitimacy, baby-farming, and disinheriting—all of which he disapproves of. Along the way, a competent, motherly young woman detective discovers her true vocation. †††

Terror Keep. 1927. One of Wallace's best series characters is J. G. Reeder, a quiet, middle-aged former banker who assists the Yard in cases of bank robbery or counterfeiting. In this book, he's marked as a target by two determined people: an escaped convict with murder on his mind and a young woman with matrimony on hers. ††††

The Traitor's Gate. 1927. The Tower of London with its lurid past and its Traitor's Gate has attracted many mystery writers. Wallace was one of the first. He created a cast of talkative young people, who chatter their way through a case involving the crown jewels, a kidnapping, and a regimental scandal. †††

The Green Ribbon. 1929. Inspector Luke reins in a ring of crooked bookies in an equestrian plot full of authentic detail. (Wallace was a great fan of the track.) ††††

White Face. 1930. Detective Sergeant Elk is another of Wallace's series characters. He's gloomy but persistent, and in this book he helps trap a cunning and cruel master criminal, who has been terrorizing London. †††

WESTLAKE, DONALD. Fondly known as the "king of the capers," Westlake is one of America's most inventive writers. His work ranges from warmly humorous novels of scoundrels at work and play to the extremely hard-boiled stories of Parker, the thief (appropriately written under the name of Richard Stark).

God Save the Mark. 1967. Fred Fitch inherits a stripper and three hundred thousand from an uncle, and the con men descend on him. Great fun. ††††

Somebody Owes Me Money. 1969. Chester Conway's horse comes in, but somebody has murdered his bookie. Chester starts out chasing, but soon winds up being chased. †††

Cops and Robbers. 1972. Two fun-loving cops heist ten million in securities. †††

Gangway. (Written with Brian Garfield) 1973. The authors describe it better than I can. They say, "It's the world's first comedy romance suspense pirate Western adventure novel." †††

Written as Richard Stark:

The Outfit. 1963. Parker takes on the New York mob. †††

The Man with the Getaway Face. 1963. The New York mob takes on Parker. He has plastic surgery. ††

Killtown. 1964. Parker decides to rob a whole town. †††

WHEATLEY, DENNIS. An English thriller writer similar to Edgar Wallace. Wheatley wrote several series; his most famous series character was Roger Brooke, a British spy during the Napoleonic wars. He also wrote a series featuring the Duke De Richleau whose exploits cover the late 19th century to WWII, and a series featuring Gregory Sallust, an agent in the WWII era.

The Secret War. 1937. As Mussolini invades Abyssinia in 1936, no one can stop him except perhaps the "Millers of God," a group of wealthy men dedicated to wiping out suffering. However, despite the nobility of their cause, Sir Anthony Lovelace, his friend Christopher Penn, and his beautiful fiancée find that the end does not always justify the means. †††

Faked Passports. 1940. The second in the Gregory Sallust series is set against the frozen Arctic and the closing days of the Russo-Finnish War and climaxes with Gregory's 700-mile journey through the frozen waste to save Erika von Epp. ††††

The Prisoner in the Mask.   1957. The Duke De Richleau sets out to free the heir to the throne of France, who is imprisoned and forced to wear an iron mask. It sounds similiar to the Dumas tale about *The Man in the Iron Mask.*
†††

WHITE, OSMAR.   *Silent Reach.* 1978. A British agent is assigned to check into sabotage in the Australian outback. The plot ingredients include an Australian head of a ranching and mining empire, his beautiful Russian assistant, another Australian rancher with a psychopathic son, and a group of aborigine commandos with shadowy allegiances.   †††

WHITNEY, PHYLLIS.   The author of award-winning mystery and suspense novels for teenagers, as well as gothic mysteries for a mostly female audience. She uses exotic contemporary settings, female narrators, and strongly romantic mystery or adventure plots much in the manner of Mary Stewart, although her writing and creation of mood and tension aren't quite up to Stewart's.

Columbella.   1966. Set in the sultry Virgin Islands, this is a classic "bad girl/ good girl" story about a naive young governess, a wanton sexpot, and the sexpot's darkly handsome husband. The bad girl is definitely ahead on points until someone kills her one dark night. Can the good girl solve the mystery, comfort the husband, and keep from getting killed herself?   †††

Hunter's Green.   1968. Here's a textbook example of the modern gothic novel: a brooding English mansion, complete with a lonely tower room, a nervous young woman, her estranged husband, an inheritance, a series of deadly accidents, and a lot of fog.   †††

Listen for the Whisperer.   1972. This is Whitney's best book. The heart of the story isn't the heroine's romance, although that gets plenty of play, it is the troubled relationship between young Leigh and her mother, Laura, a former Hollywood star whose maternal behavior makes Joan Crawford look like June Cleaver. The usual mystery and suspense elements are deftly handled and the setting—a film group in Norway—is offbeat and well done.   ††††

WILLIAMS, ALAN.   *Tale of the Lazy Dog.* 1973. The animal of the title refers to the call letters of the plane in which Murray, a soldier of fortune, and Sammy Ryderbeit, a South African flyboy, pull off an incredible hijack in the midst of the Vietnam War. In the background, Charles Pol, financial villain extraordinary, manipulates the moves of a gigantic double cross.   ††††

WILLIAMS, ALAN.   *Holy of Holies.* 1980. Ryderbeit, a bored flyer, baby-sitting in London, is recruited for a secret, profitable flight in a case of mistaken identity. He finds himself involved in a shocking scheme of Pol's, the fat arch-villain, which could escalate the already volatile Middle East situation into a bloody Muslim holy war. ††††

WILLIAMS, GORDON. *Pomeroy.* 1982. The story of John Stockley Pomeroy, a hard-drinking, fast-living Tennessean who is a secret-service agent for Teddy Roosevelt. Breezy and fun. †††

WILLIAMS, VALENTINE. The author of dashing pre-WWII novels of adventure, often dealing with espionage in an upper-class way. In Williams's world, as in Oppenheim's, spies are highly individual, even flamboyant, gentlemen or villains, never realistic civil servants. Best remembered today are his tales of Clubfoot, aka Dr. Adolph Grundt, a Hun as nasty as his name.

The Man with the Clubfoot. 1918. A mysterious message from his brother, lost behind enemy lines in WWI Germany, lures Desmond Okewood to Holland. He winds up posing as a German secret-service officer in a deadly game of wits with the Kaiser's chief spymaster, the odious Dr. Grundt. Okewood's mission is to find and rescue his brother, to succor a damsel in distress, and to smuggle Clubfoot's captured secrets back to Britain. ††††

The Eye in Attendance. 1927. The "Eye" in this straight mystery novel is Inspector Manderton of Scotland Yard, who solves an ugly case of double murder at an elegant country house. Scandal, blackmail, and passion are the ingredients of the case. The main plot is a little thin, relying heavily on emotional scenes between the characters, but Williams uses an entertaining romantic subplot and good comic interludes to bolster it up. ††††

The Crouching Beast. 1928. Despite his apparent demise at the end of *The Man with the Clubfoot*, Dr. Adolph Grundt is back as the almost omnipotent master-bastard of prewar Germany in this spy thriller. A young Englishwoman working in Germany in 1914 gets mixed up with a not quite respectable ex-agent of the British Secret Service who will run any risk to win back his commission. Together they try to get vital wartime secrets out of the country in a breathless combination of masquerade and manhunt, pursued by the implacable Grundt. ††††

WINWARD, WALTER. *Hammerstrike.* 1978. The story of a German attempt to rescue some German prisoners held in England in 1942. Well written and somewhat similar to *The Eagle Has Landed*. †††

WISE, DAVID. *Spectrum.* 1981. Inside the CIA is another CIA. The world hangs in the balance, and guess what—only one man can stop it. Well written, but only average in plotting. ††

WOLFF, BENJAMIN. *Hyde and Seek.* 1984. A beautiful woman hires John Hyde—a California, Vietnam vet, karate instructor, and private eye—to find her missing brother. ††

WOODHOUSE, MARTIN. *Tree Frog*. 1966. Giles Yeoman—a young research scientist and ex-RAF flyer—sees "Tree Frog," an ultralight, pilotless spy plane. He notices some design flaws, but before he can do anything about them, he and his secretary are kidnapped and tortured, and he is forced to become a reluctant hero. ††††

WYND, OSWALD. *The Blazing Air*. 1981. A romantic adventure novel about the events leading up to the Japanese attack on Malaya during WWII, and its effects on a small group of English citizens. ††

XY

YORK, ANDREW. *The Eliminator*. 1967. Jonas Wilde, a professional assassin in the mold of James Bond, begins to let his precise life-defending routine slip when he falls in love with the beautiful Jocelyn. This new live-and-let-live attitude naturally fouls up his assignment to kill a Russian scientist being held by the CIA at a safehouse in the English countryside. †††

YORK, ANDREW. *The Predator*. 1968. On the day of his forced retirement from his post as government assassin, Jonas Wilde's girlfriend and two other members of his former organization are killed, and Jonas is off to Italy on a busman's holiday. †††

YORK, THOMAS. *Trapper*. 1981. The true story of the seven-week manhunt for the "Mad Trapper of the Red River" by the Mounties. The story is the stuff legends are made of, but the slow-moving style of the book does not do it justice. †

Z

ZOCHERT, DONALD. *Murder in the Hellfire Club*. 1978. When Ben Franklin arrives in London in 1775, the murder of the porter at the Vulture Tavern draws him into a series of adventures leading him to the Hellfire Club, a notorious group devoted to acts of incredible debauchery. †††

THE
POLICE
PROCEDURAL

ALTHOUGH THIS IS THE SMALLEST of the four categories, per entry the Police Procedural novels have the greatest quality of them all. Where the romantic suspense novel and the hard-boiled detective novel rely on character, and the country-house or locked-room mystery and the thriller rely on plot, the Police Procedural needs both characters and plot, or it simply doesn't work.

Normally, the Police Procedural offers a step-by-step, in-depth look at police personnel and police methods for a given case (or cases), hence the name "Police Procedural" (or merely "Procedural" to its friends). However, for this book I have taken a bit of artistic license by including a number of entries which are not Procedurals in the strict sense, but which I allow to slip in using a very loose interpretation of the rules of the genre. (Robert Van Gulik's Judge Dee stories, and Arthur Upfield's Napoleon Bonaparte stories readily come to mind as examples of this looseness.)

Five types of stories make up the Police Procedural: Misdemeanors, Felonies, Manhunts, Trials by Jury, and the Ultimate Inhumanity.

"Misdemeanors" are novels of squad rooms, sweat, creaking leather jackets, equipment belts overloaded with revolvers, bullets, nightsticks, handcuffs, lariats, lunchboxes, screaming sirens, public defenders, and impersonal justice meted out swiftly. In these stories, the heroes beat their wives, neglect their children, and strong-arm helpless merchants into giving them free coffee and doughnuts, while the villains do even worse. Although these stories are filled with nasty people on both sides, who routinely commit random acts of violence for the most trivial of reasons, no one portrays them better or more sympathetically than Joseph Wambaugh or Ed McBain.

"Felonies" are novels which deal with the investigation of a crime, or crimes, committed by one person with a definite motive. The crime is usually murder, and the motive is usually love or money. The story takes place in a small town where the impact of the crime is felt throughout the community. The English, like Dorothy Simpson and June Thomson, do this best, and it is often a close call as to whether someone like P. D. James or Michael Gilbert belongs in the Procedural section or the English section.

"Manhunts" are psycho novels, or grisly retellings of the old fable of the tortoise and the hare. The killer is the hare, the charismatic one who draws our attention. There is a fatal beauty in his madness as he goes his merry way, gleefully cutting, chopping, chain-sawing, and shooting his way through the general populace for the flimsiest of motives. The cop—the tortoise—ploddingly pursues him, never quickening nor slowing his pace until justice is ultimately served. There is no beauty to the cop. He is as leathery and hidebound as the tortoise, and as much an outcast to his world as the tortoise is to the world of amphibians, symbolically equally ill at ease in water or on land, and seemingly suited for only one purpose—to pursue and defeat the hare. After *Crime and Punishment*, Lawrence Sanders's *First Deadly Sin* is possibly the greatest "Manhunt" novel ever written, but also deserving special mention is Thomas Harris's *Red Dragon*.

"Trial by Jury" novels are stories which build up to and center around a trial for one particular crime. These are novels written almost always by lawyers, featuring lawyers as the heroes, and hinging on a unique point of law. The most prolific and famous author of "Trial by Jury" novels was Erle Stanley Gardner with his Perry Mason series, but my personal favorites are Robert Traver's *Anatomy of a Murder* and Harper Lee's *To Kill a Mockingbird*, although the latter is rarely even thought to be a mystery, much less a Procedural.

And last of all are stories of the "Ultimate Humanity," or true crime stories, such as Truman Capote's *In Cold Blood*. True stories about which nothing flip or cute should be said. Stories of sick, twisted failures who, in that moment (or several moments) of desperation throw all semblance of humanity out the window in an act (or a series of acts) of such depravity that the only thing one can say is—"There but for the grace of God go I."

A

ARMBRISTER, TREVOR. *Act of Vengeance.* 1975. The true story of the murder of labor leader Jock Yoblonski, masterminded by union president Tony Boyle.
††††

ARONSON, HARVEY, AND MCGRADY, MIKE. *Establishment of Innocence.* 1976. A well-written psychological novel set in Long Island and involving a high-profile senator. There are some nice twists in this one.
††††

ASHLEY, STEVEN. *Stalking Blind.* 1976. In Appalachian West Virginia, Sheriff W. T. ("Cub") Hamill investigates the murder of a young man and a series of crimes immediately following, which include the death of a horse at a county fair, and the burning of his girlfriend's house.
††

AVALLONE, MIKE. *The Felony Squad.* 1967. Detective Sergeant Sam Stone and his felony squad take on a psycho who has already killed five.
††

B

BALL, JOHN. *In the Heat of the Night.* 1965. Black Pasadena detective Virgil Tibbs visits the South and encounters racial prejudice when he teams up with a local sheriff.
†††††

BALL, JOHN. *The Cool Cottontail.* 1965. Virgil Tibbs investigates the murder of an inventor. Nowhere near as good as *In the Heat of the Night.*
††

BALL, JOHN. *The Eyes of Buddha.* 1976. Virgil Tibbs tries to establish the identity of a murdered young woman while at the same time trying to find a missing heiress. The trail takes him to Katmandu. ††

BALL, JOHN. *Chief Tallon and the S.O.R.* 1984. Chief Jack Tallon of the Whitewater police department is caught in the middle when Reverend Ezekial Moses sets out to break up the convention of the Society for Open Relationships, and murder occurs. Not a bad book to pass a hot day with. ††

BARNETT, JAMES. *Palmprint.* 1980. Inspector Owen Smith is called in to solve the murder of an American in a British Caribbean possession. Even though I don't care for novels set in the Caribbean, I liked this one. †††

BARNETT, JAMES. *The Firing Squad.* 1981. One of the most interesting police procedurals I have read in years. The setting is England. The time is the present. The remaining members of a WWII British army unit execute their former commander, and it falls to Inspector Smith to capture them. The middle of the book contains a diary, which really makes the men come alive. ††††

BARTHEL, JOAN. *A Death in Canaan.* 1976. The true story of the murder of a sleazy New England woman, and how, when her son is accused of the crime, the town and many celebrities as well come to his defense. ††††

BARTHEL, JOAN. *A Death in California.* 1981. The bizarre true story of Hope Masters, a pretty California wife whose husband is brutally murdered by a psychopathic killer, who then rapes her physically and mentally until she falls in love with him and winds up on trial for her husband's murder. ††††

BAYER, WILLIAM. *Peregrine.* 1981. The story of a New York madman who uses a falcon to do his dirty work, and the female TV newscaster who must follow through on the story to keep her job. Be prepared for a really offbeat ending. †††

BAYER, WILLIAM. *Switch.* 1984. The title comes from the discovery of two decapitated female bodies whose heads have been switched by the killer. †††

BENSON, BEN. A police procedural writer from the 1950s who deserves the occasional light read. His heroes change, but the stories deal with the Massachusetts state police. The writing is good, crisp, and clean.

The Burning Fuse. 1954. Detective Inspector Wade Paris has twenty-four hours to stop a killer with a load of dynamite. ††

Broken Shield. 1955. Trooper Ralph Lindsey's partner is killed, and the men of the force blame him. The only way he can regain his esteem is to capture the killer. ††

Seven Steps East. 1959. Ralph Lindsey investigates the murder of trooper-trainee Kirk Chanslor and finds loose women in the background.   ††

BLOCHMAN, LAWRENCE.   He wrote short stories about Leonidas Prike, a police detective in British India, and also some slangy mystery novels.

Bengal Fire. 1937. One of the best of Blochman's work. The energetic Inspector Leonidas Prike solves a Calcutta case involving smuggling, murder, and a maharajah's missing jewels. Blochman deserves credit for ingenious, logical plotting and especially for the offhand, casual tone of his setting.   ††††

See You at the Morgue. 1941. This book has it all: Irish policemen with brogues as thick as the soles of their boots, glamorous stolen fox pelts, a 1941 state-of-the-art forensics lab, and a triple murder, including the slaying of a good old-fashioned gigolo. The heroine is one of a group of telephone-answering clerks, who were then called "phantom secretaries." This is not one of his police procedurals, but it deserves mention.   ††††

BOLITHO, WILLIAM.   *Murder for Profit.* 1926. This is not exactly a police procedural, but is a good example of the early true-crime account. Bolitho summarizes the careers of six real murderers, who slew for money, including Burke and Hare, the Edinburgh grave robbers, and Landru, the French "Bluebeard."   †††

BOYLE, THOMAS.   *Only the Dead Know Brooklyn.* 1985. An inventive tale in which a psycho with a large head is stalking the women of Brooklyn. It takes a nice turn when the kidnapping of a scholar seems to tie in somehow.   †††

BRADLEE, BEN, JR.   *The Ambush Murders.* 1979. The true story of the murder of two Riverdale, California, cops, and the throw-away-the-book, revenge-motivated manhunt that tore apart the black community.   †††

BUGLIOSI, VINCENT, WITH HURWITZ, KEN.   *Till Death Us Do Part.* 1978. Bugliosi, the prosecutor who put Manson behind bars, tells of his most difficult case, a double murder among the California well-to-do. Bugliosi must go to trial with no witnesses, no weapon, and no physical evidence to aid him in his case.   ††††

BUGLIOSI, VINCENT, AND HURWITZ, KEN.   *Shadow of Cain.* 1981. On Christmas Eve 1959, Raymond Lomak went on a killing spree, which took the lives of six people. Twenty-one years later, against psychiatric advice, he is paroled. Everything seems to be going well until two murder victims turn up, and the evidence points to Lomak. Is he guilty, or not? A true story.   †††

C

CAUNITZ, WILLIAM J. *One Police Plaza.* 1984. A New York homicide detective is assigned to find out who killed a travel-agency employee. A simple crime of passion from the look of it. Before it is over, Israeli intelligence, the PLO, a police unit in deep cover, the Catholic Church, a highly placed blue-blooded WASP, and the final verse of the Eighty-third Psalm combine to lead Lieutenant Malone to a deadly confrontation on the Pulaski Bridge. ††††

CONSTANTINE, K. C. Author of a series featuring Chief Mario Balzic. Constantine's settings in the western Pennsylvania coal mining town of Rocksburg, make him one of the best writers working today in terms of atmosphere. His plots, as mysteries, are a bit thin, leaning more toward the straight novel than the mystery, but well worth reading. His main character, Mario Balzic, is so well drawn that I hate him, because he typifies to me all the narrow-minded priggishness of small-town sheriffs I have known over a lifetime.

The Rocksburg Railroad Murders. 1972. The first of the series. Balzic investigates the murder of John Andrasho, who was beaten to death with a Coke bottle. †††

The Man Who Liked to Look at Himself. 1973. My favorite of the series because Chief Mario Balzic gets bitten by a dog while on a hunting trip. If that's not enough, the dog digs up a human thigh bone which turns out to be part of a local butcher who has been missing for a year. †††

The Blank Page. 1974. Balzic investigates the murder of a local coed. ††

A Fix Like This. 1975. Balzic investigates the stabbing of a minor local hood. ††

The Man Who Liked Slow Tomatoes. 1982. Jimmy Romanelli, an out-of-work coal miner, disappears, and it has something to do with drugs. †††

Always a Body to Trade. 1983. The death of an unknown young woman leads to deeper crime involving narcotics agents. While trying to solve the crime, Chief Mario Balzic also has to educate a new mayor about the facts of life. †††

CUNNINGHAM, E. V. Long before Eddie Murphy strutted onto the scene, Masao Masuto was the original Beverly Hills Cop. Masuto is a Nisei, a second-generation Japanese, who practices Zen and the art of criminal detection for the Beverly Hills police force. His best feature is that he can't help getting involved with the people in his cases, no matter how hard he tries. Another interesting point about Cunningham is that he is actually best-selling writer Howard Fast.

The Case of the Angry Actress. 1967. Five show-biz execs, who participated in a bit of casting-couch group sex eleven years ago, are now getting knocked off one by one. At least that's how it looks until Masuto goes to work on the case. As always, the solution is simple, obvious, and well-camouflaged until the end of the book. †††

The Case of the One-Penny Orange. 1977. The Orange is an extremely rare and valuable stamp. A seemingly routine burglary investigation leads first to the murder of a stamp dealer and then to a Nazi war criminal. Masuto exercises his ability to spot links between unlikely bits of evidence. †††

The Case of the Russian Diplomat. 1978. Masuto's traditional, Japanese-style life is rudely interrupted when terrorists kidnap his daughter in this tale of double murder and international espionage. East Germans, Zionist Jews, Russians, and the exotic inhabitants of Beverly Hills are mixed up in a complex plot. †††

The Case of the Poisoned Eclairs. 1979. Eclairs are mysteriously delivered to a quartet of Hollywood wives at a bridge party. They don't eat them, but the maid does and dies. Cunningham updates Berkley's *Poisoned Chocolates* with Masuto at the helm. ††††

The Case of the Sliding Pool. 1981. A mud slide moves a pool in an exclusive Beverly Hills neighborhood and unearths a mysterious thirty-year-old skeleton. My favorite of the series. †††

The Case of the Kidnapped Angel. 1982. A Hollywood star's wife is kidnapped, and the ransom is a million dollars. But the wife disappears and so does the money. There are some nice twists here. †††

D

DALEY, ROBERT. As a former New York deputy police commissioner, Daley is especially qualified to write about the NYPD. When you couple this special knowledge with his writing ability, you have a police procedural writer of considerable skill.

Target Blue. 1971. A scattershot picture of the New York Police Department. Even though it is episodic and has no real story, the episodes are interesting as hell. †††

Prince of the City. 1981. A true inside story of police corruption in the big city. ††††

Year of the Dragon. 1981. An excellent story of corruption in New York's Chinatown, the Chinese mafia, and the heroin trade. ††††

Hands of a Stranger. 1985. The author gives us an excellent lead character in New York Asst. D.A. Judith Adler as she grapples with a series of rape cases. But that's not all—there's a strong emotional plot as well between Adler, Joe Hearn—a New York cop—and his wife. Daley is really at the top of his form with this book. ††††

DIEHL, WILLIAM. In addition to the fine thriller *Chamelion*, the author has given us two noteworthy police procedurals.

Sharkey's Machine. 1978. An Atlanta-based, fast-moving police procedural that reads as though it was written for the late Steve McQueen. Sharkey, a Bullitt-like character, races around Atlanta trying to keep a beautiful call girl from becoming a victim. ††††

Hooligans. 1984. A well-written but overlong "corrupt town" type of police procedural in which Vietnam vet Jake Kilmer proves that you can't go home again—not even with a task force the size of the Mississippi National Guard to back you. Lots of action. †††

DILLINGER, JAMES. *Adrenaline.* 1985. A reverse police procedural told from the point of view of two gays, who are on the run after innocently blowing away a couple of cops for interrupting their fun. There is some very graphic sex and brutality in this one. ††

E

ELLROY, JAMES. A rising, young mystery writer filled with an immense brooding power. Although, like many writers, he owes inspiration to Ross Macdonald, his landscape has more of the bleakness of James M. Cain and Cornell Woolrich than a rehash of the familiar Macdonald style.

Blood on the Moon. 1984. A dramatic entrance for Los Angeles cop Lloyd Hopkins, who pursues a sex killer in a deadly game. †††

Because the Night. 1984. A much bigger story as Lloyd Hopkins investigates the disappearance of a legendary cop, a murder with a pre-Civil War pistol, and an encounter with a deadly psychiatrist known as the "Night Tripper." ††††

F

FISH, ROBERT L. Author of a series featuring José da Silva, a Brazilian Interpol agent. The plots are good, the character is engaging, and the setting colorful enough to make you samba.

The Fugitive. 1962. The award-winning first in the series. It is about the Nazi underground in contemporary Brazil, and one man's noble but clumsy attempt to smash it. He runs up against not just neo-Nazis, but the Jewish underground and Interpol as well. Da Silva emerges as a competent, compassionate, interesting character. †††††

FOX, PETER. *The Trail of the Reaper.* 1983. A well-written psycho novel in which the "Reaper" stalks the streets of London while Detective Inspector Jack Lamarre tries to stop him before he can kill again. The author gives the clearest definition of a psychopath and a psychotic I have ever seen, and the plot hinges on the subtle distinction between the two. †††††

FREELING, NICHOLAS. His mysteries are usually compared to Simenon's Maigret books, and they are similarly slow-paced, conversational, and full of local details. But Freeling's books are longer and more political. They feature the introspective Inspector Van der Valk of the Amsterdam Police, whose wife, Arlette, solves some of his mysteries, or Henri Castaing of the French Police Judiciare. Like Simenon, Freeling pays a lot of attention to mealtimes. He employs an abrupt, impressionistic style that occasionally makes you wonder if the printer left some of the words out by mistake.

Question of Loyalty. 1963. Van der Valk and Arlette become involved in a case of revolutionary politics, idealism and—incongruously enough—butter smuggling. The unconventional Van der Valk, never very patient with bureaucracy, is a revolutionary in his own way and acts as judge and jury at the case's conclusion. †††

The King of the Rainy Country. 1965. Two missing-persons cases converge in a murder in the story of a dynastic power play among the very wealthy. Van der Valk is able to muse a bit on class differences while skiing after his quarry in a posh resort. †††††

Criminal Conversation. 1965. In this strange book, narrated in part by the murderer, Van der Valk poses as a patient to check out a neurologist suspected of murdering an artist. Van der Valk analyzes the doctor, who in turn analyzes him. There's a shortage of action, but more than any other of Freeling's novels, this one explores the curious love affair between the hunter and the hunted. †††

The Dresden Green. 1966. Louis Schweitzer, a translator who works for a European peace organization, takes a day in the country and becomes mixed up with multiple murders and a famous diamond, the Dresden Green, lost in WWII. A passive, ironic man, he is forced into action, but this book is really about the consciences of nations. †††

Tsing Boom! 1969. The title is taken from Alban Berg's opera *Wozzeck*, about a soldier who murders his lover. In this book, the midday murder of a housewife has all the marks of a professional assassination, leading Van der Valk into an encounter with two veterans of the French war in Vietnam. †††

The Lovely Ladies. 1971. Van der Valk witnesses a fatal stabbing in the Amsterdam market. His investigation leads him to Dublin. It's a strange setting for a Dutchman, but the mystery, the characters, and Van der Valk's involvement with them are all well done. ††††

Aupres de Ma Blonde. 1972. Van der Valk experiments in detection and compares himself to Maigret, Holmes, and Marlowe. Unlike these fictional heroes, though, Van der Valk is mortal, and this book kills him off. Arlette tracks down his killers. †††

The Bugles Blowing. 1975. A high government official calls Henri Castaing to confess to an ugly triple murder. The book is less a mystery than an examination of the French legal system and the issue of sanity and responsibility. †††

The Widow. 1979. In this novel of character, Arlette remarries and opens her own detective business. At fifty she's an unusual but effective sleuth. †††

The Back of the North Wind. 1983. Henri Castaing, his wife Vera, and his colleague, Commissaire Richard, deal with teenage prostitution, murder, and worst of all—office politics. Freeling makes his characters confront the failures of the body and mind that come with age. On the whole, it is depressing, but well written. †††

G

GILL, BARTHOLOMEW. Gill's Inspector McGarr police procedurals may be the best mystery novels ever written about Ireland. His plots are good, but his setting and characters are better. Pour yourself a pint of Guinness and settle back.

McGarr and the Sienese Conspiracy. 1977. The weakest of the lot. Inspector McGarr goes to Italy, and interestingly enough, Italy—the land of intrigue—does not work well in a mystery. †††

McGarr and the Politician's Wife. 1977. The inspector investigates a straight-forward assault case, which turns out to have political overtones. †††

McGarr on the Cliffs of Moher. 1978. My favorite of the series. McGarr investigates the murder of a female New York reporter involved with the IRA. ††††

McGarr and the P.M. of Belgrave Square. 1983. McGarr investigates the death of a Dublin art dealer and the theft of a valuable French painting. †††

McGarr and the Method of Descartes. 1984. His most ambitious plot to date. Inspector McGarr, with the help of his assistant, Ruth B. H. A. Bresnahan, and the logic of Descartes, tries to find a murderer before he can assassinate the Reverend Ian Paisley of the Ulster Protestants. †††

GODDARD, KENNETH. *Balefire.* 1983. A respectable police procedural in which an assassin single-handedly takes on the police department of Huntington Beach, California, with a series of police killings prior to moving on to bigger things. It is interesting that the story doesn't have a designated hero. †††

GRANGER, BILL. *Public Murders.* 1980. A gritty police story set in Chicago, in which a serial killer is on the loose and killing women. What is interesting here are the social and political ramifications of the police methods used to bring the killer to justice. †††

GRAYSON, RICHARD. *The Monterant Affair.* 1980. Sophie Monterant, a young actress, is poisoned, and Inspector Gautier of the Sureté investigates. This late 1800s mystery is not exactly a police procedural, but it is close, and it is a fun read. ††

GREENBERG, DAN. *Love Kills.* 1978. Although still offbeat, Greenberg turns away from the humor which has marked his *Playboy* articles to give us a story of a psycho on the loose in New York. While it is a procedural, the procedure is unorthodox in that a young homicide cop teams up with a clairvoyant woman to bring the story and the killer to an end. ††††

GUTHRIE, A. B., JR. *No Second Wind.* 1981. A police procedural set in Montana's modern West. Sheriff Chick Charleston and his young sidekick, Jason Beard, are on the trail of the perpetrator of ritual cattle killings, while the miners and ranchers of the area are embroiled in a strip-mining dispute. Then murder strikes, and the whole community chooses sides, as the two laymen draw a net tighter around the murderer. Lots of character and atmosphere. †††

H

HARDWICK, MICHAEL. *Bergerac.* 1982. This police procedural derives from a BBC television series by an author known mostly for his Regency stories and pastiches of Sherlock Holmes. Here he depicts a policeman on the Isle of Jersey, recently returned to duty after a crippling injury, who solves three interlocking cases involving his best friend's murder, his own wife and father-in-law, and an alcoholic officer whose forthcoming book on the Korean War makes him the target of a vendetta. †††

HARRIS, THOMAS. *Red Dragon.* 1981. Quite simply, one of the best psycho novels ever written. Parts of it are so chilling that you may want to check the locks on your doors, parts of it are unbelievably gruesome, and in the end, you get the feeling that there may be nothing good on this earth. After this novel came out, I imagine the author's friends looked at him strangely when he came to parties. †††††

HARRISON, RAY. *Why Kill Arthur Potter?* 1983. I really enjoyed this story of the murder of a hardworking clerk in Victorian London. The lead characters— Detective Sergeant Bragg and Constable Morton—are well drawn and the story moves at a lively pace. ††††

HEBDEN, MARK. *Death Set to Music.* 1979. Every weird member of the family has an alibi. It is up to Inspector Pel to figure out who killed Madame Chenandier. †††

HEBDEN, MARK. *Pel and the Faceless Corpse.* 1979. The European version of the corrupt town novel. Pel investigates a series of murders in a small French town which was a Resistance center during WWII. †††

HEBDEN, MARK. *Pel and the Predators.* 1984. Pel has been promoted to chief inspector when a series of murders begins. Someone is killing the women of Burgundy and leaving them in unsightly places like the beach and local caves. †††

HENTOFF, NAT. *Blues for Charlie Darwin.* 1982. A beautifully drawn Greenwich Village is the scene for this police procedural featuring Detectives Noah Green and Sam McKibbon. ††††

HENTOFF, NAT. *The Man from Internal Affairs.* 1985. Officer Noah Green has his hands full as a killer keeps stuffing bodies into garbage cans on New York's East Side. If that's not enough, Internal Affairs is investigating him at the same time. Well written, chock-full of great street humor. ††††

HICHENS, ROBERT. *The Paradine Case*. 1932. While it is not strictly a police procedural, in many senses this is the essential trial novel. The barrister falls in love with his beautiful client accused of murder. ††††

HILL, PETER. *The Liars*. 1977. Chief Inspector Staunton and Detective Inspector Wyndsor of Scotland Yard are called to the isolated fishing village of Crukenporth to look into the death of a local fisherman whose body is found hanged in a manner dictated by a two-hundred-year-old legend. ††††

HILTON, JOHN BUXTON. *The Sunset Law*. 1982. Retired Superintendent Kenworthy visits his daughter and her policeman-husband in Florida, where he becomes involved in some pretty shady affairs. Two prostitutes are murdered after accusing the son-in-law of conspiracy, and the son-in-law disappears. †††

I

IANNUZZI, JOHN NICHOLAS. *Part 35*. 1970. An excellent trial novel about two drug addicts, accused of being cop killers, and the crusading lawyer who takes their case. ††††

IBARGUENGOITA, JORGE. *The Dead Girls*. 1981. A novel based on the story of two Mexican sisters who, in 1963, killed six young prostitutes and buried their bodies in the backyard of the brothel which they owned and operated. An excellent read from an internationally acclaimed author. ††††

J

JAHN, MICHAEL. *Night Rituals*. 1982. Detective Donovan of the NYPD finds the nude body of a teenage girl, who has been "sacrificed" in Central Park. †††

JANCE, J. A. *Until Proven Guilty*. 1985. Seattle homicide detective Beaumont investigates the murder of a little girl, which is linked to a weird religious cult run by a nasty, old preacher like the one in *Night of the Hunter*. ††

JAPRISOT, SEBASTIAN. I know he really doesn't belong in this section. But he does deserve to be in the book, and the readers of police procedurals, especially the European ones, are those most likely to enjoy his work.

The 10:30 from Marseille. 1963. A woman is found murdered on a night train, and all of the others in her compartment are suspects. But before Inspector Grazzi can question them, they are each being murdered in turn. A clever puzzler, strong on character. The inspector is a kind of French Martin Beck, troubled and unhealthy, but relentless. ††††

Trap for Cinderella. (n.d.) The beginning of the book is sure to grab you. It is told in the first person by a young girl who awakes in a hospital after a fire, only to find her identity obliterated by burns and her memory gone. Another girl, the same age, was found dead in the same fire, and it appears that she was murdered, perhaps by our heroine. †††

One Lonely Summer. (n.d.) In a French country village an odd, wild, young woman marries a nice young man. At first it seems just an innocent passion, but, in fact, it is the first step in an elaborate plot of revenge. The French countryside never seemed more vivid, and there has rarely been a heroine more sensual. †††

JENKINS, ELIZABETH. *Harriet.* 1934. Although not long on page count, this novel of Victorian evil is filled with substantial details about a handsome fortune hunter who approaches Harriet, a wealthy but half-witted young woman. Taken from the files of the Old Bailey, this story shows the depth to which someone will sink for personal gain. ††††

JOEY. *Killer.* 1973. Supposedly the true story of a Mafia hit man who has killed thirty-eight people. ††

JOHNSON, SANDY. *The Cuppi.* 1979. The title stands for "circumstances un-determined pending police investigation" in this gritty police drama about child prostitution and sexual violence. ††††

JOHNSON, SANDY. *Walk a Winter Beach.* 1982. A mad killer plays matchmaker and brings together Jake Ryan—a cop whose only thought is revenge for the death of his wife—and Scotty Stanton—a rich and beautiful woman who is trying to find herself—on the Montauk shores. †††

JONES, ELWYN. *Barlow Comes to Judgement.* 1974. A novelization of a BBC television series. Chief Inspector Barlow discovers a body on the moors during a visit to his home. That, coupled with a mutilated photograph, takes him on a lengthy chase, ultimately leading back to London. †††

K

KAMINSKY, STUART. *Black Knight in Red Square.* 1984. A nice touch in a Russian police procedural. This time the terrorist group attacks *them* instead of us. †††

KASTLE, HERBERT. *Death Squad.* 1977. They were cops by day, vigilantes by night. They were what the title implies. ††

KATZ, WILLIAM. *Open House*. 1985. A misfit New York cop tracks a
psycho.   †

• A *few things to read when there is snow on the sidewalk, and the
Florida ads on TV sound so good, but you can't get away because your
mate has the flu:*

DEATH SAILS THE BAY by John R. Feegel

THE DREADFUL LEMON SKY by John D. MacDonald

THE HEAT OF THE SUMMER by John Katzenbach

HURRICANE SEASON by Mickey Friedman

THE SAILCLOTH SHROUD by Charles Williams

KEATING, H. R. F. Many of Keating's mysteries feature Inspector Ganesh
Ghote of the Bombay Criminal Investigation Department. Having staked out
India as his territory, Keating has performed the difficult feat of creating a
detective who is as exotic as his setting, but as likable as a good neighbor. Canny
and patient, Ghote never falters in his duty of bringing legal order to the formless
chaos of India, and his insights into his people's lives and world are unobtrusive
but always vital to the structure of the books. In his non-Ghote novels, Keating
experiments with other styles and settings.

The Perfect Murder. 1964. This novel, which introduces Ghote and the India-
in-transition in which he must try to operate, won a Crime Writers Association
award for the best novel of its year.   †††

Is Skin Deep, Is Fatal. 1965. It's a case to die for. Inspector Ironside of the
Murder Squad investigates the murders connected with a local beauty pageant.
The suspects are a bevy of beauties. The setting is Soho.   ††

Death of a Fat God. 1966. An amusing tale of murderous goings-on in a small
English opera company. Exaggerated characters and dry wit add luster to a story
fraught with artistic temperament. There are more operatic allusions here than
in a year's worth of *New York Times* Sunday crosswords.   †††

Inspector Ghote Breaks an Egg. 1970. Ghote must tread carefully as, disguised
as a chicken-feed salesman, he probes a murder committed fifteen years earlier
in a small village ruled by a tinpot politician. Unfortunately, his investigation
shakes up the town, but, after all, you can't make an omelet...   ††††

A Remarkable Case of Burglary. 1975. Set in Victorian London, this book
chronicles the obsessive, destructive relationships between a criminal drifter and
two women he loves and uses. Not really a mystery, more a novel of social
observation in the vein of Dickens.   ††

The Murder of the Maharajah. 1980. In the Imperial India of 1930, Detective Superintendent Howard matches wits with the murderer of an eccentric, capricious, indecently wealthy potentate. Is the culprit the taciturn American millionaire? The stoical British legate? The luscious chorus girl? The maharajah's rebellious son? Wry humor, atmosphere, and period details are smoothly inserted into this Indian version of the traditional country-house mystery.   ††††

Go West, Inspector Ghote. 1981. This one could be called Inspector Ghote Meets the Valley Girls. On the track of a runaway Indian heiress, Ghote visits Los Angeles. There's the locked-room murder of a swami to be dealt with, but the real fun is the satirical counterpoint of the earnest oriental's reactions to the best—and worse—the West has to offer, from the vending machines in men's rooms to dune buggies.   †††

KEECH, SCOTT. *Ciphered.* 1980. A young police inspector faces the challenge of a double murder in his midwestern college town. Already, the college is being looked at askance because of explosions, peculiar smells, and other unsettling incidents. To solve the murders of the science department head and his wife, Jeff Adams uses many of the principles of Sherlock Holmes to reach an appalling yet satisfactory denouement.   ††††

KEMP, SARAH. *No Escape.* 1984. A nice touch in a police procedural—a female forensic pathologist, who chases down a female, psycho, slasher, eye-gouger, and all-round nasty person. A quick breezy read which is long on dialogue and short on description.   †††

KNOX, BILL. *Bloodtide.* 1982. The English coastguard vessel, *Marlin*, with first mate Webb Carrick, docks at Port Ard to investigate the murder of a seaman on a fishing boat that was selling fish to the Russians.   †††

KRASNER, WILLIAM. *Walk the Dark Streets.* 1949. A would-be actress does dirty things to get her big break in show biz. When someone returns the favor in spades, it is up to homicide detective Sam Birge to find out who.   ††††

KRASNER, WILLIAM. *Death of a Minor Poet.* 1984. What looks like an ordinary death by mugging turns out to be much more, as detective Sam Birge investigates in a somewhat Simenon-like story.   †††

L

LaROSA, LINDA J., AND TANNENBAUM, BARRY. *The Random Factor.* 1978. The New York police are plagued by a seemingly senseless series of murders. What is the common denominator of the victims? Why are there four different modi operandi? The police commissioner pools the best brains in his department with a noted criminologist and his daughter, an assistant district attorney. This leads to a deadly game with the killer and rolls on to a shattering conclusion.   †††††

LIEBERMAN, HERBERT. *Nightbloom.* 1984. This is the story of a psycho killer loose in New York, with the cop personally drawn into the search. He is sometimes aided, sometimes hampered, by a hypochondriacal medical genius who is the outstanding character in the book. ††††

LIEBMAN, RON. *Grand Jury.* 1983. A young, ambitious U.S. attorney comes into possession of some hot information concerning powerful people and decides to go it alone in a rather questionable manner. †††

M

McBAIN, ED. The author of a series featuring the men of the 87th Precinct (and their women). His setting is Isola, which is Manhattan in disguise. McBain's specialty is the procedural novel, in which he guides you through every step-by-step detail of routine police work. He can—and does in one book—spend more than a page telling you how the police scientists make a plaster cast of a footprint in dogshit. For all their detail, these books are generally fast-moving, with a minimum of scene-painting and character study. Readers love them or hate them, with no middle ground.

Cop Hater. 1956. One of the first and still one of the best, this book shows the 87th Precinct in action against a murderer who's picking off detectives. The ending isn't the surprise it's supposed to be, but that doesn't spoil the story. ††††

He Who Hesitates. 1965. McBain deserves credit for experimenting with quite a few different kinds of stories in the 87th Precinct series. Here the detective division is seen from the outside, through the eyes of a sexually disturbed young man who toys with the idea of confessing to a murder. It's a grim story, but well written and suspenseful. †††

Doll. 1965. This book opens with the brutal murder of a fashion model and goes on to explore various permutations of sex, beauty, and death. Detective Steve Carella, one of the cornerstones of the series, is the victim of a particularly sadistic plot. †††

Hail, Hail, The Gang's All Here! 1971. This book chronicles the events of twenty-four hours in the 87th Precinct. Half a dozen or so cases are investigated, and McBain focuses on the nitty-gritty of police work, complete with reproductions of arrest sheets and other paperwork. †††

Hail to the Chief. 1973. Detectives Steve Carella and Bert Kling start the day early with a pile of quick-frozen corpses found in a ditch. There's a big gang war brewing, and Carella and Kling are literally under the gun as they struggle to identify the victims and the killers. †††

Heat. 1981. Like the earlier *Cop Hater,* this book makes much of the murder-inciting, midsummer, urban heat wave. Two cases are skillfully intertwined: the suicide or murder of an alcoholic artist, and the dangerous infidelity of Detective Kling's wife. Both are convincing and well plotted. †††††

The McBain Brief. 1982. This collection of short stories receives high marks for its occasional black humor and its vivid portraits of characters on both sides of the law. McBain's touch is light; his dialogue and descriptions less repetitive than in his novels. "Hot Cars" and "Kid Kill" are two stories especially worth reading, the first for laughs and the second for shudders. ††††

Ice. 1983. Kling, Carella, and the rest of the regulars are back on the job in this long novel, which links rape, murder, robbery, and drug crimes in a plot that's just a bit too slippery. McBain has always used a lot of dialogue, especially interrogations, and he uses it well here to vary the pace and keep *Ice* from freezing up. †††

Jack and the Beanstalk. 1984. One of McBain's few novels not about the 87th Precinct. This is a sultry tale of semi-tropical skullduggery. Lawyer Matthew Hope turns detective to investigate the savage stabbing of a boy who had wanted to buy a bean farm. †††

McClure, James. He uses a South African setting and a pair of oddly compatible detectives, Lieutenant Tromp Kramer and his Bantu sidekick Sergeant Mickey Zondi, of the Trekkersburg Police Force. Pious social commentary is pleasantly absent. The closest McClure comes to making a political statement is when he has Zondi solve the case for Kramer. Description and dialect are colorful, but not overdone, and the characters are solid and well realized.

The Steam Pig. 1971. McClure's first book about Kramer and Zondi goes right to the guts of the race business. It's about the murder of a white woman killed with a Bantu weapon. It turns out that the dead woman has a secret past—a dark one. This story is about apartheid, but only in a wry, indirect way. It's also a meticulously plotted procedural and an impressive work. ††††

The Caterpillar Cop. 1972. This book is worth reading if only for the horrific, funny, seduction scene which opens it. From there, the plot is one of McClure's favorites: two seemingly unrelated crimes that turn out to be part of the same case. In this case, it's sex murders. ††††

The Gooseberry Fool. 1974. When a mild-mannered civil servant is murdered, his servant is the obvious, and only, suspect. But Kramer and Zondi discover that there's more to the case than they thought. The well-written conclusion combines scientific criminology, good deduction, and a surprise plot twist. †††

Snake. 1975. Kramer and Zondi must solve not one but two baffling cases: a series of petty robberies and the murder of a snake dancer who is strangled with her costar. Kramer provides the muscle and Zondi the brains. †††

The Sunday Hangman. 1977. Kramer and Zondi track the cleverest and most dangerous criminal of their careers: a vigilante whose hobby is hanging. With each book, the relationships among members of the police crew become more interesting and more important to the story. ††††

The Blood of an Englishman. 1980. Once again, it's a case of two separate crimes combining into one investigation, as Kramer and Zondi search for clues to two bizarre murders. The trails converge in some unfinished WWII business. †††

The Artful Egg. 1984. McClure's most recent is one of his best: sardonic, full blooded, well plotted. A case that begins with the murder of a famous and controversial woman novelist goes on to involve more death, blackmail, and dirty secrets both personal and political. ††††

McGinniss, Joe. *Fatal Vision.* 1983. The story of Dr. Jeffrey MacDonald, the Green Beret captain convicted of murdering his wife and children. I don't usually like true crime stories, but I could not put this one down, nor could anyone else I know. †††††

McIlvanney, William. *The Papers of Tony Veitch.* 1983. Laidlaw investigates the murder of a derelict, and in so doing uncovers the involvement of a large number of people from both sides of Glasgow society. The link between the two groups is Tony Veitch, a student who disappears abruptly. Also, be sure to read *Laidlaw*, the first novel in this, so far, short series. †††

MacNamara, Joseph. *The First Directive.* 1984. A first novel by a California police chief, this is a police procedural plodding its way through Silicon Valley and a labyrinth of computer scams, political corruption, and high-priced porn. The narrator and his two assistants risk life and limb to solve two murders. †††

Mantell, Laurie. *Murder in Fancy Dress.* 1978. Detective Arrow disregards the confession of a retarded teenager in the death of a policeman and continues his investigation against the colorful backdrop of Petone, New Zealand's celebration of Ponderosa Day in honor of the TV show "Bonanza." †††

Mantell, Laurie. *Murder and Chips.* 1982. A New Zealand police procedural in which Sgt. Steven Arrow investigates the murder of a biker. ††

Marshall, William. Author of a series of Hong Kong police procedurals featuring Chief Inspector Harry Feiffer and the boys of the Yellowthread Street station. They are very well written and have more humor in them than any other police procedural series that I can think of. Don't miss them.

Skullduggery. 1979. A raft comes floating into the harbor. On it is a skeleton with its feet tied together, a dead fish, some sweet potatoes, and a length of drain pipe. The Yellowthread Street boys investigate what turns out to be a twenty-five-year-old murder. †††

Sci-Fi. 1981. My favorite of the series as the "Spaceman" moves through costumed crowds attending the All-Asia Science Fiction and Horror Movie Festival, incinerating those in his path with a ray gun. It is up to Yellowthread Street station to stop him. ††††

Perfect End. 1981. It appears that six cops have been killed by some kind of huge cat, and it is up to Inspector Feiffer to solve the case before an impending hurricane can hit. ††††

MAXIM, JOHN. *Who Was Abel Baker Charley?* 1983. The FBI, the CIA, the Mafia, and a couple of good-looking women are all looking for a psycho. †††

MILLS, JAMES. *On the Edge.* 1971. The story of a cop and the Times Square scene which is driving him crazy. ††

MILLS, JAMES. *Report to the Commissioner.* 1972. A police procedural complete down to photostats of the forms. It features an internal affairs investigation. ††††

MINAHAN, JOHN. *The Great Hotel Robbery.* 1982. John Rawlings investigates the robbery of a midtown Manhattan hotel. Parts of it are funny. The characters are well drawn and nicely different. ††††

MINAHAN, JOHN. *The Great Diamond Robbery.* 1984. In a search for missing diamonds, John Rawlings works his way through some street thugs, looking for Mr. "Big," and eventually winds up in England. ††††

MOORE, CHRISTOPHER. *His Lordship's Arsenal.* 1985. A very offbeat book about a Canadian judge who develops writer's block while writing an opinion on an arson case. The way he combats his block is to tell us his entire life story from college onward. There are some nice scenes, but, on the whole, it was a somewhat unsatisfactory read for me. ††

MOORE, ROBIN. *The French Connection.* 1969. The story of a huge drug shipment coming in to New York. I can't imagine that there is anyone out there who hasn't heard of this one. ††††

MORTIMER, JOHN. There are five volumes of the Rumpole of the Bailey series. All of them are excellent. The crusty Rumpole is the most engaging trial lawyer since Charles Laughton's film performance in Agatha Christie's *Witness for the Prosecution.* The five volumes are: *Rumpole of the Bailey, Trials of Rumpole, Rumpole's Return, Rumpole for the Defense,* and *Rumpole and the Golden Thread.*

N

NABB, MAGDALEN.   A "must read" for fans of Sjowall and Wahloo, Simenon, Freeling, and Van de Wetering.

Death of an Englishman.   1981. The body of a quiet, unassuming Englishman is found in Florence during the Christmas season, which proves a well-drawn backdrop in this Simenon-like novel. Marshal Guarnaccia investigates what life had been like for the dead man.   ††††

Death of a Dutchman.   1982. Again very Simenon-like as Guarnaccia goes to visit an old lady and stumbles across a dying man.   ††††

Death in Springtime.   1983. Even though Simenon himself wrote the introduction, this book marks a style change as Nabb writes a kidnapping story with more meat in it. This time the style is closer to Van de Wetering than Simenon.   ††††

Death in Autumn.   1984. Two Swedish tourists discover the body of a woman in the river. Guarnaccia has to ferret out identity, background, and motive as the author again returns to the Simenon-style.   ††††

NEWMAN, G. F.   *Trade-Off*. 1977. Detective John Fordham of the NYPD is a man who likes to take shortcuts wherever possible. He has a habit of trading lighter sentences for the names of people higher up in the crime world. This works well until it backfires in an Attica escape linked to a major crime figure.   †††

NORMAN, CHARLES.   *The Genteel Murderer*. 1956. This book is for you if you enjoy true-crime stories or Victoriana, or both. It is an examination of the criminal career of Thomas Griffiths Wainewright, who died in 1852. A dilettante artist and essayist, he prided himself on his friendships with Charles Lamb, Byron, and others. He also forged financial documents and probably poisoned three members of his family.   ††††

O

O'DONNELL, LILLIAN.   Author of two series of police procedurals. Of the two—the first featuring Sgt. Norah Mulcahaney of the New York Police Department, and the second featuring Mici Anhalt—the Norah Mulcahaney series is far and away the best.

The Children's Zoo. 1981. Sgt. Norah Mulcahaney investigates a series of teenage terroristic acts that turn the streets of New York into a jungle of gang violence, only this time rich kids, instead of ghetto kids, are involved. The opening pages of this story have so much violence that it made me not want to finish it. †

Cop Without a Shield. 1983. Norah takes a vacation from the force and goes to York Crossing, Pennsylvania, where she witnesses the kidnapping of a young woman. When her body is found in a quarry ditch, Norah's vacation turns into a busman's holiday. †††

Ladykiller. 1984. Norah tries to catch a psycho who is running around New York slashing the throats of young women. The tie-in is that each has recently had a love affair with a mysterious stranger, the kind of man you don't bring home to mama. ††††

OLCOTT, ANTHONY. *Murder at the Red October.* 1981. A Russian police procedural in which a hotel security officer finds the body of an American, who is staying at the hotel. Very similar to *Gorky Park*, with one exception, it is a much better story. ††††

ORMEROD, ROGER. *Seeing Red.* 1985. A well-written "almost procedural" in which suspended Detective Harry Kyle tries to get to the bottom of a death by auto accident involving a traffic signal and a color-blind man. †††

P

PACE, TOM. *Fisherman's Luck.* 1971. A good police procedural, with a well-drawn Florida setting, in which the first mate of a fishing boat falls overboard and is thought to have drowned. However, when the body is recovered, Chief Ben Garden discovers he was shot. †††

PAUL, BARBARA. *Kill Fee.* 1985. An excellent story with an offbeat twist. A hit man named "Pluto" works "on spec.," which is to say that he selects the victim, kills him, and then presents a bill to the person most likely to benefit from the service. ††††

PIKE, ROBERT L. *Bank Job.* 1974. Things are going smoothly enough in a routine payroll heist from a San Francisco bank until a cop is killed, and Lieutenant Rierdon of homicide takes over. ††

PIKE, ROBERT L. *Deadline 2 A.M.* 1976. A cop is kidnapped, and Lieutenant Rierdon has to handle the negotiations for his release—negotiations which seem to have a double meaning. ††

QR

RATHBONE, JULIAN. *The Euro-Killers*. 1979. EUREAC is about to build a huge industrial complex when the head of the organization disappears. Police Commissioner Jan Argand takes on the investigation.   †††

REEVES, JOHN. *Murder by Microphone*. 1978. The general manager of the Canadian Broadcasting System is killed by the proverbial blunt instrument, and a Toronto homicide duo have to find out which of his most likely successors did the deed. The author overcomes unlikely motivation with some knife-edged satire on the radio business, and programming double entendre which, by itself, will satisfy many readers.   †††

REILLY, HELEN. Author of a procedural series featuring Inspector McGee of the Manhattan Homicide Squad.

The Canvas Dagger. 1956. Inspector McGee has to figure out which of eight suspects killed Grant Melville.   †††

Ding Dong Bell. 1958. Inspector McGee solves the murder of a blackmailing private eye.   †††

Certain Sleep. 1961. A case of murder among the "swells" has Inspector McGee up to his elbows in the upper crust.   ††

S

ST. PIERRE, DENNIS. *The Marshall*. 1981. A solid police story in which the ghost of Wyatt Earp decides to clean up Los Angeles. Good-quality writing keeps this rather offbeat plot under control, and the result is a tightly written story.   †††

SANDERS, LAWRENCE. When you think of Lawrence Sanders one word comes to mind—superstar—and deservedly so. His career has been one fueled by brilliance and versatility, but it is his tremendous police stories featuring Edward X. Delaney that has boosted him to his present pinnacle of success.

The Anderson Tapes. 1969. A brilliant combination of the diary novel and a caper story. Quite by accident the long ear of "Big Brother" hears of a caper set to come off soon, but it is a case of one hand not knowing what the other is doing. There is a moderate amount of lightly handled but kinky sex.   ††††

The First Deadly Sin. 1973. His masterpiece. The tortoise and the hare story of Capt. Edward X. Delaney as he tries to catch Daniel Blank, a New York psycho killer. Possibly the most accurate fictional portrait of the mental break-down of a human being ever drawn. †††††

The Second Deadly Sin. 1977. Edward X. Delaney tackles the murder of a disagreeable artist. Nowhere near the power and scope of *The First Deadly Sin.* ††††

The Sixth Commandment. 1979. A straight, private-eye story beautifully told, in which an investigator for a charitable foundation checks out an evil doctor about to receive a big grant. There is a touch of Frankenstein madness here.
††††

The Tenth Commandment. 1980. Joshua Bigg, a 5-foot-3¼-inches-tall in-vestigator for a law firm looks into the apparent suicide of a wealthy client of the firm. †††

The Third Deadly Sin. 1981. This time Edward X. Delaney is after a female psycho driven to murder by a problem bordering on pre-menstrual syndrome.
††††

The Case of Lucy Bending. 1982. The story of a sexually precocious eight-year-old girl. †††

The Seduction of Peter S. 1983. Great fun. The story of a lovable New York male hooker who runs afoul of the mob. ††††

The Fourth Deadly Sin. 1985. The fourth deadly sin is anger, an anger so great that it explodes into the murder of a prominent psychiatrist. Retired Chief of Detectives Edward X. Delaney has to find who, among a list of offbeat suspects, is *that* angry. ††††

SCOTT, JACK S. *The View from Deacon Hill.* 1981. Sergeant Rosher takes a visiting American cop named Hooper on a tour of the countryside, where they happen to witness a murder. When they report it, nobody wants to believe them. ††

SCOTT, JACK. S. *A Death in Irish Town.* 1985. In the throes of a mid-life crisis, Inspector Rosher returns to his first beat—Irish Town—to investigate a fire. †††

SCOTT, JACK S. *A Time of Fine Weather.* 1985. Although this is not exactly a police procedural, Scott apparently still had more to say about arson than he used in *A Death in Irish Town,* so he wrote this story of the fiery death of two people. This is not an Inspector Rosher story. †††

SELA, OWEN. *The Kremlin Control.* 1984. A grim police procedural set in Moscow in which a black-marketeering general is found murdered, and no one cares except KGB officer Yuri Raikin. Another novel similar to *Gorky Park*.

†††

SHANNON, DELL. I was quite surprised to find that the author of the "Luis Mendoza" series of procedurals is a woman. Their fast pace and hard-boiled tone seems more like the work of a man. There is no masterpiece in the series, but each book is a well-written succession of incidents in the lives of Mendoza and his men. The series has great appeal to women because of the care taken by the author in developing the background, subplots, and characters.

The Death Bringers. 1965. In the middle of a hot September, a lone bank robber keeps knocking off banks at will, until he angers Lieutenant Mendoza by killing one of his men.

†††

Murder with Love. 1971. After an earthquake, Los Angeles detective Lieutenant Mendoza investigates the murder of a cop as he gets ready to go to work, the murder of a john by a hooker, and the murder of a doctor, his wife, and nurse.

††††

The Ringer. 1971. Mendoza investigates a series of apparently motiveless female homicides in which the victims are beaten to death, but not raped or robbed. Also, one of Mendoza's cops is accused of heading a stolen-car ring.

††††

Spring of Violence. 1973. Bank holdups, the murder of a city employee, the theft of a rare tropical fish, and the usual assortment of minor crimes makes March a tough time for Lieutenant Mendoza.

††††

Appearances of Death. 1977. Things begin quietly enough for Mendoza with a missing person's report on a nurse and her car. Then a woman is killed in a phone booth in the rain, and an old man holds up a store, as the week starts to heat up.

†††

Cold Trail. 1978. A rapist and child molester is on the loose who continues to evade Mendoza. A chain of robberies occurs, and dead bodies start to turn up.

†††

Destiny of Death. 1984. A little weaker than some of the others. The story of the young girl who is held prisoner by her mother is interesting, but the one about the blind man and his seeing-eye dog is less so.

††

SIMENON, GEORGES. The author of many non-series crime novels, he is best known for his long string of books about Jules Maigret of the Paris police. Short on clues and action but long on psychology and conversation, these books seem aimless at first but are in fact detailed accounts of investigation, as opposed to detection. Their best feature may be the brief but vivid glimpse they offer of Paris and French life.

Maigret and the Spinster. 1942. An unattractive spinster complains to Maigret that her furniture moves at night. When her murdered body is found in a broom closet, Maigret blames himself for not having taken her seriously. He seems especially French by comparison with his partner in the investigation, a Philadelphia cop, whose presence is mysterious but amusing.   †††

Maigret's Rival. 1944. Maigret unofficially investigates a political scandal, which soon becomes a scandalous murder. He matches wits with a private investigator—known as "Inspector Cadaver"—who was thrown off the police force. This book is as funny as Simenon gets.   ††††

Maigret Afraid. 1953. When Maigret looks into a series of seemingly unrelated murders, his intuition and deduction tell him that the next skull to be fractured will be his own. As often in Simenon's books, the resolution of the case comes almost as an afterthought. This book is one of Maigret's few encounters with true insanity.   †††

Maigret Sets a Trap. 1955. Maigret masterminds a plot to catch a killer who is working his way through the women of a Paris neighborhood. The murderer's motives are murkily Freudian, but not too murky for Maigret.   †††

Maigret and the Headless Corpse. 1955. Strange clues, including a headless body fished out of the Seine, lead to an unusual version of the good old-fashioned French *crime passionel.* Maigret engages in a duel of wits with his rival and enemy, the examining magistrate.   †††

Maigret and the Black Sheep. 1962. This book opens with a quiet neighborhood, a loving wife, and a man murdered in the stronghold of bourgeois respectability. Maigret's investigation reveals the victim's secret life.   ††††

Maigret Loses His Temper. 1963. In a seedy Montmartre setting of nightclubs and Apaches, reminiscent of early Edith Piaf, the usually impassive or melancholy Maigret becomes angry when his reputation is threatened by the murder of a cabaret owner.   †††

Maigret in Vichy. 1968. Away from Paris, with nothing to do but drink Vichy water, Maigret has a busman's holiday and compiles a dossier on a mysterious fellow visitor. When she is murdered, he feels it is his duty to assist the local "flics."   †††

Maigret and the Killer. 1969. A wealthy perfume manufacturer's son enjoys slumming in the smellier quarters of Paris—with a tape recorder in his pocket. The motive for his murder raises the question of guilt or insanity.   †††

Maigret and the Loner. 1971. The roots of murder often lie in the distant past, as Maigret points out during the investigation of this particular slaying: a well-groomed corpse found in squalid surroundings. Nothing is quite as sordid as the really slummy parts of Paris in August. ††††

SIMPSON, DOROTHY. *The Night She Died.* 1981. An excellent police procedural fully in the league of Michael Gilbert and P. D. James. Inspector Luke Thanet investigates the murder of a beautiful but cold young woman. Simpson takes this ordinary plot and turns it into a gem by her fine writing and meticulous attention to detail. ††††

SIMPSON, DOROTHY. *Six Feet Under.* 1982. Inspector Thanet investigates the murder of the village busybody—a woman that everyone has a reason to wish dead. †††

SIMPSON, DOROTHY. *Last Seen Alive.* 1985. Luke Thanet, a very likable and well-drawn English "copper," investigates the death of Alice Parnell, a girl he went to school with more than twenty years before. †††

SJOWALL, MAJ, AND WAHLOO, PER. This Swedish husband-and-wife team wrote ten novels about Stockholm policeman Martin Beck before Wahloo's death in 1975. This series is as fine a body of police-procedural writing as has ever been done. Because of the emphasis on the individual rather than the system, the heavy European flavor, and the gloominess, feel free to suggest the Martin Beck stories to anyone who goes to movie festivals, haunts the liquor store in search of a great cheap wine, or has a pair of earth shoes gathering dust in the closet.

Roseanna. 1965. Martin Beck investigates the rape/murder of a young woman. ††††

The Man Who Went Up in Smoke. 1966. Beck goes to Budapest to search for a missing Swedish journalist. ††††

The Man on the Balcony. 1967. Summer gets hot in Stockholm, too—especially for Martin Beck as he investigates a series of muggings and child murders. ††††

The Laughing Policeman. 1968. Beck investigates the murder of the passengers on a Stockholm bus. †††††

The Fire Engine That Disappeared. 1969. Beck investigates an apartment house explosion and the fire engine that disappears on the way to the fire. †††††

Murder at the Savoy. 1970. Beck investigates the murder of a Swedish industrialist making a dinner speech at the Hotel Savoy. ††††

The Abominable Man. 1971. Beck hunts for the murderer of a police captain. ††††

The Locked Room. 1972. A decayed corpse is found in a locked room as Sjowall and Wahloo try their hand at the classic type of puzzle in the tradition of Ellery Queen and John Dickson Carr. ††††

Cop Killer. 1974. Beck goes to the country to investigate a shooting between the cops and some teenagers. ††††

The Terrorists. 1975. Beck is assigned to protect an American senator from Stockholm terrorists. ††††

SMITH, DENNIS. *Glitter and Ash.* 1980. A novel of insurance fraud, hot women, and even hotter fires. †††

SMITH, MARK. *The Death of the Detective.* 1973. A classic psycho novel, set in Chicago. †††††

• *Some good, hard-boiled, detective novels that are* not *set in California or Boston:*

DECOYS by Richard Hoyt
THE LAST GOOD KISS by James Crumley
THE MIDNIGHT LADY AND THE MOURNING MAN by David Anthony
SARATOGA HEADHUNTER by Stephen Dobyns
TRUE CRIME by Max Alan Collins

SMITH, MARTIN CRUZ. *Gorky Park.* 1981. An excellent book, the first police procedural to be set in Russia. Chief homicide investigator Arkady Renko investigates the murder of three corpses found frozen with their faces and fingers missing. The plot is average, but the picture it gives of the life of the average Russian is fascinating. ††††

STRANGE, JOHN STEPHEN. *All Men Are Liars.* 1948. This book stars Capt. George Honegger of the New York Police Department, one of Strange's series characters. It's a courtroom drama with a psychological slant in which a playboy is accused of murdering a garage mechanic. †††

STRANGE, JOHN STEPHEN. *Eye Witness.* 1961. Honegger returns in this story of a week in the life of the chief witness to a murder. Actress Lily Logan tells the police what she knows about a killer, and Honegger tries to catch him before he catches Lily. ††

T

THOMSON, JUNE. Author of the "Inspector Rudd" series of English police procedurals. The strength of the series lies in its slow-moving, meticulous detection. Inspector Rudd is a good character but not a charismatic one.

Death Cap. 1977. A village shopkeeper, Mrs. King, is killed by a poisoned mushroom. Rudd is very graphic about what happens to a person who is poisoned in that manner, and it isn't pretty, but it is still a great idea for a murder. †††

Case Closed. 1977. Inspector Rudd is being followed by a stranger. This unnerves him to the point that it temporarily distracts him from the murder of a young girl, whose strangled body was found in the bushes. †††

A Question of Identity. 1977. Rudd investigates a modern corpse in an archeological dig. †††

The Habit of Loving. 1979. Rudd investigates a love triangle between a young man passing through the village, a woman who sees him as the son she never had, and a young woman marked for death. †††

Alibi in Time. 1980. Rudd investigates the death of a very nasty writer. †††

TRAVER, ROBERT. *Anatomy of a Murder.* 1958. Possibly the greatest trial novel ever written. A Michigan ex-district attorney defends a young soldier for killing a bar owner who had raped his wife. What a great book! Do yourself a favor and read it. †††††

TRAVER, ROBERT. *People Versus Kirk.* 1981. A trial novel set in the Michigan peninsula in which a young man is accused of murdering his rich lover. The story—almost all dialogue—is built around an interesting point of law. †††

TREVANIAN. *The Main.* 1976. The story of a broken-down cop in a broken-down section of Montreal. It is a story told with a minimum of action and a maximum of sensitivity. †††

TURNBULL, PETER. *Fair Friday.* 1983. On the eve of Fair Friday, a reporter is badly beaten. He regains consciousness only long enough to utter the word "Gilheaney," a word which stretches back to another murder on a Fair Friday some years earlier. My only complaint is that I would have liked a bit more description of the interesting Glasgow scene. †††

U

UHNAK, DOROTHY. A top-flight police-procedural writer. She has no series character, choosing instead to build from scratch to fit the situation.

The Ledger. 1971. Not one of her best stories. The Ledger is a hooker with an evil boss, and together they provide violent interaction which drives the story forward. †

The Investigation. 1977. A fictional accounting of a famous murder case in which a mother is accused of murdering her children. As Sgt. Joe Peters begins to investigate, he starts to believe in her innocence. ††

UPFIELD, ARTHUR W. His series of Australian mysteries stars Inspector Napoleon Bonaparte, a half-caste aborigine detective who uses bush craft and charm to solve his cases. The settings are not only intrinsically interesting but integral to the fabric of the plot. In his quiet way, Bony is one of the most colorful detectives of fiction.

Death of a Swagman. 1945. Merino is an isolated town in New South Wales. Posing as a laborer, Bony goes there to investigate the murder of a vagrant and soon discovers a murderous tangle of motives and suspects. There are some very engaging characters and some excellent tracking scenes leading to a suspenseful finish. ††††

The Bachelors of Broken Hill. 1950. Who's killing the unmarried old men of Broken Hill, and why? Bony arrives in the silver-mining town to solve two old murders and a new one. He enlists the help of an unlikely assistant to prevent a fourth poisoning. †††

The New Shoe. 1951. Bony investigates a month-old murder in a seacoast community, where he feels out of his element near the ocean. The melodramatic mystery—hocus-pocus with coffins—matches the moody setting. The tone is somber, but, as in most Upfield books, there's one especially sympathetic character who befriends Bony and cheers things up. †††

Sinister Stones. 1954. Bony comes up against an aborigine tracker, the chief suspect in the murder of a policeman, in this battle of wits and wills in the outback. The mystery itself is as good as the bush scenes. ††††

Death of a Lake. 1954. A lucky lottery winner went swimming in the lake and never came out. Now the lake is drying up, and Bony and others are waiting to see if the lake's bottom holds a clue to the fate of the swimmer—and the money.

Bony's advantage is that only he understands and is comfortable with nature as an amoral, living presence.   †††

Bony and the Kelly Gang.   1960. Using his favorite trick of posing as a casual wanderer, Bony visits an unusual setting: a remote, paradisiacal valley settled by Irish immigrants. The investigation of a death in the past leads to an unexpected crisis in the present, as Bony sifts through the ashes of time to unravel the identity of the killer.   ††††

The Will of the Tribe.   1962. Upfield's best book is an empathetic—not sympathetic—look at the position of aborigines in modern Australian society. More than any other book, it shows Bony as a creature of two cultures that can never fully mesh. The discovery of a white man's murdered body in a meteor crater leads him to a conflict with an aborigine tribe. Social commentary doesn't get in the way of a good mystery.   †††††

V

VAN DE WETERING, JANWILLEM.   A widely traveled man who has lived in Maine and Japan, and has served in the Amsterdam police department. He has used all three locales in his excellent police procedurals, but mainly they are set in Amsterdam, and feature Dutch detectives Grijpstra and de Gier. While they can be compared to Simenon, Freeling, Sjowall and Wahloo, or McClure, I feel they have one quality that sets them apart from the others—a touch of humor and gentleness, and maybe even incurable optimism, where the others tend to work with a pretty bleak outlook.

Outsider in Amsterdam.   1975. This murder mystery introduces Grijpstra (amiable, middle-aged family man), de Gier (free-living, philosophical young bachelor), and the Commissaris, their senior officer (wise, old statesman of the force). A murder case linked to drug smuggling leads them through Amsterdam's Old Town. The outsider is their unlikely suspect-ally, a native Papuan policeman.   ††††

Tumbleweed.   1976. Grijpstra and de Gier look for the killer of a pretty woman and find a number of lovers who might fit the bill. But the real killer could be the black magic she claimed to practice—in which de Gier becomes dangerously interested. A colorful and unusual mystery, but somewhat unsatisfying because of its inconclusive Zen-like ending. What is the sound of one handcuff clapping?   †††

The Corpse on the Dike.   1976. A mysterious recluse in a shabby quarter of Amsterdam is shot in the head, and Grijpstra and de Gier must discover who he was, what he lived on, and why anyone would want to kill him. They meet the exotic inhabitants of the Dike, a community of borderline criminals, Arabs, and high-class whores.   †††

Death of a Hawker. 1977. Grijpstra and de Gier investigate the murder of a street vendor with a terrifying homemade weapon. The pace quickens when the murderer strikes again, at an elderly transvestite ex-cop. A collection of oddball characters and stray vignettes somehow coalesces into a highly satisfying story.
††††

The Japanese Corpse. 1977. In a bizarre plot that works amazingly well, Grijpstra and de Gier follow a case to Japan to zero in on a gang of Japanese mafiosi. It's a long and intricately plotted novel, somewhat like a cross between Sherlock Holmes and *Shogun*. The picture of the Japanese criminal underworld with its samurai heritage is fascinating.
††††

The Blond Baboon. 1978. When a wealthy businesswoman is murdered, some look no further than the obvious suspect—her young lover, known as "the baboon." But Grijpstra and de Gier learn that others in her life also had reason to wish her dead. This is a fairly straightforward case of embezzlement, fraud, and medical chicanery.
†††

The Mind Murders. 1981. Other mystery writers have asked the question: can an attack on the spirit be fatal? De Gier saves the life of a would-be suicide and winds up searching for the man's vanished wife. The case leads to a character with a strange talent for pestering people to death.
††††

Inspector Saito's Small Satori. 1985. This is a new direction for the author— a collection of short stories fitted harmoniously together, featuring Matsuo Satori of the Kyoto police department. Kyoto is the holy city of Japan where the author studied Zen Buddhism, and the Zen tone predominates in these tales. The stories are concise, colorful combinations of humor, logic, action, and wry reflections on the interaction of East and West.
††††

VAN GULIK, ROBERT. A noted orientalist—author of such scholarly works as *Sexual Life in Ancient China*—Van Gulik based his series character on the historical personage Dee Jen-djieh (A.D. 630–700), a magistrate of the T'ang dynasty, who was famous as a solver of mysteries. Many of Van Gulik's plots are drawn from Chinese criminal records. His books are notable for deft historical detail, satisfying plot resolution, and a faint odor of sexual corruption. Some editions feature the author's illustrations, mostly of bare-bosomed beauties.

De Goong An (Celebrated Cases of Judge Dee). 1949. Van Gulik translated this 18th-century account of three cases in which Judge Dee encounters murder on the silk route. Judge Dee was the Sherlock Holmes of China long before Conan Doyle ever put pen to paper.
††††

The Chinese Bell Murders. 1951. The first Judge Dee novel involves Dee and his faithful sidekicks, including two highwaymen converted from their evil ways by the force of the judge's benevolent personality. This is the Chinese version of the Hatfield-McCoy feud, with gang-rape in a monastery thrown in. †††

The Chinese Lake Murders. 1953. As magistrate of Han-yuan on the shore of a strange, haunted lake, Judge Dee investigates crimes of greed and forbidden passion among the district's famous flower boats (floating brothels). He acquires his fourth sidekick, a shrewd, old gambler-philosopher who appears in most of the later books. †††

The Chinese Gold Murders. 1959. At the beginning of the Judge's career, he is called on to solve three interlocked cases. The Chinese conquest of Korea, which took place in A.D. 661 while the real Dee was alive, figures in the plot. †††

The Emperor's Pearl. 1963. An old mystery—the theft of the Emperor's Pearl a century before—is part of a series of mysterious events at the annual festival of dragon-boat races. The Judge makes a rare mistake, but manages to solve a case involving rape, murder, theft, and madness. †††††

The Red Pavilion. 1964. During the Festival of the Dead, Judge Dee visits Paradise Island, a sort of early Chinese version of Club Med, where sex and gambling are the order of the day. He becomes entangled with a notorious courtesan and peers beneath the idyllic surface of island life to discover greed and twisted passion. ††††

The Monkey and the Tiger. 1965. Two short novels involving ancient Chinese astrology. The Judge de-sheets a couple of murderous ghosts. ††

The Willow Pattern. 1965. Judge Dee is in charge of the Imperial capital during a fearsome plague epidemic. Of the three intertwined mysteries he is called on to solve, the best is that of the old puppeteer, his twin acrobat daughters, and an ancient crime commemorated in a china pattern. ††††

The Phantom of the Temple. 1966. A haunted Buddhist temple, a series of grisly murders, and the theft of the Emperor's gold keep Judge Dee busy. The setting is a remote border town in western China, with simmering political unrest added to the criminal brew. †††

Judge Dee at Work. 1967. Eight short stories reveal the wit and wisdom of Judge Dee, as well as Van Gulik's skill at tight plotting and concise characterization. The judge is far from infallible, but with the help of a keen eye and some surprising witnesses, he always gets the guilty one. †††

Necklace and Calabash. 1967. Perhaps the best of the Judge Dee books. Love, incestuous and otherwise, is the motive behind three tangled plots. A runaway wife, a princess's stolen necklace, and the judge's cryptic double are the main plot ingredients. Along the way, a beautiful young girl tests the Judge's virtue with a midnight swim. †††††

WXYZ

WAINWRIGHT, JOHN. *All Through the Night*. 1985. A straight police procedural which takes you through an "ordinary" night at the fictional Radholme, England, police department. A good read for McBain fans. ††††

WAMBAUGH, JOSEPH. A former cop himself, Wambaugh is one of the finest writers ever to tackle the police story. His stories are generally memorable not for their plots but for his characters, who are drawn with humor and insight so sharp that they seem to walk off the page and into your living room.

The New Centurions. 1970. The story of a group of cops which includes a tough ex-marine, a baby-faced cop who likes to entrap hookers, and a liberal who really isn't. ††††

The Blue Knight. 1972. The story of Bumper Morgan, a Los Angeles patrolman who has seen everything and knows it all. ††††

The Onion Field. 1974. The true story of a California cop murdered by a couple of two-bit thugs and how the justice system sees to their punishment. A classic. †††††

The Choirboys. 1975. The story of a bunch of hard-drinking, fast-talking lovable cops. Hilarious. ††††

The Black Marble. 1978. A dognapping story set in sunny California. †††

The Delta Star. 1983. A really offbeat one for Wambaugh in which a Russian sub, run aground in Swedish waters, plays a part, but so does the death of a hooker, a stolen credit card, a dog named Ludwig, and love affairs galore. ††††

The Secrets of Harry Bright. 1985. The author's closest attempt at a straight private-eye novel. Two L.A. cops on vacation investigate the death of a young man, the son of a rich father, some seventeen months earlier in a desert resort town. †††

WEBSTER, NOAH. *An Incident in Iceland*. 1979. Inspector Gaunt is given the unpleasant task of going to Iceland to sell an airplane and airstrip willed to Queen Elizabeth. Trouble turns up when the business is found to be tied in to a bootlegging scheme. †††

WESTLAKE, DONALD. *Levine*. 1984. A collection of short stories about Abraham Levine of the New York Police Department. †††

WILCOX, COLIN. The author of a well-written series of police procedurals featuring Lieutenant Hastings of the San Francisco Police Department.

The Disappearance. 1970. Lieutenant Hastings investigates the disappearance of a predatory, bed-hopping woman. †††

Doctor, Lawyer. 1976. A nursery-rhyme killer named the "Masked Man" is giving Hastings a lot of trouble as he goes through the doctor, the lawyer, the merchant—his next victim will be Chief Dwyer of the San Francisco Police Department. ††††

WILTSE, DAVID. *The Serpent*. 1983. A creepy, gruesome, bloodthirsty, psycho novel full of scenes with snakes. Tom-Tom, the killer, turns the table on the cop who is chasing him and sets his sights on the cop's pregnant wife. ††

WOOD, TED. *Dead in the Water*. 1983. Winner of the Scribner Crime Novel Award. A solid police procedural set on an island off the coast of Canada where the local police chief has to contend with bikers, vacationers, and drugs, as well as solve a series of murders beginning with a boating accident. †††

WOOD, TED. *Murder on Ice*. 1984. Police Chief Reid Benett investigates the kidnapping of a winter festival queen. But that's not all. There's murder, snowstorms, and CLAW (Canadian League of Angry Women) as well. †††

WOODS, STUART. *Chiefs*. 1981. An excellent story of three generations of police chiefs in a small Georgia town, and their efforts to bring in a sex murderer, whose escapades cover a half century. ††††

WRIGHT, ERIC. *The Night the Gods Smiled*. 1983. Inspector Charlie Salter of the Toronto Police Department investigates the murder of a college professor. At first I was not taken with Inspector Salter as a character, but as the story progressed, I found myself liking him more and more. By the end I was a fan. †††

WRIGHT, ERIC. *Smoke Detector*. 1984. Inspector Charlie Salter investigates the death of an antiques dealer who died in a fire caused by arson. Between the well-drawn pilot and Charlie's problems at home keeping his fourteen-year-old son away from girlie magazines, you will find this one hard to put down. ††††

WRIGHT, ERIC. *Death in the Old Country*. 1985. A joy to read. Toronto Inspector Charlie Salter and his wife, Anne, go to England for a holiday. While Charlie is discovering a passion for English beer and horse racing, their hotel is plagued by a peeping tom, and then there's murder. The atmosphere is great. It presents England as you've never seen it. †††